THE
WESTERN ISLES

by

ALASDAIR ALPIN MACGREGOR

Illustrated and with a Map

London
Robert Hale Limited
18 Bedford Square W.C.1

First published 1949

PRINTED IN GREAT BRITAIN BY
NORTHUMBERLAND PRESS LIMITED
GATESHEAD ON TYNE

PREFACE

"My complaint as a reader, as a critic, and as an inhabitant against some of the numerous works published during the last decade about the Western Isles is not so much of their superficiality as of their effort to make the Islands and the Islanders conform to a sentimental preconception in the minds of their authors. . . . This nebulous twentieth-century impressionism will be of as much service to historians in the future as the posters of esurient railway companies."

In these words, Compton MacKenzie prefaces his contribution to *The Book of Barra*;[1] and it is because I so heartily agree with him that I have included in the latter chapters of this volume a great deal of matter which, though by no means complimentary to the Islanders, is true.

The biography of a people, like the biography of a person, is true only if it show both sides of the picture. Otherwise, historically and sociologically, it is valueless.

I confess to having been one of those who, in earlier years, enjoyed looking at the Hebridean people through coloured spectacles. However, on this occasion, one feels some measure of responsibility to the reader, if not also to society at large. I have made no attempt in these pages to gloss over the less pleasant things, therefore. On the contrary, I have endeavoured to give a contemporary account of the Islanders and their ways, free from any "nebulous twentieth-century impressionism".

I shall assume that no one will desire to challenge the facts upon which the criticisms made in the last few chapters are based. After all, many of these facts have been appearing in the local press, continuously, year after year, in the form of letters-to-the-editor frequently written by natives themselves, and of reports on police court proceedings and matters discussed at meetings of public bodies, such as the town council of Stornoway. These facts are no less true because they now appear between the covers of a book.

ALASDAIR ALPIN MACGREGOR

CHELSEA, S.W.3.

[1] Routledge, 1936.

CONTENTS

CONTENTS

ILLUSTRATIONS

ILLUSTRATIONS

facing page

ILLUSTRATIONS

ACKNOWLEDGMENT

*All the illustrations are reproduced from
photographs taken by the author.*

CHAPTER I

GENERAL SURVEY

LYING athwart the Atlantic tides, and at a distance from the north-west coast of Scotland varying from about thirty miles to fifty-four, are the Western Isles, or the Outer Hebrides, a chain of islands and islets, reefs and skerries, often called the Long Island, as though they were one long, continuous island.

Measured from Barra Head, in the south, to the Butt of Lewis, in the north, this defiant fragment of the very ancient world is roughly a hundred and thirty miles in length. Between these two extremities lie some quite large islands, and innumerable islets of every shape and size, and varying considerably in character.

Let us enumerate the more important of them.

The southernmost group in the chain is that known as the Barra Isles. It includes Berneray (or Barra Head, as it is sometimes called), Mingulay, Pabbay, Sandray, Vatersay, Muldoanich, and of course Barra itself, largest and most important of them. Then, in turn, come South Uist, Benbecula, and North Uist. To the north of North Uist is the island of Harris; and to the north of Harris is Lewis, which is by far the largest and most important of all the Western Isles, although so much of its area consists of loch and intractable moorland.

Geographically speaking, Lewis and Harris form one island. Yet it is customary to refer to them as though they were separate islands. The isthmus between the fiords of East and West Loch Tarbert connects North and South Harris.

The Western Isles, in addition to these main components, include literally hundreds of lesser isles. The larger and more important of these lie between Barra and South Uist, in the Sound of Barra, and between North Uist and Harris, in the Sound of Harris. Of the innumerable isles in the former seaway, Eriskay is the chief: included in the latter

1

are Berneray, Killegray, Pabbay, and Shillay. Berneray, the largest of them, is usually referred to as Berneray, Harris, in order to distinguish it readily from the island of the same name already noted as being one of the Barra Isles, and also from the largest of the Bernera(y)s, which is that situated off the north-west coast of Lewis. This last named is one of a series of rugged and remote islands in or about the entrance to Loch Roag. This series includes the Great Bernera, the Little Bernera, Pabbay, Vacsay, Berisay, and the Old Hill.

Besides the main chain and its more immediate satellites, several groups of still more remote islands fall to be noted. They are the Shiant Isles, Heiskeir or the Monach Isles, the Flannan Isles or Seven Hunters, North Rona, Sulasgeir, the St. Kilda group, and, finally, Rockall, the most distant speck of Britain, lying out in the Atlantic a hundred and eighty-four miles west of St. Kilda.

All these islands together form the Western Isles of Scotland, or the Long Island, or the Outer Hebrides. The *Inner* Hebrides, which embrace Skye, Mull, and many another well-known island, are closer to the Scottish mainland, and are therefore much less remote.

In the minds of many, there exists considerable confusion as to which are, and which are not, the Western Isles. It may be as well, therefore, that we should be clear as to the exact scope of this volume, lest we be criticised for the omission of matter more appropriate to our proposed companion volume, which will deal as exclusively with the Inner Hebrides (including Skye) as the present volume deals with the Outer.

In olden times, and indeed until fairly recently, it was customary to include, under the general title of the Western Isles, both the Inner and the Outer Hebrides. Since 1918, however, when the Outer Hebrides became a separate parliamentary constituency known as the Western Isles, their true geographical position in relation to the many other islands found off the west coast of Scotland has been more fully recognised. They are, in fact, the only islands entitled to this distinctive name; and the tendency at the present time is to apply this name exclusively to them—that is to say, to the islands comprising the Long Island.

Nevertheless, railway and steamship companies, as well as the proprietors of hotels and boarding-houses, still find the title an attractive one when advertising many of the more accessible of the *Inner* Hebrides. Who has not seen, for instance, those alluring posters in our railway-stations publicising cruises from Oban to the Western Isles? Those cruises, for the most part, are short sea-trips to Mull, to Iona, to Fingal's Cave, in Staffa. Then, from time to time one finds in the *Spectator* and periodicals of like character an advertisement of the Western Isles Hotel, inviting you to "spend your holidays amid the peace and beauty of the Western Isles". This establishment is situated, not in the Outer Hebrides, as one might suppose, but in Tobermory, in the Isle of Mull.

Until the parliamentary constituency of the Western Isles was created, Lewis, by far the largest and most populous of the Hebrides, formed part of the County of Ross and Cromarty, for parliamentary purposes; while Harris, together with its own islands (Scarp, Scalpay, Taransay, and the isles in the Sound of Harris) and all the Outer Hebrides to the south of it were included in Inverness-shire. For purposes of local administration, Lewis still forms part of Ross-shire—part of Ross and Cromarty; while Harris, North Uist, South Uist, Benbecula, and the Barra Isles belong to Inverness-shire. Lewis, for county purposes, is administered from Dingwall, the county town of Ross-shire. The remainder of the Western Isles, as now defined, are administered for like purposes from Inverness.[1]

The Minch (cf. *La Manche*, The Sleeve) is the name given to the sea intervening between the Western Isles and the

---

[1] By those who urge that the Western Isles should form an independent administrative unit, as well as a separate parliamentary constituency, it has been pointed out that their combined population of approximately 40,000 exceeds by a considerable margin that of no fewer than thirteen of the thirty-three counties of Scotland. Their population is nearly seven times that of Kinross, five times that of Nairn, nearly thrice that of Peebles or of Sutherland, and almost twice that of Orkney, Shetland, or Selkirk.

In population the Western Isles also exceed Caithness, Berwick, Wigtown, Kirkcudbright, and Clackmannan. Indeed, they approximate in this respect to Kincardine.

Lewis, taken by itself, and having a population equal to that of Caithness or of Berwick, is more populous than half the counties we have named. Lewis and Harris, taken together (geographically, as we already have seen, they form one island, though divided administratively between two counties) exceed Wigtown in the matter of population, and almost equal Kirkcudbright and Clackmannan.

mainland of Scotland. This sea, notorious even among the Hebrideans and the West Highlanders for the stormy passages many have experienced upon it, and actually dreaded by not a few of the less adventurous inhabitants of the seafaring communities dwelling on its fringes, is narrowest off the north-west coast of Skye, where it contracts to about fourteen miles. To the north and to the south it widens considerably. The Butt of Lewis, in the extreme north of the island, is thirty miles from the Sutherlandshire coast; while Barra Head is fifty-four miles from Ardnamurchan Point, which, as every Scottish schoolboy is obliged to learn at an early age, is the most westerly promontory of his country's mainland.

The area of the Western Isles is roughly 809,000 acres, or approximately 1,264 square miles. According to the figures given to me recently by the Director-General of the Ordnance Survey, it is made up as follows:

AREA (in acres) OF THE OUTER HEBRIDES

ISLANDS	LAND	INLAND WATER	SALT-MARSH	FORESHORE	TIDAL WATER	TOTAL
Barra Isles	22,221·968	98·752	–	2,595·599	–	24,916·319
North Uist	75,436·337	8,845·206	76·369	18,446·275	910·832	103,715·019
South Uist, including Benbecula	90,093·607	9,196·851	–	10,577·510	345·323	110,213·291
Harris	123,751·901	3,109·139	–	6,212·185	104·665	133,177·890
Lewis	404,183·255	24,862·857	229·777	7,775·454	149·985	437,201·328
Total Acreage	715,687·068	46,112·805	306·146	45,607·023	1,510·805	809,223·847
					Square Miles	1,264·4

Only the merest fraction of this vast area is cultivated; and it is doubtful whether, in a sense truly economic, much more is cultivable. Indeed, one might be excused for enquiring whether even such of it as is cultivated is worth the labour expended upon it. Various benefactors have spent considerable sums at different times in an endeavour to improve the husbandry of these islands, but with little success. To their well-intentioned efforts we refer in detail in our concluding chapter.

The population of the Long Island has shown little change during the present century, despite considerable emigration in the early nineteen-twenties. Emigration on a large scale took place from Lewis in 1923 and 1924. It is difficult, however, to say just how many left the island then. In a report published recently by the Lewis Association, the figure is put at 3,000. This, I am inclined to think, is an over-estimate. I should say that roughly a thousand Islanders left. They went to Canada, for the most part, aboard the *Metagama* and the *Montcalm*, vessels owned by the Canadian Pacific Railway.

The latest figures available are those of the census of 1931, when the total population of the Outer Hebrides was estimated at slightly under 39,000. Lewis accounted for approximately two-thirds of this number. The remaining third was scattered throughout Harris, the Uists, Barra, and the lesser isles adjacent thereto. These figures, taken in conjunction with the areas of the various islands, show at a glance how very sparsely peopled are the Western Isles. Roughly 39,000 inhabitants to 715,000 acres of land gives an average of but one-twentieth of a person to the acre, or $18\frac{1}{3}$ acres per person.

The rural population of Lewis at the present time is scattered throughout nearly a hundred villages of varying sizes. With the exception of the three small villages of Achmore, Cliascro, and Lochganvich, not one of these is situated farther than a mile from the sea, the narrow, coastal strip being almost the only cultivated land in the island. Those tens of thousands of acres of moorland and swamp in the centre are quite unreclaimed, quite uncultivated, and probably quite uncultivable. They are fit only for the grazing of a limited number of sheep throughout the year, and perhaps for cattle during the summer months.

Only in the town of Stornoway, in the villages situated in its immediate neighbourhood, in the peninsula known as Eye, or Point, reaching out into the Minch to the east of Stornoway, and in Ness, the northern parish of Lewis, is there any great concentration of population. Stornoway proper had just under 4,000 inhabitants in 1931. This number is somewhat increased, of course, at the height of the herring fishing season, on account of the great number of East Coast drifters operating from this port. Point and Ness, where so many crofting townships are contiguous, are extremely densely populated—populated far in excess of what the land available could ever support in any degree of comfort. When one subtracts from Lewis's population of 25,000 the population of these three areas, it leaves about 400,000 acres to the merest sprinkling of people. The same is true of the rest of the Outer Isles. Deduct the population of Tarbert, Lochmaddy, Lochboisdale, and Castlebay from roughly 14,000, and you see how few people inhabit 310,000 acres. It must not be supposed, however, that these islands are capable of carrying, *economically*, a larger population. Indeed, it is my considered opinion that, as in past years, they are burdened with a population far in excess of what they can reasonably be expected to support. Only by the continuance of much gratuitous assistance from outside, as we shall see later, is their present economy the least workable. They constitute a very heavy drain upon public revenue. One realises, of course, that this statement will be immediately challenged by those who take the popular and emotional view of the Isles and their inhabitants.

There was a time, of course, when many of the Western Isles carried a much larger population. The half-buried ruins of small townships and of some quite considerable villages are still to be seen on some of the lesser and more remote of them, which were deserted during the nineteenth century. In our own century, such islands as Mingulay, St. Kilda, and Heiskeir (the Monach Isles) have been evacuated.

Several of the smaller islands, now deserted, appear to have been inhabited and cultivated when Dean Monro visited them about the middle of the sixteenth century. The Dean refers to many "ane guid ile for corne, store, and fisching", and to many an isle " inhabit and manurit, fertill and fruit-full", that, for well over a hundred years, has been given over to the sea-birds, and possibly to a few sheep pastured upon it.

Dean Monro's account of the Long Island is the earliest we possess of any value. In 1549, when, in his capacity as High Dean of the Isles, he travelled to most of the Inner and Outer

Hebrides on a pastoral itinerary, several islands long since abandoned were inhabited and tilled. Take, for instance, the Little Bernera, in Loch Roag. "This ile," he writes, "is weill inhabited and manurit, and will give maire nor two hundred bows of beire [bolls of barley] with delving onlie."[1]

Martin Martin, writing of the Western Isles as he found them in 1695, gives their population at about 40,000. If this computation be an accurate one, as it may well be, it would seem as though the total population has altered little since the close of the eighteenth century.[2]

Remote as are the Western Isles, their chief centres of population are in regular sea communication with the mainland of Scotland all the year round. Six days a week, the mail-steamer sails to Stornoway, the metropolis of Lewis, from Kyle of Lochalsh, the rail-head in Wester Ross. Twice or thrice weekly, weather permitting (and it is seldom that our West Highland seamen allow anything as unexceptional as stormy weather to interfere with their routine), Castlebay, in Barra, and Lochboisdale, in South Uist, are reached by similar means from Oban; while Tarbert, in Harris, and Lochmaddy, in North Uist, are served by the mail-boat sailing on alternate days from Kyle, or from Mallaig, the latter being the terminus of the Old West Highland Railway. This means that Mallaig is in direct communication with King's Cross.

Besides these regular sailings, small cargo vessels ply at intervals between the Clyde ports and the Western Isles. During the summer months, even St. Kilda, until 1930 the remotest of the inhabited Hebrides, was visited by a Glasgow ship every fortnight or so, by way of the Sound of Harris. With the evacuation of St. Kilda in the autumn of that year, these visits ceased.

Between Stornoway and Tarbert (that is to say, between Lewis and Harris) there is no direct steamer service. To accomplish such a journey by sea, one would have to cross the

---

[1] *A Description of the Western Isles of Scotland called Hybrides*, by Sir Donald Monro, High Dean of the Isles, first published from the manuscript in 1774, and printed by William Auld, Edinburgh.
[2] *A Description of the Western Islands of Scotland (circa 1695)*, by Martin Martin, Gent. Printed for Andrew Bell, at the Cross-Keys & Bible, in Cornhill, near Stocks-Market, 1703.

Minch to Kyle of Lochalsh, and change steamers there. However, these two centres of population and of industry, situated thirty-six road miles apart, are connected by motor-bus, as indeed are nearly all the townships of the Outer Hebrides nowadays, even some of the most distant and remote of them. Almost every day of the week, excepting Sundays, improvised motor-buses of none too comfortable a kind run from many of the extremities of Lewis and of Harris to Stornoway, where most of them remain until after the arrival each evening of the daily mail-steamer from Kyle, whence it is scheduled to cross in approximately five-and-a-half hours.

Inseparably bound up with sea transport in these parts is the name of David MacBrayne, Limited, the steamship company formed nearly a century ago by Mr. David MacBrayne with a view to developing a regular service between Glasgow and the Western Highlands and Islands, where, hitherto, such means of communication had been spasmodic and uncertain. As has been said of the founder of the company, "he made circumstances, sending his steamers into Scottish undeveloped ports, and encouraging the crofter-fisherman to send his stirks, fish, and produce to the markets of the south". This was certainly more remunerative for the Islanders, especially when such traffic became regular and reliable. At the outset, one of the company's vessels sailed twice monthly from Glasgow to the Outer Isles, by way of Portree, in the Isle of Skye. Soon afterwards it became necessary to have a vessel based on Portree, in order to maintain a service thrice weekly between that port and the Outer Isles ports of Rodil and Tarbert, in Harris, and Lochmaddy, in North Uist. In 1880 MacBrayne acquired the Highland Railway Company's passenger and mail services to Portree and to Stornoway from Stromeferry, then the western terminus of the Dingwall-Skye railway. Eight years later, the services of the Highland Company's Inner Island Route, which operated from Oban, were incorporated in his organisation. In 1919 the sailings to the Outer Isles from the rail-heads at Kyle and Mallaig were reorganised, so as to meet a change in conditions brought about by the First World War. The Small Isles (Eigg, Rum, and Canna) and also Lochboisdale, were now included in a regular circuit.

The Second World War placed a very serious burden upon the company's personnel, especially on such members of it as were charged with the duty of actually navigating its steamers. Throughout the war, the masters of vessels serving the Outer Hebrides had considerable dangers to contend with. War risks were by no means negligible in these waters; and anyone familiar with them in daylight can well imagine the strain entailed in sailing them in the dark, without lights, and with a minimum of those navigational aids to which seafarers are accustomed in times of peace. Moreover, these vessels, throughout twelve months of the year, were then carrying not only very heavy cargoes of perishables, but also a passenger traffic formerly handled only during the peak days of the summer holidays.

Here, indeed, was a service demanding no less skill, endurance, and fortitude than were required on any battlefront; and it redounds to the glory of our West Highland sailors, as well as to those who had to organise matters in Glasgow under most trying circumstances, that there occurred not a single mishap of any gravity, and that even the *Lochmor*, the Stornoway boat, rarely failed through stress of weather or other circumstances to carry out her schedule.

For many years now, it has been customary to criticise, and with some bitterness, the Glasgow and Highland Royal Mail Steamers as operated by Messrs. MacBrayne; and I must confess that, in my earlier and less responsible days, I myself joined lustily in the declamatory chorus. However, when one realises to the full the circumstances under which the service has been run, not overlooking the totally uneconomic nature of so many of the islands served, and that a considerable government subsidy must be paid each year in respect of the mails carried by these steamers, even to some quite remote places, there is little cause for complaint under existing conditions. This does not mean, of course, that one is not aware of the extreme discomfort in which passengers are often obliged to cross the Minch.

Inter-communication among the various islands is sometimes more difficult than is communication between the principal islands and the mainland. This may appear surprising to those who, not knowing the Outer Hebrides, would naturally assume that, once you have disembarked at one of them, the others must be reasonably accessible. Islands where population is small are usually difficult to reach, and equally difficult to quit. Thus, it is no easy matter to obtain transport between the north of North Uist and Rodil, at the southern extremity of Harris; and it is almost impossible to reach the more southerly of the Barra Isles even from Castlebay, the port nearest to them. The difficulty in the case of the latter may be excused on the ground that, with the exception of Barra itself, and of Vatersay, the Barra Isles, though still used for grazing purposes, are now uninhabited. The only regular means of communication with Berneray, or Barra Head, is the motor-boat which, at stated intervals, sails from Castlebay to effect the relief at the lighthouse there.

Yet, he who desires to be independent of sea travel can accomplish much on foot. If he follow the islands' main roads, such as they are (stretches of them are exceedingly good, considering the sparse population they serve), and study carefully the state of the tides, he may pass, dryshod, from Pollachar, in the south of South Uist, to the Leac Bhan, the northernmost tip of North Uist, a total distance of fifty miles. When the tides are suitable, he may cross the North Ford, between Benbecula and North Uist. But this passage is a dangerous one; and the stranger, therefore, would be well advised to consult the natives as to how and when it should be attempted. There are quick-sands in this neighbourhood; and drowning accidents have occurred here from time to time, despite the fact that the various recognised ways across the ford are indicated by prominent cairns.

The South Ford, situated between the inn at Carnan, in South Uist, and Creagorry, in Benbecula, no longer con-stitutes a problem. The long, single-carriageway bridge now spanning it, constructed a few years ago, enables pedestrian and wheeled traffic alike to pass freely between South Uist and Benbecula at any hour of the day or night. It stretches firmly across the vast sands and shell-beaches; and the manner in which it has simplified transport between these two islands has encouraged the notion that before long further public funds may be forthcoming for the building of another bridge across the *North* Ford. However, not only is this ford thrice the width, but it would appear as though much greater difficulties are likely to be encountered in finding a series of firm foundations upon which the piers might be built. In any case, the cost of such an undertaking would be exorbitant, especially in these days of expensive materials, and having regard to the ridiculously high rate of wages now being paid in the Isles and elsewhere for dilatory and totally unskilled labour. The public, which has been excessively generous in recent years where the Western Isles are concerned, cannot be expected to finance a proposal, the cost of which would be colossal, and would far outweigh the benefit to be derived from it by a few thousand unproductive and largely indolent islanders. One cannot see how the mass of the crofters inhabiting these islands would benefit at all. A few of the more enterprising might.

A much more feasible proposition is the erection of a bridge across the narrow Sound of Earshader, in western Lewis, thus linking the large island of Bernera, in Loch Roag, with the Lewis mainland. The agitation for a bridge at this point has been going on for years; and it now looks as though something is to be done about it. As recently as the autumn of 1947, the highways committee of the Ross-shire County Council recommended to the Ministry of Transport the building of a nine-span, ferro-concrete structure, some 300 feet in length, at an estimated cost of £43,000. The actual bridge, it is said, will cost £30,250. The approach roads will cost £9,400, and land wayleave £200. Engineering construction charges have been estimated at £3,150. The Ministry, it was stated, would provide toward the total cost a grant of 60 per cent. The Department of Agriculture for Scotland promises a grant of 25 per cent. This leaves 15 per cent, which the Secretary of State for Scotland, when on a recent visit to Lewis, undertook to find.

The natives of Bernera have been expecting this bridge ever since 1932, the year in which their Member of Parliament, when opening the road to Earshader, pointed across the Sound and indicated that the next demand should be for a bridge. That very day there began what in Lewis is known as the "Battle for the Bernera Bridge". The County Council's approval of plans for a bridge to cost £43,000 is regarded as the Islanders' first signal victory in this protracted warfare.

Bernera's case for such a bridge is a reasonably good one, although the writer must confess to serious misgivings about the enormous public expenditure in which the Western Isles are involving the nation, and with remarkably little to show for it, except further incessant, and often unreasonable, demands. To this matter we shall return in general terms in a subsequent chapter.

The peat resources of Bernera, an island the surface of which shows much outcropping rock, are nearly exhausted. Quarrels between its townships over the few remaining peat-banks are numerous and bitter. Some of these have had to be settled by the Land Court. For several years now, the inhabitants of Bernera have been cutting peats on the Lewis mainland adjacent to them, and have ferried them over the narrow Sound of Earshader.

Then the Bernera shielings (the island's summer grazings) are also situated on the mainland of Lewis. This obliges the crofters to swim their cattle over the strait twice a year—from Bernera to the Uig moors in the early summer, and home again in the autumn. They contend that not only is this a hazardous undertaking, but that it is also bad for the cattle. I myself have witnessed this annual exodus to the summer shielings scattered about the vast moorland upon which the Bernera people has had grazing rights for a very long time. Indeed, for centuries, the swimming cattle, on their way to or from the shielings, have been towed across these narrows at low, slack tide. This method of transport need not necessarily be hazardous. If carried out on a calm day, it seems simple enough. Many of the Bernera cows have swum so often that they seem to think little of it. In fact, some of them would appear to enjoy it, especially when returning to their native isle in the autumn.

While on this pastoral topic, it might be mentioned in passing that this locality has grim associations with the Highland and Island agrarian troubles of the nineteenth century. It was on the hillside at Earshader, close to the site for the proposed bridge, that the angry crofters of Bernera defied Donald Munro, the Baron Bailie of Lewis, as he was termed. Donald threatened to bring a detachment of the Volunteers from Stornoway to drive the rebellious islanders into the sea! This was one of the earliest revolts against the tyrannical conduct of the factors. It helped to precipitate the state of affairs which ultimately led to the Crofters' Act.

. . . .

A little beyond the township of Newton, in North Uist, and a couple of miles short of the Leac Bhan, the road comes to an end at an inconspicuous jetty on the fringe of a white, sandy inlet at a place appropriately named *Port nan Long*, the Ships' Harbour. Thereafter the traveller must proceed along the hillside, selecting the more direct of the tracks made by the crofters' sheep, and by the few who, from time to time, cross between North Uist and Berneray, largest and most populous of the isles in the Sound of Harris. When winds and tides are suitable, he may avail himself of the Newton Ferry, enabling him to reach any of the isles in the Sound from this jetty, or to land at Rodil, in the south of Harris, a dozen miles away. He may then traverse the entire distance of eighty miles between Rodil and the Butt of Lewis without interruption, except that his progress may be a little retarded by mountains which are in no way formidable.

The difficulty often experienced in procuring transport by small boat across the Sound of Harris is also to be met with when seeking to cross the Sound of Barra. In neither case is there a regular ferry service. Occasionally a boat, under sail or perhaps motor-driven, may reach Pollachar from Eoligarry, the northernmost district of Barra, ferrying across the Sound of Barra Islanders who probably have relatives or business on both sides of it. Since the construction of the slip at Kilbride, a mile or so to the east of Pollachar, and therefore somewhat better situated in relation to Eriskay, much ferrying has been diverted from Pollachar, with the result that the old inn, standing there on the fringe of the sea-rocks, is less frequented than in former years. Most of the Eriskay traffic now by-passes it, finding the jetty at Kilbride, or that at Ludaig, more convenient, both as regards distance and as regards shelter from winds and crowding seas. Passengers *do* come and go by Pollachar, however, more especially those arriving direct from, or leaving for, Eoligarry.

At Pollachar one may obtain, at almost any hour, an excellent and inexpensive tea. Here, furthermore, those addicted to the dram (and they are notoriously numerous in the Highlands and Islands) may be served with such satisfaction as their purses will allow, this inn being the only licensed premises in South Uist south of the spacious hotel at Lochboisdale.

The inn at Pollachar, the new proprietor will tell one, is built on sand—" a *hard* sand ", he will add. If you ask him how he became aware of this, he will explain how he recently discovered it for himself, when delving to renovate the inn's drainage. More than two centuries ago, the lime used in building this inn was procured from shells shipped across the Sound of Barra from the Great Cockle Shore. Its roof, the old people of South Uist delight in telling one, was just being put on in July, 1745, when Charles Edward Stuart landed on the strand in Eriskay, but two or three miles away. When Miss Ellen Brown, the present licensee at Pollachar, applied for her licence in 1945, the solicitor representing her explained to the licensing court in Lochmaddy that the application was in respect of premises where, according to tradition in the Isles, " Prince Charlie had his first ' half '—his first taste of real Highland whisky—while on his way to Milton to see Flora MacDonald." The tradition is certainly a picturesque one, if nothing else!

This inn, which lies roughly six miles from Lochboisdale, contains some fine wood panelling and wood ceilings, all of which are said to have been hand-sawn in olden times from driftwood cast on the shore, so close at hand.

The trout-fishing of all the Uist lochs to the south of Lochboisdale go with the inn at Pollachar; and the crofters at Kilbride readily assure one that the lochs lying among the hills so near to them are as full of brown trout as any in South Uist, a part of the Outer Hebrides famous for its loch fishing.

The Uists, so teeming with lochs, are the anglers' paradise. Devotees of the rod proclaim that South Uist is considered better than North Uist for their purpose, though the lochs of the latter are by no means lacking in the requisite amenities. Since South Uist is the anglers' principal paradise among the Western Isles, the hotel at Lochboisdale must necessarily be their Mecca. In any of its apartments, and at almost any hour, you may hear the most trifling minutiae concerning fish and loch, rod and reel, line and fly. The problem as to whether this hook or that knot is the better may be debated there for months on end, without anyone's being a whit more convinced that his own particular preference is not the superior.

It is the boast of those who, year after year, use the Lochboisdale hotel as a base from which the innumerable lochs everywhere around it may be fished, that all catches measuring less than fifteen inches, or weighing under twenty-four ounces, are instantly replaced in the water whence they were taken. Moreover, the maximum number of rods allowed to operate at one time is so strictly observed that the angler returning to the hotel with an empty basket is regarded as being unworthy of what Izaak Walton called " the contemplative man's recreation ", this being the sub-title of his famous treatise.

If the traveller do not happen to be related in some way to the ferryman, or perhaps to the people inhabiting one or other of the isles between which he is desirous of passing, he is liable to find inter-island transport both difficult and unreasonably expensive. For example, it will cost him seven-and-six to cross from South Uist to Eriskay, a distance from Ludaig to Haun of not much more than a mile. One is aware, of course, that the boat conveying him may have to return without a passenger. But, even if he go by the motor-boat employed in carrying the mails, and subsidised for so doing, he may be charged five shillings for the single journey. Indeed, the Islanders, in their excessive greed for money, now sting the stranger whenever they can. This certainly disheartens the tourist with limited means, as does also the cavalier manner in which many of the hotels treat the *bona fide* traveller seeking a night's shelter, or even a simple meal. Hotel proprietors or their gauche underlings will refuse accommodation when there is plenty of room. They often cannot be bothered with people wanting board and lodgings. The sale of liquor is the great thing with most of them. It brings in ample revenue; and often the management, or some ill-mannered person acting perfunctorily on its behoof, will show little interest in the slower ways of turning a few honest shillings. The traveller, with whom they do not happen to be personally acquainted,

15

is inclined to be looked upon as a nuisance, and particularly so if he be one of those odd creatures who do not patronise the hotel bar, or order drinks between or with his meals. The conduct of all such affairs in the Isles is very arbitrary indeed. The stranger arriving at a hotel there is apt to be bewildered by the casual manner in which he is accepted as a guest, or by the unhelpful tones in which he is turned empty away. Perhaps, as a special obligement, when tarrying an hour or two before proceeding with his journey, he may be given some food, rather grudgingly, upon his asking for it. Yet, as often as not, a series of petty pretexts will be proffered for alleged inability to satisfy, even in some small degree, his physical needs. The excuse that, owing to rationing and a shortage of food, there is nothing available for the casual client is hardly a valid one in the Western Isles, *where there is no food shortage*. In comparison with such as is to be had elsewhere in the country, food is superabundant in these parts, and there is much irregular trafficking in it. Ask for alcohol, however, and it is very unlikely that it will be refused you! Most of the inns in the Isles, as presently run, would seem to be doing everything in their power to discourage tourist traffic.

. . . .

Scotland is said to be one of the most air-minded countries in the world!

There is a tendency to think of air travel in terms of vast and luxurious airway terminals at London, Paris, or New York, where almost prohibitively expensive air-liners await the pleasure of business magnates, of film stars and government agents, and of wealthy play-boys and their women. Air travel, however, is essentially a utilitarian means of transport. The aeroplane defeats mountain barriers and seas. And no civilised country in the world is so surrounded, crumpled, divided, defended, and gloriously endowed by encircling waters, lochs, mountains, and highlands as is Scotland. The Scots, as it happens, are an air-minded nation, and have been so for many years. The crofters, shepherds, and small farmers of the Western Isles and of the Orkneys and Shetlands have accepted the aeroplane as part of their everyday existence.

The story of Scotland's air-lines is that of the men who surveyed and pioneered the routes, often at their own expense.

Stornoway from the Gallows Hill

In the far north of the country, Captain E. E. Fresson, until recently Area Manager of the British European Airways in northern Scotland, was seeking new ground for his five-shilling joy rides, when he realised that there was a demand for an air service across the stormy Pentland Firth. In 1933 he founded Highland Airways, Ltd., when a regular service with a single four-seater was started between Inverness and Kirkwall. In 1934 the company received the first internal air-mail contract to be granted in Britain. The same year saw also the inauguration of a service from Aberdeen to Kirkwall, and an inter-island service connecting Longhope (Inverness), Westray, Sanday, Stronsay, and North Ronaldsay with Kirkwall. The following year the Inverness-Orkney service was extended to Lerwick, in the Shetland Isles.

The immediate success of the first Scottish air-line occasioned some misgivings. It was said that at the take-off and return times at Inverness, and in all weathers, there was always a well-dressed character in a bowler hat watching in the background. It was discovered that the L.M.S. Railway was interested in the venture, and was zealously counting the number of passengers. Subsequently, in a spirit of *noblesse oblige*, the pilot, when on the point of taking-off, would yell to this bystander, holding up his fingers to indicate the number he had on board. In course of time the watcher vanished.

During the same eventful year—1934—Mr. George Nicholson decided at Renfrew to test the scope for air services to the Outer Hebrides. With a capital of £7,000, he formed Northern and Scottish Airways, Ltd., and opened his first Scottish route to Campbeltown and Islay. In 1935 a service between Glasgow and Skye was started; and by the following year a circular return service was in operation between Glasgow, Skye, North Uist, South Uist, Barra, and Glasgow.

Mr. Nicholson and Captain David Barclay, his chief pilot, carried out in the Western Isles widespread air surveys for landing-grounds, most of which were developed at the company's expense. When they found a likely spot, agreement with the local landholders was not always easy. The local Sheep Grazing Committee had to be consulted; and deadlock in negotiations often resulted. In one instance, what seemed

Mr. MacKenzie, proprietor of Carnish Inn, North Uist, arriving in Benbecula by way of the North Ford

to be insurmountable difficulties melted away like magic in face of the formidable supply of whisky thoughtfully brought on the scene at the critical moment!

In 1937 these two pioneer companies amalgamated to form Scottish Airways, Ltd. The crofters and small farmers of the Isles were now to become quite accustomed to air travel, and to the sight of aircraft gliding between the channels of the islands, often no more than a hundred feet above the water.

In the meanwhile, private companies were being formed throughout the United Kingdom to take advantage of the growth in air travel. From 1934 the number of air-line companies had been increasing steadily; and there was a considerable amount of competition, with the result that almost all of them were running at a loss. The largest of these concerns, Railways Air Services, Ltd., realising that nothing was to be gained by trying to force each other out of business in starting competitive air routes, did its best to enter into agreement with various operators with a view to pooling experience, reducing costs, and offering to the public the best possible facilities. As a result, between 1934 and 1939 many private companies, including Scottish Airways, entered into working agreement with the railway's network, or were peaceably absorbed, until, at the outbreak of war, co-ordination had been achieved with most of the companies operating air services within the British Isles.

Scottish Airways, Ltd., during its first year, carried 13,207 passengers, while its aircraft flew 1,082,316 passenger miles. Its development was steady and encouraging; and in 1945 it carried 41,830 passengers, and had a passenger mileage of 5,840,500. No fewer than ten routes were then in operation.

As an example of the local difficulties experienced in operating the Island services, one recalls the story of the ancient Islander who booked a seat on one of the Hebrides services while Double Summer Time was in force, and who turned up at the aerodrome two hours late. When told that his plane had gone two hours previously, he remarked, " Oh! *you* go by the new time: *I* go by God's Time."

The amalgamation of Highland Airways, Ltd., and the Northern and Scottish Airways, Ltd., added impetus to the development of air transport in Scotland; and by May, 1938, a Glasgow-Perth-Inverness service was in operation, linking the northern and southern routes. By establishing connections at Glasgow with Railway Air Services, it became possible for the first time to travel by regular air service from the Shetlands to London, to the Channel Isles, and to the Continent.

With the outbreak of hostilities in September, 1939, all internal air services in the British Isles were instantly suspended. However, less than a fortnight after the declaration of war, the government's approval was obtained for the restoration of restricted services on the Glasgow-Campbeltown-Islay and the Inverness-Orkney-Shetland routes. These were the first war-time services to be authorised within the British Isles. By this time, Scottish aircraft and crews had proceeded to their stations in the south of England to undertake communication work, which they did until the fall of France in 1940. Much might be written about the feats performed by Scottish aviators in those difficult days. The following example is typical.

A few days before France capitulated, one of the company's De Havilland Rapides was as far south as Bordeaux, with the enemy sighting the town. Given the alternatives of undertaking an extremely hazardous flight to England over enemy-occupied territory, or of abandoning his aircraft and returning to England by sea, the pilot chose the former. Under the eyes of the enemy, he took off safely; but, owing to the inferior quality of the oil picked up in France, engine trouble soon developed, with the result that he was forced to land in Jersey. By a piece of good fortune, there was on Jersey's airport a De Havilland 86, which had been undergoing annual repair, and had of necessity to be abandoned. Working overnight, the flight engineer, with the assistance of the pilot and radio officer, was able to extract the unserviceable engine, and replace it with one of the engines from the abandoned craft. The pilot then flew his passengers safely to England. This machine was one of the last to leave the Channel Isles before the Germans occupied them. This crew of three is now on the staff of British European Airways. Captain Donald Prentice, the pilot, is Flight Captain at Aberdeen. Mr. J. Rawes is Maintenance Control Engineer at Renfrew. The

Radio Officer, Mr. J. Mitchell, is a Navigation and Telecommunication Officer at Renfrew.

After the fall of France, the various aircraft returned to their bases in Scotland, whence, throughout the whole of the war, they operated the restricted services with 98 per cent regularity. Two De Havilland Rapides belonging to Scottish Airways had a plaque placed in the front bulkhead, each bearing the aeroplane's registration, and the words, "War Service in France, September, 1939, to June, 1940, with Scottish Airways Crews."

In August, 1946, the Civil Aviation Act received the Royal Assent, and the British European Airways then came officially into existence to operate British internal lines. In Scotland the air lines continued to be run by Scottish Airways, Ltd., until February, 1947, when they were handed over, and the Scottish Division of the B.E.A. was formed.

Despite the tremendous amount of reorganisation which, without interrupting the normal services, had to be effected, the most comprehensive schedules in the history of Scottish aviation were put into effect in May, 1947. One noteworthy feature of this summer programme was the inauguration of the longest internal air route in the United Kingdom—over six hundred miles—between London-Edinburgh-Aberdeen and Shetland. In connection with this route, Turnhouse Airport, Edinburgh, was brought into use for the first time as a civil airport on a joint-user basis with the R.A.F. The number of daily flights in the Scottish Division increased at the same time from 52 to 93; while aircraft mileage jumped from 4,500 to 10,900 per day on regular services. The number of flights between Glasgow and London and between Prestwick and London was increased, and the capacity of the services between Scotland and Northern Ireland was considerably augmented with the introduction, on the London-Glasgow and Glasgow-Belfast routes, of the luxury passenger air-liner, the Vickers Viking.

By August, 1947, the B.E.A. in Scotland were operating over seventeen routes, providing a total of 382 services weekly.

Vickers Viking, and D.C.47 air-liners, with their silver elegance, have brought added comfort and speed to the Scottish routes. These modern aircraft on regular services with the British European Airways have armchair seating and heated passenger cabins. There is also a fully licensed bar aboard all these air-liners; and cigarette smoking is permitted. This means that, even in the air, the nation may indulge freely two of its major obsessions! The D.C.47 carries a crew of four, and seats twenty-one passengers. The Viking seats twenty-four passengers, and also has a crew of four.

The growth of air travel in Scotland may be seen from the following comparative statistics of Scottish Airways, Ltd., between February and December, 1946, and of British European Airways in Scotland for the corresponding period in 1947:

	Service Miles Flown	Passengers Carried	Passenger Miles Flown
British European Airways (Scottish Division) Feb./Dec., 1947	2,341,406	103,703	17,577,201
Scottish Airways, Ltd. Feb./Dec., 1946	1,546,539	59,629	8,487,002

An interesting aspect of air transport in Scotland is the air-ambulance service between the Islands and the mainland. This has resulted in the saving of many lives. The inhabitants of the Western Isles and of the Orkneys and the Shetlands all stress the relief of mind the aeroplane has brought them. Before the arrival of the air-ambulance, serious illness, climbing and shooting accidents, and complicated child-birth cases meant either death or an agonising and hazardous sea-trip to the mainland. This service is carried out entirely by De Havilland aircraft. By removing the passenger seats, and rigging special stretchers, all the service aircraft can be converted quickly for air-ambulance purposes. In 1935 the County Councils responsible for the administration of the Islands decided to include the air-ambulance service in their scheme to supply medical assistance to the Highlands and Islands; and the local doctors of the Highland Medical Service were empowered, at their discretion, and with the approval of the Department of Health for Scotland, to call upon the company for an air-ambulance at any time. Scottish Airways carried in ten years over a thousand ambulance cases.

As indicating the time-saving advantage which the air-ambulance provides for the inhabitants of the Hebrides, the following emergency flights are typical. An urgent call was received from the Isle of Colonsay; and arrangements were made for the patient to be taken by speed-boat to Port Askaig, in Islay, and thence by road-ambulance to the aerodrome at Port Ellen. There the aircraft took over, and the journey to Glasgow was completed by air. A landing was made just before midnight. In all, the patient's journey from Colonsay to Glasgow took less than three hours, whereas the steamer was not due to call at Colonsay until the following day, after which a journey, by land and sea, of some fifteen hours would have to be undertaken.

During the war a direct request was received from the Department of Health for Scotland for an air-ambulance to proceed to Barra, where six sailors, whose ship had been torpedoed in the Atlantic, had been washed ashore, after drifting many days in an open boat. The aircraft made a landing on the beach, picked up the men, and flew them to Glasgow for the medical treatment they so urgently needed.

Of the air services to and from the Hebrides, I can write from personal experience. I was one of the first to drop out of the skies on the golden sands at Northton, in Harris, when they were the only landing-ground in use in the Outer Isles. This was some years before the establishment of a civil airport either in Lewis or in Benbecula. By arrangement, some days later, a 'plane landed on these same sands to pick me up and carry me off to Renfrew.

I shall never forget my sitting alone by the fringe of the Northton Sands on a quiet, sunlit forenoon, waiting for a pilot friend who was not due for half an hour or so. Could I have been dreaming? I asked myself—dreaming that, quite shortly, something with wings was to descend near by, and taxi across the sands to within a foot or two of the very spot where I was seated with my suitcase? Such a thing seemed incredible, fantastic. Yet, there, before me, in the sand, were the tyre-marks of the 'plane which had deposited me here but a few days earlier. Our Hebrides had been noted for their remoteness, for their inaccessibility; and here was I, waiting confidently at this spot, several miles removed from any of the island ports at which the mail-boats from the mainland are wont to call. And then I detected a droning in the distant sky. Sure enough, my friend was keeping his tryst. It was now about 11 a.m. Two hours later, I was lunching in Glasgow. The Hebrides were now far away. Something revolutionary had happened. The wonder of it all haunted me for days.

The other day I flew from Inverness to Stornoway's airport, on a visit to kinsfolk living close at hand. In an hour's time I was stepping down to familiar turf, within a couple of miles of their threshold. That seemed even more incredible, as I began to reflect on the long and wearisome journeys by rail and sea, to which I had been accustomed.

Recently I alighted on the Great Cockle Shore of Barra, surely one of the loveliest scenes in all the Hebrides. I had known the Cockle Shore in earlier years, when nothing swifter than a cart or a bicycle passed this way. To-day, at least one 'plane lands there every day, except on Sundays, and runs up to the shore at Suidheachan, a spot noted as being the abode of Highland faeries. What the faeries must think of the aeroplanes' invasion of their domain, we do not know. But we do know that their coming to the Isles has brought comfort and relief to the seriously ill, and to those who dread a tardy sea-voyage. There are many people in the Hebrides, as also in the Northern Isles of Scotland, who never visited the mainland until these air services were inaugurated. The stormy Minch and the restless Pentland Firth were more than they could face.

Nevertheless, for all this development in air transport, our Western Isles remain remote on the whole; and therein lies much of their charm and attraction. Indeed, parts of them are exceedingly remote. There are small, crofting communities and isolated homesteads situated in Lewis and in Harris, by the shores of their wild, rocky fiords, which must be the loneliest and remotest in all Britain. I know in these Isles solitary homes removed eight or ten miles from their nearest neighbour. And not just any ordinary eight or ten miles, which one can travel not too uncomfortably and inconveniently in a vehicle, but miles of trackless moorland, of rocks, of lochs and swamps, of streams, of acres of naked gneiss—barren distances, which are often interrupted by dangerous tideways. It is not so much the actual distance to be covered that matters in such circumstances as the nature of the surface intervening. Two or three miles an hour is good going on foot in some of the wilder parts of the Western Isles; and even these parts are accessible only to the surest-footed and the soundest in wind and limb.

Let us now look at the surface of this ancient land.

The eastern coast-line, from the Butt of Lewis as far south as the Sound of Harris, rises for the most part in cliffs, with off-lying skerries. Thereafter it is inclined to be flatter, until it reaches the lofty and precipitous cliffs of the Barra Isles. The east coast, furthermore, is penetrated in places by long, deep fiords, and by ample bays such as Stornoway Bay and Castle Bay. In contrast with this is the west shore, with its wide stretches of machar or meadow-land, covered largely with bent-grass, and fringed by sweeping bays, the margins of which are usually characterised by enormous crescents of white shell-sand piled up through the ages by Atlantean winds and tides. Many of these bays are extremely beautiful, especially when sunlight emphasises the natural colourings of earth and sea and sky. Under certain conditions, the colourings of Uig Bay, in western Lewis, for instance, or of the sandy crescents on the Atlantic side of southern Harris, are too exquisite to admit of description.

Lewis has many fiords, both on its east and on its west coasts. Among the larger and better known of these pene-trating sea-lochs are Loch Luirbost, Loch Erisort, Loch Odhairn, Loch Shell, Loch Seaforth, Loch Resort, and Loch Carloway. In Harris one finds such considerable inlets as East Loch Tarbert and West Loch Tarbert, and also fiords like Loch Stockinish and Loch Finsbay. In Benbecula and the Uists there is none on the west coast, but several of note on the east. The innermost inlets of Loch Eport, in North Uist, are many miles from the open sea. So, also, are those of Loch Boisdale and Loch Eynort, in South Uist.

Some of these sea-lochs, where they run for great distances into the land, tend to insulate considerable areas of the larger islands. An isthmus of but half a mile in width links North

Harris and South Harris. So far inland does Loch Seaforth reach that its northern shore is but a mile and a half from the head of Loch Erisort. This comparatively narrow strip of intervening moorland is all that unites to the rest of Lewis the large district known as Pairc, or Park. The head of Loch Resort, that long, narrow loch penetrating eight or ten miles on the Atlantic side, is not much more than four miles from Kinloch Roag and the salmon-pool where the river from Loch Morsgail meets the sea at Little Loch Roag. The salt-marshes of Loch Eport are not much more than half a mile from the point whence it is possible at certain tides to cross on foot to Baleshare, the large island lying off the west coast of North Uist. That half-mile or so unites the southern part of North Uist with the northern. Loch Eynort and Loch Boisdale, in similar fashion, almost divide South Uist into three large islands, the smallest of which would be about the size of Barra.

Ancient the Western Isles certainly are. Indeed, the archaean rocks comprising their foundation are gneiss—Lewisian gneiss, as geologists term what they believe to be the oldest of rock formations. Geikie pronounced this gneiss to be the oldest fragment of Europe. Subsequent geologists of equal standing have not merely confirmed this opinion, but are largely agreed as to its being the oldest portion of the world's surface.

At this point a brief geological survey may not appear inappropriate.

From Barra Head to the Butt of Lewis, and including such far-flung outliers as the Flannan Isles or Seven Hunters, Sulasgeir, and North Rona, the Outer Hebrides are strongly and enduringly built of some of the oldest rocks known. They are almost entirely pre-Cambrian in composition, and are highly metamorphosed. They belong to what is referred to as the Lewisian Series of Scotland. Although they are developed most extensively in the Long Island, large exposures of them occur in the Inner Hebrides, and also along the western seaboard of Sutherland, Ross, and Inverness-shire. These pre-Cambrian rocks, spoken of affectionately as "The Old Boy", fall into two groups. One of these is the interesting series of

gneisses and schists, which were originally sedimentary rocks
—sandstones, shales, and limestones—all of which were first
formed under water, and were highly metamorphosed at a
later date to form the group known collectively as paragneisses. The second and more widely distributed group
of gneisses and schists is the orthogneisses. These are the
metamorphosed equivalents of granites, gabbros, and other
intrusive, igneous rocks. The paragneisses are found only
to the north of the Sound of Harris, and chiefly in two belts
running north-westwards from Rodil and from Loch Finsbay
to Toe Head and to the vicinity of Borve Lodge, on the west
coast of Harris.

By far the most spectacular geological feature of the
Western Isles is the great belt of crushed rocks extending from
Sandray and Vatersay, two of the Barra Isles, up the east
coast to Tolsta Head, in Lewis. Along this coastal belt, and
reaching inland sometimes to a depth of from five to six
miles, the bright, mica-spangled gneisses and dark-green and
black hornblende rocks have been so intensely sheared that
their original coarse granitic appearance has been altered to
a very fine-grained dull green or dull grey. Beneath this zone
of crushing lies a great thrust-plane, dipping eastward at a
low angle towards the Minch. The crushed rocks, known as
crush-breccias and mylonites (milled rocks) lie for the most
part above the thrust-plane. The pressure, which caused
the rocks to move gently up this inclined plane, came from
the east. It was so powerful that in many places near the base
of the plane of movement the gneisses, by a process akin to
melting, were converted into a black, glassy rock known as
Flinty Crush, because of its dark blue or black colour, and
its tendency to splinter. It splinters very easily.

Younger than the gneisses, though probably also of pre-
Cambrian age, and composed of fragments of these older rocks,
is the great thickness of conglomerate, or pudding-stone,
known as the Stornoway Beds. This is to be found to the
north, east, and south of the town of Stornoway, in Lewis, and
also round the western shore of Broad Bay, but two or three
miles away. These boulder beds, in the absence of convincing evidence, have been classified by geologists as Torridonian,
Old Red Sandstone, or Triassic; but the view is held that per-

haps they ought to be regarded as part of the pre-Cambrian Torridonian Series, which is so strongly developed above the Lewisian gneiss along the north-western coast of the Scottish mainland.

Apart from the intrusion of some igneous dykes in Tertiary times, when the volcanoes of the Inner Hebrides are said to have been active, there is little to record in the geological history of the Outer Isles until we reach the Pleistocene period, or Great Ice Age. It would appear that twice at least the immense ice-cap from the mainland ploughed its way across the Minch to cover practically the whole of the Long Island. Only the peaks of Ben More and Hecla, in South Uist, and of the Clisham, in North Harris, and some of the higher mountains situated in the north-west of Lewis (the mountain-peaks of Uig) would seem to have raised their heads clear of the icy waste. There is good evidence of a third glaciation, when the Long Island nursed its own small ice-sheet.

To-day, quite obviously, the scenery bears the imprint of this prolonged invasion. Glacial striae or scratchings scored across the polished rocks, innumerable gravel-dammed lochs, lochans, and tarns gouged out of the solid rocks, and the ubiquitous, dolphin-backed exposures of naked rock (commonly called *roches moutonnées*) are the most conspicuous marks of the passage of the ice. Boulder-clay or till, where the latest glaciation and the present-day streams have not already conveyed it out to sea, lies strewn in many patches, varying in size, beneath the peat or thin soil. Though some of the boulders in the clay are of local origin, others have been transported from the mainland by the débris-laden ice.

Raised beaches have not been discovered in the Outer Hebrides. The reason for their absence may possibly be that the islands have suffered depression in our own post-glacial time. In several places around the coast, buried peat and tree-stumps have been found lying far below present-day high-water mark. Line-fishermen in the Sound of Harris have often brought to the surface such wasting remnants of a former land vegetation. Martin Martin mentions such tree-stumps covered by the sea in this locality. Referring to Berneray, one of the isles in the Sound of Harris, he writes: "The west end of this island, which looks to St. Kilda, is called the wooden harbour, because the sands at low water discover several trees that have formerly grown there. Sir Norman MacLeod told me that he had seen a tree cut there, which was afterwards made into a harrow."

The constructive and destructive forces of Nature are never at rest. To-day the great rollers from the open Atlantic, aided by strong, westerly winds, are smashing to a fine powder the shells of the seashore. This powder the winds carry inland to enrich the fertile machar-lands fringing so much of the western seaboard of the Western Isles. The long, narrow *geos* and *slocs* are also the work of the sea, which has excavated the coast-line along prominent joint-planes in the gneisses. Even many of the inland lochs have been invaded by the sea as the result of the depression of the land surface already referred to. The Uists and Benbecula abound in such lochs. The Outer Hebrides, like the Orkney Islands, exhibit a drowned topography.

The St. Kilda group of islands, lying some forty miles to the west of the Long Island, is, in all likelihood, the basal wreck of a stupendous volcano. Except for the lonely out-post of Rockall, it forms the most westerly focus of volcanic eruption in what geologists term the Brito-Icelandic Igneous Province, which once extended from the Mountains of Mourne, in Ireland, to Hecla, in Iceland, and perhaps even as far as the east coast of Greenland.

Our present-day differentiation between the Outer Hebrides and the Inner is justified on geological grounds, as well as on those topographical grounds which we discussed earlier. Whereas the former are composed of the primeval gneiss, the rocks of the latter would appear to belong to an age much more recent in the earth's history. For the most part, they are Tertiary rocks of volcanic origin. In many of the Inner Hebrides, notably in Skye and in Mull, great cliffs of basalt, rising precipitously from the sea in a series of terraces, form extensive table-lands, which are generally flat, and are covered with a characteristic sward affording pastur-age for sheep and cattle. Here and there the basalt, at a much later date, has been penetrated by igneous intrusions of considerable magnitude, producing such mountain masses as the Coolins of Skye and the Coolins of Rum. The islands, however, lack that fertility one usually associates with volcanic deposit. The glaciers of the Ice Age carried away from the land—from its glens and plateaux—such rich detritus as must have accumulated here in some previous geological era. Thus good cultivation is possible only in the base of the wider valleys, where such glacial action may have left a layer of boulder clay. ' The enormous deposits of peat in the Isles, suggesting a moist climate promoting the growth of a dense vegetation, has done much to protect the underlying rocks from further denudation by epigene agents.

. . . . . .

It cannot be said that the Outer Islands are mountainous in the sense in which mountaineers would use the term. Only in Lewis, Harris, and South Uist will the serious mountaineer discover anything worthy of consideration. Even in these islands, he will not be able to ascend above sea-level higher than 2,622 feet—the height of the Clisham, in North Harris.

On the other hand, the rock-climber will have little difficulty in finding opportunities for testing his fortitude and sureness of foot, not only in the three main islands mentioned, but also in many of the lesser isles. The Outer Hebrides possess some of our finest and most formidable rock-faces; and there is reason for believing that, with the appreciable growth in the membership of the rock-climbing fraternity in recent years, they may soon be attracting adventurous spirits who, hitherto, have regarded their mountains as undeserving of attention. The sea-cliffs on the western side of Berneray and of Mingulay, with their myriads of wild-fowl, would try the most intrepid rocker no less than did those of the St. Kilda group of islands before the evacuation of Hirta in the autumn of 1930. The north face of Conachar, the highest point of Hirta, principal island of the group, drops almost perpendicularly to the Atlantic thirteen hundred feet below, thus constituting the loftiest cliffs in the British Isles.

South Uist possesses three distinct groups of hills, all of which are confined to a belt running down the island's eastern side. The southern group, situated to the south of Loch Boisdale, offers little attraction for the hill-walker, and none at all for the mountaineer. It consists of a series of rounded hills. Easaval, the highest of them, is no more than about eight hundred feet.

Ten distinct hills, two of which exceed a thousand feet in height, compose the second group, which lies between Loch Boisdale and Loch Eynort, and which, for the most part, is covered with grass or heather, and has little rock out-cropping. Stulaval, the highest of them, is 2,227 feet, and may be ascended without much difficulty from more than one direction.

Of much greater interest is the third group, lying between Loch Eynort and Loch Skiport, in the north. It embraces two noteworthy peaks—Ben More and Hecla, which are 2,034 and 1,988 feet, respectively. The former includes a line of formidable precipices extending half a mile to the east of its summit, with an average drop of nearly nine hundred feet. These precipices are extremely steep. A number of narrow gullies and chimneys divides them into frowning buttresses, upon which may be found several hazardous climbs as yet not fully worked out by those whose delight it is to risk themselves in such adventure, and to plot in minutest detail the routes by which conquest may ultimately be achieved.[1]

Benbecula is a flat island—an island of low land and of innumerable freshwater lochs. Rueval, its only hill, is a little over four hundred feet; and only at two other points does the surface exceed a hundred feet. Benbecula is of immense interest to the archaeologist and the historian, but of little to him seeking physical exertion and hazard. Anyone with a knowledge of mountains will be inclined to regard the island merely as a stepping-stone in the midst of the Great Fords, which he must needs cross when passing between the Uists.

What North Uist lacks in high ground is certainly compensated for in low ground and in loch. Apart from Eaval (1,138 feet) its highest hill, rising in the south-east corner of the island, and for North Lee (823 feet) and South Lee (920 feet) lying between Loch Maddy and Loch Eport, it has no

---

[1] The mountaineer or rock-climber contemplating an expedition to these cliffy mountains could not do better than consult beforehand the appropriate volume published by the Scottish Mountaineering Club—*The Islands of Scotland* (excluding Skye), edited by W. W. Naismith. Edinburgh, 1934.

notable eminences. The three hills mentioned would appear
to be but the northern extension of those on the east of South
Uist, to which we have already alluded. North Uist, like Benbecula, contains an amazing complexity of freshwater lochs
and lochans, a feature of these particular islands upon which
every competent topographer has enlarged.

On the whole, the islands in the Sound of Harris are low-
lying and grassy, providing excellent pasturage. Berneray
is hilly, however; and it should be noted that Beinn a' Char-
nain, the peak on Pabbay, second largest and, excepting
Shillay, remotest of the islands in the Sound, is well over six
hundred feet.

When we cross over to South Harris, we are again approaching mountainous country, though by no means as mountainous as *North* Harris, the much more extensive portion, lying
beyond the isthmus at Tarbert. The only hills in South
Harris of any magnitude are Beinn Dubh (1,654 feet) one
of the Luskentyre Hills, and Roneval (1,506 feet) situated
behind Obbe, or Leverburgh, a place about which we will
have occasion to say something when reviewing the late
Lord Leverhulme's enterprises in the Outer Hebrides.
Yet, the whole of this area, except for the machar-lands
fringing its beautiful bays of sheen-white sand, is decidedly
hilly.

The Luskentyre Hills, rising between the southern shore
of West Loch Tarbert and the Luskentyre Sands, form part
of one of the loveliest settings in the Outer Hebrides. They
embrace two main peaks—Beinn Dubh, which we have
already mentioned, at their western end, and Ceann Reamhar,
at the eastern, the latter attaining, at 1,529 feet, an altitude
but 125 feet less than that of the former. On the north side
they rise very steeply from the shore; and I well remember
an exploit I once had in attempting to scale Uamascleit, the
splendid rock-face of Ceann Reamhar, their eastern summit.
This rock-face towers nigh a thousand feet; and it occurs to
me that the more youthful and agile among those who, perhaps, learn of its existence for the first time from these pages,
may like to give it a thought when on the outlook for
unknown and untried rock-climbs. Its base is situated at no
great distance from Tarbert. At Beesdale, a little farther to

the west, one finds a steep glen by which it is possible to reach the summit of Beinn Dubh without undue exertion.

Much of South Harris is depressingly rocky and barren. The road from Obbe or from Rodil to Finsbay (if by a word as concrete it may be termed) and the ill-defined tracks to such clachans as Meavaig, Stockinish, Manish, and Grosebay, all of them set down in extreme isolation on the east coast, traverse sheets of outcropping gneiss many acres in extent, and completely devoid of vegetation, except where heather and deer-grass and stunted moorland plants are able to survive in crevices, or in shallow hollows filled with a thin layer of peaty soil. Browning, when penning those weird, Spenserian stanzas he entitles *Childe Roland to the Dark Tower Came*, could not have had in mind a scene more gloomy, more hopeless, more sterile and foreboding than this.

> *So, on I went. I think I never saw*
> *Such starved, ignoble nature; nothing throve:*
> *For flowers—as well expect a cedar grove.*
> *But cockle, spurge, according to their law,*
> *Might propagate their kind, with none to awe,*
> *You'd think; a burr had been a treasure-trove.*
>
> *No! penury, inertness, and grimace,*
> *In some strange sort, were the land's portion.*

To him who, for the first time, makes his way toward any of these remote and ancient places, there comes the feeling that, maybe, he ought not to proceed farther into a country so desolate, so inhospitable, so utterly wanting in anything the least hopeful. He may begin to wonder whether the road shown on the map as leading to Finsbay, or that which ends abruptly at Geocrab, will ever bring him to a township so named, or indeed to any inhabited place at all. He will ask himself whether it can really be true that he is moving in the direction in which human beings can possibly have lived, continuously, for centuries. On a day of rain, I can well imagine anyone, unaccustomed to spaces so wild, open, and solitary, losing heart, and turning back from a scene, the grimness and forebodement of which seem to increase with every outward step.

32

The Inn at Pollachar, South Uist

Notwithstanding, people do live among these hills of naked rock; and one can only assume that some bond, unbreakable, binds the Islanders to a land so stern and unproductive. The keen of eye may notice, afar off, and probably some time before anything in the nature of a dwelling becomes visible, one or two peat-stacks, their chocolate-brown colour rendering them the more conspicuous against a background of bleached stone. Or he may observe on the hillside, at irregular intervals, and sometimes on the skyline, the funeral cairns upon which the Islanders throughout the centuries have rested the coffin, when conveying a corpse to some wonted place of burial, such as Rodil or Luskentyre. Somewhere amidst this grim welter, and usually at no great distance from the peat-stacks, a dwelling-house must lie. A drift of blue peat-reek upon the hillside, or maybe the scent of it borne on the breeze, is often further evidence of the existence of such, long before it comes into view, for it may nestle in a *lag* or coomb affording it what little shelter from the winds of winter may be had in a land so exposed, so windswept. If the roof of the dwelling be of thatch, as indeed were the roofs of all such dwellings in the Hebrides up till a few decades ago, the traveller, unaware of its existence, may not notice it until he actually stumbles upon it, because the old " black houses " of the Isles merge so completely with their background. No camouflage would ever be necessary to conceal them from an enemy: so perfect is their natural, protective colouring. The newer houses, built of dressed stone and faced with plaster, are much more noticeable. Yet even *they* may be difficult to locate among these wastes of primordial rock.

Go where you will among the Western Isles, even to the most fertile of them, that passage from Boswell's *Life of Johnson* keeps on recurring to one: " Sir Allan bragged that Scotland had the advantage of England by its having more water." To this Dr. Johnson replied, " Sir, we do not have your water. . . . You have too much. . . . Your country consists of two things, stone and water. There is indeed a little earth above the stone in some places, but very little, and the stone is always appearing. It is like a man in rags: the skin is always appearing."

The stranger who, in reading this passage, turns to a good

The afternoon plane at Suidheachan, Isle of Barra

topographical map of Scotland soon realises the truth of this statement. What is true in this regard of the Scottish mainland is trebly true of the Outer Hebrides, where the total area of cultivated or cultivable ground is negligible in comparison with that occupied by fresh or by brackish water, by mountain, and by bare, outcropping stone. Scan from any of the higher hills—from Ben Obe, in Barra, for instance, from Hecla or from Ben Tarbert, in South Uist, from Eaval, in North Uist, or from the hill-tops overlooking the watery wastes of Harris or of Lewis—these eerie expanses of water and land, of land and water, each interlocking with the other like a gigantic jigsaw puzzle, and you will get the impression, especially on a dull, wet day, that they may just have been born out of primeval chaos, and that one might have to wait a long, long time before the land dried sufficiently to allow of herbage and zoological life to exist upon it and multiply. Yet, there is some reasonable prospect that, with the development of water power under the Hydro-Development (Scotland) Act of 1943, even these islands may turn to profitable account that very excess of water about which Dr. Johnson was so scornful.

The stranger to these islands is either attracted to them or repelled by them. He will either love them intensely or hate them intensely: he will never be merely indifferent about them. If he love them, he will tolerate gladly all their inconveniences such as the primitive nature of their sanitation, the awkward journey often entailed in reaching his destination, their wild, wet weather, and perhaps also the palpable shortcomings of the people. Even the sea voyage to them, during which he may have to suffer grievously, will fail to dispel the sense of an irresistible allurement. It is true that his feelings on arrival will be much influenced by climatic conditions prevailing at the time, as indeed they would be anywhere else. But, if he be attracted to the Isles, as so many are, neither seasonal inclemencies nor human limitations are likely to diminish his ardour.

On the other hand, if he dislike them, nothing will ever alter his attitude to them. He will find their barrenness and sterility depressing, their seas fraught with sadness, with melancholy. To their quite remarkable colourings under certain conditions, he will remain blind, to their sweetest sounds deaf, to their fragrance insensitive. The coloured moors, the coloured waters laving coloured shores, the cry of seabird or of moorland fowl, the scent of wild flowers growing in such profusion on some of the isles, and especially on their machars—all these will be lost on him.

No one is ever half-hearted about the Western Isles. I have met people so responsive to them, so hynotised by them, that they never want to leave. But I confess to having also met people who, having been obliged to reside in them, perhaps in some official capacity, have prayed devoutly for the day when they might quit them for ever.

So far as the natives are concerned, the farther removed they are from their belovèd island-homeland, the greater is their love for it. People have gone from these Isles to settle in the remotest corners of the earth. Many Hebridean families have been long established in the Dominions and Colonies, speaking the Gaelic language as fluently to-day as did their emigrant ancestors. Like other Celts, and particularly the Irish, they are never without that yearning for a whiff of peat-reek, or for a glimpse of the shieling of bygone years. And in what is the Hebridean's nostalgia more memorably, more faithfully, recorded than in those verses generally known as *The Canadian Boat-Song*, which first appeared among the *Noctes Ambrosianæ* in *Blackwood's Magazine* in September, 1829? The matter of their authorship, however, is still in dispute. They are claimed to be a translation from the Gaelic. The second verse has been much quoted in recent years, especially at times of emigration from the Highlands and Islands. It was much in mind when, in 1923, and again in 1924, Canadian Pacific liners (notable among them the *Metagama*) arrived off Stornoway to bear some hundreds of Islanders to exile in Canada, where already so many of their stock had made good. Emigration had been no new thing to the Long Island. Indeed, it had been going on, intermittently, for a couple of centuries. It is estimated that, during the early twenties of the present century, about two thousand left Lewis alone.

THE CANADIAN BOAT-SONG

Listen to me, as when ye heard our father
    Sing long ago the song of other shores!
Listen to me, and then in chorus gather
    All your deep voices as ye pull your oars!

Fair these broad meads, these hoary woods are grand;
But we are exiles from our fathers' land.

From the lone shieling and the misty island
    Mountains divide us, and a waste of seas;
Yet still the blood is strong, the heart is Highland,
    And we, in dreams, behold the Hebrides.

Fair these broad meads, these hoary woods are grand;
But we are exiles from our fathers' land.

We ne'er shall tread the fancy-haunted valley,
    Where, 'tween the dark hills, creeps the small,
        clear stream,
In arms around the patriarch banner rally,
    Nor see the moon on royal tombstones gleam.

Fair these broad meads, these hoary woods are grand;
But we are exiles from our fathers' land.

When the bold kindred, in the time long-vanished,
    Conquered the soil and fortified the keep,
No seer foretold the children would be banished,
    That a degenerate Lord might boast his sheep.

Fair these broad meads, these hoary woods are grand;
But we are exiles from our fathers' land.

Come foreign rage! Let discord burst in slaughter!
    O then for clansman true, and stern claymore:
The hearts that would have given their blood like
    water
    Beat heavily beyond the Atlantic roar.

Fair these broad meads, these hoary woods are grand;
But we are exiles from our fathers' land.

Both to the ear and to the eye, the very name of our Western Isles, namely, the Hebrides, has something fascinating about it. Yet, nothing of historical nor of ethnological import can be inferred from it. We know little of the ancient inhabitants of these islands whom the rieving Northmen found when they came over the sea from Lochlann, as the Gaelic people call Norway. Neither do we know precisely what the islands were then called. The origin of the name, Hebrides, is believed to be the Greek, Ἐβοῦδαι, mentioned by Ptolemy, and used earlier by Pliny in the Latinised form of *Hæbudes*, or *Hebudes*. Geographers of old referred to these islands as the *Ebudæ*, or *Hebudes*. Philologists have suggested that the name, Hebrides, is a ghost-word, which arose from an error in transcribing as *ri* the *u* in the penultimate syllable of Pliny's *Hebudes*. Be this as it may, the name in the form in which we have become so accustomed to it carries with it something which stirs the imagination. It is one of the loveliest in our language.

To the Gael, the Western Isles are known as *Innse-Gall*, the Islands of the Strangers, probably a reference to the Northmen, who dominated them until after Haco's defeat off Largs in 1263, when Norway's sovereignty over so much of our northern and western seaboard came to an end.

CHAPTER II

THE WESTERN ISLES IN HISTORY

THE earliest known references to the Western Isles are those contained in the Sagas; and it is unfortunate that even these are both scanty and vague. It is just possible, however, that in the ancient Irish records there may be allusions one might justifiably regard as referring to them. No written records of pre-Norse times exist.

In the ancient stones of these islands there is much pre-history. The duns and brochs, the menhirs and stone circles, the chambered cairns—all these, though mute enough in one sense, are eloquent in another. It would appear from them as though the Western Isles had been peopled by an organised society long before the Norsemen sailed over to the Scottish Isles—to the Orkneys and the Shetlands, as well as to the Hebrides—to conquer, to take possession, to settle down in numerous communities. The Standing Stones of Callernish were old when Rome was yet unborn, as W. C. MacKenzie puts it in one of the works from which we have already quoted. Ancient structures, such as the broch known as Dun Carloway, were in use centuries, if not millenia, before our northern kingdom became known as Scotland. The subterranean dwellings and stone huts of the Isles must have been very old, indeed, by the time the Scots crossed over from Ireland to Dalriada, in Argyll.

From the eighth century onwards, the Norsemen of Viking times continued to come over the seas and settle in these parts. They came not just as plunderers, ready to depart whenever they had despoiled the countryside: on the contrary, they arrived with the intention of remaining. And they certainly remained some centuries. But for the defeat and destruction of King Haco's fleet at Largs in 1263, there is no saying how long thereafter the Norse domination of the Western Isles might have continued.

The physical characteristics of the Norsemen are still obvious among the Islanders; and, curiously, although the former did not replace the ancient Gaelic language with their own, they did succeed in bequeathing to the toponomy of these islands several thousands of names which are purely Scandinavian in origin. There is scarcely a *geo*, or creek, in the Hebridean coast-line without its Norse name, hardly a promontory. In Lewis, however, there are more Gaelic place-names than Norse, though it must be added that, in the case of farm names, the preponderance is the other way.

The Norsemen, when at the height of their power, dominated Scotland's islands as far south as Arran and Bute. The Kintyre peninsula also came under their sway. It was agreed between Magnus Barefoot and the King of Scotland that the former might claim for Norway any territory on the west coast of Scotland, round which his galley could be steered, and that, in order to embrace Kintyre, he sat at the helm while his warriors dragged his galley over the isthmus linking Kintyre with Knapdale—that is to say, between West and East Lochs Tarbert. If the etymologists be right, it would seem as though the Norsemen were in the habit of transporting their craft across similar isthmuses, such as that between East Loch Tarbert and West Loch Tarbert, in Harris, and possibly the isthmus between Loch Long and Loch Lomond. The Tarberts, or Tarbats (literally, "draw-boats") were simply shortcuts to avoid the longer journeys by sea.

So thorough was the Norse domination of the Hebrides that they were known among the ancient Gaelic-speaking people of the Highlands as *Innse-Gall*, the Strangers' Isles. By this name they are still referred to, collectively, in the Gaelic.

. . . .

By the time the history of the Western Isles becomes less obscure, five main clans shared them, each having a region of its own. The Clan MacNeil possessed Barra and the isles pertaining thereto. The Uists and Benbecula were the patrimony of the MacDonalds—the brave and adventurous Clan Ranald of the Isles. Harris belonged to the MacLeods of Harris, a branch of the MacLeods of Skye, or of Dunvegan. Lewis was divided between three powerful clans. In Ness, the northern part, the Morisons were in control. In Uig, the western and remotest part, the MacAulays flourished. The rest of the island belonged to the redoubtable MacLeods of Lewis, who, in the early years of the seventeenth century, were displaced by the artful and ambitious MacKenzies, who were, perhaps, a little more civilised. Two other Lewis clans of minor importance ought to be mentioned in passing, namely, the MacIvers, and the MacNicols or Nicolsons. There is a tradition that the latter were in possession of Lewis prior to the MacLeods.

The MacIvers, like the MacRaes and others who are of no great numerical significance in Lewis, are regarded as a fairly recent importation—recent, at all events, in comparison with the MacLeods, the Morisons, and the MacAulays, whose roots were deeply embedded there some centuries earlier. The MacIvers, like the MacLeods and MacAulays, are of Scandinavian origin; and it would appear as though most of them arrived in the island with the MacKenzies, as the MacRaes, a Celtic clan, certainly did.[1] At the present day, MacIvers are to be found all over Lewis. They used to be most numerous in the neighbourhood of Achmore and Loch Ganavich (Gainmheich) two townships situated about ten miles to the south-west of Stornoway, on the road to Uig. Some twenty years ago, relatives living in Lewis took me on a visit to an old crofter named MacIver, living in a tumbledown, thatched cottage not far from the roadside at Loch Ganavich. This old man was regarded in Lewis as the Chief of the Clan MacIver—a piece of harmless nonsense, I had better add, lest some reader should feel himself called upon to initiate a newspaper correspondence, as the Scots are so prone to do in matters of clan-ship and genealogy. The MacIvers, one may safely say, had no chief in the accepted sense.

To this day, these seven surnames—MacNeil, MacDonald, MacLeod, Morison, MacAulay, MacIver, and Nicolson—are by far the commonest in the Western Isles; and to a large extent they have retained their ancient geographical distribution. MacKenzies, of course, are to be found all over Lewis, and especially in and around the town of Stornoway, where

[1] " The common inhabitants of Lewis," according to an account of Lewis in 1750, " are the Morisons, McAulays, and MacKivers, but when they go from home, all who live under Seaforth call themselves MacKenzies."

the first contingents of them landed early in the seventeenth century.

There are other surnames well known in the Western Isles, of course, among which might be mentioned MacAskill, and MacSweyn or MacSween. The name, MacAskill, is indeed ancient. In the *Annals of Ulster*, in 1171, one reads of "Ascall, son of Torcall, King of Ath-Cliath". Then the name of one, Gilbert MacAskill, appears in 1311 in connection with lands included in the bishopric of Durham. Askill is a name of Norse origin.

Of an origin no less ancient are the MacSweyns, if we believe their progenitor to have been Sweyn Asleifsson, one of the last of the Vikings. Somewhere about the year 1160, this illustrious sea-rover and all his men were ambushed and killed at Dublin, which they had captured and sacked. Sweyn was quite a common Scandinavian name.

And one might just add a word or two about my own surname, proudest and most romantic of any, if I may be forgiven for reminding you of this. MacGregors are not numerous in the Western Isles. They are to be found almost exclusively in Lewis, where a fugitive from Perthshire—from Loch Katrine-side—sought refuge in the days when the Clan Gregor was persecuted, and the very name of MacGregor proscribed. This fugitive settled in the west of the island, at a place called Tolsta Chaolais, by the shores of Loch Roag. The small colony of MacGregors still residing there are descended from him; and so am I.

How far the island clans were of Norse or of Celtic origin, or how far an admixture of both, it is impossible to say. Their descendants in the Isles at the present day exhibit marked characteristics of both. The Norse were like sandwiches between two layers of Celts. Then there were, at all times, the descendants of the prehistoric people, still much in evidence in some parts of Lewis, especially in the parish of Barvas, where one finds traces of the Iberians.

Besides the descendants of the Norse, whose Scandinavian characteristics are obvious, the main body of the Western Islesmen is composed of Celtic stock, Gaelic in speech. In certain parts of Lewis, too, descent is traceable from the short, dark, swarthy, prehistoric people once inhabiting the island. A commingling of the different races is, of course, an ethnological fact. In some districts, the Nordic predominates: in others, the Celtic.

It has often been questioned how far the Celts, as a race, are adapted to a seafaring life. So far as the Norsemen are concerned, however, no one would dispute their seamanship and love of the sea. Their roving and rieving proclivities, as we know, brought them much farther a-field—much farther a-sea, one might say—than the Hebrides, and at a time when navigation elsewhere in western Europe was in a primitive state. One thing is certain: obscure as may be the ethnological origin of our Hebridean clans, the Norse infusion imparted to them a fondness for, and a familiarity with, the sea not to be found in peoples more purely Celtic. Take, for example, the maritime exploits of the MacNeils of Barra, those irrepressible pirates of the sixteenth century and the early years of the seventeenth. Or take the Clan Ranald, whose warlike history in these parts was so closely bound up with their birlinns, those war-galleys which were common to *all* the maritime clans. The seamen of the Hebrides at that period were as familiar with the coasts of the Western Highlands and Islands as the Vikings were with those of Norway. They knew the wild sealochs of the Western Isles as thoroughly as Haco's galley-men ever knew the Scandinavian fiords. As terminations in the names of our sealochs, the Norse fiords appear in various forms—*ford, fort, ord,* and *ort.*

The MacDonalds, including that powerful and colourful branch known as Clan Ranald of the Isles, claim descent from no less distinguished a personage than Somerled, who was probably of mixed origin, and whose name is still revered by members of this clan. From the MacDonalds came the Lords of the Isles, who, for all their warring, contributed much to Highland tradition and romance.

The MacLeods, likewise, are of Norse origin. They are the descendants of Leod; and who was Leod (if tradition be reliable) but a son of Olaf the Black? Olaf ruled the petty kingdom of Man and the Isles. He was, in fact, one of the Kinglets of the Isle of Man and the Hebrides.

Leod, his son (from whom, according to popular, if inaccurate, etymology, the island of Lewis derives its name) married the daughter of MacCrailt Armuinn. By her he had two sons, Torquil and Tormod, two Christian names still very popular with the MacLeods. Torquil is regarded as having been the founder of the Lewis branch of the Clan MacLeod, the branch known in Highland history as the *Siol Thorcuil*, the Seed of Torquil. From Tormod the MacLeods of Skye and Harris trace their beginning. They are known as the *Siol Thormoid*, the Seed of Tormod, or Norman. The Chiefs of the MacLeods of Dunvegan, as the MacLeods of Harris and Skye are sometimes called, because Dunvegan Castle, in the Isle of Skye, has been their ancestral home for many centuries, were in direct descent from Tormod, son of Leod. The last of these Chiefs (each of whom in more recent times has been known as MacLeod of MacLeod, or as MacLeod of Dunvegan) in the direct succession from Tormod died a few years ago. He was Roderic, XXVth Chief of this historic clan. The heir to the chiefship was his son, Iain Breac, who was killed in action in France in 1915, while serving with the Black Watch. Iain Breac was the last male heir of his line.

Of MacCrailt Armuinn we know very little. The surname, MacCrailt (sometimes spelt MacRailt, and said to be the same as MacHarold) survives in Skye, but not in Lewis, although there is a belief that, like the Nicolsons, the MacCrailts preceded the MacLeods in the ownership of that island.

In Ness, the northernmost part of Lewis, the Morisons held sway. In this clan was vested the hereditary brieve-ship, or judge-ship, of the Island of Lewis. Hence they were known as the *Clann na Breitheimh*, the Clan of the Brieve, or Judge. Their judicial seat was at a place called Habost, to-day a typical Hebridean crofting township.

For a great number of years, the Morisons and the MacLeods lived as peacefully together as neighbouring clans ever could. It was only right and proper that the Morisons, who were the dispensers of justice in the island, should have set an example by abstaining from those acts of aggression to which the other clans of the Highlands and Islands were all too prone. During the closing years of the sixteenth century, however, a serious feud between the Morisons and the Mac-Leods took root. It began as a minor domestic dispute, but eventually involved both clans in their entirety. This feud, prosecuted by both sides with the utmost zeal and ferocity, led to the decline and ultimate ruin of the MacLeods.

In mediaeval times, and even subsequently, the Brieves were greatly respected in Lewis. Their verdicts were accepted as final: their knowledge of ancient law and usage was never questioned. Indeed, where matters juridical were concerned, they held a position almost identical with that of the Brehons in Ireland. The basis of their jurisprudence was the *eric*. That is to say, the compensation paid by offenders judged guilty. The *eric* corresponded with the Welsh *galanas,* and with the Teutonic *weregild.* To the Brieve went an eleventh part of the compensation claimed. To the relatives of the victim, as in the case of murder, went the remainder, after the chief had taken what he considered to be *his* share.

Of course, in this somewhat primitive and arbitrary administration of justice there must have been much that, to-day, we should regard as highly improper. Yet, the position of the hereditary brieve continued unchallenged in Lewis for many a generation. Eventually, it was displaced by the system of heritable jurisdiction. This increased enormously the power and authority of the chiefs, with their right of pit and gallows. Indeed, it is more than probable that justice, as administered in Lewis by the Brieves, was much closer to our modern concept of what constitutes justice than was that of many a chief exercising his authority as a hereditary judicator.

For all this, the Brieve-ship survived long after it had become an anachronism, as did also the principle of hereditary jurisdiction. The latter, long before its abolition, which followed the final defeat of the Jacobites at Culloden, had become intolerable, as had, in fact, many another remnant of feudalism, swept away about the same time. Such power in the hands of a cruel and unscrupulous chief, as so many of them were, must have resulted in untold misery and oppression. We like the romantic idea that the chiefs of old were all generous and magnanimous men. But this idea is soon demolished when one delves into the social and domestic

44

history of the times. They were good and bad, just like the rest of us, though some of them were excessively bad.

The Brieve was to be found elsewhere than in Lewis. It would appear that, during the heyday of the Lords of the Isles, every island of any size and importance had its own Brieve, whose powers, however, may not have been quite so extensive as those exercised by the Morisons. Such judges acted in matters of local import. Where minor disputes were concerned, they probably had complete autonomy. In the days of the Lords of the Isles, the principle Brieve in the Hebrides resided in Islay, southernmost of the Inner Isles. As there seems to have been a right of appeal to him, he was, in effect, what W. C. MacKenzie suggests, namely, Lord Chief Justice of the Isles.[1]

Remnants of the species of justice obtaining in the Western Isles in the days of the Brieves survived there, at any rate in spirit, long after these hereditary judges had become but a historical memory. MacKenzie cites the case of a sheep-stealer who, in 1788, was placarded and led through the streets of Stornoway by the common executioner, to receive, upon his bare back, and at each of five appointed places, no fewer than ten lashes. What the culprit must have looked like, and felt like, at the last stance, if indeed he were capable of feeling anything at all, one must leave to the imagination. Of course, we do very much the same sort of thing in our prisons at the present day, with this difference, that the flogging now takes place in camera, a provision which, in my view, greatly hinders fundamental penal reform.

Banishment, either for life or for a long period of years, usually followed public whippings for such offences as sheep-stealing which, in olden times, was considered as heinous an offence as anyone could commit.

A woman convicted of theft in 1820 was sentenced to be led from prison by a rope tied round her neck, and to carry on her breast a placard proclaiming her, in large letters, to be a habitual and reputed thief. Thereafter she was put in the pillory for a couple of hours. Her sentence included seven years' banishment.

Traditions concerning the Brieves persist in Lewis to this

[1] See his Book of the Lews, p. 164 et seq.

day, especially in Ness, where they lived and functioned. The folk-tales of this island are full of references to them, as also to the instances in which they and their Morison clansmen came to bloody blows, either with the MacLeods or with the MacAulays.

The Brieves are also remembered in Sutherland-shire, where Morison is by no means an uncommon surname. Indeed, one of the several islets situated off Eddrachillis, a coastal parish in the north-west of the county, is named *Eilean a' Bhreitheimh*, the Brieve's Island. Here, towards the close of the sixteenth century, were interred the bowels of John Morison, Brieve of Lewis at the time. Morison and a handful of his henchmen, while in Assynt, came to daggers with a party of MacLeods. All the Morisons were slain in this encounter, which appears to have been one in which the MacLeods were anxious to get even for some insult they had suffered. Now the galley, aboard which the Brieve's body was placed, attempted to sail for Lewis; but contrary winds cast her ashore on this isle. There, according to tradition, the corpse was disembowelled, and the bowels buried.

The other great tribe of undoubted Lewis origin is the Clan MacAulay. It occupied the wild and remote west of the island—that part of it known as Uig. Aulay, of course, is really the Norse, Olaf, or Olave; and there is reason for believing, therefore, that the MacAulays have a Norse ancestry similar to that of the MacLeods. It is the proud boast of the Lewis MacAulays that the forebears of one of the most distinguished of their name—Thomas Babington MacAulay—lived at Breidhnis, a crofting township by the Atlantic seaboard of Uig. The ruins of their humble home are still pointed out by the older inhabitants. At the present time, MacAulays are almost as numerous in Uig as are Morisons in Ness.

Of the internecine struggles in the Western Isles one might write much. They would appear to have been the principal concern of the inhabitants, continuously, throughout the fifteenth and sixteenth centuries. It is doubtful whether anywhere else in Britain, in historic times, so much blood was spilt in proportion to the population. Warfare between the Morisons and the MacLeods was no less ferocious than that

between the Morisons and the MacAulays. Even more sanguinary, however, was the protracted feud between the Mac-
Donalds and the MacLeans, conducted in the more southerly
of the Hebrides. In fact, the history both of the Inner and
of the Outer Hebrides at this period is almost solely confined to clan rivalry and inter-family machinations, and to the
appalling waste and misery they occasioned. These are too
numerous and complicated to be of interest for our present
purpose. They may be studied in appropriate detail in
MacKenzie's monumental work, *The History of the Outer
Hebrides*, or in his *Book of the Lews*.

It should be added, nevertheless, that all this strife and
bloodshed are the foundation of an enormous amount of
island legendary, folk-tale, and tradition. Conspicuous
among the recorders of these, and perhaps the most indefatigable prior to the present century, was John Morrison. (He
spells his name with an extra *r*, although the Morisons of the
islands usually have only one.) John Morrison was born in
Harris in 1787. Most of his youth was spent in Uig, in which
parish he was, for a time, a schoolmaster. Uig was then
unbelievably remote. Immense moorland, diversified with
lochs and swamps, isolated it from the rest of the Northern
Hebrides. Among the valleys intervening between its lovely
hills, or by such stretches of its Atlantic seaboard as allowed
of a certain amount of fishing and crofting, its inhabitants
lived very much *inter se*—very much as a people apart. Only
when foraging on neighbours' territories did its men-folk
leave their own confines. This isolation meant that the
ceilidh[1] (the social gathering, usually held round the peat-fire
in the evening, for the telling of folk-tales and the singing of
folk-songs) remained the sole venue of social intercourse at
a time when, perhaps, its importance was already diminishing
elsewhere. At the Uig ceilidhs John Morrison, in early man-
hood, was afforded the unique opportunity of hearing many
a story recounted in the ancient, traditional fashion of the
Isles. These he diligently noted down.

Morrison eventually removed to the town of Stornoway,
where he was employed none too felicitously as a shop-
assistant. Later he earned a livelihood there as a cooper. He

[1] Pronounced *kay'-lee*.

47

was the father of twelve children, and he died in 1834, at the age of forty-seven. He occupied his spare time in collecting, collating, and recording such traditions as were then to be found abundantly in the Western Isles. The result of his labours, as we can now appreciate, has been most gratifying, particularly when we consider the handicaps under which he must have worked. He possessed no desk of any kind. His MSS., now bound in seven volumes, and containing nearly a hundred stories of varying length, were written with " only a board across his knees ". They represent a colossal amount of industry and application, of which those of us belonging to, or interested in, the Western Isles cannot be too apprecia-tive, for he rescued from oblivion much to which we now have access. His MSS. were entitled:

TRADITIONS OF THE WESTERN ISLES
By JOHN MORRISON

The Conflicts of the Western Highlanders; or the Various and Repeated Struggles of the Most Illustrious Heroes of the Isles of Lewis, Harris, Uist, Barra, as well as of the Mainland, Skye, Eigg, Mull, etc.

Also

The Various Forays committed by the Clans upon each other, and how the same were resented, bravely repulsed, or retaliated; during a period of 263 years.

On Morrison's death, these MSS. passed into the posses-sion of Captain Thomas, R.N., a careful and enthusiastic antiquary who, about 1880, contributed to the *Proceedings of the Society of Antiquaries of Scotland* two lengthy papers based upon them. Later, they became the property of Sir Arthur Mitchell, another noted antiquary and archaeologist. On Mitchell's death they were sold to the firm from whom W. C. MacKenzie, mentioned so often in these pages, bought them. MacKenzie appropriately presented them to the public library in his native town of Stornoway, where they are acces-sible to anyone who may care to consult them.

. . . .

48

The airport, Isle of Barra, on the fringe of the Great Cockle Shore

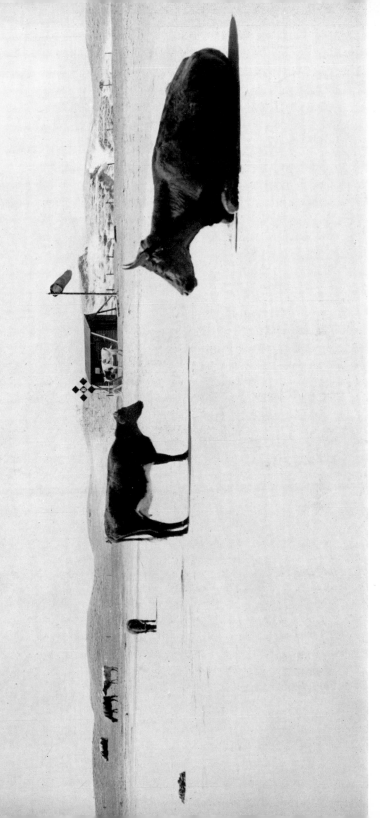

The impoverishment of the Western Isles by clan and tribal strife may well be imagined. Murder and rapine were the order of the day. Lawlessness and destitution stalked the land. This was as much the case in Barra and the Uists as it was in Lewis and Harris. Yet, the Islanders, on their limited and precarious resources, managed to conduct warfare abroad as well as at home. Fifteenth-century records are full of their exploits elsewhere than in and about their own particular isles. They raided the Scottish mainland frequently, and on more than one occasion visited the Orkneys with fire and sword. Under the banner of Donald, Lord of the Isles, who claimed the Earldom of Ross, the MacLeods of Lewis and of Harris fought at Harlaw in 1411.

Scarcely a home in the Western Isles was not affected by the feud between John, Lord of the Isles, and Angus, his bellicose son. This feud, one of the bitterest in the annals of the Western Highlands and Islands, came to issue in that sanguinary sea-fight, the Battle of Bloody Bay, where Angus defeated his father. In this contest, the heir to MacLeod of Lewis was mortally wounded, and MacLeod of Harris was killed. Both of them fought on the losing side.

During the sixteenth century, things went from bad to worse in the Long Island. Notorious among the leaders of disorder was Roderic, almost the last of the MacLeods of Lewis. It was he who, according to Donald Monro, High Dean of the Isles, was in the habit of retiring to Pabbay, an isle in Loch Roag, " quhen he wald be quyeit, or yet fearit ".[1]

Roderic lived to a great age, despite his arduous and adventurous life. In an official document dated 1593 (written about the time of his death) he is alluded to as an old man " famous for the massacring of his own kinsmen ".

It is not surprising that Roderic should have been one of the chiefs whom James the Fifth was anxious to interview during the royal expedition to the Western Isles in 1540. This expedition, as an authority already quoted so often puts it, had a close analogy to the sporting adventure. " The King was like a Saxon sportsman in modern times, who stalks

---

[1] *Description of the Western Isles of Scotland called Hybrides (circa* 1549), first published from the manuscript in 1774 by William Auld, Edinburgh.

Ben More (RIGHT) *and Hecla* (LEFT) *from Bornish, South Uist*

game in the Isles, and carries home in triumph the trophies of the chase. Resistance to the armed forces of the Crown there was none. The chiefs were apparently paralysed by the suddenness of the descent. The main object of the expedition was to examine conditions on the spot. The legality of the holdings needed scrutiny; the administration of justice had to be placed on a more satisfactory footing; the resources of the Isles as centres for the development of the fishing industry called for examination. But the main object, clearly, was to secure some cessation of the interminable quarrels among the Islesmen themselves, and to break down their resistance to the authority of the Crown. All the proprietors of the Western Isles were compelled to be unwilling passengers with the Sailor King, who was thus provided with an unequalled opportunity for acquiring the same proficiency in the Gaelic language as his father had possessed. One cannot help associating the expedition of James the Fifth to the Isles, with the fact that he was, when Heir Apparent, the first to bear the title of ' Prince of Scotland and the Isles '; and he had visited Lewis four years previously, apparently to see for himself what some of his Isles were like."

The King's visit to this outlying part of his kingdom was not altogether barren of results, since it was followed by a period of unusual calm there. For a time, at any rate, the warring elements engaged in more peaceful pursuits. The detention as hostages of the more troublesome may have accounted for this temporary spell of quiet.

The dynastic troubles ever brewing during Roderic MacLeod's lifetime became accentuated at his death. Rival factions now asserted their claims to the ownership of Lewis in a manner which paved the way for the MacKenzies of Kintail, who ultimately succeeded the MacLeods as overlords of Lewis. The MacKenzies, like the Campbells, had always been on the side of the Crown in any dispute it had with the lawless clans. With commendable patience and consistency, they bided their time, and with results by no means unprofitable to themselves. By their upholding the Crown's authority, not only in Lewis, but also in Barra, where the MacNeils were continually giving trouble, they indeed waxed powerful. In Lewis their opportunity came when the last of the MacLeods resisted to the death the attempts made by the Fife Adventurers to colonise the island.

During the sixteenth century, the fishermen of various European nations discovered that the waters of the Western Isles abounded in fish. Among the first to exploit the fishings were the Spaniards and the French, who were actually fishing our sea-lochs before King James's expedition in 1540 suggested any official recognition of the islands' commercial possibilities. By 1580, fishermen from the south and east of Scotland were beginning to take an interest; and by the close of the century the Dutch were also busy in Hebridean waters.

So far as the Crown was concerned, as little profit accrued from these potentialities as went to the natives. Turbulence in Barra, in Uist, and in Lewis made it impossible to organise anything where the native population was involved. Trade, in the accepted sense of the term, was quite impracticable amid the squalor and confusion then obtaining. Any profits, such as were derived from the seas and fiords of the Western Isles, went, therefore, to strangers.

The people of Lewis, according to an official report on their condition at the time, were "voyd of ony knawledge of God or His religioun". Moreover, they had "gevin thameselfis over to all kynd of barbaritie and inhumanitie".

How was the island to be redeemed? How was it to be brought into line with the rest of the kingdom? How were the Islanders to be encouraged to abandon their old ways, and to respect the King's authority?

Unfortunately, there was no appealing either to Roderic MacLeod of the Lewis and his partisans on the one hand, or to his equally ruthless enemies, on the other. Neither side had retained a vestige of civilisation. Each was resolved to exterminate the other by fair means or foul. Yet, it was this very anarchy which, in due course, provided the Crown at least with the pretext for intervention. Truth to tell, however, the scheme now sanctioned by James the Sixth, ostensibly for the purpose of civilising the island, was, in fact, nothing more or less than a commercial venture, calculated to enrich the King at the expense of the Islanders, and to ensure that, hereafter, there should be some reasonable prospect of his being able to collect from the MacLeods certain dues, such as *maill* and *greffum*, to which the Crown was entitled, and of which, for many a year, it had been deprived. So the Fife Adventurers, or the Gentlemen Adventurers from Fife, as they are sometimes called, made their first expedition to Lewis late in 1598, in an endeavour to gain a permanent footing there. Though they took Stornoway Castle, they were unable to make much headway. The hostility of the Islanders, now banded together against them under the leadership of the intrepid Neil MacLeod, one of Roderic's five bastard sons, soon proved to the would-be colonists that they would have to abandon their enterprise, at any rate for the time being.

In 1605 they made a second attempt; but again Neil was able to organise sufficient local opposition to render their permanent settlement impracticable, if indeed it did not entail their slow extermination. Four years later, the Fifers made their final bid to establish themselves in Lewis, and to bring the island and its none too lucrative resources under their control. Again they failed.

All this time, the wily Kenneth MacKenzie of Kintail had been waiting an opportunity of making good his own claim to Lewis. The opportunity came in 1610 when, with the collapse of the Fife Adventurers' third attempt, they sold to him their charter rights in Lewis, and also such rights as they had in the Trotternish district of Skye. Just before their final debâcle, Kenneth had been raised to the peerage, ostensibly for the assistance the Crown imagined he had given to the Fifers in their struggle against the lawless and dauntless MacLeods. As Lord Kintail, and with the support of his brother, Roderic, he landed in Lewis with a strong contingent of his clansmen. In a short time the island was under his control, though for a year or two Neil, the last of the MacLeods of Lewis, held out. Neil and a number of his confederates eventually took refuge on the islet known as Berisay, in Loch Roag, which they fortified, and from which they pursued a reckless career as pirates. The story of their ultimate dislodgement from Berisay, and of how Neil himself went to his execution "verie christianlie", is narrated in the chapter dealing more particularly with the several attempts that have been made to improve the island of Lewis economically, since the days of the Gentlemen Adventurers.

The MacLeods of Lewis, hapless as they were feckless, now disappear from the history of the Western Isles, although from time to time thereafter they engineered spasmodic insurrections, and gave trouble through their piratical behaviour. They had been in possession of Lewis for three-and-a-half centuries.

Lord Kintail soon proved himself to be a conqueror who was both competent and conscientious. In matters of administration, he was as efficient as his predecessors had been incapable. He took over the control of the whole of the island. This was an onerous undertaking, as one realises from contemporary documents. The chaos and conflict he found there can scarcely be imagined. All respect for authority had gone. Murder and robbery were the order of the day. With the help of clansmen from Wester Ross—from Kintail and the surrounding country—MacKenzie and his successor, Colin, first Earl of Seaforth, earnestly strove to introduce some measure of civilisation into an island that, hitherto, had known little, if indeed any. Yet it seemed impossible to do this without recourse to methods of extreme stringency. At the outset, therefore, he assigned to his brother, Roderic Mac-Kenzie (known as the Tutor of Kintail, which was the title given to the heir's guardian) the task of bringing the rebellious MacLeods completely under his control.

Roderic was as bold and resolute a fellow as was to have been found anywhere. By one means or another, he had already proved himself more than a match for those who had tried to circumvent his clansmen in attaining the ambition upon which their hearts had long been set, namely, the taking over of the island of Lewis for their own purposes. It was he who, by stratagem, dislodged from Berisay that desperado, Neil MacLeod, together with his sea-rieving band, and in so doing broke the back of all serious resistance to the Clan Kenneth—to the Clan MacKenzie.

It may be said of the MacKenzies that they applied themselves conscientiously to the bettering of the island. During the two-and-a-half centuries they remained its overlords, the condition of the inhabitants improved out of all recognition. "At the end of the seventeenth century," writes W. C. Mac-Kenzie, "the picture we have of Lewis is that of a people pursuing their avocations in peace, but not in plenty. The Seaforths had been extravagant, and the people had to pay for their extravagance; they were politicians, and the people had to suffer for their politics. Yet it is clear that, besides establishing orderly government in the island, they had done a good deal to rescue the people from the slough of ignorance and incivility in which they found themselves immersed. But in the sphere of economics their policy apparently was of little service to the community."[1]

Certainly, the closing years of the seventeenth century and the first few decades of the eighteenth saw considerable poverty and wretchedness among the inhabitants. To his report in 1721 that they were amenable to the government's authority, Zachary MacAulay, Seaforth's Chamberlain in Lewis, appends the following rider: "But I can assure yee, yee shall find one rugged hag that will resist both King and Government, vizt., Poverty."

It cannot be doubted that this poverty, by no means confined to the Outer Hebrides, was greatly accentuated by the wholesale spoliation of one clan by another. Where there was no security against rievings and raidings by neighbours, there could be little foundation upon which to build an economy calculated to improve the conditions of the people. The whole of Celtic Scotland (that is to say, the Highlands, as well as the Western Isles) remained impoverished by this kind of thing long after the Lowlands were settling down to civilised habits and peaceful pursuits. Theft from a member of one's own clan was considered an offence of the utmost gravity, whereas theft from someone belonging to another clan was not merely excused, but extolled. It was regarded as right and proper. Indeed, the greater such theft, the more commendable. The larger the spreagh driven off in some murderous foray, the more did the chief and his clansmen approve this mode of acquisition. But the clan enriched to-day by

[1] *The Book of the Lews*, p. 167.

such means might be the clan reduced to-morrow to direst straits. However, as long as the ordinary people were buoyed up with the notion that retaliation would more than recoup them for any loss they had sustained, this reckless attitude to life continued.

In Barra and in Uist there existed a similar state of affairs. The MacNeils and the Clan Ranald spent much of their time in despoiling one another, or, perhaps, in despoiling their neighbours on the Scottish mainland. Both of these clans had their pirates; and, indeed, it was doubtful at one time which of them was to gain the mastery of the island seas. The tide of fortune ebbed and flowed between them for many a day. In the end, the MacNeils won. There was a period during which the piratical enterprises of the Chiefs of Barra exercised not merely James the Sixth of Scotland and Queen Elizabeth of England, but also the courts of France, of Spain, of Portugal. With the NacNeils, piracy was a highly organised profession during the closing years of the sixteenth century, and the first decade or two of the seventeeth. Reprisals led to reprisals, as reprisals always do, until in the end there arises a state of utter desperation and callousness. We have only to look at our own twentieth century to realise the truth of this; and, having done so, we can scarcely feel ourselves justified in criticising the conduct of the clans in earlier and, presumably, less enlightened centuries.

From such records as are available, it would appear as though the condition of the inhabitants of the Western Isles at the end of the eighteenth century showed little improvement upon that obtaining at the end of the seventeenth. The Rev. John Lane Buchanan, who visited the Long Island at this time, paints in his *Travels in the Hebrides* a pathetic picture of circumstances there. The tacksmen, or tenant farmers, had reduced their sub-tenants to a state of abject misery. Especially was this so in Harris. Lane's testimony is supported by others.

On the whole, it seems as though conditions in North Uist and in Barra were slightly better at this time. Lord Mac-Donald in the former, and MacNeil in the latter, were pursuing a policy designed to reduce the size of the tacksmen's holdings, and to substitute for the somewhat arbitrary tenure then prevailing a system devised to give greater security to the ordinary inhabitants.

In Lewis the Seaforths had done little to rescue agriculture, if indeed it could ever be rescued in the true agricultural sense. They were too preoccupied with their richer possessions on the Highland mainland to be much bothered with an island, the climatic and natural conditions of which, in their view, offered little prospect of a return on capital they might have sunk in it. They, therefore, tended to regard Lewis as a sort of romantic adjunct; and, albeit they had done something to replace with a better conception of society the former lawlessness based on mutual pillage, their neglect had serious repercussions. True, they could not have been held responsible for the weather, nor for the failure of crops largely resulting therefrom, nor yet for an increase in the native population in excess of what the island, in its primitive condition, was able to support. On the other hand, there was much within their power which they might have done to ameliorate the poverty of the people.

The only member of the family to show any real concern for the welfare of the island was the last Lord Seaforth. He did much to improve the town of Stornoway by extensive building schemes. He encouraged fishing and agriculture, and did his best to wean the natives from many of their less economical methods of tillage. He developed the burning of kelp, built roads as well as houses, and took an interest in education. He even resided for some months of the year in Lewis, a matter which helped considerably, for it is difficult to estimate the harm which, throughout many generations, absentee landlordism has wrought in the Highlands and Hebrides. Indeed, it has been as great a curse as alcohol! Of the Islanders' long-standing partiality to the bottle, you will hear something later.

.   .   .   .

It was during the Seaforths' tenure of Lewis that there took place in Britain two events of major political and historical significance, which had far-reaching repercussions even in the Western Isles. The first of these occurred during the Cromwellian period. The other was the series of attempts, known as the Jacobite Risings, made during the earlier half of the eighteenth century to restore the Stewarts to the throne. Hitherto, the Isles had played little part in Scotland's political intrigues. Trouble they certainly had given to the central authority, as we have seen; but at no time previously had the conduct of the island chiefs threatened the security of the established order by their taking sides with the not inconsiderable forces sworn to oppose and, if possible, overthrow it.

George, second Earl of Seaforth, had spent much of his active life in opportunist ways. His sympathies were divided. At one moment he showed himself a half-hearted Royalist: at another a half-hearted Covenanter. At Auldearn in 1645, however, he supported the Covenanters, when Montrose routed them, decimating the large contingent of Lewismen Seaforth had brought with him into the field. In the end, he joined Montrose; and he died a Royalist.

Five years after Auldearn, the national levy reached the Hebrides. There the historic cry, "For King and Covenant", found many a sympathiser, which explained, among other things, how Colonel Norman MacLeod of Bernera, in Harris, fought at the Battle of Worcester with a force of MacLeods believed to have been a thousand strong.

That year—1651—Earl George died. He was succeeded by his son, Kenneth Mor, third Earl of Seaforth. Kenneth, then a lad of sixteen, and full of the fervour of his years, was even more Royalist in his sympathies than his father had been. He was prominent among those who refused to submit to the dictates of General Monk, then commanding in Scotland on behalf of the Commonwealth. The young Earl was by no means in a negligible position, for by this time the Seaforths had waxed powerful—so much so that in a Commonwealth news-sheet it was said of them that in Lewis they "played Rex". It was known that, at a moment's notice, Kenneth Mor could muster several hundred men. That, in itself, was regarded as some threat to the Commonwealth, and doubly so when, with the outbreak of hostilities between the Commonwealth and Holland, the young Earl disclosed his Royalist sympathies by openly supporting the latter. The danger that the Royalist clans might coöperate with the Dutch was one with which the Commonwealth dealt promptly. Thus the Western Isles were fortified by English garrisons against the possibility of a Dutch occupation. Attempts to dislodge the garrison in Lewis were unsuccessful. Cromwellian troops remained in Stornoway until all Highland and Island resistance to the Commonwealth had either been crushed, or had petered out. During their stay in the island, they built for themselves a fort, not a trace of which remains. Before finally quitting Lewis, they reduced to ruins old Stornoway Castle, once the stronghold of the MacLeods.

Peace between the Commonwealth and the Dutch came so unexpectedly that it "did strike all dead". It placed young Seaforth in a position so invidious that, before long, he was obliged to seek conciliation with the English.

Not in all Scotland was there a man more rigorously opposed to the accession of William and Mary than the Romanist, Kenneth Og, or Young Kenneth, fourth Earl of Seaforth. After the Revolution, he steadfastly espoused the cause of the exiled James, who in course of time created him Marquis of Seaforth in recognition of his services. In 1689 Kenneth Og landed with James in Ireland, where he took part in a number of Jacobite enterprises, including the siege of Londonderry. When he crossed over to Scotland, in order to assist in the Jacobite Rising there, ill-fortune attended him. Circumstances compelled him to surrender to the Government. He was afterwards granted his release on finding caution for himself and for some of those who had been associated with him in his rebellious behaviour. The year, 1691, saw him once more in conflict with the government; and a year later he was arraigned for treason "for his invasion with forces from Ireland, and his behaviour since". Until 1697 he was a prisoner in Inverness Castle. On his release, he went to France, where he died in 1701.

Kenneth Og's misfortunes in no way cooled the Jacobite ardour of his son, *Uilleam Dubh*, or Black William, who, when still a lad, succeeded him as fifth Earl of Seaforth. William, like his father, was a Catholic, so that everything he stood for seemed bound up with the interests of the Old Chevalier. So whole-heartedly did he throw himself into the Jacobite cause that, in the summer of 1715, he was attainted for treason, and his estates were forfeited to the Crown. No one was more active in 'The Fifteen' than he. With a force of two thousand foot and five hundred horse, he joined the Earl of Mar, and fought at Sheriffmuir, where many a Jacobite Islander fell, prominent amongst them being young Clanranald, a chief of much promise, and dearly beloved by his clansmen. So indecisive was this battle that the Jacobites were hopeful of yet another opportunity of proving their loyalty to the Stewarts. That opportunity came soon afterwards, when the Old Chevalier himself landed in Scotland, and Seaforth and Sir Donald MacDonald of North Uist took a leading part in the abortive measures that followed the Battle of Sheriffmuir.

Seaforth's participation in 'The Fifteen' had made things pretty unsafe for him, even in Lewis, which was now occupied by a Hanoverian garrison in order to restrain him and his partisans, just as the Cromwellian garrison had restrained his grandfather. So he betook himself to France, the country where so many of the more prominent Jacobites had found asylum. But he returned to Scotland to take a leading part in 'The Nineteen', the plans for which Rising were actually laid at Seaforth Lodge, on the site of which Lewis Castle now stands. At the Battle of Glen Shiel, where, yet again, the Jacobites were routed, Seaforth fought bravely, and was badly wounded. He left the field accompanied by Tullibardine and George Keith, and remained in hiding until he managed to escape to France once more. In 1726 he returned to Scotland, when he was granted a pardon. His adherence to the Jacobite cause had cost him dearly; and there is no saying what it must have cost his poor tenants in Lewis. His property was taken over by the Commissioners and Trustees of Forfeited Estates, to be administered with the object of reducing the enormous debts incurred in these Jacobite ventures of his.

In 1740 William, fifth Earl of Seaforth, died in Lewis, attainted; and it is believed that he was buried within the old Church of St. Columb, at Eye—at Aignish—near Stornoway, among the Chiefs of the old MacLeods of Lewis, whom his ancestors had so successfully dispossessed.

Little wonder that Earl William's son, Kenneth, kept clear of Jacobite politics! Five years after his father's death, 'The

Firty-five' was upon Scotland. Kenneth was resolved not to be drawn into it, which meant that the island of Lewis was in no way involved in the last and greatest endeavour of the Jacobites to recover their throne. This gave the inhabitants some respite, which they greatly needed. It may be remembered that, when Prince Charlie and his faithful pilot, Donald MacLeod of Gualtergill, landed near Stornoway after Culloden, the townsfolk showed them open hostility, fearing, no doubt, lest they might again be embroiled in circumstances like those which, but thirty years earlier, had placed upon them and their resources so heavy a strain.

Although Lewis took no active part in 'The Forty-five', the more southerly of the Western Isles did. Barra, Benbecula, and South Uist were all Catholic in religion, and Jacobite in sympathy. Their people succoured the Prince during his wanderings; and from South Uist came the heroine who, more than anyone else, enabled him to reach the French privateer which bore him away to permanent exile.

The opening years of the nineteenth century found the Seaforths so much in debt, and their properties so heavily entailed, that in the spring of 1825 the Island of Lewis, excepting the parish of Stornoway, was exposed for judicial sale in Edinburgh. The sale realised £160,000, more than £22,000 in excess of the upset price. The purchaser was Mr. Stewart-MacKenzie. He retained it for nineteen years. In 1844 it passed finally from the ownership of the Seaforths, whose connection with it had lasted two hundred and thirty-four years, during which period their influence on the tenantry of the island had been great, and, on the whole, beneficial. During their suzerainty, the name of Seaforth had become synonymous with Lewis, and Lewis had become synonymous with Seaforth. Memories of them persist in the island, where still reside many of the name of MacKenzie. They took their title from Loch Seaforth, that long, narrow sea-loch penetrating far inland between Harris and Park, or Pairc, the southernmost parish of Lewis. And we must not forget that they raised the Seaforth Highlanders, the county regiment of Ross and Cromarty.

It was in 1787 that, in an endeavour to attract recruits to

the army, Lord Seaforth first offered to raise, for the King's service, a regiment from his own estates. Not until 1793, however, on the outbreak of war with France, was he permitted to do so, with himself as Lieutenant-Colonel Commandant. At his bidding, notices of a recruiting campaign were posted throughout the county, and also in the Island of Lewis, encouraging "all lads of true Highland blood" to sign on for a period of service, such as would afford them an opportunity of dealing "a stroke at the Monsieurs". The response was immediate. Recruits came in so rapidly that within a few months Lieutenant-General Sir Hector Munro was able to inspect the first battalion of them at Fort George. Encouraged by this notable achievement, Seaforth sought permission the following year to raise a second battalion. After some vexatious delay, permission was granted; and the regiment became known as the Ross-shire Buffs. In 1796 the Seaforth Highlanders had their beginnings, when Seaforth's two battalions were amalgamated to form the second battalion of the Seaforth Highlanders, a regiment largely recruited from Lewis, not only at that time, but also during the two major wars of the present century.

Though Seaforth did not actually accompany the regiment overseas, his services to king and country in connection with it were recognised in 1797, when he was raised to the peerage of the United Kingdom by the titles of Lord Seaforth and Baron MacKenzie of Kintail. He also became Lord-Lieutenant of the County of Ross; and for six years (1800-1806) he administered Barbadoes. In 1808 he was made a lieutenant-general.

Ever since those days, the martial tradition of Lewis has been associated with the exploits of the Seaforth Highlanders, just as the martial tradition of the remainder of the Outer Hebrides (Harris, North and South Uist, Benbecula, and Barra) has been associated with those of the Cameron Highlanders, the county regiment of Inverness. The proportion of Lewismen serving with the Seaforths during the two wars of the present century was indeed high. Such of the islanders as were not already serving in the Navy, primarily through their connection with the Naval Reserve, were to be found in one of the several battalions of the Seaforths.

The MacKenzie origin of the regiment is perpetuated in the tartan it still wears, which is the MacKenzie tartan, and in its crest and motto, which are those of the MacKenzies of Seaforth—the *cabar feidh*, or deer's antlers, with the motto, *Cuidich 'n Righ!* Help the King! Crest and motto are said to have had their origin in the tradition concerning Colin Fitzgerald, the legendary founder of the Clan MacKenzie. Colin, in answer to a summons for help, rushed forward and rescued the King of Scotland (according to legend, Alexander the Third) from an infuriated stag which had attacked him. This legend has been conveyed to canvas by Benjamin West, from whose oil painting the famous engraver, Bartolozzi, perpetuated the legend in his fine engraving of the supposed event.

In 1844 the Seaforths were succeeded in Lewis by the Mathesons. That year, Mr. (later Sir) James Sutherland Matheson, a native of Achany, in Sutherland, who had made a considerable fortune in the East (he was one of the founders of the house of Jardine, Matheson, & Co.) purchased the island from the trustees of the Seaforth Estates for the sum of £190,000. In May, 1844, Mrs. Stewart-MacKenzie, the previous proprietor, brought before Parliament a Bill for "investing in trustees certain parts of the entailed estates of Seaforth to be sold, and the price applied in payment of en-tailers' debts, and the surplus laid out in the purchase of other lands; for enabling the heiress in possession to borrow a sum of money on the credit of the said entailed estates; and for other purposes connected therewith". The Bill passed both Houses of Parliament, and two months later it received the Royal Assent. In this wise, Lewis, an island which had had so many ups and downs, passed from the gay and historic Seaforths to the Mathesons.

For many years, Sir James Matheson sat as Member of Parliament for Ross and Cromarty. With the handsome fortune he had behind him, he sought to improve Lewis in a variety of ways, and to an extent hitherto undreamed of. The financial outlay his schemes entailed was enormous. In 1878 he died without issue, leaving to his widow the life-rent of the heritable estate. Lady Matheson survived her husband by eighteen years, during which she endeared herself to the

Islanders. She was not so popular, however, as was her mother, Mrs. Percival, of whose goodness the oldest inhabitants still speak as though she had just departed from their midst. In Stornoway, especially, Mrs. Percival is remembered for her munificence in large ways, and her generosity in small. Her name survives in Percival Square, where the island's pipe band, in colourful regalia, disports itself in the summer evenings.

When Lady Matheson died in 1896, her estate, in virtue of the entail, passed to her husband's nephew, Mr. Donald Matheson, who, three years later, and two years before his death in 1901, handed it over to his son, the late Lieutenant-Colonel Duncan Matheson, my father's friend and contemporary.

The Mathesons' connection with Lewis came to an end in 1918, the year in which Colonel Matheson was constrained to sell the island to Lord Leverhulme. They had been in possession for less than three-quarters of a century. Yet, they had built up between themselves and the Islanders a bond of affection and esteem so largely absent elsewhere in the Outer Hebrides, as between proprietor and people.

. . . .

Lord Leverhulme's advent looked promising at the outset. I well remember his discussing with my father in Edinburgh the projects he had in mind. The latter assured him that, whereas it was doubtful whether he would ever live to take a penny out of Lewis, he would find in its peat-mosses ample scope for sinking a million or two. However, Leverhulme was not to be discouraged by such frank talk, for he was a visionary as well as a man who had been highly successful in the world of business. For the failure of his gigantic schemes in the Long Island (in Harris as well as in Lewis) he was little to blame, as we shall see later. An unfortunate concatenation of circumstances obliged him to abandon Lewis and all his vast works then in progress there, and to devote himself to the development of Harris instead. In Harris he began to sink wealth as he had been doing in Lewis. Not until after his death in 1925 were his Harris projects brought to an end.

Leverhulme was not the last benefactor to arrive in Lewis with ideas as to how the island's resources might be tapped, and the condition of the islanders materially improved in consequence. Scarcely had he shaken the dust of Stornoway from his brogues when there arrived on the scene from Canada the late Thomas Basset MacAulay, of Montreal, grandson of a Lewisman, and a descendant of the MacAulays of Uig, to whom we alluded earlier. MacAulay had the romantic notion that the island of his fathers possessed considerable agricultural possibilities, if only it could be reclaimed from peat. This idea was no new one, even where Lewis was concerned. Had not Sir James Matheson brought to Lewis Alexander Smith, that celebrated reclaimer of waste land? Smith, who hailed from the Perthshire village of Deanston, is said to have converted many of the bogs of Scotland into fertile farmlands. The Carse of Gowrie is given as an instance of his success in this field as a thoroughly competent agriculturist. But the moors of Lewis proved more intractable than the Carse, even though Sir James placed at Smith's disposal so handsome a sum of money for their exploitation, if not actually for their reclamation.

There is reason for supposing that Lord Leverhulme (in addition to his believing, as did the Fife Adventurers and others before him, that the prosperity of the island depended on the proper organisation of the fishing industry) was not averse from considering what might have been done by way of land reclamation, and the utilisation of any mineral resources the island might possess. I think he was also interested even in the possibility of exploiting its peat deposits. According to the report on such matters, which was prepared for him by an expert, " Lewis has 710 million tons of peat, containing a valuable proportion of carbon and nitrogen, two of the most crying and essential needs of the day. Is it an asset? What can be the economic contribution of Lewis to the world? Can the peat, before and after use, be profitably cultivated at an expense not materially exceeding that of cultivation on an average soil? "

All these vicissitudes in Lewis throughout the centuries had their repercussions upon the other inhabitants of the Western Isles. The chiefs of the other isles viewed with growing concern, for instance, the fact that a band of Lowlanders

The sterile wastes between Obbe and Finsbay, South Harris

had dared to make an attempt to dispossess their Lewis neighbours. Whatever feuds they had amongst themselves, they were united when it came to foreign intervention, such as they certainly regarded this to be. If the Fifers succeeded in gaining a foothold in Lewis, what next? How soon would it be ere they tried to establish similar settlements at Lochmaddy, at Lochboisdale, at Castlebay? If the lure of fish had taken them to Stornoway, how long would it be before the same lure brought them south to Barra, off which lay some lucrative fishing-grounds? They therefore decided that attack was the best defence against any such contingency. To begin with, they did all in their power to hamper the Adventurers from behind the scenes. However, when it looked as though the Adventurers meant to go on trying, they felt themselves called upon to render aid in a form more tangible. Thus, in course of time, contingents of MacNeils from Barra and of MacDonalds from Uist arrived in Stornoway, and attacked the Fifers' encampment there, committing " barbarous and detestable murthouris and slauchteris upon thame ".

Apart altogether from the temporary fear that they, too, might be invaded by such speculators, matters were anything but agreeable in the more southerly of the Outer Isles. In Barra, the MacNeil chiefs were even more lawless than their subjects. Indeed, they greatly encouraged the latter to follow their example. In South Uist and Benbecula, rival claims by the two principal branches of the powerful Clan Donald kept the country in a constant state of tension. Things were no better in North Uist, where MacDonald of Sleat and MacLeod of Harris strove for the ascendancy. In all this the Crown, to some extent, was involved; but, as a rule, it acted in such matters in the interests of expediency. As it seemed incapable of taking over and pacifying the Isles, it pursued the only course open to it, namely, that of playing the chiefs off against one another as best it could.

Nevertheless, during the opening years of the seventeenth century, the Crown did make some attempt to bring the Western Isles into line. The Statutes of Iona were designed solely with this object in view. Yet, the more recalcitrant of the chiefs, in their relations with the Crown, maintained an air of contempt and defiance. Among the worst offenders was

F   65

Where the Red River flows through the sands of Uig Bay, between Carnish and Ardroil

Clanranald himself. No statutes were going to curtail *him*, if he could help it! He meant to continue as he and his proud forebears had always done. He well knew that the Crown's invitation to a parley was but a prelude to the pruning of his autonomy; and he was resolved to combat *remis atque velis*— with oars and sails, tooth and nail—any encroachment upon his lawless existence. The mainlanders found him particularly trying. At the instance of the Scottish Burghs, he was summoned to compear before the Privy Council on a charge of interfering with fishermen peacefully pursuing their calling in Hebridean waters. He and his seamen, as is stated in the charge, had made a practice of boarding Lowlanders' smacks, destroying their nets, and seizing their catches. There is actually recorded an instance in which Clanranald compelled the owner of a fishing-boat he had taken to buy it and its lastage back from him at an extortionate price! For the three lasts of herrings she had aboard her, he demanded one hundred and twenty pounds per last, and for each of the three nets forty pounds.

In order to protect against such unscrupulous conduct the fishermen frequenting the Hebrides, the Council compelled Ruairi (Roderic) MacLeod, Donald Gorm of Sleat, Clanranald of the Isles, Ranald MacAllan of Benbecula, and Sir Lachlan MacKinnon of Strath to enter into a bond that they would behave themselves, and at the same time see that others did so too. The first of them openly to break this bond was Clanranald. So in 1625 Ruairi MacLeod, " all excuissis sett asyde ", was directed by the Council to assist in bringing him to account. Ruairi was none too willing to coöperate in such an undertaking, since Clanranald happened to be his son-in-law, and a good fellow-pirate to boot. But the Council, distrustful of Ruairi, and not without reason, made it plain to him that in no way could he " eshaip the weyght of his Majesteis arme ". Under pain of heavy penalty, therefore, it was determined to enforce his compliance with this direction, for he had given a deal of trouble, and the Council's patience was now exhausted. Only a month or two previously, he had been held responsible, along with Clanranald and MacLean of Coll, for fostering piracy in the Hebrides.

In face of Ruairi's record, it is comical that, in August,

1622, a letter should have been addressed to the Privy Council, on behalf of himself and his son-in-law, complaining of the hardships it had imposed. Ruairi found it irksome that, in such a "dilectable tyme of peax", he should be obliged to enter an appearance annually before the Council for his good behaviour! He even went so far as to petition the Council to be permitted to stay at home, undisturbed and unmolested, for the next seven years, so that he might improve his property, and thus pay his clamouring creditors. As Clanranald's financial position was even worse, Ruairi petitioned on his behalf that he might be immune for seven-and-a-half years from all civil actions brought against him in respect of the monies he owed. They were anything but blate, those unruly chiefs of the Western Isles!

It was at this time that the MacLeods, the MacNeils and the MacDonalds resorted to wholesale piracy, robbing ships of wines and spirits, and carousing and quarrelling for days thereafter. One of the Privy Council's main indictments against the islanders in 1622 was that they seized any cargo of wine, and spent "bothe dayis and nightis in thair excesse of drinking". The Council therefore enacted that masters of vessels should carry no more wines to the Isles. It has been suggested that, as a result of this and similar measures, which were calculated to reduce insobriety, the islanders may have first resorted to a practice for which they long remained notorious—the illicit distilling of whisky. When the wines of France and Spain were no longer procurable, either through peaceful trading or through piracy, they may have turned with determination to whisky, Scotland's national beverage, and her greatest curse, even at the present day.

The first half of the nineteenth century saw great changes in the ownership of the various islands comprising the Outer Hebrides. With those affecting Lewis, we have already dealt in some detail. In 1834 MacLeod of Harris sold his patrimony to the Earl of Dunmore for roughly £60,000. In 1868 Dunmore sold North Harris to the Scotts. In 1858 General MacNeil, last of the MacNeils of Barra, sold his estate to Lieutenant-Colonel John Gordon of Cluny. Soon afterwards, both South Uist and Benbecula were in the market; and in 1856 North Uist, the last island of any size to remain in the hands of its old proprietors, was sold by Lord MacDonald to Sir John Orde. Long before the closing years of the nineteenth century, not one of the Western Isles was owned by any of the old, Hebridean families. The MacLeods and the MacKenzies had each lost Lewis in turn. The MacLeods had parted with Harris, the MacDonalds of Clan Ranald with Uist and Benbecula, and the MacNeils with Barra.

Lady Gordon Cathcart, who had inherited from her first husband, John Gordon of Cluny, aforementioned, the estates of Barra and South Uist, together with Eriskay and Benbecula (a total of roughly a hundred thousand acres) died in 1935. She had already sold the Barra estate (excluding Vatersay and the north end of Barra, which had been bought for land settlement purposes by what was then known as the Board of Agriculture for Scotland—now known as the Department of Agriculture) to Robert Lister MacNeil, XLVth Chief of the MacNeils of Barra, who lives in New York. MacNeil owns approximately 8,000 acres of the isle of his forebears.

At Whitsun, 1944, Lady Gordon Cathcart's trustees sold the residue of her island estates (that is to say, some 92,000 acres) minus the north end of Benbecula (which the Air Ministry had purchased from them in 1942) to Herman Anton Andreae, a London banker, for a sum in the region of £75,000. South Uist, which represents roughly nine-tenths of the area, is essentially a sporting estate. From nothing else but its shootings and fishings could any revenue be derived under existing circumstances. The general poverty of these properties is shown in their comprising the lowest rented estate in the West Highlands and Islands. A total of about 1,200 small-holding tenants, representing a population of between six and seven thousand, on an area of approximately 92,000 acres, has an annual rental value of no more than £4,000, even when the landlord, or the factor acting on his behalf, is able to collect *all* the rents due. In South Uist, as elsewhere in these parts, many of the crofter-tenants are often years in arrears with their rents. If less were spent on alcohol, few would be in arrears. All of these tenants come under the Small Landholders' (Scotland) Acts of 1886 and 1931, which give them complete security of tenure, provided they pay the very reasonable rents fixed by the Land Court,

and comply with modest requirements as regards good husbandry. However, their husbandry is seldom good. The
crofters who husband well are few.

As an example of how little they are asked to pay, a crofter
with, let us say, eighty acres (twenty arable and sixty rough
pasture) usually pays no more than six pounds annual rental.
At the other extreme come the crofters in Eriskay. There the
most highly rented holding is but thirty shillings a year. Most
of the Eriskay holders, however, pay rents ranging from no
more than five shillings to seven-and-six.

Apart from what is known as the South End Shoot (that is
to say, the South Uist shootings to the south of Daliburgh,
which are let to the proprietor of the Lochboisdale Hotel at
the negligible rental of ten pounds a year) and the South
Uist fishings situated to the south of the Bornish road (in
which, meanwhile, the hotel proprietor, aforesaid, at an
annual rental of £114, and Mr. Andreae have coëqual rights)
and excluding Loch Bharp, at Lochboisdale (the fishing
rights of which the hotel proprietor purchased outright) the
new owner of these estates does not let the shootings and
fishings, but reserves them for his own private enjoyment. A
good deal of poaching goes on in his absence, however, as I
myself have seen. In the Western Isles, crofters and professional people, alike, have no qualms about other people's game
preserves and fishing rights. But they would very soon squeal
if the landlord in any way encroached on *their* rights! The
wholesale introduction into the Islands of the motor-car in
recent years has made poaching much easier than it used to
be. It enables the owner to reach, in ease and comfort, many
a distant loch noted for its brown trout, or a remote spot
where a bit of shooting can be done on the sly. He will often
pack into his car such of his friends as know precisely where
the best sport may be poached. Much of this poaching is
done at night, of course, when conditions are favourable. The
whisky-bottle is usually an indispensable accessory on such
unlawful occasions.

Chapter III

NATURAL HISTORY

To those who have derived their knowledge of the Western Isles from books, from casual sailings about their coasts, or from hurried excursions into their rocky, treeless wastes, it may seem surprising that from the botanist's point of view they are of immense interest. This is shown by the vast and varied data on their flora collected in recent years. Although the survey in this field is not yet wholly completed, a great deal of serious work has been accomplished. It represents, for the most part, the labours of several expeditions organised by the Department of Botany of the University of Durham, between the years 1935 and 1940. These labours began in 1935 with an examination of the flora of Barra and South Uist, and concluded with that of Benbecula, by which time all the major islands and very many of the smaller and less important ones had been visited and carefully investigated. These embraced Lewis, Harris, the Great and the Little Bernera belonging to Lewis, Taransay, Scarp, Pabbay and Berneray, in the Sound of Harris, North Uist, Grimsay, Ronay, Baleshare, Heiskeir or the Monach Isles, Benbecula, South Uist, Eriskay, Fuday, Fiaray, Barra, Vatersay, Flodday, Muldoanich, Sandray, Mingulay, and the two Barra Isles of Pabbay and Berneray, or Barra Head. Under the direction of Professor W. J. Heslop Harrison, F.R.S., of the University of Durham, to whom I am indebted for guidance in the matter of these pages, there will be published eventually a volume dealing with the flora of the Inner, as well as of the Outer, Hebrides. This will be much more comprehensive than the *Preliminary Flora of the Outer Hebrides*, which came from the same source some little time ago. The Professor's ardent collaborators have also done much entomological research in this region; and it would indeed be ungracious of me not to allude to the work of Miss May Campbell, a competent botanist who, a few years ago, issued an account of the flora of Uig, remotest and westernmost parish of Lewis. Miss Campbell is on the point of publishing an exhaustive work along these lines, dealing with the Outer Hebrides as a whole. Botanists now give the name of *Euphrasia Campbellæ* to the species of Eyebright she discovered in the Islands. Curiously, this species was found simultaneously in the Outer Hebrides by Dr. W. A. Clark, and by Jack Heslop Harrison, son of the professor already mentioned. It was noted in a florula of theirs, published in 1940.[1] Miss Campbell's name is scientifically associated with it, however, through the happy accident that her specimens were the first to reach the Eyebright specialist.

Had it not been for the serious dislocation publishing has suffered as a result of the war, her brother, James Campbell, as accomplished an ornithologist as his sister is a botanist, would have published by this time a corresponding work on the birds of the Outer Hebrides. This work ought to be available in the next year or two.

To the botanist, the Long Island is essentially a region of moorland interspersed with loch, bog, marsh, burn, and rather low mountain masses, through which sheets of bare, grey, Lewisian gneiss protrude. Rocky hill-slopes, fine sea-cliffs, and sandy or shingly bays add variety to the plants' habitats. Behind the sand-dunes by the shore stretch the machars, those rich areas of more stable sand upon which the natives pasture their cattle in common. Indeed, the machars are the common grazings of the Isles.

On the low-lying west coast of the Uists, and fringed by great bays of sand, these machars are of considerable extent. Owing to the highly calcareous nature of the sand, which is composed so largely of comminuted shells, the machars support a wonderful flora. This calcareous sand, blown inland over the rocky slopes in the neighbourhood, tends to neutralise the acidity of the peat, thus contributing to a pasture rich in plants. These sanded areas provide the Western Isles not only with good grazing, but also with most of their best cultivable land. Here and there among the rocks, cultivation

[1] *Noteworthy Plants from the Great and Little Bernera (Lewis) Pabbay and Berneray (Harris) and the Uig District of Lewis.*

is sometimes made possible by heaping into narrow strips such soil as may be available. These strips, known in the Isles as lazy-beds, are often sloped and curved for drainage purposes. Many of them are very ancient indeed, having been sown, reaped, and manured with cow-dung or with seaweed each year for countless generations. The deep drainage channels between the lazy-beds are often brightly coloured by Purple Marsh Orchids, or filled with Yellow Rattle. The cultivated ground, as a rule, is exceedingly weedy. Sometimes it is a mass of yellow or of gold, since Corn Marigold, Golden Wild Radish, and Charlock thrive upon it.

The casual visitor to the Isles, seldom venturing far from the beaten track, is as little aware of their floral richness as is the native crofter. Both are inclined to regard the mountains and moorlands, the lochs and shores, as remarkably sterile. However, before the enthusiastic naturalist, not afraid of long and arduous wanderings over ground seldom trodden by mankind, a very different picture unfolds itself. He investigates the secluded gorges, often supporting woodlands in miniature; the sea-shore, the sea-cliffs and the mountain-cliffs, harbouring many a rare plant; the lochs and lochans, often so full of Water-lilies, and sometimes fringed with Royal Ferns, or with Rowan-trees, the fruit of which glows scarlet in the September sunshine; the verdant islets studding many of the inland lochs, their lush vegetation lending to them the appearance of emeralds set in still, blue pools; the coombs and cliffs clad with Purple Heather, or with Foxgloves, gently nodding in the breeze as they do so memorably in Devon; the machars bright with countless wild flowers, and fragrant in summer with the scent of various Clovers; the hill rocks, occasionally supporting Holly and Ivy and prostrate Juniper; the moorland ponds, zoned by Bottle Sedge, or Smooth Water Horsetail, and usually containing most of the plants found in water deficient in mineral salts; the streams debouching over the sand, affording a habitat for such species as Water Speedwell; the mountain rocks and the gullies bearing those alpines which, because of the lowness of the mountains and the mildness of the climate, are so rare; the salt-marshes with their sward of *Armeria* or Sea Pink, Sea Plantain, and Sea Milkwort, affording such excellent grazing for sheep, their surface the dark green of a billiard table except when the *Armeria* in flower transforms them into the most wonderful expanses of pink; the corners where one finds "Atlantic" species, and occasionally some belonging to the "Southern Element" of our British flora. Apropos the last mentioned, a recent discovery is the Cornish Moneywort, found in 1946 in the grounds of Lewis Castle, at Stornoway, its previously known distribution in the British Isles being Kerry, southern Wales, and southern England as far east as Sussex. Abroad, it occurs only in France, Spain, and Portugal.

An Alpine rarity is the Yellow Saxifrage which, as recently as 1947, Jack Heslop Harrison found most unexpectedly in Barra, between the peaks of Heaval and Hartaval.

The noteworthy features of the Long Island's flora might be summarised thus:

(1) the "floriferousness" of the machars.

(2) the extraordinary abundance and variety of Orchids, Yellow Rattles, Eyebrights, Heaths and Heathers.

(3) the extreme rarity of such mainland common plants as Strawberry, Herb-Robert, Woundwort, and Wood Pimpernel, and the complete absence of others, such as Wood Anemone, White Dead Nettle, Ground Ivy, and Cowslip.

(4) the predominance of yellow- or gold-flowered weeds of cultivation.

(5) the golden-brown tidal zone of coastal rocks and skerries, due to the luxuriant growth of Sea-wrack.

(6) the rich cryptogamic flora, including great numbers of Ferns and fern allies, Mosses, Lichens, and Algæ.

It may be said without exaggeration that the Outer Hebrides possess a rich flora, for, within their limits, no fewer than seven hundred and fifty species of flowering plants and ferns have been collected. These plants are by no means restricted to the more southerly of them, which are more favourably situated: on the contrary, the flora of Lewis and of Harris is almost as varied as is that of the Barra Isles.

To the uninitiated, one of the most surprising features in a list of Long Island plants is the number of native trees. On almost every island from Lewis to Barra, the Silver Birch is anything but rare, even as a tree fairly well grown. It is also found on several of the smaller islands, such as Scotasay, in Harris, and Wiay, in Benbecula. On cliffs and in sheltered valleys, from the Great and the Little Bernera to Sandray, the Hazel abounds. Professor Heslop Harrison tells me that on several occasions he has collected quantities of hazel-nuts in South Uist, to the astonishment of the native populace, which was unaware of their existence on the island.

Quite common, too, are the Aspen, the Rowan or Mountain-ash, various species of Sallow, the Bramble, Honeysuckle, and many kinds of Wild Rose. Most unexpected is the Holly, the range of which is more limited. It is to be found only on the cliffs of Lewis and of North and South Harris, where, in winter-time, it displays great clusters of its red berries.

The principal plant habitat in the Hebrides is the machar, stretching behind the sand-dunes, intermittently, all the way from Lewis to Mingulay, and reaching its greatest extent in the Uists. Its light soil, so heavily charged with shell sand, supports a luxuriant growth of Grasses and Clovers, supplying food for the herds of cattle belonging to the various town-ships having communal pasturage rights in it, or yielding, when manured with seaweed, good crops of little, black oats, of bere, rye, and potatoes.

To the botanist the machar calls irresistibly. Its flowers range from multitudes of such plebeian plants as Ragwort, Buttercups, and Daisies to the lordliest Orchids. No fewer than fourteen species of the Orchid are known in these Islands, ten of which thrive on the machar. Outstanding among them are the Fragrant Orchid and the Pyramidal. These two are restricted to the lush machar-land of Fuday, one of the lesser of the Barra Isles, lying off Northbay, and renowned as an island visited in great numbers by the barnacle goose. (See photograph facing page 128.)

Much more widely distributed, and also more abundant, are the Common Twayblade, the Marsh Orchid, the Early Purple, and the Frog Orchid. The Spotted Orchid (*Orchis Fuchsii* var. *hebridensis*) is endemic to the Hebrides. It occurs plentifully in Coll and Tiree, and sparingly in Rum.

Among the other plants characteristic of the Hebridean machar might be mentioned the Kidney Vetch, Bird's-foot

Trefoil, Tufted Vetch, Gentian, Centaury, Yellow Pansy, Yellow Bedstraw, Stork's-bill, Lamb's Lettuce, Eyebrights, Knapweeds, Creeping Willows, and some peculiar Dandelions. Two ferns—the weird-looking Adder's Tongue and the Moonwort—are unique in that they can stand machar conditions.

Outcropping rock found on the landward side of the machar is often clad with stunted Grasses, with scrubby Heather, with Thyme, Bird's-foot Trefoil, and the Mountain Everlasting. The last named of these persists far up the mountain-slopes. On Fuday, and rarely elsewhere, as at Corodale, in South Uist, the Thyme is parasitised by the strange, lurid-red Broomrape.

On and just behind the sand-dunes, and in a giant guise, the Harebell (known in Scotland as the Bluebell) puts in a welcome appearance; whilst on Vatersay alone the machar and dunes yield Restharrow and Field Scabious. The marram-covered dunes themselves support many other plants, such as Sand Sedge, Burdock, Sand Rue, and Thistle.

One rarity, wishfully supposed to favour only a particular stretch of the shore-land of Eriskay, is the Sea Convolvulus known to botanists as *Calystegia Soldanella,* but popularly spoken of in the Isles as Prince Charlie's Flower, or simply as the Prince's Flower, because it is believed to grow nowhere except on that little beach on Eriskay called the *Coilleag a' Phrionnsa,* the Prince's Strand. Here the Prince first set foot on the kingdom of his ancestors, in his bold endeavour to win back a throne lost to him by their folly. According to Hebridean tradition, this plant sprang from a few seeds the Prince had brought with him from France, and scattered there on disembarking. Unfortunately or otherwise (and I must confess to a twinge of personal regret in the matter!) this Sea Convolvulus is also to be found, and in abundance, on the Traigh Varlish, one of the shores of Vatersay.

The shallow lochs sometimes to be found about the machars are also of botanical interest, since the presence of shell sand renders them suitable as habitats for aquatic vegetation. They usually abound in many species of water plants, including Water Crow's-foot, Bur-reeds, Milfoils, a variety of Starworts, the Greater and the Lesser Water Plantains, the two Bulrushes, Water Persicaria, and the Marsh Horsetail. By their marshy shores may be seen Meadow-sweet, Marsh Cinquefoil, Willow-herbs, Brook-weed, Celery-leaved Crowfoot, Watercress, Forget-me-Nots, Angelica, Mare's-tail, Ragged Robin, Water-mint, Great Water-speedwell, Devil's-bit Scabious, Marsh Arrow Grass, Marsh Orchids, Yellow Irises, and very occasionally the Slender Naiad—an American plant, and therefore noteworthy in the Hebrides. Near Loch Ardvule, in South Uist, there occurs a novelty in the form of the Purple Loosestrife.

In passing to the moorlands we find, in South Uist and Benbecula, that the lochs situated in the transition zone between machar and moor are often fringed with Sweet Gale and Sallows, the former again making its appearance after a great gap. It is to be found at Soval, in Lewis, a good deal farther north.

On the actual moorlands, the lochs, often lying in rock basins gouged out of the solid gneiss in glacial times, are deep and peaty. The surface of the more sheltered of them is decked as a rule with a magnificent array of waxen-white Water-lilies, while their fringes are sometimes occupied by slender Reeds, nodding their purple tassels in the breeze. In the lochans—the *little* lochs—near Loch Minish, in South Uist, one finds, rather unexpectedly, the Yellow Water-lily, a species more modest than the waxen, but none the less beautiful. Often, too, the Water Lobelia, the Bog Bean, and the Bladderwort poke their spikes of curious blossom through the surface of our Hebridean lochs.

The Bladderwort is much commoner in these parts than is generally believed. Masses of its feathery ropes, each with those strange traps for catching minute water creatures, are inclined to clog the pools. Of the Pond-weeds, only the floating variety (*Potamogeton natans*) and its ally, *P. polygonifolius*, have been recorded from moorland waters. Other Potamogetons belonging roughly to ten other species occur in machar lochs. A particular loch in Benbecula provides most of them, including three exceptionally rare hybrids.

In the lochs, as well as on such islets as remain untrodden by man and ungrazed by beast, masses of tangled vegetation flourish. These are usually impenetrable without the aid of some sharp, cutting implement clearing the way before one. Here Honeysuckle and Bramble compete with one another for the ascendancy, and in so doing sprawl over the stunted Rowans, Sweet Gale, Aspens, Sallows, and Royal Ferns. These islets are frequently the relict stations where plants such as Garlic, long since extirpated elsewhere by human hands, linger as remnants—linger as survivals of the more extensive woodlands of a past age. The presence of a ruined dun upon many of these islets and the existence of a curved causeway leading out to it (now largely submerged in most cases) show that in ancient days such islets were used as places of refuge. Nowadays, their most regular residents are usually a pair of swans.[1]

Around many of the lochs lie boggy expanses. These are often deep with Sphagnum Moss. Here the Bog Pimpernel, with its pink stars, crawls far and wide: here, also, the tiny Bog Orchid finds a home. Among the other plants to be seen near our lochs in the Outer Hebrides are the Cuckoo-flower, Marsh Marigold, Lesser Spearwort, Lesser Skullcap, the Marsh Pennywort, Willow-herbs, together with several species of Grasses and Sedges.

Where such boggy territories end, the moorland proper begins. Here one arrives at those glorious stretches of true Heather, intermingled, where conditions allow, with cross and with fine-leaved Heaths. Each of these three species produces white-flowered forms; and all of them are richer of hue than are many of the mainland representatives of the same species. Common, moreover, are the Black Crowberry, and, where drier conditions prevail, the Bracken and the Bilberry. At intervals in the damper zones, no fewer than five insectivorous plants expand their leaves to catch the unwary fly. Three of these are Sundews, and two of them Butterworts, occurring near lochs.

Among the Heather, and often replacing it, numerous Grasses and Sedges occur, the Mat-grass preferring the drier regions, the Purple Moor-grass the damper. The whole field tends to be relieved by frequent patches of colour, introduced by such plants as Tormentil, Milkwort, beautiful St. John's

[1] A fine example of an islet with dun and causeway may be seen in the illustration facing page 145.

77

Wort, Violet, Devil's-bit Scabious, Heath Bedstraw, Bird's-foot Trefoil, Yellow Rattle, and several Eyebrights. Of the Orchids, the Spotted variety is the commonest; while the tiny Twayblade is able to maintain itself in a fairly flourishing state wherever the canopy of Heather or of Bracken permits. On rare occasions, as on Stuley Island, and also on the South Uist mainland, the Twayblade may be accompanied by relict patches of Bluebells and Wood-sorrel.

From Lewis to the Pabbay which constitutes one of the Barra Isles, the moorlands of the Outer Hebrides are inter-sected by mountain torrents which, in rushing seaward through the ages, have carved out for themselves deep ravines with rugged, cliff-like sides. Occasionally, the floors of these gorges form shelves a few yards in width. Upon these shelves, as also upon cliffs where they are protected from gales, tiny relict woodlands persist. In this connection there comes to mind the gorges through which flow such streams as the Trollamarig, in North Uist, the Amhuinn Gillan Talleir, in South Harris, the burn running south-east between the North Lee and the South Lee in North Uist, and so on.

Although botanists in general have not studied great num-bers of these miniature woodlands, those of King's College, Newcastle-upon-Tyne (University of Durham) have done so. Indeed, the latter may be said to have discovered them, botanically. Certainly, they have worked them thoroughly. Their favourites seem to be those lying along the Allt Volagir, a stream tumbling southward from Ben More to Loch Eynort, in South Uist. In May, the deep coombs of this water-course are gay with Primroses, Bluebells, and Garlic: in August they are richly coloured by Heath and Foxgloves. The Sallow and the Hazel are the commonest trees in such woodlands. They are accompanied by Honeysuckle, Rasps, and Brambles, usually in abundance. The Allt Volagir woodland, however, is of the birch-hazel type; but it also contains many Aspens, Sallows, Rowans, Junipers, Honeysuckle, and Brambles. Its cliffs, in places, are hidden by cascades of Ivy, Bearberry, and Ferns.

Even more wonderful is the ground flora, which closely resembles that of a wood on the mainland. In springtime, under the Hazel canopy, appear beds of Bluebells, Primroses,

Violets, Garlic, and Wood-sorrel. These in August give place to Foxgloves, Wood-sage, Strawberry, Herb-Robert, Yellow Pimpernel, the Pyramidal Bugle, Golden Rod, Wild Thyme, and the like.

One need hardly say that few of our copses are as rich in flora as is that on the Allt Volagir. However, most of them can boast Hazels, Aspens, Sallows, Rowans, Honeysuckle, Wild Roses, Brambles, and Ivy. Those found in North Uist and in Harris produce the Bearberry and the Pyramidal Bugle. In Harris, curiously enough, the Holly manifests itself; and in the ravine of the Bun na Gill, in South Harris, enormous Whins may be seen, their stems as thick as a man's arm. Whins also grow in quantities in the Uists, in Barra, and in the locality of Steinish, Culrigrein, and Stoneyfield, on the outskirts of Stornoway.

In the gorges between Loch Eynort and Loch Boisdale a fresh group of plants makes its appearance—Common Bugle, Agrimony, Hedge Woundwort, and Tuberous-rooted Bitter Vetch. And once again, as if to remind us of the woodlands covering so much of the Western Isles in some past age, the Wood Vetch turns up at Hellisdale, in South Uist, on Scarp (an island situated off the west coast of Harris), and in Glen Rodil.

Let us now consider the mountains themselves.

Prior to the researches recently carried out by Professor Heslop Harrison and his colleagues, it was thought that northern and Alpine plants were confined to the mountains of Lewis and Harris. It has now been established that they occur in South Uist, on the Ben More-Feavalleach-Hecla massif. From among such as have been found there, let us mention the Alpine Rue, the Alpine Scurvy Grass, the Cushion Pink, the Mossy, the Starry, and the Purple Saxifrage, the Viviparous Knotgrass, the Alpine Saw-wort, Roseroot, the Mountain Sorrel, the Alpine Willow-herb, the Dwarf Willow, together with some rare Grasses and Sedges.

The shady crags and mountain gorges of South Uist harbour a rich and rare variety of Ferns, the most delicate of which is the Filmy Fern, which is by no means uncommon there. Other attractive Ferns are the various Spleenworts, the Parsley Fern, the Brittle Bladder Fern, the Scented

Buckler and the Mountain Buckler, the Beech Fern, and the Common Polipody.

The mountains of Harris provide many similar species, and in addition to them some strange forms of Cow-wheat, the new hermaphrodite Crowberry, and the Spiked Woodrush.

To our list of northern and Alpine forms, other islands have added their quotas. Berneray and Mingulay, for example, have supplied us with the Cushion Pink; Pabbay and Mingulay with the Mountain Sorrel. The Pyramidal Bugle has been collected on Barra, Muldoanich, and North Uist. Benbecula has contributed the alpine Mouse-ear Chickweed. The Cushion Pink, it should be noted in passing, has been found at sea-level at Uig, in western Lewis, and on the island of Little Bernera, approximately in the same locality.

Needless to say, islands characterised by lofty, spray-drenched cliffs have a vegetation appropriate to these habitats. Such vegetation is well developed in the Outer Hebrides. Generally speaking, the plants mainly represented are the Sea Pink, the Sea Campion, Sea Pearlwort, Scurvy-grass, Scottish Lovage, Thrift, English Stonecrop, Rose-wood, the Sea and the Stag's-horn Plantains. Among the Ferns thriving under such conditions are the Sea Spleenwort and, very occasionally, the Hart's-tongue Fern.

Vegetation strongly reminiscent of woodlands flourishes on the more sheltered cliffs, such as those by the shores of East Loch Tarbert, in Harris, and of Loch Eynort, in South Uist. Such vegetation is considered to represent traces of the more general mantle of trees once covering the Islands. In these localities a rich and varied flora occurs, including the Red Campion, which grows abundantly on the cliffs of Muldoanich, of the Shiant Isles, and of South Uist. Nowhere else but on the cliffs of the last mentioned has the Figwort been observed.

A remarkable plant, usually confined to the cliff-tops, is the Vernal Squill. It has been noted at Ard Uig, in Lewis. After a huge distributional gap, it reappears on Barra and on all the major islands to the south of it. It is common on Vatersay. On Sandray, at a height of 678 feet above sea-level, it reaches the summit of the highest hill.

Finally, we come to the vegetation of the salt-marshes and

Isle of Barra from Isle of Vatersay, with Heaval in the distance

the sea-shore. In the Western Isles salt-marshes are numerous. They are confined for the most part to estuaries and the heads of the sea-lochs, and are of greatest extent in South Uist and in Benbecula, where the entire range of plants associated with them occurs, including the Sea Aster, Thrift, Glasswort, Sea Blite, Parsley Water Dropwort, Sea Milkwort, Sea Spurrey, Sea Plantain, several species of Scurvy-grass, Sea Arrow-grass, and a variety of Rushes.

The most interesting plants found on the sandy shores are the Sea Holly (occurring from Mingulay to North Uist), the Sea Rocket, the Sea Kale (found only on Eilean a' Mhorain in North Uist), Prickly Saltwort, the Oraches, and Ray's Knotgrass. On the shingle beaches one finds these plants in company with masses of Goose-grass, Docks, and Silverweed.

So windswept are the Islands that trees and shrubs, which might otherwise flourish upon them, often grow no more than a few feet. Yet, as we have seen, there was a time when they must have been both heavily wooded, and covered by a dense undergrowth. In the peat the remains of Scots Firs are constantly being found. The tree which, though not a native, would appear to stand the climate best, is the Sycamore.

The few plantations throughout the Western Isles occur in valleys, usually near human habitations, where it was hoped they might serve as wind-breaks. There is one such pine plantation at Northbay, in Barra, in the midst of which Wild Hyacinths and Primroses grow profusely.

By far the greatest concentration of trees and shrubs in the Outer Hebrides exists in the grounds of Lewis Castle, at Stornoway. These were planted by a proprietor of Lewis well over a century ago, and are a conspicuous feature of the landscape when entering the harbour and approaching the quays. Enormous bushes of Rhododendron have been allowed to run wild among them, attaining in places a height of as much as fourteen feet, and in June, when they are in full bloom, presenting a remarkable spectacle.

Extensive damage was done to the few plantations of trees, both in the Inner and in the Outer Hebrides, by the terrific gale which swept them on March 21st, 1921. It was estimated that in the Dunvegan Castle policies alone, no fewer than 40,000 trees were uprooted and cast down on that

G   81

Where the Uig road peters out near Mealista, in western Lewis

occasion. An earnest attempt to make good as far as possible this enormous loss was begun almost immediately by the planting of young trees. Owing to the comparative shallowness of the soil, resting as it does on rock at no great depth, the roots of the trees in the Western Isles are unable to penetrate sufficiently far to ensure the trees' surviving such a gale as that which visited the Islands in 1921. Great numbers of those growing in the Castle grounds at Stornoway were also blown down that year; and many of them still lie as they fell.

There is no contradicting the geological and botanical evidence that once upon a time both the Outer and the Inner Isles supported dense forests. We know this from the great roots and boles of decayed trees uncovered so often in the peat-mosses. However, it seems unlikely that trees, in any great numbers, flourished there within historic times. Yet Adamnan tells us that Saint Columba had an encounter with a wild boar in the woods of Skye. Furthermore, this same island, if we accept the testimony of Dean Monro, possessed, in the middle of the sixteenth century, " maney woods, maney forrests, maney deires, faire hunting game ".[1]

The limits within which a sketch of this nature must necessarily keep obliges one to omit mention of many species of great botanical interest. Yet, from the preceding pages it will be seen that, bare as these Islands must appear to the casual observer, especially if he be accustomed to abundant verdure and foliage, their flora, by no means negligible, presents the scientist with many a problem worthy of patient research. To the trained eye, the rocks which seem barest are often as covered with a profusion of wild flowers as are the roadside ditches of the Uists. Nature, it would appear, abhors a vacuum anywhere.

.   .   .   .

Flora suggests insect life; and it is not surprising that, with this abundance of wild flowers on moorland and machar, many species of insect should be common in the Outer Isles. Even Butterflies, which are supposed to avoid wet areas, are numerous, individually, if not so numerous in the number of species.

Probably the finest butterfly in the Outer Hebrides is the

[1] *Description of the Western Isles (circa* 1549).

Dark Green Fritillary, which may be seen flitting from place to place throughout July and August, wherever the violet grows. Common as it is, and occurring in a very special Hebridean form which rarely reaches the mainland, one often looks for it in vain in the orthodox textbook. Distantly related to this fine butterfly is the Small Tortoise-shell, which thrives everywhere from the Butt of Lewis to Barra Head, and is particularly plentiful where there are colonies of nettles.

A recent arrival, in Barra at least, is the Peacock butterfly; whilst almost every year the Painted Lady and the Red Admiral, after their long journey from Northern Africa, breed in the Islands, providing a fresh brood in August and September. Migrating with them, often in considerable numbers, is the Large Garden White, and, in very small numbers, the Clouded Yellow, which my entomological friends tell me has been reported from Barra to Harris.

A genuine native of the Outer Isles, discovered as recently as 1938, is the Green Veined White, a species much attracted to water-cress and to the cuckoo-flower. It has been seen from Barra to Benbecula, on both machar and moorland. On the boggy moors especially, and feeding there on the Blue Moor Grass and the Beaked Rush, the Large Heath is to be found in a guise peculiarly Hebridean. It has been captured from Lewis to Mingulay, and is more plentiful towards the north. Its relative, the Small Heath, doubtfully reported from St. Kilda, has been shown to occur quite freely from Mingulay to Harris. In the same family, and found in crowds on moor and machar from Barra Head to the extreme north of the Long Island, is the Meadow Brown, which in these parts assumes a striking appearance. Replacing it on the sand-dunes to a certain extent, and also occasionally on the low, heathery hills, is the Grayling, a species not so far reported anywhere north of South Uist. Here, again, we are dealing with a special Hebridean race.

Lastly, we come to the Common Blue, a butterfly which frequents all stations where bird's-foot trefoil grows—that is to say, on every island, great and small. In the Common Blue we have a magnificent insect, beside which the average English, Scottish, and Continental forms are insignificant. The males are glorious in their rich blue: the females, instead of their being brown, are largely blue also. Forms anything like them are to be seen only in certain localities of Ireland, on the Durham coast, and casually in some habitats on the Scottish mainland.

The listing of the Moths of the Western Isles would be a tedious undertaking. Yet, to the investigator of the early natural history of the Islands, they are all of extreme interest. Many of them, such as the Gray Dagger, indicate woodland conditions at a period not very long ago in the earth's ageless history.

Prominent amongst the larger and more striking moths which should be mentioned is the Emperor, a truly magnificent creature. It is found feeding on heather anywhere between the Butt and Barra Head, from June until August. Its great enemy is the hoodie (hooded) crow.

With this moth may be found the Oak Eggar, which also is a heather feeder, and the Fox moth, the yellow and black furry caterpillar of which occurs in multitudes during the autumn, and is known to the Islanders as "bratag". Recently, and unexpectedly, the Pale Eggar was discovered near Strone Scourst, in North Harris, and in a form which could be described as anything but pale.

Other fine moths frequenting the moorlands are the Wood Tiger and the Ruby Tiger, both small in size, but glorious in colouring. The Common Tiger, their larger and even more lustrous ally, its caterpillar the common "Hairy Worm", may be seen everywhere, on all types of ground, though it would appear to prefer cultivated territory and the macharlands. To the same group belong the two Ermines, the White and the Buff, the former recorded only on Barra, the latter very recently discovered in a single colony in South Uist, at Loch Eynort.

Another beautiful moth—the Puss moth—having an equally striking caterpillar is to be sought wherever aspens and sallows abound. It occurs from Lewis to Pabbay, in the Barra Isles. Of the Prominents, only the Pebbled has been observed. It was added to our Hebridean lists as recently as 1938, the year it was discovered in South Uist. In 1941 it was noted in North Harris. In the Barra Isles, as well as in South Uist, the delicate Chocolate Tip may also be seen.

Of the other moths met with in the Outer Hebrides, we must single out for particular mention the lovely Six-spot Burnet, the Ghost moth, the Beautiful Golden Y, the Gold Spot, the Burnished Brass, and the Gold Spangle. All these occur sporadically in the more southerly of the Isles. More widely distributed is the Silver Y, a migrant which, in favourable years, has been seen everywhere, gaily darting from flower to flower.

Now a word or two on the Bees, the Wasps, and the Ants.

At the outset, one is surprised at finding among the Western Isles such great numbers of Bumble-bees. Surprise tends to diminish, however, on realising how prevalent and profuse are such flowers as clover.

The bees of the Isles are an interesting lot. One of them (*Bombus jonellus* var. *hebridensis*) ranging from Barra Head to the Butt, is found nowhere else in the world. It affords a clear illustration of evolution at work. Moreover, *Bombus smithianus*, swarming in the Outer Isles and also in certain of the Inner, fails completely on the mainland. To entomologists, this bee is known familiarly as the Ginger bee. It, also, has an interesting history. Its peculiar distribution speaks eloquently of its having passed part of the Glacial Period as a survivor in the Hebrides.

Among the other bees noted are *Bombus hortorum, B. lucorum*, and *B. distinguendus*.

Of the Wasps, only *Vespa sylvestris* (one of the social wasps) and *Ancistrocerus pictus* (representing one of the solitary varieties) have been observed, the former only on Barra, the latter more widely. With the latter is to be found the brilliant, metallic *Chrysis ignita*, its parasite. So much for the bees and wasps.

Three species of small, red Ants have been listed; and these occur freely.

Ants have fascinated me ever since I first began to watch them working feverishly in the Gearrchoile, that woodland I knew so intimately during my boyhood years in Ross-shire. Men have studied their development from an entomophagous existence, through the aphidicultural or pastoral, to the fungicultural, which is agricultural and vegetarian. Like men, as Maeterlinck observed, they have been, in turn, hunters, herdsmen, and agriculturists. These are the three main stages of human development recognised by Auguste Comte; and they correspond with conquest, defence and industry.

Is all this mere coincidence? One can hardly think so!

We now arrive at the Dragon-flies and Caddis-flies.

With such an abundance of lochs, lochans, streams, and marshy ground, it is not to be wondered at that Dragon-flies are common during the summer and autumn months. Eight species of them are represented. Many species of the Caddis-fly are also to be found; and these at the moment are being scientifically tabulated under the direction of Heslop Harrison, aforenamed.

A word or two on the Beetles of the Outer Hebrides.

Most striking of these are the brilliant Carabids, of the genus, Carabus. Three species of these are to be sought underneath stones and driftwood.

The Islands also possess several kinds of Whirligig beetles, as well as of Diving beetles, large ones and tiny ones.

Only one Lady-bird has been noted, and that was a very special form—*Coccinella 11-punctata*, Eleven-spotted Lady-bird.

To the entomologist looking for a field likely to provide him with a rich harvest, one could safely recommend the Beetles of the Hebrides. Such of their history as is known is indeed engrossing. The study of them, together with that of the other insects we have dealt with all too superficially, may give some clue as to when the Outer Hebrides and the mainland became separated from one another.

Since the appearance of J. A. Harvie-Brown's well-known work, *A Fauna of the Outer Hebrides,* innumerable notes and papers on the ornithology of this fascinating field have been printed in various scientific publications. During that interval many changes of ornithological import have taken place in this locality, as elsewhere. The Outer Isles are a particularly difficult area to work, as any scientific investigator readily discovers, be he geologist, folklorist, botanist, or ornithologist; and, albeit so many of them have been studied carefully in more recent decades, parts of them still remain largely unexplored by any competent ornithologist. In order to bring our knowledge of the bird-life of these Islands up to date, and to correlate much information at present available only in journals rather too scientific and technical for most of us, a new and comprehensive work is needed. But for the war, such a work by James Campbell, already alluded to, would have been obtainable by this time. Over a great number of years, Campbell has spent long periods on the various islands, collecting fresh data about their bird-life, as well as verifying much which has been taken for granted. The results of his research are expected to find their way into our bookshops within the next year or so.

To deal adequately in a few pages with the bird-life of an area so diverse is no easy task. The Islands, as the trained ornithologist is aware, provide numerous scientific peculiarities, and even pitfalls. Many of the species found have a very local distribution, so that, in all probability, the enthusiast setting out in the hope of finding certain of them will be disappointed, unless he has received prior information concerning localities. Then the bird-life of a moorland loch during the summer in, say, Lewis, is very different from that of a Benbecula machar loch at that time of year.

The Western Isles (including, of course, those outlying groups—the Shiants, Heiskeir or the Monach Isles, Haskeir, the Flannans, North Rona, Sula Sgeir, St. Kilda, and Rockall) possess an interesting bird-life; and our present task may be simpler if we now proceed to give a classified survey, in the hope that in this form such features as are of peculiar interest may be seen at a glance.

Certain Geographical Races or Sub-species:
These include the St. Kilda Wren, the Hebridean Song Thrush, the Hebridean Stonechat, the Hebridean Hedgesparrow, the Hebridean Rock-pipit, and the Hebridean Wren.

Whilst the first named has not been found elsewhere than on St. Kilda, it is now known that certain of the so-called Hebridean sub-species are not confined to the Outer Isles. For example, it has been shown that the race of Song Thrushes breeding in Skye is the same bird as that known as the Hebridean Song Thrush. Then the breeding race of Starlings in the Outer Isles is similar to that found in Shetland; while the Dipper and the Red Grouse are of the Irish race. So far as Grouse are concerned, however, it should be remembered that, in addition to the *native* race, others have been introduced into the Islands from the mainland at various times.

Certain Rare Breeding Species:

Among these should be mentioned the Short-eared Owl, Hen Harrier, Grey-lag Goose, Leach's Fork-tailed Petrel, the Red-necked Phalarope, and the Arctic Skua. These species, as well as others, have suffered greatly in the Outer Isles at the hands of egg-collectors. Their eggs are still so much in demand among collectors that particulars of their breeding quarters are kept very secret by those who share them. The Short-eared Owl, found on the heathery hills and marshes of the Islands, is the only member of his kind found there which habitually hunts during the daytime and in full daylight. It is looked upon as the keeper's friend, since it lives mainly on voles, rats, and mice. Rats are numerous, and are believed to destroy much on our moorlands. Keepers certainly do not regard the Short-eared Owl as they do the Merlin, that dynamic, little hawk preying so largely upon small birds.

Sea Bird Colonies:

This heading instantly brings to mind such islands and island groups as St. Kilda, Sula Sgeir, the Flannans, Mingulay, and Barra Head. St. Kilda and Sula Sgeir are famous for their Gannets. Boreray of St. Kilda, the third island of the St. Kilda group in point of size, is undoubtedly the greatest gannetry in the world. The Gannets there are the most amazing spectacle of their kind the writer has ever witnessed. They also breed in great numbers on Stac an Armuinn and on Stac Lee, two famous pinnacles of rock adjacent to Boreray.

In times less strenuous, and indeed until a few years ago, the natives of Ness, in northern Lewis, used to organise an annual expedition to Sula Sgeir (or Sulisgeir) for the purpose of bludgeoning on their nests, and thereafter bringing home for human consumption, the *gugas*, as the young Gannets are called in the Western Isles. The Ness-men visited Sula Sgeir for this purpose in 1947. The Gannets' colonisation of this remote and desolate isle is perpetuated in its very name, *Sula Sgeir*, the Gannets' Rock. "Be sexteen myle of sea to this ile [North Rona] towards the west," writes Dean Monro about the middle of the sixteenth century, "lyes ane ile callit Suilskeray, ane myle lang, without grasse or hedder, with highe blacke craigs, and blacke fouge thereupon part of thame. This ile is full of Wylde foulis, and quhen foulis hes ther birdes, men out of the parochin of Nesse in Lewis use to sail ther, and to stay ther sevin or aught dayes, and to fetch hame with thame their boitt full of dray wilde foulis, with wyld foulis fedders."

No less astounding than the cliffs of St. Kilda, of Mingulay, and of Barra Head are the myriads of seafowl breeding upon them. If you approach these cliffs during the nesting-season and make the smallest disturbance, the sky overhead instantly becomes darkened by birds in a great, protesting pother. The noise everywhere around one is indescribable. The birds' screaming and screeching, together with the beating of their wings, create a pandemonium recalling those lines in which the auld Scots poet, William Dunbar (1465?-1530?), describes the Bass Rock, the gannetry situated near the mouth of the Firth of Forth:

> *The air wes dirkit whith the foulis,*
> *That cam whith yawmeris and youlis,*
> *Whith shrykking, screeking, skyming, scowlis,*
> *And miklie noyis and shoutis.*

Vagrants:

The Outer Hebrides provide us with a long and interesting list of such birds. Only a few of the more important we need mention—the American Water-pipit and the American Bittern, the American Widgeon and the American Snipe, the Carolina Crake, and the Green-winged Teal.

The Uists and Benbecula:

These islands, so full of lochs of every size and shape, have long been famed for the great numbers of Snipe, Duck, Geese, and Swans found there in winter. The extensive machars of these islands attract such birds in flocks. In summer the machars are the principal pasturage of the islanders' live-stock: in winter they used to be the chief feeding-ground of the Barnacle Goose, which recently has become rather scarce in these parts.

Birds to be seen in the Minch:

Many of these are regularly seen: others are not. Since most visitors to these Islands still come by way of the Minch, the following list of some of the more important birds may be found useful:

> Long-tailed Duck (winter)
> Eider Duck
> Cormorant
> Shag
> Gannet (mainly in spring, summer, and early autumn)
> Storm Petrel
> Manx Shearwater (in spring, summer, and autumn)
> Great Shearwater (in summer and autumn)
> Sooty Shearwater (mainly in autumn)
> Fulmar
> Black-throated Diver
> Red-throated Diver
> Great Throated Diver
> Common Tern (in spring, summer, and autumn)
> Arctic Tern (in spring, summer, and autumn)
> Gulls: (Black-headed, Common, Herring, Greater Black-
>   backed, Lesser Black-backed, and the Kittiwake)
> Arctic Skua (in spring, summer, and autumn)
> Razorbill (mainly in spring and autumn)
> Guillemot (mainly in spring, summer, and autumn)
> Black Guillemot (all the year round)
> Puffin (spring, summer, and autumn)

In season, all these birds are moderately regular. In addition to them, one sometimes sees, in winter, Glaucous and Iceland Gulls, and also Little Auks. Many of these species frequent the Minch when fishing; and many use it as a highway when passing to and from their breeding quarters. The greatest concentrations of birds in the Minch during the breeding season occur near such breeding stations as the Shiant Isles, and off Canna, in the Inner Hebrides.

In summer, the Black-throated Diver, one of the handsomest of British Birds, haunts the larger and lonelier of our lochs. It builds its nest but a few inches from the water's edge, thus enabling it to dive straight from its eggs. Consequently it seldom takes to the wing during the nesting season. The nest is usually to be found on an islet which at the same time is being occupied for like purposes by one or more species of Gull. The latter, as co-inhabitants, are destructive, readily devouring the Diver's eggs or chicks, if left unprotected.

Divers generally have to "tummy crawl" a short distance from nest to water. It is believed, however, that the nesting lochs provide them amply with food, which is probably the reason why they fly little in the breeding season, although in some places they do move on the wing quite a bit.

On damp moorland, or on a knoll among the marshy ground often fringing such lochs, the Arctic Skua, in midsummer, makes the little hollow in which she lays her two dark eggs, so remarkable for the way in which they blend with their surroundings. No better example of protective colouring can be seen. This graceful bird is swift in flight. Against a headwind, it wings at an almost incredible speed, either over land or over water. When anyone approaches the nest, the sitting bird, having already observed the trespasser a long way off, leaves the eggs as unostentatiously as it can, and then begins to flap its wings, and to drag them along the ground as though it were wounded. Seton Gordon tells me that, of the many birds habitually resorting to this type of stratagem after their young are hatched, the Arctic Skua is the only one which does so while sitting on its eggs. Other ornithologists assure me, on the other hand, that they have seen this happen, with eggs, in several other species.

The Arctic Skua is noted for the way in which it subsists so largely upon the fish it compels Gulls and other species to drop when it pursues them so swiftly, so powerfully, so unrelentingly.

* * * * * * *

Although the main island groups have many characteristics in common, they differ so much topographically that one may find it simplest to deal with the birds ecologically. Let us now proceed to tabulate them in this way.

East Coast of the Outer Hebrides:

Generally speaking, the rocky east coast of the principal islands attracts comparatively few rock-breeding birds. There are exceptions, however, as, for example, "scattered" Gulls nesting there (Herring and Greater Black-backed) and a few Shags and Black Guillemots. The caves on the east coast are the home of the Rock Dove; and the Rock Pipit is common in suitable areas.

Hereabouts, moreover, the Oystercatcher, the Peregrine Falcon, the Raven, and the Hoodie Crow are seen. The last named, haunting all habitats in the Outer Isles, is common here.

Wherever inlets occur, not only is the bird population greater, but so also is the number of species. In such surroundings, especially where there are also skerries and low, rocky islets, the Heron, Curlew, and Redshank are by no means scarce. Many birds of the Minch frequent the east coast bays of the Islands.

The Sounds and Fords:

The bird population of the sounds and fords separating the main islands is large and varied. Waders, Ducks, Divers, and Seabirds occur among them. The Sound of Harris, habitat of the Long-tailed Duck, is particularly interesting in this regard. So, also, is the Sound of Barra, the larger isles in which—Fuday, especially—are a well-known haunt of the Barnacle Goose. This fine bird arrives in these parts in October, and remains all throughout the winter, flying northward again in April or May.

The Moorlands:

There are various types of moorland birds in the Outer Hebrides. The most extensive tracts of moorland are, of course, in Lewis. This habitat carries the lowest bird population of all. Indeed, parts of the moorland, especially in wintertime, are almost bird-less.

Among such moorland birds as are to be found there in the breeding season, we might mention the Hoodie Crow, Twite,

Skylark, Meadow Pipit, Song Thrush, Stonechat, Hedge-sparrow, Wren, Cuckoo, Merlin, Golden Plover, the Red Grouse. In certain parts of the Islands, the Eider Duck is a moorland breeder.

It should be noted, with reference to this list of moorland birds, that the type of moorland and the quality of the heather growing upon it have important effects on the distribution of the various species. For example, the Song Thrush, the Hedge-sparrow, and the Stonechat prefer heather which is really rank and old. The Golden Plover, on the other hand, likes those parts of the moorland where the vegetation tends to be tundra-like in character.

Hoodies in the Outer Hebrides regularly nest and roost in long heather. On the more open parts of the moorland, a few scattered pairs of Peewits breed; and on stony ground, and in the vicinity of old ruins, Wheatears occur during the nesting-season. Both of these birds, however, are commoner on the fringes of the moorland than on the actual moorland itself. This is true also of the Cuckoo, a bird frequently to be seen by the side of such roads as intersect moorland country. In autumn, Kestrels are at times conspicuous in the moorland, particularly in roadside areas.

Many parts of the Hebridean moorland are unbelievably bird-less during the winter. I have tramped several miles of the Lewis moors on a winter's day without putting up a single bird. Nevertheless, at this time of the year the moorland is the haunt of the migrant Woodcock; and in some of the wetter areas groups of White-fronted Geese winter.

It should be borne in mind that, even throughout the main island groups, the distribution of several species differs remarkably. South of the Sound of Harris, for instance, the Golden Plover is a scarce breeder at the present time, whereas it is quite common in the areas north of it, especially on the great moorlands of Lewis.

The Curlew, I am told, does not breed in the Islands. Grouse are scarce; and those which do frequent these parts sit so tight that one can tramp for days in their haunts, seeing very little of them except their droppings. In time of migration, some quite unexpected species are encountered—the Blackbird and the Redwing, for example.

Inland Cliffs and Rocky Escarpments:

Breeding thereon are the Hoodie Crow, Raven, Starling, Kestrel, and Common Buzzard. All these birds, with the exception of the Starling, have their roosting haunts there in winter.

Cultivated Areas:

Here the Corn Bunting, the Peewit, and the Corncrake breed. Mixed flocks of Corn Buntings, Twites, Sparrows, and other species use the cultivated areas in winter. Snipe visit the flooded stubbles, which the Rock Doves glean. The Grey-lags graze on the grass; and the Mallards often raid the cornfields in autumn. The Hoodie is also common in such regions. Conspicuous, too, particularly in the neighbourhood of Stornoway, is the Rook.

Human Habitations:

In these the Starling and the House-sparrow breed. However, the birds do not find all types of Hebridean dwellings attractive. Houses are often used as song perches by the Hebridean Thrush and by such unexpected birds as the Rock Pipit. Steadings and stackyards are the haunts of many of the small birds at all seasons of the year. Twites and Corn Buntings frequent them, especially in autumn and winter. So do Greenfinches and Chaffinches.

Gardens:

Gardens, as found in territory where the soil is richer and the climate less inimical to profuse flowering, are almost unknown in the Western Isles. Yet, in such as there are, the Twite, Song Thrush, Blackbird, Robin, Hedge-sparrow, and Wren breed. Owing to the general scarcity of cover, our island gardens attract several kinds of small birds during migration periods.

Woodlands:

So scarce in the Outer Hebrides are trees that even such natural woodland as scrub, composed for the most part of Rowan or Willow, has a noticeable effect upon their bird-life. Among such scrub, which, as we have seen earlier, occurs on islets in freshwater lochs, the Hoodie Crow, the Reed Bunting, the Song Thrush, the Hedge-sparrow, and the Heron breed.

Among the few plantations the Islands possess, several of the commoner species nest, such as the Chaffinch, Willow Warbler, Song Thrush, Blackbird, Hedge-sparrow, and Wren.

It must be remembered, of course, that in the Western Isles certain species are very local breeders. For example, the Chaffinch and Sedge-warbler have a very restricted breeding range in the Islands, and are absent from some areas which would seem quite suitable for their requirements. It is anomalies like this which make it difficult to compile a brief account of the bird-life of the Outer Hebrides.

The most extensive woodland in these Islands, as we have seen, is that at Stornoway, comprising so much of the policies in the immediate neighbourhood of Lewis Castle. From an ornithological point of view, it is by far the most important. In addition to many of the birds already mentioned, Jackdaws, Greenfinches, and Wood-pigeons breed here. There is also a large Rookery in these woods.

Other birds found therein are the Goldcrest, Missel Thrush, and Tawny Owl. For reasons which are obvious, the breeding population of the Song Thrush and of the Blackbird is higher here than anywhere else in the Outer Hebrides.

Machars:

Here the Skylark, Ringed Plover, and Peewit nest. So also does the Dunlin, in the swampier parts. In winter-time a great concourse of fowl, many of them migratory, may be seen on the machars, among them Golden Plover, Peewit, Redshank, Curlew, at least three kinds of Geese, and several Gulls. Many of the last mentioned remain in the Hebrides throughout most of the year. Very few of the Lesser Black-backs do, however.

Strands:

The strands of the Outer Hebrides, as we have seen, are to be found on the Atlantic or western seaboard, and mainly to the south of Harris. The west coast of Lewis and of Harris is more rocky, although there are fine stretches of sand at Suainabost, in the north of Lewis, at Uig, in the west, and at Luskentyre, Scarista, and Northton, on the west side of South Harris. These, however, are negligible when compared with the vast expanses of sand in the Uists and Benbecula, and even in Barra, where the Great Cockle Shore, adding much poetry and loveliness to the Hebridean scene, is peopled by so many birds.

Commonest of those breeding among our strands are the Oystercatcher, the Common Tern, and the Little Tern. In winter the strands are thronged with all kinds of birds—Raven, Hoodie Crow, Snow Bunting, Brent Goose, Widgeon, Oystercatcher, Ringed Plover, Redshank, Greenshank, Bar-tailed Godwit, Curlew, and Sanderling.

Where reefs and skerries occur along these strands, the Turnstone and the Purple Sandpiper are not uncommon. During migration various other waders, such as the Grey Plover and the Whimbrel, turn up on the strands.

Lochs:

The number of lochs in the Western Isles is enormous. Indeed, they may be said to be literally innumerable. More-over, there are so many different types and sizes—large, fresh-water lochs with islets in them, lochs with reed beds, lochs entirely devoid of cover, semi-tidal lochs, brackish lochs, moor-land lochs, lochs in the machar, hill lochs, and so on. A glance at the map readily shows one how much of the surface of the Islands between the Sound of Harris and the Sound of Barra is occupied by lochs of every size and of every con-ceivable shape. Look at the extent of Loch Bee, in South Uist, or of Loch Druidibeg! Run your eye along the road leading in a south-westerly direction from Lochmaddy, in North Uist, and mark the welter of water it traverses! Little wonder these areas attract so many kinds of wild-fowl!

Many birds nest among these lochs, including several kinds of Duck, and also the Grey-lag Goose. In the breeding season, the following, arranged thus for ready reference, may be found among them:

96

Castlebay at noontide in autumn

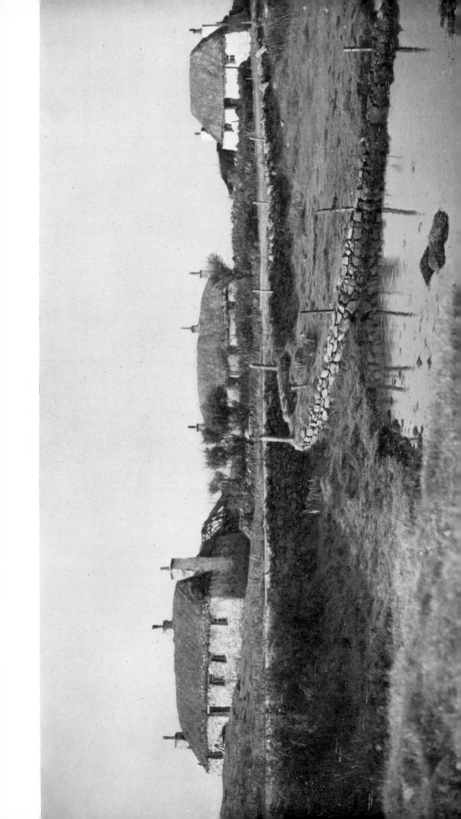

Heron
Mute Swan
Grey-lag Goose
Shel-duck
Mallard
Teal
Widgeon
Shoveler
Tufted Duck
Eider
Red-breasted Merganser
Red-throated and Black-throated Divers
Coot
Oystercatcher
Common Sandpiper
Common and the Arctic Tern
Black-headed, Common, Herring, Lesser Black-
   backed, and Greater Black-backed Gulls

The variety of Duck in winter is considerable. Besides Mute Swans, many Whoopers are to be seen, and occasionally a pair of Bewick's Swans.

Swamps and Marshes:

Here breed the Reed Bunting and the Sedge Warbler, the Dunlin, the Snipe, and the Moorhen. So also does the Black-headed Gull. In winter such areas are much visited by various kinds of Geese, Duck, and Waders, by Snipe, Water-rail, and Moorhen.

Rivers and Burns:

Here we find the Dipper and, very occasionally, the Water Wagtail; and, in summer, the Common Sandpiper. The Robin flits merrily along such water-courses.

In the Western Isles, migration is not so extensive a movement as may be witnessed on the east coast of Great Britain. Nevertheless, these Islands, from the ornithologist's view-point, are an interesting field to work. Apropos migration, St. Kilda and the Flannan Isles, when visited by Dr. W. Eagle Clarke just prior to the outbreak of war in 1938, furnished some useful data.

The subject of migration is too vast and intricate for our

H   97

Wayside cottages at Linicleit, Isle of Benbecula

present purpose. Yet, it should be remembered that many species seen in the Outer Hebrides in spring and autumn are passage migrants. Such, for example, are the White Wagtail and the Whimbrel.

.   .   .   .

The Western Isles are entirely free from Newts, Frogs, and Toads. Professor Heslop Harrison tells me that he has seen one Viviparous Lizard on Vatersay. It is commonly seen, I believe, in Coll and in Rum, two of the Inner Hebrides.

Vipers are reported from Lewis, although there is still some doubt among naturalists whether there really are any in the Long Island.

The absence of Newts, Frogs, and Toads is explained by their having been exterminated at the onset of the Great Ice Age. During the last Inter-Glacial Period (a time of high land levels, when *terra firma* was continuous from the Scottish mainland to a line far to the west of the present western shores of the Outer Hebrides) the ice left the land. Thus, the area under review was opened for an influx of immigrants which might re-populate it with their kind. Most of the present population of plants and animals entered then, or at some period of temporary climatic amelioration during the last Pleistocene Glaciation. However, before the Newts, Frogs, and Toads could re-colonise the area, or more suitable habitats become available for them, the Islands were once more cut off by the sea, and all admission ceased.

Rabbits, occasionally, are plentiful on the machars, but rare on the moorlands. The Common Hare and the Blue Hare have been introduced. The former is still found, but sparingly, in Lewis and in Harris. The latter, like the Marten, which was so common in the Islands seventy or eighty years ago, is now thought to be extinct there. The Polecat, Weasel, and Badger are not found. The Otter is to be met with throughout the entire length of the Long Island.

Among the other rodents might be mentioned the special Field Mouse (*Apodenus hebridensis*). It occurs on most of the islands, indicative of their former woodland conditions. The Pigmy Shrew, though scarce, may be seen everywhere.

All the islands as far north as North Uist harbour Voles. They are entirely absent from the isles in the Sound of

Harris, from Harris itself, and from Lewis. The House Mouse and the Rat are all too plentiful in places.

The one Bat is the Pipistrelle, which is rare. It has been found at Rodil, near the southernmost tip of Harris.

The Red Deer, which would appear to be natural in some parts, but to have been introduced into others, roams the moors and hilly fastnesses of Harris and of North Uist. A considerable herd flourishes on Pabbay, largest of the isles in the Sound of Harris. Deer were once common on many of the islands from which they have now disappeared completely, having been exterminated by the human species.

By no means uncommon around the entire coast of the Long Island is the Porpoise. The Pilot Whale and the Common Rorqual are seen but rarely. The former, on the few occasions upon which it has put in an appearance, has been seen in numbers. At the present moment there lies off the west coast of the island of Baleshare, in North Uist, the skeleton of a whale which is probably a Rorqual.

The Blue Shark, which the natives of the Hebrides used to hunt for its oil, is not rare, and may be seen anywhere from the Butt to Barra Head. The Basking Shark, seen much more frequently, is still taken for its oil. Indeed, this species appears to be so plentiful at the moment about the Outer and the Inner Hebrides, and in the Atlantic waters beyond, that an industry has recently been established at Soay (Skye) to deal with the sharks now being landed there. During the closing years of the eighteenth century, the men of South Uist profited considerably by the valuable oil obtained from the Basking Sharks they hunted in adjacent waters.

The fish in which the Hebridean lochs and streams abound are the Trout, the Salmon, and the Salmon Trout. The last named are very plentiful. The patient and observant may see them entering the Harris streams in great numbers.

The Eel is common in the lochs, as is also the Three-spined Stickleback, especially in the more brackish lochs. The Charr, though by no means rare, is seldom caught.

Among the salt-water fishes, some of which are common, some of which are rare and erratic, may be mentioned the Thornback and other Rays, Skate, Mackerel, Dog-fish, Cat-fish, Lumpsucker, Two-spotted Goby, Grey Mullet, Wrasse,

Cod, Haddock, Whiting, Coal-fish, Pollack, Hake, Ling, Halibut, Turbot, Plaice, Flounder, Sole, and of course the plentiful Herring. The prosperity of Stornoway, as a base of the Scottish Herring Fleet, still rests much on the Herring. From Castlebay, in the last decade or so, the herring fishing industry has disappeared almost entirely.

Line-fishing is prosecuted mainly for purposes of local consumption. Of an evening, the crofter-fisherman frequently goes out to fish with lines off the rocks near his home.

It was held some twenty years ago that the line-fishing banks of the Hebrides were largely ruined by trawlers operating illegally within the statutory three-mile limit. Vigilance on the part of our Fishery Cruisers has greatly reduced this offence, which is regarded by the Western Islander as one of the most dastardly crimes of which men are capable.

In British waters live two kinds of seals, namely, the Common Seal, and the Grey or Atlantic Seal. Only the latter frequents Hebridean waters. According to Seton Gordon, it is " the largest British mammal, and one of the most robust ". The Common Seal brings forth her young in the early summer, whereas the Grey Seal seldom drops her pup before the end of September, and may do so even as late as the end of November. In fact, the breeding season of the latter is almost invariably the months of October and November. It is now protected during September, October, and November. Yet, incursions upon its nurseries do occur occasionally. In olden times such incursions were frequent. Indeed, in the Outer Hebrides they were made annually and were regarded as an integral feature of the year's routine.

The pup of the Common Seal, usually born on a skerry or tidal rock, takes to the water almost immediately. It certainly begins its swimming life on the first day of its existence. On the other hand, the young of the Atlantic Seal is dropped inland, and often at some height and distance from the sea, on one of the many remote and uninhabited islands of the Hebrides, or of the Orkneys and Shetlands. For the first few weeks of its life, therefore, it is essentially a land mammal, its mother actually deserting the sea to suckle and guard her young, often at a spot from which the sea cannot even be

100

seen. It is believed, in fact, that, during the first few weeks of the pup's life, the mother remains constantly with it, not even leaving it to feed, but subsisting on her own accumulation of fat.

The island chosen for breeding is usually remarkably inaccessible. Take, for example, Shillay, lying a mile or two north of Pabbay, off the western end of the Sound of Harris. Or take North Rona, situated forty-five miles west of Cape Wrath, and but a mile less in a north-north-easterly direction from the Butt of Lewis.

The Atlantic Seal, unlike the Common, breeds in considerable numbers as a community. In the late autumn or early winter, I have seen hundreds of them congregated on the high, rocky promontory of Fianuis, at the north end of Rona. In November these barren rocks are littered with white, silky pups, usually asleep on their backs, with their small heads tilted upwards, or asleep in curled-up fashion, like a domestic pet. There they lie, often completely exposed to inclement weather. November and December can, indeed, be rude and boisterous months in the Western and Northern Isles.

Shillay, like Rona, is out of reach for the greater part of the year. Only during calm weather can a landing be made on either. The seals begin to assemble at Shillay in the autumn. By October, when breeding is in full swing, it is difficult to move on the island without treading upon them. Travelling well inland, they mingle with the fifty black-faced wedders which Mr. Simon MacKenzie, tenant of the island, winters there. They cover entirely the summit and sides of the eminence above the beach where a landing is usually made. Much of Shillay is grassless and slushy as the result of their constantly moving backwards and forwards upon it.

"When the Atlantic Seal nursery is disturbed," writes Seton Gordon, "most of the mother seals hasten to the safety of the sea. The minority remain to guard their young, and if the human intruder ventures too near, make threatening darts towards him, the while roaring and moaning with wide-open mouths. The baby joins in the querulous moaning, pitched in a higher key. But, if the human observer should stand quietly, a mother seal may in time become reassured and may suckle her baby—and then it is seen that her teats are normally hidden beneath her thick skin, in order to shield them from injury when moving across the rocks, or even when lying basking in the sun, as the Atlantic Seal often does at low tide on some low skerry. I have sometimes seen a seal on a summer day looking like a double-prowed Norwegian skiff, as it held head and tail beyond reach of the rising tide, which at last washed it off its warm perch into the cold water."

If you watch a seal coming ashore, and rather laboriously flopping its way some little distance inland, among rocks and boulders, you would think that a mammal so clumsy of movement on land would be easily caught on land. This is far from so, however. Once the nursery receives the alarm of human intrusion, it is amazing the rapidity with which the adult seals flop and flap to the cliff's edge, and plunge for safety into the sea. I once thought I would stalk a colony of seals on Fianuis; but, when still some hundreds of yards off, lying very quietly and unseen in a slimy hollow in the rocks, I heard much splashing ahead of me. Rocks and skerries which had been so closely packed with seals basking in the late autumn sunshine were completely cleared. The stampede had lasted but a few seconds; and the neighbouring waters were now as densely populated with seals as had been the rocks from which they had slithered in what seemed to me an incredibly short space of time.

Though many of the Western Islanders had great compunction about shooting or killing the seals, or even about molesting them in any way whatsoever, these creatures, in former times, were much persecuted. Martin informs us that " they are ate by the meaner sort of people, who say they are very nourishing. The natives take them with nets, whose ends are tied by a rope of the strong alga, or sea-ware, growing on the rocks ".

Those were the times when the Hebrideans annually made expeditions for the sole purpose of hunting the seal. Perhaps the most famous and savage of these was the excursion to the rock known as Cousamul, which is situated off North Uist. Let me again quote Martin in this connection, and at some length: " On the western coast of this island," he writes, when dealing with North Uist, "lies the rock Cousmil, about a quarter of a mile in circumference, and it is still famous for the yearly fishing of seals there, in the end of October. This rock belongs to the farmers of the next adjacent lands: there is one who furnisheth a boat, to whom there is a particular share due on that account, besides his proportion as tenant. The parish minister hath his choice of all the young seals, and that which he takes is called by the natives Cullen-Mory, that is, the Virgin Mary's seal. The steward of the island hath one paid to him, his officer hath another, and this by virtue of their offices. These farmers man their boat with a competent number fit for the business, and they always embark with a contrary wind, for their security against being driven away by the ocean, and likewise to prevent them from being discovered by the seals, who are apt to smell the scent of them, and presently run to sea.

"When the crew is quietly landed, they surround the passes, and then the signal for the general attack is given from the boat, and so they beat them down with big staves. The seals at this onset make towards the sea with all speed, and often force their passage over the necks of the stoutest assailants, who aim always at the forehead of the seals, giving many blows before they be killed; and if they be not hit exactly on the front, they contract a lump on the forehead, which makes them look very fierce; and if they get hold of the staff with their teeth, they carry it along to sea with them. Those that are in the boat shoot at them as they run to sea, but few are caught that way. The natives told me that several of the biggest seals lose their lives by endeavouring to save their young ones, whom they tumble before them towards the sea. I was told also that 320 seals, young and old, have been killed at one time in this place. The reason for attacking them in October is because in the beginning of this month the seals bring forth their young on the ocean side; but those on the east side, who are of the lesser stature, bring forth their young in the middle of June."

.   .   .   .

I am tempted to conclude this chapter on a happier and, perhaps, more personal note than the slaying of seals, for, whenever I think of our Hebridean birds and beasts, flowers and butterflies, there come to mind two localities which have ranked high in my affections, ever since I began to take an interest in the Western Isles. One of these is the bird-haunted Sound of Harris, with its islands and islets, its skerries and tumultuous tides, its legends of the Widgeons and of the Seal-folk. The largest and most important of its islands are Berneray, Pabbay, Boreray, Killegray, Ensay, and Shillay. I have visited all of them at the time of year when the wild flowers of the Hebrides are at the height of their splendour. I have been there in the springtime when the lapwings, in great numbers, were beginning to assemble on the lovely machar of Berneray, upon which they nest in early summer. I have wandered along the shores of Loch Bhruist, the large, fresh-water lake situated about the centre of this same island, when the swans were wintering there, and have listened to their weird singing in the night. With my camera, I have stalked the deer on Pabbay, and the seals of Shillay. On Boreray—ah! that isle which calls so tenderly, as if welcoming the visitor who, perhaps, may tell its ancient stones how fare the descendants of those who, long ago, quitted its shores for lands more prosperous—I have examined, with an eye all too amateurish, butterflies and moths, few of the names of which I then knew. I have waded, literally knee-deep, through the wild flowers of Ensay, and more than once risked my life in a small boat among the fickle tides and currents swirling un-ceasingly on every side of it. What a paradise is the Sound of Harris for the naturalist who can sail his own boat in waters so perilous!

The other locality I have in mind is Eoligarry, tucked away among smooth, soft, rounded hills of emerald, beyond the Great Cockle Shore, in the north of Barra. In springtime these hills, right up to their very summits, are covered so thickly with primroses that one can scarcely move among them without trampling upon their faint-scented loveliness. Likewise with the Eoligarry shorelands, where even the bent-grass fails to limit the primroses' ubiquitous profusion. Now glance at the photograph facing page 112, for it will give you some conception of what the shoreland pastures of Eoligarry looked like when I visited them with my camera late in May, 1948. Primroses can be picked at Eoligarry at the end of September; and I have found them blooming there well into October.

CHAPTER IV

ARCHAEOLOGY

THE distribution map of cairns, stone circles, and standing stones, reproduced in that scholarly volume published by His Majesty's Stationery Office in 1928,[1] suggests that in times prehistoric the Outer Hebrides may have carried a population much in excess of what is to be found there to-day. Certainly, the Inventory, which comprises so large and valuable a part of this volume, and supplies details of all manner of ancient structures in these Islands, assigned to a date before the year, 1707, shows how rich a field they are for the archaeologist.

Generally speaking, such isolated objects as have been recovered, though relatively few in number, would appear to indicate the three phases of cultural and economic development which, for purposes of convenience, if chronologically not too accurate, we term the Stone Age, the Bronze Age, and the Iron Age. But, whereas it may be deemed convenient to attribute this or that ancient monument to a particular phase, it must be remembered that such classification can have reference only to one of the three recognised stages of development. Although one uses these terms when denoting, in a general way, the phases through which man has passed in his progress toward what is called civilisation, one realises that they cannot be regarded as indicating even approximate dates, and are merely the lines along which economic man would seem to have travelled. In other words, the inhabitants of the Western Isles, owing to their remoteness and isolation, may have reached, say, the Bronze Age at a date much later than did peoples living a less isolated existence—an existence more directly in contact with civilising influences and agencies.

[1] *Ninth Report of the Royal Commission on the Ancient and Historical Monuments of Scotland, with an Inventory of Monuments and Constructions in the Outer Hebrides, Skye, and the Small Isles.* (Edinburgh, 1928.)

In the Western Isles, up to the present time, there have been discovered no monuments of any kind which archaeologists, with confidence, could assign to the Stone Age; while the relics associated with that era, which have been found there, are few in comparison with those discovered in certain parts of the mainland. This does not necessarily mean that the Western Isles never knew a Stone Age, such as seems so clearly defined elsewhere. It merely means that, so far, no monuments indisputably of Stone Age origin have been discovered in these Islands. The view has been advanced, however, that beneath the peat, which in places is of considerable depth, monuments of great antiquity, and possibly also contemporaneous relics, may lie buried.

In relation to area, the greatest concentration of ancient monuments occurs in North Uist: the least is in North Harris and in Lewis. Many of these monuments, of course, are sorely dilapidated. Where Lewis is concerned, it must be borne in mind that peat, several feet in thickness, now overlies much of the ground which, in some pristine era, may have been cultivated and habitable, and that buried beneath this peat are probably the remains of many very old constructions. Who knows but that one day we may discover among our immense Hebridean peat-mosses a Stone Age monument comparable with that to be found anywhere?

It should be added, moreover, that the denuded condition of not a few ancient structures in the Isles has resulted largely from the way in which, from time to time throughout the centuries, their stones have been carried away by the inhabitants, so as to provide ready material for the building of houses, dykes, byres, sheep-pens, jetties, and the like. Nevertheless, the Outer Hebrides are by no means deficient in archaeological remains. Scattered throughout them are chambered cairns, small cairns, duns or forts built in lochs, by the seashore, or on promontories, hut circles, earth-houses, beehive shielings, galleried duns, brochs, standing stones, stone circles, and ecclesiological ruins.

Let us now look, if but superficially, at a few of these ancient remains.

Those structures known as duns, especially of the type believed to have been used for defensive purposes, are indeed common throughout the length and breadth of the Outer Hebrides. On almost every island of any size may be found the ruins of at least one.

Good examples of defensive duns constructed upon islets in freshwater lochs are to be seen in Dun Cromore, in the Lochs region of Lewis, and in that situated in Loch Bharabhat, in the Uig parish of the same island. A stone causeway connects each with the nearest point on the shore of the loch. Such causeways seldom run straight across: they are usually curved, or proceed in zigzag fashion. Some of them have gaps, made for the purpose of ensnaring or impeding an enemy: some have a knocking-stone—a stepping-stone so poised that the weight of the human foot upon it rocked it sufficiently to warn the dun's inmates that someone was approaching. It is interesting to find that, after so many centuries, several of these knocking-stones still knock, even when lightly trod upon, so carefully were they placed in position at the outset.

Nowadays, many of the stone causeways connecting such islets with the shores of the lochs in which they stand lie submerged, at any rate for the most part. In the case of the two duns just mentioned, however, they are clearly seen, especially in time of drought. As a rule, the islets chosen for such constructions were exceedingly small, with the result that their walls encircled the entire area.

One of the best known duns among the Barra Isles is that situated on an islet near the eastern shore of the small loch to which it gave the name of Loch an Duin. This loch lies a little over a mile to the east of Cuier, in Barra itself; and the islet is plainly visible from the roadside as one proceeds toward Northbay. The dun, though by no means inconspicuous, is now in a very ruinous condition, as may be seen from the photograph of it facing page 145. Most of its stones were borne away for incorporation in the dam built at the loch's outlet many, many years ago, in order to raise its level. In a green hollow by the edge of the road, where it follows the steep valley through which runs the stream flowing from Loch an Duin to the sea at Northbay, stands the disused mill which the raised waters of the loch once worked.

On the western side of the islet, the ruins of the dun,

though now little more than a heap of tumbled blocks, are still some six feet in height: on the eastern, all the large stones have been removed, leaving nothing but a rickle of small stones not required when the dam was being built. The outer face of such of the dun as remains shows evidence of its having been a circular structure. According to the Inventory, over a length of thirty feet on the north-western curve, several courses remain in position to a height of between three and four feet. The dun also exhibits slight traces of a gallery, which, when considered in conjunction with its dimensions and general character, suggest that this particular structure may have been a broch, the type of ancient monument sometimes referred to by antiquaries as a Pictish tower.

The external diameter of this ruin measures nearly fifty feet. A causeway some fifty-five feet long, and as much as seven feet broad, connects the dun with the extremity of a small promontory on the east side of the loch. Usually, most of the causeway is visible a few inches above the surface of the water.

Popularly, but erroneously, the brochs are believed to be of Norse or Scandinavian origin. Archaeological research has shown that they belong to a period much earlier than that during which the Norse dominated the Western Islands.

It is curious that, although this occupation extended over four-and-a-half centuries, and was of the utmost importance, both historically and ethnologically, the Norse did not replace with their own tongue the Gaelic language of the Celtic inhabitants whom they found there, and with whom they intermingled much and inter-married. Yet, even the most superficial examination of the place-names of the Inner and Outer Hebrides shows that, with a few notable exceptions, they are of Scandinavian origin. Among the well-known exceptions might be mentioned Eigg and Skye, both of which, in one form or another, were current before the Norse invasion began. The former is obviously the *Egea*, and the latter the *Scia*, of which we read in Adamnan's *Vita Columbae*—his *Life of St. Columba*—written towards the close of the seventh century.

The place-names of the Hebrides are a study in themselves. For the benefit of those anxious to pursue such in reliable and authoritative company, one cannot do better than recommend what has been written on the subject by W. C. MacKenzie, upon whose scholarship the writer has so frequently had occasion to draw.

Among the commonest suffixes in the coastal place-names, not merely of the Hebrides but of Scotland generally, is *ness*, signifying a promontory or headland. This, of course, is derived from the Norse, *nos*, which is closely connected with our English word, nose.[1] Throughout the Western Isles, there are literally hundreds of examples of the Gaelicised form of this suffix, either as *nis* or as *nish*—Arnish, Bornish, Breidhnis, Duirinish, Ranish, and so on. One could extend the list indefinitely. A few mainland examples occurring to one are Berridale Ness, Binsness, Buchan Ness, Caithness, Clyth Ness, Durness, Girdle Ness, Inverness, Tarbat Ness, Trotternish, and Waternish.

In the Isles there are also numerous place-names ending in *bost*, a Norse termination denoting a farm-steading or a homestead. As examples of such we might mention the following well-known place-names in Lewis, where this suffix is particularly common: Crossbost, Garrabost, Habost, Luerbost, Melbost, Shawbost, and Suainabost.

We have our *shaders* as well as our *bosts*, signifying, as a rule, summer pasturage, such as one would associate with the Gaelic, *airidh*, a shieling. Examples of this are found in Caryshader, Grimshader, Kershader, Lamishader, Sheshader, Ungashader, and Shader itself, a populous croft community on the west coast of Lewis.

In the suffix, *bhal*, survives the Norse, *fjall* (or variants of it) denoting a hill. Like *mh*, *bh* (as in *bhal*) is pronounced *v* in Gaelic. Phonetically, therefore, *bhal* becomes *val*, as in the first syllable of "valley". In the names of the hills and mountains of the Western Isles, this Norse suffix occurs almost to the exclusion of others. Among such as come to mind are Ainebhal, Chaipaval, Cracabhal, Easaval, Griomabhal,

---

[1] The name survives in Noss, the island lying to the east of Bressay, in Shetland, the highest part of which consists of the remarkable cliffs known as the Noup of Noss, which the writer visited with his camera last May, while myriads of seabirds were nesting upon them.

Hartaval, Heaval, Mealasabhal, Rueval, Roneval, Stulaval, Taithabhal, and Ullaval.

Commonest of the loch terminals is *bhat* (pronounced *vat*) which comes to us from the Norse, *vatn*, water, or a loch. The names of inland lochs ending in *bhat* are usually prefixed by the Gaelic word, *loch*, which means precisely what it does in English. Thus we have such tautological examples as Loch Bharabhat and Loch Hungavat, Loch Langabhat and Loch Steisevat.

The Norse influence is also prominent in the number of place-names ending in *cleit* or *cleat*, a Gaelic form of the Norse, *klettr*, a crag or rock. We find it in such names as Breascleit, Einacleit, Hacleit, Malacleit, and Inacleit, the last mentioned being the Scandinavian name for that part of the town of Stornoway now known as Newton.

No less numerous are the names ending in *dal* or *dail*, which corresponds with our English word, dale, and is derived from the Norse, *dalr*. (*Cf*. Welsh, *dol*.)

Probably the commonest of all the terminations derived from the Norse is *ay*, or *ey*, denoting an island or islet. In Gaelic this termination is usually rendered *aidh*. The names of innumerable islands in the Hebrides so suffixed immediately occur to one—Berisay, Berneray, Ensay, Eriskay, Flodday, Mingulay, Pabbay, Sandray, Scalpay, Scotasay, Taransay, Vacsay, and Vatersay.

One might pursue indefinitely the subject of place-names, giving examples of other suffixes, all of which go to show how thoroughly the Norse domination of the Western Isles impressed itself upon their toponomy. However, when we turn our attention to the ancient monuments of these Islands, we are astonished at finding how very few of them can be said, with any certitude, to be of Scandinavian origin. Indeed, it is extremely doubtful whether there exists throughout them the remains of a single structure which could be assigned to the centuries during which the Norsemen remained in control. A few personal relics of the period have been found, nevertheless. These consist of some oval brooches; a pair of brass scales, and a little hammer, found in a grave on Ensay; the bronze hilt and pommel of a Viking sword; some brass pins; and seventy-eight chessmen of walrus ivory. Eleven of the last mentioned are in the Scottish National Museum of Antiquities: the rest are in the British Museum, together with fourteen draughtboard pieces and a buckle, all found in a sandbank in a gully by the south shore of Uig Bay, in western Lewis. This hoard was discovered by accident in 1831: a cow, rubbing herself against the sandbank, brought it to light.

The only outstanding object which one can associate fairly confidently with the Scandinavian occupation is the rune-inscribed slab found in the old churchyard of Kilbar, at the north end of Barra, and now an exhibit in the National Museum of Antiquities, at Edinburgh. Not only is this the sole object of its kind ever discovered in the Outer Hebrides, but it is unique in that the erection of sculptured stones was not customary among the Scandinavians in their own country. The practice is one they appear to have adopted through contact with the Celts, among whom they settled in such numbers, and with whom they remained until Norway's colonial power collapsed with Haco's misfortune at Largs in 1263.

This rune-inscribed stone stands four-and-a-half feet in height. Its breadth varies from twelve inches to sixteen; and it is ten inches thick. On the front of it is a Celtic cross, which would appear to be entirely free from any Norse influence. The whole of the back, however, is covered with the runic inscription, an adequate interpretation of which has yet to be given. Many of the runic letters are lost where the end of the slab has been broken. Such as remains would seem to read as follows:

UR THUR KIRTHU STI[N-]R
RISKURS S[ ]RISTR
[ ]

It is nearly three-quarters of a century since that eminent antiquary, Dr. Joseph Anderson, in subjecting the broch to critical examination, showed fairly clearly that it could not be attributed to the Norsemen.[1] Not a single broch, he

[1] " Notes on the Structure of the Brochs ", in the *Proc. Soc. Ant. Scot.*, xii (1878).

pointed out, had been found in Norway, nor in any of the territories colonised by the Norse, with the exception of Northern and North-western Scotland. Furthermore, the Norsemen of Viking times built of wood, as we know from their literature. Towards the close of the ninth century, according to various Sagas, Orlyger, the Norseman, who had been reared by Patrick, Bishop of the Isles, went to Iceland as a missionary, taking with him from the bishop, *inter alia*, wood for the erection of the church he built there and dedicated to St. Columba, and also consecrated earth to place under the church's corner-posts.

Moreover, edifices of drystone masonry, though usual in Scotland and in Ireland during the Celtic and Early Christian period, were totally unknown in Norway in Viking times, or even later. Consider, in conjunction with this, that relics discovered in brochs excavated in Caithness and in Orkney are akin to such as have been found in other Scottish dwellings of the period, notably in the earth-houses, which are unquestionably pre-Norse. Dr. Anderson's evidence, although largely of a negative nature, was confirmed in 1891 during excavations of a mounded enclosure at Torwoodlee, Selkirkshire, when the foundations of a broch were brought to light. Among the relics found on the floor were fragments of Samian ware, a variety of Romano-British pottery, some glass, and a single coin—a denarius of Vespasian. All these would seem to point to the broch's having been occupied as early as the first century, A.D.

What applies to the brochs, which, as we have now seen, cannot be regarded as Scandinavian, probably applies also to the great number and variety of duns, particularly to those showing certain well-defined broch-like affinities. They, also, must be pre-Viking. With the brochs and earth-houses, the duns, for equally good reasons, may be assigned to the Early Iron Age. Exactly what their uses were remains in doubt, though relics found in them would seem to indicate that they continued in constant use while the Romans were in occupation of the rest of Britain.

Of the forty-four brochs noted in the Outer and Inner Hebrides (more than half of them, by the way, are found in Skye) very few now stand more than three or four feet above

Primrose-time at Eoligarry, Isle of Barra

their foundations, so very dilapidated have they become through one cause or another. To-day the only broch of any magnitude is that known as Dun Carloway, perched conspicuously on the crest of a rocky slope on the west coast of Lewis, near the crofting township of the same name, and overlooking much of Loch Roag. It is circular in plan, and has an average external diameter of forty-seven feet. Its walls vary in thickness from ten to twelve feet. Although far from complete, it is in a much better state of preservation than is any other in the Western Isles. Its ancient walling still rises, on the east side, to a height of thirty feet.

Dun Carloway, after the broch on the island of Mousa, in Shetland, is probably the finest example in the country, excepting not even the two excellent specimens preserved in Glen Beag, not far from Glenelg, in western Inverness-shire. Without going too much into architectural detail, and giving a list of measurements conveying little to anyone but the expert in such matters, one might mention that it is constructed of two concentric drystone walls, roughly built to courses with stones averaging only one-and-a-half feet by six inches. On the north-west a doorway measuring approximately three feet by three-and-a-half gives access to the court. The massive monolith forming the lintel is obviously the largest stone in the building.

In ancient times Dun Carloway was known as Dun Dearg, signifying the Red Dun, or Red Fort. It seems curious that Martin Martin never alludes to it in his invaluable account of the Western Isles. He does, however, mention Dun Bragair, the ruined broch standing on the low-lying strip of land protruding into Loch an Duna, at Bragair, about eight miles to the north-west of Carloway. "Some few miles to the north of Brago," he writes, "there is a fort composed of large stones; it is of a round form, made taperwise towards the top, and is three stories high: the wall is double, and hath several doors and stairs, so that one may go round within the wall." It is scarcely likely that this broch, at the time of Martin's visit, stood in a better condition than did Dun Carloway.

Tradition in Lewis has it that as late as the seventeenth century both Dun Carloway and Dun Bragair were occupied. In the former, one of the Morison brieves, or judges, of the

I   113

A corner of the Great Cockle Shore of Barra

Lewis, together with his family, is said to have taken refuge from the fury of a certain Donald Cam MacAulay, a desperado who figures much in the folk-tales of western Lewis. With the aid of a couple of dirks, the dauntless Donald scaled the walls of the old dun in the dead of night, and suffocated his Morison foes by dropping great bundles of burning heather into the dun's interior.

The people of Lewis say that Dun Carloway, like all the other brochs in the Islands, was built by the Picts. They sometimes refer to them as Pictish Forts, or Pictish Towers. But who were the Picts? And whence came they? Are not these amongst the many questions upon which ethnologists, as well as archaeologists, are much at variance?

In his *Scottish Place-names*, W. C. MacKenzie has put the facts of the Scottish brochs in this succinct form: "Scottish archaeology preserves an open mind about the origin of the brochs; but opinion has hardened in favour of assigning as their probable date a post-Roman and pre-Viking limit. That would make their chronology coincide, more or less, with the time when, as we are told, the Picts commenced to settle down in the country."

As for their purpose, MacKenzie doubts whether they fulfilled the same functions as the (British) hill-forts, but suggests that they may have been admirable safes for plunder. Most of them are so situated, he adds, as to justify the view that they were used as watch-towers.

.   .   .   .

In Lewis, Harris, North Uist, and Benbecula many circles of standing stones are to be seen. South of Benbecula there is none to be found to-day, though this does not necessarily mean that South Uist and the Barra Isles never possessed such monuments. All one can say is that at the present time none is visible among the more southerly Isles. As for what remains of such circles in the Long Island, the greatest number of them occurs in the west of Lewis, within a comparatively small compass, round the head of Loch Roag. Here stands the famous circle known as the Callernish Stones, which, and although occupying an area less than does either the Ring of Brodgar, in Orkney, or the better-known circle at Avebury, is regarded after Stonehenge as being the most important Bronze Age monument in Britain. Of the eleven stone circles recorded in Lewis, no fewer than seven lie within a radius of four miles of the Callernish Stones, which, along with two of the other circles in this neighbourhood, would appear to have enclosed a chambered cairn. One of the other two—the Steinacleit circle, near Shader—gives the impression of having once possessed an outer ring of single monoliths surrounding an area roughly elliptical, in the south-west segment of which the circle proper is to be found. Near Garynahine, and also near Callernish, is a circle embracing a small cairn; but in neither of these cases is it now possible to say with any confidence what either of these cairns may have looked like originally, since they are both thoroughly collapsed.

At Garrabost, not far from the town of Stornoway, is an ancient ruin strongly resembling that of a dolmen. It is that of a megalithic chambered cairn and stone circle. The chamber appears to have been situated within four corner stones and a single capstone. These five blocks lie prominently on the sward of the common grazing at Garrabost. The whole construction is very much denuded, and so few loose stones now lie about it as to justify the view that in olden times the cairn must have been used extensively as a quarry for the houses and byres in Garrabost, as well as in those of the townships in the immediate neighbourhood.

Two stone circles situated at Breascleit, near Callernish, show that, when complete, each of them consisted of two concentric rings. Each of these smaller stone settings is referred to locally as a Tursachan. What this word actually means, we know not, though it seems probable that it has some connection with the Gaelic adjective, *tursach*, meaning sad or sorrowful, mournful. If this be so, it may arise from the belief that ancient monuments such as these were in some way associated with death and burial. The name, Tursachan, is also applied in the Western Isles to groups of standing stones not necessarily erected in a circle. The name, in the singular form, is sometimes used to denote a solitary standing stone. Three standing stones and a prostrate pillar stone at Barraglom, by the narrows separating the Great Bernera from the Lewis mainland, are spoken of by the natives as the Tursachan, though these monoliths are also referred to as *Na Fir Bhreige*, the False Men. The latter term is the one most frequently applied by the Islanders themselves, even to the Callernish Stones. Then the name, Clach an Tursa, given locally to a monolith on the hillside above Loch Carloway, is an example of the Tursachan conception persisting even in the case of a single standing stone.

In a vague sort of way, the Islesfolk ascribe all the standing stones, whether occurring singly or in circles, to the Druids. They regard them as the giants of eld—some of them ancient Fingalians, perhaps—turned to stone by the magic wand wielded by a Druid priest.

Pre-eminent among the solitary standing stones in the Western Isles is that known in the Gaelic as the *Clach an Truiseil*, popularly spoken of as the Thrushel Stone. This splendid menhir is reared on the gentle slope of a hillside in the north of Lewis, at the township of Balantrushal, in the parish of Barvas—" about ¼ mile northwest of the fifteenth milestone on the Stornoway and Ness road ", to quote from the precise Inventory once again. Nineteen feet of this celebrated stone are above ground. It is about six feet in width, and nearly four at its maximum thickness. The stone's girth at its base falls but a few inches short of sixteen feet.

There is a tradition in Lewis (not a very convincing one, we might observe) that the Thrushel Stone was erected by the Morisons of Ness to commemorate an outstanding victory in their long feud with the MacAulays of Uig.

If Lewis can boast its Thrushel Stone, North Uist can boast its Ultach Fhinn, the gigantic pillar—" Fingal's Armful ", as the words would seem to suggest—lying prostrate on the southern shoulder of the hill called Craonaval. Reclining in a hollow upon several small blocks of stone, clear of the ground, it is more than twenty-two feet in length, and six at its greatest width. Experts say that it shows every sign of its having been moved by human hands.

Stone circles are not common elsewhere in the Outer Hebrides. Only one has been noted in Harris, and two in Berneray, largest and most populous of the isles in the Sound of Harris. There are two in Benbecula, and six in North Uist, two of which enclose a chambered cairn.

Single menhirs occur frequently, however. In addition to those already noted, we might mention a few others which come to mind, namely, that at Borvemore, in Harris, which appears to have been one of a circle, the remaining stones of which lie their full length near by, and are largely buried in peat; the stone known as *Clach MhicLeoid* (MacLeod's Stone) situated on a sloping promontory at Nisabost, in Harris; the three "False Men" on the hillside at Blashaval, not far from Lochmaddy, in North Uist; the standing stone on the edge of the rocks by the shore, just below the church on Boreray, one of the islands, now uninhabited, in the Sound of Harris; and the fine stone standing by the sea-rocks close to the inn at Pollachar, at the southern extremity of South Uist. Scattered throughout the Long Island are numerous menhirs such as these.

Let us return for a moment to the megalithic avenue, circle, and associated cairns at Callernish, since these far outweigh in importance anything else of the kind in the Hebrides. This wonderful array of ancient stones, standing on the ridge of a promontory running from the southern end of the village of Callernish towards Loch Roag, is a conspicuous landmark from several points of the compass. It is cruciform in shape. The site is not more than a hundred feet above sea-level. Towards the south it rises gently in a hillock known to the natives of western Lewis as *Cnoc na Tursa*. This ancient construction, the axis of which runs approximately north and south, consists of an avenue two hundred and seventy feet long and twenty-seven feet broad, composed of nineteen monoliths. This avenue terminates at its southern end in a stone circle thirty-seven feet in diameter, and comprising thirteen monoliths. To the east and to the west of the circle extend transverse rows of four stones each. To the south but six stones remain. These look as though they once formed part of another avenue twelve feet wide.

With the Callernish megaliths are associated two cairns. One of these, lying within the circle, is the chambered cairn, upon which the other cairn impinges.

From the central megalith, such as remains of the south avenue runs almost due south. From the same point, the north avenue deflects ten degrees towards the east. The eastern limb deviates slightly to the northward; while the western runs almost due east and west.

All of these massive monoliths are of the Lewisian gneiss. They vary in thickness from six inches to twenty; and, except for their having been cleft, they are entirely unwrought. Each stone is inserted some distance into the ground, the base in every case being packed tightly with small stones.

The central stone, which is the largest of them, stands fifteen-and-a-half feet in height. Its weight has been estimated at between five and six tons. The smallest stone, occurring in the north avenue, is but three feet six inches high. It would be interesting to know just how much of the larger stones is underground, and it is not unlikely that, during the unchronicled centuries they have stood upon these windswept wastes, they have sunk a good deal into the peat.

Between 1857 and 1858, by which time the peat had accumulated to a depth of five feet round the packing of the stones, Sir James Matheson, then proprietor of Lewis, caused the peat to be removed from the site of this ancient construction. It was then that the chambered cairn within the circle came to light. Few relics were found, however—merely some fragments of human bones, and a dark, unctuous compound thought to have been partly of peat and partly of animal substance.

There is a belief among the Lewis people that no one can count the Callernish Stones accurately. A similar belief exists in Ireland in regard to the ancient cursing-stones to be found inside a cashel, such as that on Tory Island. It is, indeed, seldom that two or more persons counting the Callernish Stones at the same time have arrived at the same figure; and I will admit that, from attempts I myself have made, I have had pretty conflicting results!

There are, in point of fact, forty-eight stones at Callernish; but even the careful counter may have difficulty in finding more than forty-seven, or perhaps less than forty-nine! I have been in the act of photographing this splendid monument when groups of sightseers have arrived on the scene from Stornoway, and each individual, prompted by the knowledge of such a belief in the Isles, has gone forth with an air of confidence, if not actually of defiance, to count these mighty megaliths; and I have listened thereafter to arguments as to whose total was the correct one. This has sometimes resulted in a series of recounts, with results even more divergent!

Of the scores of islands comprising the Outer Hebrides, a surprising number possess the ruins of some ancient ecclesiological structure. Even the remotest and smallest of them often have such ruins. Yet, when one remembers the nature of the Old Celtic Church—its monastic basis, and the hardship and solitude its devotees sought in furtherance of their mission—this should not astonish one. Wherever you find in the Isles a place-name beginning with Kil (Gaelic *cill*, from the Latin *cella*, a cell, such as a hermit would occupy) you may be certain it notifies the site of an ancient Celtic church or chapel, and of a burial-place attached thereto, or maybe the simple cell of Celtic saint or monk, who found his way there in the course of his missionary wanderings, establishing wherever he could some nucleus for Christian worship, however small, however primitive. Such place-names are very common throughout Celtic Scotland, and also, of course, throughout Ireland; and the religious foundations they denote are sometimes of considerable antiquity.

In the Isles, as might be expected of a region for which Ireland, by way of Iona, was responsible in the matter of religion during the early centuries of Christianity, the Kils commemorate Celtic saints. In the name of only one ancient church would there seem to be commemorated a saint who was obviously not a Celt. This is St. Aulay's, at Gress—the church in Lewis to which Martin (*c.* 1695) refers as that of " St. Aula (*i.e.*, Olaf) in Grease ". The walls and gable of this rather featureless little church still stand. It is roughly twenty feet by fourteen. Over the doorway occur the initials, I B and M K, together with the date, 1681. The foundation is very much older than this, of course, though the date given may be that at which it underwent some restoration. The excellent state of its gables would seem to suggest that it may have had some such attention about this time. The dedication is patently of Norse origin. With Aulay, or Olaf, is connected MacAulay, the name of one of the four principal clans of Lewis in olden times, and a surname still very common in that island, particularly in the Uig district, which was their patrimony.

It does not necessarily follow that all the ancient churches and chapels named after Celtic saints were established during the years that the Old Celtic Church held sway in the Isles. Indeed, it is known that some of them were founded subsequent to the Synod of Whitby, which took place in 664, whereafter the Celtic Church was gradually superseded. In such cases, where the influence and memory of a good and holy Celtic missionary persisted locally, it would be deemed proper that his name should be perpetuated there in the dedication of any post-Celtic place of worship and of burial.

The saint whose name occurs most frequently among the early dedicated structures in the Hebrides is Columba. His name is to be found in Lewis, in Harris, and in South Uist, although Columba, so far as we know, never visited any of the Outer Isles. He did visit Skye, of course; and his name is likewise commemorated there. In religious matters, however, his influence throughout the Isles was paramount; and it is interesting to note how, even at the present day, his name, like that of Iona, is revered in these parts, especially by the better educated.

The Irish saint, whose name survives in Barra, is St. Barr. Barra, or Barray, as it used to be spelt in olden days, is simply Barr's Isle, the Norse termination, *ey*, signifying an island, and showing that this saint was associated with Barra *before* the Norse arrived there. At Kilbar, in the north of the island, stand the old religious buildings bearing his name. The same applies to Taransay, an island off the west coast of Harris. The Norse, *ey*, or *ay*, was added to Ternan, or Taran, a name which one supposes to be Pictish in origin.[1]

A religious significance also attaches to those islands called Pabbay, denoting in each case the priest's isle. There are four well-known Pabbays in the Outer Hebrides, and one in Skye. Each of these, doubtless, had its monastic cell in preNorse days, the importance of which increased in later centuries.

Situated in the old kirkyard at Balnacille, near the southern

[1] Adamnan, in his *Vita Columbae* (*lib. ii, cap. xxiii*) mentions a Pictish noble named Tarainus.

shore of Pabbay, second largest and remotest of the many isles in the Sound of Harris, are the ruins of an ancient building known as *Teampull Mhoire*, Mary's Temple. Within a dozen feet of it lie the ruins of a similar, though smaller, structure called *Teampull Beag*, the Little Temple. This word, *teampull*, is, of course, a Gaelic form of the Latin, *templum*. It occurs frequently throughout the Western Isles, though fewer ruins are denoted by it than by *cill*, or kil.

Older than either of these as an ecclesiastical term still surviving in the Islands is *annat*. Authorities on place-names believe this word to have originated with the Celtic Church. It is not uncommon in parts of the mainland of Celtic Scotland; and there are several examples of it in Skye. At Kilbride, for instance, in the Strath parish of that isle, is a well named *Tobar na h-Annait*, and a stone, *Clach na h-Annait*. The ruined church at Killegray (an isle in the Sound of Harris) and the fine spring situated a quarter of a mile to the south of the church are, in all probability, the *Teampull na h-Annait* and the *Tobar na h-Annait* mentioned in *The Statistical Account*.

At Shader, in Lewis, this ancient word occurs in the plural form, *Na h-Annaidean*—the Annats. This is applied to a stretch of pasture extending inland roughly a couple of hundred yards from the shore at Shader, and situated at no great distance from *Teampull Pheadair*, Peter's Temple, one of the several ancient *teampulls*, the ruins of which are located in this neighbourhood.

It is thought that in Celtic Scotland, as in Ireland, *annat* may have been applied to the site of the earliest Christian settlement in any particular locality. The compilers of the Inventory believe that, structurally, it is represented solely by the example in Skye, which is known simply as Annat. It is situated in the parish of Duirinish, not far from the Faery Bridge, on the road between Portree and Dunvegan. This is the Annat which Dr. Johnson and James Boswell visited in 1773, in company with Mr. MacQueen, the parish minister, who supplied them with antiquarian information regarding it which they seemed none too inclined to accept. "The first thing we came to," writes Boswell, "was an earthen mound, or dyke, extending from the one precipice to the other. A little farther on, was a strong stone-wall, not high, but very thick, extending in the same manner. On the outside of it were the ruins of two houses, one on each side of the entry or gate to it. The wall is built all along the uncemented stones, but of so large a size as to make a very firm and durable rampart. It has been built all about the consecrated ground, except where the precipice is steep enough to form an enclosure of itself. The sacred spot contains more than two acres. There are within it the ruins of many houses, none of them large— a *cairn*—and many graves marked by clusters of stones. Mr. M'Queen insisted that the ruin of a small building, standing east and west, was actually the temple of the Goddess Anaitis, where her statue was kept, and from whence processions were made to wash it in one of the brooks. There is, it must be owned, a hollow road visible for a good way from the entrance; but Mr. M'Queen, with the keen eye of an antiquary, traced it much farther than I could perceive it. There is not above a foot and a half in height of the walls now remaining; and the whole extent of the building was never, I imagine, greater than an ordinary Highland house. Mr. M'Queen has collected a great deal of learning on the subject of the temple of Anaitis . . ."

Well within living memory, I have been assured, the corpses of unbaptised children have been buried in this enclosure.

While on the topic of worship and sanctity as indicated by place-names, we might mention the Shiant Isles, that cluster of precipitous and rather inaccessible islands lying in the Minch, some four miles off the south-east corner of Lewis. Here we find yet another Annat—probably that from which, in olden times, these isles derived their repute for the sanctity which gave to them their name. Shiant is but an Anglicised form of the Gaelic word signifying " charmed ". Indeed, the Shiants were sometimes referred to as the Charmed Isles, their name having its origin in the Gaelic, *seun*, meaning a charm or amulet.

With the channel separating the Shiant Isles from the Lewis mainland are associated the Blue Men of the Minch, the best known of our Hebridean water-kelpies. The channel which they frequent, and in which they often lured seafarers to their doom in the days of the sailing-ships, is known in our island legendary as the Stream of the Blue Men.

We may now examine in a little detail the more important ecclesiological monuments in the Outer Hebrides.

In the shadow of Ben Eoligarry, at the north end of Barra, are the ruins of the church and of the two detached chapels of Kilbar, to which we already have made passing reference. These buildings, dedicated to St. Barr, are oblong in shape. They are composed of rubble built in lime mortar, and pinned up with shells. Little now remains of their gables. The church, within walls, measures roughly thirty-eight feet by thirteen. The walls themselves are about two-and-a-half feet in thickness. This is the " paroche kirke, namit Killbare " mentioned by Dean Monro.

Associated with Kilbar in olden times were some interesting customs and observances, upon which Martin Martin writes interestingly:

" The church in this island is called Kilbarr, i.e., St. Barr's Church. There is a little chapel by it, in which Macneal and those descended of his family are usually interred. The natives have St. Barr's wooden image standing on the altar, covered with linen in form of a shirt; all their greatest asseverations are by this saint. I came very early in the morning with an intention to see this image, but was disappointed; for the natives prevented me by carrying it away, lest I might take occasion to ridicule their superstition, as some Protestants have done formerly; and when I was gone it was again exposed on the altar. They have several traditions concerning this great saint. There is a chapel (about half a mile on the south side of the hill near St. Barr's Church) where I had occasion to get an account of a tradition concerning this saint, which was thus: ' The inhabitants having begun to build the church, which they dedicated to him, they laid this wooden image within it, but it was invisibly transported (as they say) to the place where the church now stands, and found there every morning.' This miraculous conveyance is the reason they give for desisting to work where they first began. I told my informer that this extraordinary motive was sufficient to determine the case, if true, but asked his pardon to dissent from him, for I had not faith enough to believe this miracle, at which he was surprised, telling me in the meantime that this tradition hath been faithfully conveyed by the priests and natives successively to this day. . . . All the inhabitants observe the anniversary of St. Barr, being the 27th of September; it is performed riding on horseback, and the solemnity is concluded by three turns round St. Barr's church. This brings into my mind a story which was told me concerning a foreign priest and the entertainment he met with after his arrival there some years ago, as follows: This priest happened to land here upon the very day, and at the particular hour, of this solemnity, which was the more acceptable to the inhabitants, who then desired him to preach a commemoration sermon to the honour of their patron, St. Barr, according to the ancient custom of the place. At this the priest was surprised, he never having heard of St. Barr before that day; and therefore knowing nothing of his virtues, could say nothing concerning him: but told them, that, if a sermon to the honour of St. Paul or St. Peter could please them, they might have it instantly. This answer of his was so disagreeable to them, that they plainly told him he could be no true priest, if he had not heard of St. Barr, for the Pope himself had heard of him; but this would not persuade the priest, so that they parted much dissatisfied with one another. They have likewise a general cavalcade on St. Michael's Day, in Kilbar village, and do then also take a turn round their church. Every family, as soon as the solemnity is ended, is accustomed to bake St. Michael's cake, as above described; and all strangers, together with those of the family, must eat the bread that night."

The largest ecclesiological ruins in the Outer Hebrides are those of the *Teampull na Trionaid*, Temple of the Trinity, at Carinish, in North Uist. In length, from east to west, they measure over sixty feet: in width they are twenty-one. The walls, except at the south-east, where they are greatly dilapidated, still stand nearly twenty feet in height; and they are three-and-a-half feet thick. Built of rubble in lime mortar, they have in them a number of beam-holes. In the east wall, ten feet above ground, there is an aumbry. A doorway in the east end of the north wall opened on to a vaulted passage leading to another building resembling a dwelling-house, which it probably was. To this part, which would appear to be of a date much later than that of the actual church, the natives give the name of MacVicar's Temple. The church itself is thought to be sixteenth century, though some archaeologists are of opinion that parts of it suggest the fourteenth.

According to Dr. Alexander Carmichael, whose name one immediately associates with *Carmina Gadelica*, that valuable collection of Celtic runes, incantations, and invocations, the portion of this edifice known as MacVicar's Temple received its name from some families of that surname who had taken it over as a burial-ground for themselves and their kinsfolk. Tradition in North Uist has it that, during the sixteenth century, much of that island was owned by one, Donald MacVicar, who was known locally as *Am Piocar Mor*, the Big Vicar; and it is thought that, rather than occupy, for domestic purposes, the actual church and its adjoining apartments, he built for himself that part of the Temple of the Trinity which ever since has been known as MacVicar's Temple.

Dr. Carmichael, in a note he wrote (probably about 1880) to that indefatigable folklorist, Captain Thomas, R.N., mentions that an old man named John MacVicar, then living in North Uist, had told him that he remembered the time when the roof of the Temple of the Trinity was thatched with heather. If this were so, it must have been as late as the closing years of the eighteenth century, or the opening years of the nineteenth, which would seem incredible.

In St. Clement's, at Rodil, in the south of Harris, we have the most outstanding church building in the Hebrides. Architecturally and artistically, it puts to shame all the other religious edifices, which, by comparison, are mainly primitive, and therefore unornamental. Standing upon an eminence in the valley sloping seaward to Loch Rodil, but a few hundred yards away, it was planned so as to suit its rocky foundation. It is built of rubble, dressed with schist, and with freestone which must have been imported for the purpose. Being cruciform, it has a nave, choir, and two transeptal aisles. In the north wall of the nave is the main entrance. The continuous roof covering nave and choir is somewhat higher than are the roofs of the aisles.

At the western end of the church stands the tower, culminating in a slated roof, pyramidal in shape, and built within an embattled parapet. Owing to the great unevenness of the site, the tower's foundation is nearly a dozen feet higher than the level of the floor of the church. Much quarrying of very hard rock was avoided by founding the tower at the higher level. A portion of the rock on which it stands protrudes through the floor of its lowest apartment. A door in the west wall of the nave enables one to enter the tower from the church itself. Admittance is gained from outside by a door on the west. The tower rises to a height of fifty-six feet from the rock on which it stands.

Much of St. Clement's beautiful fabric is enriched by carvings and by sculptured panels. One or more such panels may be seen on each of the tower's four outer walls. In the north wall a central panel bears a bull's head. A nude woman in a bent posture, nursing an infant, occurs on the panel in the south wall. One of the two weathered panels in the east wall depicts a horse: the other represents a couple of fishermen in their boat, with a net hanging overboard, astern. In a canopied niche in the west wall, above the tower's entrance, is an effigy of St. Clement.

But who was St. Clement? No one appears to be able to say. It is unlikely that he was Pope Clement. The suggestion has been made that this ancient church at Rodil may have been dedicated to Clement, who was Bishop of Dunblane in the earlier half of the thirteenth century. This seems improbable, however. The name is singular, so far as the Outer Hebrides are concerned. The only other example of its use in the Western Highlands and Islands, so far as I am aware, occurs in Skye, where, near the old church in Strath Suardal, one finds a well known as Clement's Well.

St. Clement's appears to have been a Priory Church, dependent on the Abbey of Holyroodhouse. Of its origin and early history, we know surprisingly little. Some have attributed it to David, the Sair Saint: others believe it may have been founded by MacLeod of Harris and Skye—that is to say, by MacLeod of Dunvegan, to whom Harris, for centuries, belonged. Indeed, Rodil was the burying-place of the chiefs of the MacLeods of Skye—the burying-place of the *Siol Thormoid,* the Seed or Progeny of Norman, by which patronymic they were distinguished from the MacLeods of Lewis, the senior branch of this powerful Hebridean clan, known as the *Siol Thorcuil,* the Seed of Torquil, whose chiefs lie buried at Eye, near Stornoway.

The earliest record of a church at Rodil would appear to be Dean Monro's. In the south of Harris, he tells us, " lyes ane monastery with ane steipill, quhilk wes foundit and biggit be McCloyd of Harrey, callit Roodill ". Though, officially speaking, the dissolution of the monasteries had taken place before the time at which the Dean was writing (that is to say, prior to the middle of the sixteenth century), and in the absence of evidence that there existed any other such building in this locality, it must be assumed that the Dean used the term, monastery, to denote this particular church. A few years later—in 1561, to be precise—we find " the personage of Roidill in Herris " listed among the livings pertaining to the Bishop of the Isles.

St. Clement's is fortunate in that it has been restored more than once, and at a time when other places of archaeological interest throughout the Isles were being allowed to fall into greater ruin. We know that the church was repaired during the first half of the sixteenth century by Alexander MacLeod of Harris, the chief who is better known to Highland litera-ture as Alasdair Crotach, or Alexander the Hunchback. Alasdair died in 1547; and at St. Clement's may be seen his remarkable tomb, to which we will refer in a moment. The church was repaired in 1784. Then, in 1787, it was restored by Captain Alexander MacLeod when he purchased the estate of Harris. A marble slab in the north wall of the nave commemorates this restoration; and the inscription the slab carries testifies to the conventual character of the previous edifice.

The most thorough and imaginative restoration, however, was that for which the Countess of Dunmore was responsible in 1873, the Earl of Dunmore having bought Harris in 1834 from the bankrupt MacLeods. In 1868 the Earl sold the northern part of Harris to the Scotts, who came to live at

Amhuinnsuidhe:[1] the southern part he retained. The Countess was greatly beloved in Harris, not only for what she did to preserve St. Clement's, but also for what she did for the people of the island. She was among the first to organise the Harris tweed industry, and to ameliorate the condition of the fisher-folk.

The most remarkable of the tombs within St. Clement's Church is that built into the south wall of the choir. This is the tomb of Alasdair Crotach, that chief of the Dunvegan MacLeods, to whom we have already alluded. It dates back to 1528, which means that Alasdair prepared it for himself nineteen years before he died. Elaborately wrought, and bearing an inscription in Latin, it consists of nine panels beautifully sculptured, and of the recumbent effigy of an armour-clad warrior, with ornamented bascinet and camail, with a sword held by hilt and quillon perpendicularly between the thighs, and a hip belt richly adorned. Round-toed sabbatons cover the warrior's feet, which rest upon a large reptile resembling a lizard. Where the tomb projects at head and foot, a lion is represented, the one at the head being much worn.

We cannot pass on from St. Clement's and Rodil without mentioning at least one of the many interesting occurrences associated with them. The one I propose mentioning is that of which Sir Norman MacLeod of Berneray, in Harris, told Martin Martin. It relates to what is termed Highland Second-sight—*First*-sight, as it ought to be called. Some of the natives of Harris, endowed with this faculty, were in the habit of seeing a certain man with an arrow in his thigh. They regarded this as an omen that one day, perhaps in some brawl, he would receive an arrow in this part of his body. When he died, his corpse was conveyed to St. Clement's for burial in the usual way. However, when the funeral party arrived there, it discovered that another party was approaching this consecrated ground with another corpse. A row now ensued as to which interment should be given precedence. Soon the parties were at blows, in the course of which one of

[1] It was while J. M. Barrie was the guest of Sir Samuel Scott at Amhuinn-suidhe Castle that he conceived the idea of *Mary Rose*, the theme of which is undeniably Hebridean. The Isle that Likes to be Visited is situated in this locality.

Isle of Fuday in May, from the sand-dunes at Eoligarry

the mourners discharged from his bow a number of arrows. When the dispute was brought to an end by the intervention of Sir Norman, aforementioned, it was found, as foreseen by the seers—as foreseen by those natives endowed with the Second-sight—that, while the body of the man in question lay on the bier just prior to burial, an arrow had actually entered his thigh.

An interesting account of this incident is included in a letter written by Lord Tarbat to Mr. Boyle in 1699, and afterwards sent by Lord Reay to Samuel Pepys, who at the time was seeking evidence of the Second-sight, a faculty "of which", as he wrote, "the people were so persuaded in the Highlands and Islands, that one would be more laught at for not believing it there than affirming it elsewhere".

At Aignish, a few miles to the east of Stornoway, and just beyond the isthmus linking the populous peninsula of Eye (more commonly referred to nowadays as Point) with the rest of Lewis, stand the ruins of St. Columba's Church, much the more important of the two religious edifices in Lewis dedicated to this saint. The other, known as St. Columb's Church, stands in the graveyard on the island in Loch Erisort called *Eilean Chaluim Chille*, St. Columb's, or St. Columba's, Isle. It measures, internally, twenty-nine feet by thirteen (quite a large building on so small an island), and its walls still exist to a height of six feet on an average. Of this island church we know nothing apart from its name.

St. Columba's at Eye is surrounded on three sides by an old burying-place where dockens and nettles hide many an ancient tombstone, recumbent underfoot. On the fourth side lies Broad Bay, that great, tidal basin which, until a decade or so ago, was encroaching so rapidly on the land at this point that steps had to be taken to prevent its undermining the church's north wall. It had already eaten away that part of the ancient burying-ground which once stretched on that side of the church, laying bare from time to time the bones of islanders long since interred there. A substantial sea-wall has now arrested further erosion at this spot, thus saving St. Columba's from the fate which otherwise would have overtaken it in a very few years.

Berneray, or Barra Head, from Mingulay

Tradition has it that the oldest part of the church owes its origin to one of the chiefs of the MacLeods of Lewis, who built it on the site of St. Catan's cell. Whether this be so or not, St. Columba's at Eye—at Ui, as it used to be spelt, this having been the name of the parish of Stornoway in olden times—was closely associated with the Lewis MacLeods for several centuries. As many as nineteen of their chiefs are buried there, it is said, although their graves cannot be identified at this distance of time. This old place of burial is now quite full: those who now die in this neighbourhood are laid to rest in a new graveyard near at hand.

St. Columba's is one of the twenty-three ecclesiastical buildings in Lewis enumerated by Martin. He refers to it as " St. Collum in Ey ". Its ruins are by far the largest of any ancient church in the island. Though roofless, its walls are intact. They are built of native rock—the primeval Lewisian gneiss —intermingled with a red, coarse-grained sandstone quarried nearby, and used abundantly in the repair of the church's walls at different periods. According to the *New Statistical Account*, the south-west end of the church, at the middle of the nineteenth century, was still roofed and slated.

Originally, St. Columba's consisted of a single apartment roughly sixty-two feet by seventeen. In the fifteenth century, or quite early in the sixteenth, an extension, approximately twenty-three feet by sixteen, was made at its western end, the west gable being retained as a partition between the two main apartments thus formed, and an arched doorway having been placed in it in order to provide passage from one to the other. Near the centre of the south wall is the church's entrance.

We know little of the early history of St. Columba's, at Eye—at Aignish, as the Lewis people usually speak of it, that being the name of the small crofting township not much more than a stone's-throw from it. Such scant records as exist show that in 1506 John Poylson (Polson), precentor in Caithness, received a presentation to the rectory of Eye conditional upon its having to be vacated by a certain John MacLeod. During the next half-century or so, St. Columba's is described in a number of documents as a rectory. The year after the Reformation it is referred to as a parsonage. The rector about

1535 was Sir Magnus Vaus. In 1552 it was Sir Donald Monro, doubtless the Dean who toured the Western Isles a few years previously, and consequently furnished us with one of the earliest accounts of the remote Hebrides which we possess.

On the floor of the church there formerly lay two carved memorial slabs which, some years ago, were affixed in an upright position, the better to preserve them. They were found there, among débris and vegetation, during some excavations, and were thus placed by the late Colonel Duncan Matheson, the proprietor of Lewis from whom Lord Lever-hulme purchased the island in 1917. The colonel had shown great interest in the archaeology of Lewis, especially where it concerned the ancient MacLeods, the hapless Seed of Torquil. He lived in Kensington during the closing years of his life; and it was in his home there, many years ago now, that he and I collaborated in the newspaper correspondence, and sub-sequent mild agitation, which culminated in St. Columba's being brought under the care and protection of the Office of Works. Whenever I visit the old church and see the stone breastwork protecting its north wall from being undermined by the sea, I like to remind myself that in some degree I, too, was responsible for its construction.

The slab on the south wall shows a figure in high relief, wearing a pointed bascinet, and a quilted coat reaching down to the knees. Neck and shoulders carry a camail or tippet of mail. In the Highlands and Islands the quilted coat survived until the late seventeenth century. Camail and bascinet ceased to be the vogue elsewhere during the early decades of the fifteenth century. This would not justify us in pro-nouncing the slab to be as old as that, since in these matters, as we have already seen in another connection, we cannot just apply to the Western Isles that chronology which has been so carefully tabulated in relation to archaeological remains elsewhere in Britain, or for that matter elsewhere in Scotland.

In the right hand, just below the level of the head, the figure holds a spear. The left hand rests on the hilt of a sword with pear-shaped pommel and quillons depressed towards the blade.

This effigy is pretty certain to represent a chief of the MacLeods, one of the luckless Seed of Torquil, who came to an end in the seventeenth century when the MacKenzies came over from Kintail to take from them their ancient patrimony. It is probably that of Roderic MacLeod, VIIth of Lewis. However, a stone set at the base of the effigy bears this inscription: "GRAVE STONE OF ONE OF THE MACLEODS OF LEWIS PROBABLY RODERIC II, LATTER PART OF XVTH CENTURY, FATHER OF TORQUIL IV. & OF MARGARET MACFINGONE WHO WAS MOTHER OF JOHN LAST ABBOT OF IONA."

The slab on the opposite wall shows an intricate design of carved devices, including a variety of foliage and of animals. At the top is an interwoven pattern of Celtic origin. The surface of the whole is much worn. Of the inscription cut around the slab's edges, only a few detached words are now legible. The scholarly archaeologists of Edinburgh (some of whom it has been my good fortune to have known when I lived there) think that this inscription, when complete, may have run thus: "HIC JACET MARGARETA FILIA RODERICI MEIC LEOYD DE LEODHUIS VIDUA LACHLANNI MEIC FINGEONE OBIIT M° V° iii": Here lies Margaret, daughter of Roderic Mac-Leod of the Lewis, widow of Lachlan MacKinnon, died 1503. This Margaret MacKinnon was the mother of John, last Abbot of Iona, the first and greatest of all Columban foundations in Scotland.

The burying-place here, at Aignish, was held in high esteem by the MacKenzies who, by trickery and stratagem, eventually ousted from Lewis the last of the old MacLeod dynasty, a dynasty weakened and impoverished by prolonged internecine strife. This is shown by the fact that, although the newcomers —the MacKenzies of Seaforth, as they were now to become, deriving their territorial title from the name of that great sea-loch in the south-east of the island—had their own mausoleum at Fortrose, in the Black Isle, William, fifth Earl of Seaforth, was buried in Lewis, in the old graveyard of St. Columba's, among the chiefs of the MacLeods of Lewis. William had been " out " in the Rebellion of 1715. After the Jacobite rout at Sheriffmuir, he went into exile in France, an attainted rebel.

Among the other Highland celebrities buried here is Roderic Morison, the Blind Harper, who, on leaving the service of MacLeod at Dunvegan Castle, retired to his native isle of Lewis, and died there. The spot where he lies buried is smothered in nettles. The older generation in the Isles is still familiar with his minstrelsy; and the crofters inhabiting the townships nearby—Aignish and Garrabost, Knock and Branahuie—like it to be known that, to this day, despite the nettles, they can identify his last resting-place.

Many folk-tales of Aignish are recounted at the ceilidhs round the peatfire of a winter's evening. That which comes to mind describes how a woman named MacLeod, while herding cattle on the machar near St. Columba's, was overtaken by a storm obliging her to abandon them and seek shelter in the old burying-ground, among the tombs of the chiefs of her clan. It was now dusk; and, as she lay there, out of the way of wind and rain, she suddenly heard the rushing of multitudinous feet upon the machar beyond. A band of Mac-Kenzies had descended upon Aignish with intent to drive off the cattle of the MacLeods grazing there. Up she rose, pretending to be the ghost of one of the MacLeod chiefs interred there, and shouting, *A Chlann 'ic Leod! Nach eirich sibh!* O Clan MacLeod! Will ye not rise! Instantly, the would-be cattle-lifters fled from Aignish. Never again did they dare plunder field or fold in the neighbourhood of St. Columba's, at Eye.

If you look carefully at a map showing, in some detail, the tip of the Hebridean mainland, where Ness, northernmost parish of the Outer Isles, terminates in the Butt of Lewis, you will notice, in close proximity to one another, several names in small, italicised lettering. Each of these denotes either the ruins or the site of some ancient building known among the local Gaels as a *teampull*, or temple. There is *Teampull Pheadair*, for example, and *Teampull Thomais*. Nearer the Butt we find the ruins of *Teampull fo Luith*, and the site of *Teampull Ronaidh*, the last mentioned having been dedicated to Rona, the saint associated with the remote and now unpeopled isle of the same name lying out in the North Atlantic, some forty-four miles north-north-east of the Butt of Lewis.

By far the most important of such ancient places in this locality is that situated in the heart of the populous croft-lands at Eorapie, and known locally as the *Teampull Mor*, or Great Temple, though often referred to as St. Moluag's. This pre-Reformation church is supervised by St. Peter's Episcopal Church, at Stornoway, under the auspices of which a service is held in it from time to time during the summer months. To Canon Meaden, of St. Peter's, is due the credit for having brought about its restoration, which occupied a couple of years, and which, at some considerable cost, was carried through by the Scottish Episcopal Church, in conjunction with the late Colonel Duncan Matheson, aforenamed. Donations towards the restoration fund came from all over the world.

It is claimed that this church at Eorapie constitutes the only pre-Reformation building legally secured to the Episcopal Church of Scotland; and we may safely regard it as one of the oldest and most interesting monuments of its kind, not merely in the Hebrides, but in the northern kingdom. Archaeologists assign it to the fourteenth century.

The design of the church is a simple oblong, forty feet in length. At the north-east corner is a sacristy: at the southeast is a chapel, connected with the main interior by a "squint". In their endeavour to preserve the church's original character, the restorers exercised the utmost care. Its old walls, except for a little necessary pointing, look pretty much as they must have done five hundred years ago.

In October, 1912, this ancient and remote place of worship was formally opened by the Bishop of Argyll and the Isles. In the summer of the following year, a thanksgiving service, marking the completion of the restoration, was held in it; and among those present was Anna Mary Livingstone Wilson, daughter of David Livingstone. Included in the gifts bestowed upon the restored church, shortly afterwards, was the Book of Common Prayer carried by Livingstone during his missionary travels and explorations in Africa. In order to ensure the maintenance of this gift in time to come, Mrs. Livingstone Wilson effected the presentation by means of a special deed of conveyance, assignation, and declaration of trust, in favour of the bishop and dean and the diocese and clergy in charge of St. Peter's, Stornoway, and of their successors. This Prayer Book is believed to have been the one

from which the burial service was read when, in 1861, Livingstone's heart was buried at Ilala.

Unlike the beautiful cathedrals of the world, St. Moluag's
is far from the track beaten by the ordinary tourist. Yet, it
is not so inaccessible, once you have reached Stornoway, since
there is a daily bus-service linking this island metropolis with
the many crofting townships scattered about Ness, some thirty
or more miles to the north. At the time of the restoration,
amicable arrangements were made with the crofters at
Eorapie, whose interests were likely to be affected by the
formation of a footpath, so that to-day one may wander from
the public road to St. Moluag's without let or hindrance.

The earliest allusion to St. Moluag's, or to St. Olaf's, as it
is frequently spoken of in Lewis, is that contained in the
report of Captain Dymes, who names the saint "Mallonuy".
At the time of Dymes's visit (1630) the church would appear
to have been in a good state of repair. The saint, to whom it
was dedicated, "was for cure of all theire woundis and
soares". In the healing art, as practised by him, the people
had great faith; and many a lunatic in olden times is said to
have been brought to Eorapie, and to have been cured at its
famous shrine. Moreover, it was customary for persons, who
had injured a limb, to carve out of wood an arm or a leg
(according to which was injured) and to cut out of such
wooden representation the part that seemed most seriously
affected. If the sufferer were unable to visit the shrine, a
relative or friend did so on his behalf, taking with him the
wooden limb, placing it on the altar, and then invoking St.
Moluag to effect a cure of the person whose limb was thus
represented. Dymes tells us that he saw several such wooden
limbs—legs and arms—on the altar at Eorapie.

Attached to the church at this time was a *sanctum
sanctorum*, from which women were rigorously excluded.
That the whole of the church was not held in anything like
the same veneration, however, is shown by the fact that at
Candlemas, and again at Allhallowstide, the islanders assembled there to attend what Dymes calls "General meetings".
At these it was their custom "to eat and drincke untill
they were druncke". Later, "after much dalliance", they
entered the church at night, bearing lights in their hands,

and continued their devotions all through the hours of darkness.

Such customs are very ancient and, of course, pagan in origin.

This is the church spoken of by Martin Martin as the Church of St. Malvay. If one substitute for the v in this name the letter, u (the former being the way in which u was written about this time—i.e., late seventeenth and early eighteenth centuries) one gets Maluay, which, doubtless, was equivalent to Malua, or Molua, or Moluag. In any case, there is no disputing that Martin was writing of this self-same church at Eorapie.

Martin tells us that it was the practice of the natives, when approaching the church, to fall on their knees immediately they caught sight of it, and then to repeat their Paternoster. He was informed by an accredited islander that, as a boy, he had seen people kneel and repeat the Paternoster at a distance of four miles from the church. Certainly, so far as visibility is concerned, this would not be impossible, since Ness is almost unbelievably bare. To anyone approaching the Butt of Lewis from the south, in normal conditions, an object of unusual size or shape, such as a church or chapel would be, is conspicuous at a range of several miles.

It was at Hallow-tide, according to Martin, that the natives of Lewis observed the custom of offering up sacrifice to the sea-god whom they called Shony. "The inhabitants round the island came to the Church of St. Malvay," he writes, "having each man his provision along with him; every family furnished a peck of malt, and this was brewed into ale, one of their number was picked out to wade into the sea up to the middle, and carrying a cup of ale in his hand, standing still in that posture, cried out with a loud voice saying, 'Shony, I give you this cup of ale, hoping that you'll be so kind as to send us plenty of sea-ware for enriching the ground for the ensuing year'; and so threw the cup of ale into the sea. This was performed in the night-time. At his return to land they all went to church, where there was a candle burning upon the altar; and then standing silent for a little time, one of them gave a signal, at which the candle was put out, and immediately all of them went to the fields, where they fell a-drinking their ale, and spent the remainder of the night in dancing and singing, &c."

On the following morning, the revellers returned to their homes, " being well satisfied that they had punctually observed this solemn anniversary, which they believed to be a powerful means to procure a plentiful crop ".

It was not until thirty-two years prior to the time of Martin's visit to Lewis (c. 1670) that two clergymen named Morison were able to persuade the islanders to abandon this peculiar rite—" this ridiculous piece of superstition ", as Martin terms it.

One of the most interesting features of this ancient church at the present time is the large number of relics of antiquarian import which it houses. It was hoped that these might form the nucleus of a small museum consisting of objects that, in the ordinary way, would be borne off to museums on the mainland, thus depriving the majority of the Lewis people of all opportunity of seeing their island's movable antiquities. When I visited Eorapie a few years ago, I found in the church quite a collection of interesting things—stoups, some old silver chalices, an old alms-box fastened with the original padlock, an ancient font, a prehistoric paddle recovered from a neighbouring peat-hag, a cruisie, a sheep's milking-pail, and an old Celtic cross brought thither from Rona, the distant Isle to which we alluded earlier. This cross, now well weathered, is much older than the church itself.

Once or twice during the nineteen-twenties, the church was subjected to a certain amount of vandalism. All the windows were smashed, despite strong protective wire-netting. Stones weighing four or five pounds were found inside. These had been used to break the upper windows. The lower ones were broken by means of sticks. The windows, therefore, had to be boarded up until repairs could be carried out; and the occasional services held in the church were, perforce, temporarily suspended. In one instance the church was actually entered, when many of its unique contents were smashed or scattered.

This type of vandalism is no new thing in Lewis; and whether, in the case of Eorapie, it was due to sectarian enmity or to thoughtless hooliganism, or to a mixture of both, it is impossible to say. In this ultra-Presbyterian Isle, anything savouring of Roman Catholicism or of Episcopacy is thoroughly suspect.

Not very long ago, the Lewis War Memorial, situated on the outskirts of Stornoway, suffered similar damage; and I never learnt that anything was done by the local police authorities to bring the perpetrators to account.

Anyhow, the old church of St. Moluag, one of the most interesting of our ancient monuments in the Outer Hebrides, is there for all to visit. Set among the croft-lands of Ness, it lies within hearing of the tide's murmurings, or of the breaking of seas against the cavernous cliffs at the Butt of Lewis.

. . . .

On the whole, the Western Isles are devoid of secular structures of any great dimensions, or in a reasonable state of repair. Like the ancient duns, the castles of subsequent centuries are ruinous. Few of them resemble, in construction, those with which we are familiar on the mainland. Vaulting is found very occasionally among them. Windows, doors, and other apertures are apt to be small. Fireplaces would seem to be exceptional; and it is remarkable that there is not a single example of a newel stair—the upright column about which the steps of a circular staircase wind, so characteristic a feature of Scottish architecture. The absence of such staircases may have been due to the inadaptability of the local stone.

The masonry of such secular buildings is rude. In most cases, it consists chiefly of a coarse concrete. Local building material was found quite unsuitable for dressing. The roofs were probably thatched, though some may have been slated. Many of the buildings show that the wooden framework of the roof rested on the inner edge of the walls, rather than on the outer. This antiquated arrangement persists in the Western Isles to this day, and is only now being superseded. It is conspicuous in the old "black houses" and byres, which are still so common in these parts, especially in South Uist, Benbecula, Lewis, and the remoter corners of Harris.

Some of the earliest Hebridean castles were in the shape of small towers erected on islets situated in inland lochs. Castle Bheagram, in South Uist, and Castle Sinclair, in Barra, are excellent examples. The former, standing on a circular islet, some eighty yards in diameter, in the middle of Loch an Eilein, has been encircled at the water-line by a wall. The tower, built of rubble in shell mortar, has been harled. It is oblong in plan, measuring roughly fourteen feet by ten. The walls in places are nearly five feet thick, their corners being rounded internally. Traces of the entrance occur in the east wall, where there is also a tiny window. Two other windows are still to be seen, one to the north, the other to the west. These are but seven inches square. The tower still stands to a height of twelve feet. When complete, it was two-storeyed at least.

Castle Bheagram is very old. In 1505, according to the *Register of the Great Seal of Scotland*, Ronald Alansoun then occupied " Yland-Bagrim ", as it was then called.

Similarly built is Castle St. Clair, or Sinclair Castle, situated on a much smaller islet in Loch St. Clair, the sheet of fresh water lying in the shadow of Ben Tangaval, a mile or two north-west of Castlebay. To the Gaelic-speaking inhabitants of Barra, this quaint, little ruin is known as *Dun MhicLeoid*, MacLeod's Castle. Who MacLeod was, no one can say. Nor does there appear to be current in the island any history or tradition concerning this tiny keep.

Castle St. Clair, a photograph of which faces page 208, is almost square. It measures eighteen-and-a-half feet by eighteen, over walls, and stands fifteen feet high. Its walls, built of polygonal rubble in lime mortar, are four-and-a-half feet thick. The lower four feet of them have been pointed. Though there is no evidence of a stair, it is thought that originally the castle had three storeys, and that its floors were of wood. It contains no fireplace of any description. The entrance, which is on the north side, at the level of the first floor, opens on a chamber which the great thickness of the walls restricts in length and breadth to nine-and-a-half and eight-and-a-half feet, respectively.

This ruined tower, though so small, is one of the most picturesque of the lesser ruins in the Outer Hebrides. Much of its outer walling is covered by an orange lichen, contrasting on a cloudless day with the blue of the loch, and with the olive-green pond-weeds growing about it to a height of several inches—contrasting with the grey of the rest of the stone-work, the eyot on which its stands barely holding its foundations above the level of the loch after a heavy fall of rain on the adjacent slopes of Ben Tangaval, the mountain over-shadowing it. On a calm and sunny day, the many colours of the scene are rendered the more vivid when a seagull, alighting for a moment on the ruins, turns its white breast toward one.

Among the largest secular ruins in the Western Isles are those of Borve Castle, in Benbecula, an ancient stronghold of the Clan Ranald in the days when they owned Benbecula and South Uist and much else. These ruins, now so largely amorphous that the castle's internal arrangement is but a matter for conjecture, stand on the edge of a flat, fertile field two miles north-west of Creagorry. Over walls, they measure sixty feet by thirty-six, and at one point are still as much as thirty feet high. In places the walls are of immense thickness —as much as nine feet at one end. There still remains enough of them to show that the castle had at least three storeys.

Historically, we know very little about Castle Borve. Its site possesses none of the physical advantages one associates with such places of strength. The land on all sides of it is level, and is at present somewhat encumbered by the enor-mous concentration of barbed-wire entanglements strewn hereabouts during the late war, lest some enemy should land in Benbecula, and decide to fortify himself within these ruined, shelterless walls, having seized the aerodrome near at hand. No one knows where, nor by whom, the castle was built. *The New Statistical Account* merely confirms local tradition in referring to it as " the residence of the lairds of Benbecula in ancient times ". Ranald MacDonald of Ben-becula, its occupant in 1625, was alluded to as " of Castell-borf ". In Nunton, the name of an old farm in Benbecula, survives the memory of the nunnery which, according to tradi-tion, was largely demolished in order to provide Clan Ranald with building material for Borve Castle.

It is curious that Martin does not even mention this island stronghold. He does mention Nunton, however. " There are also some chapels here," he writes, " one of them at Bael-nin-

Killach, *id est*, Nun's-town, for there were nunneries here in
time of popery. The natives have lately discovered a stone
vault on the east side of the town, in which there are abundance of small bones, which have occasioned many uncertain
conjectures; some said they were the bones of birds, others
judged them rather to be the bones of pigmies. The proprietor of the town, enquiring Sir Norman Macleod's opinion
concerning them, he told him that the matter was plain, as he
supposed, and that they must be the bones of infants born
by the nuns there. This was very disagreeable to the Roman
Catholic inhabitants, who laughed it over. But in the meantime the natives out of zeal took care to shut up the vault that
no access can be had to it since; so that it would seem they
believe what Sir Norman said, or else feared that it might
gain credit by such as afterwards had occasion to see them.
The island belongs properly to Ranald MacDonald of Benbecula, who, with all the inhabitants, are Roman Catholics;
and I remember I have seen an old lay Capuchin here, called
in the language *Brahir-brocht*, that is, poor brother, which is
literally true, for he answers this character, having nothing
but what is given him."

While on the subject of Borve Castle, it may be apposite to
mention that in 1931 there was found on the seashore, near
at hand, a carved stone ball thought to have some connection
with the remains of the Iron Age site and kitchen midden at
the south-west point of Benbecula. It is the only specimen
recorded as having been discovered in the Western Isles.

These balls, specimens of which may be seen in our Edinburgh museums, are confined almost entirely to Scotland, and
are by no means common. Always found singly, they usually
have six faces, one of which is distinctive. One of the four
faces of the Benbecula ball, a photograph of which hangs in
the lounge of the Creagorry Hotel, in that island, lacks the
encircling line. In some specimens the faces are multiple,
like a mulberry. To what use these carved stone balls were
put is not known. All kinds of uses have been suggested.
Some think they might be the mace heads displayed at warlike ceremonials. Most of them weigh just under a pound, or
exact multiples thereof.

Though historical references to Borve Castle be few, it

occupies a prominent place in the folklore of Benbecula. Who has not heard the story—so oft recounted in the Hebrides —of how the Captain of Clan Ranald of the Isles hastened from the castle, and vanished for ever from the sight of men? Lad of the Wet Foot (that unique fellow among the Highland chief's retainers who, in wet weather, would be walking in front of him, so as to take the dew or rain off grass and heather, lest the chief should get his feet wet) came upon the washing-woman by the stepping-stones at one of the Benbecula fords, as she was rinsing the death-shrouds and singing the death-dirge. "I am washing the shrouds and singing the dirge for the Great Clan Ranald of the Isles," she answered when he demanded of her that she should tell him whose death her shroud-washing foretold; "and he shall never again in his living life of the world go thither nor come hither across the clachan of Dun Borve."

In an instant, Lad of the Wet Foot snatched the shrouds, and flung them into the water. Then he sped home to Borve Castle with the washing-woman's doleful tidings. Clan Ranald, seemingly unperturbed by them, gave the instruction that a cow should be killed immediately, so that a hide might be available for a new coracle. Soon a new coracle was brought to him. The Islanders watched him as he launched it, and slowly paddled away and away from Benbecula. Never thereafter was the Captain of Clan Ranald seen by the eyes of men.

Much more recent than Borve Castle is Ormacleit Castle, which has been described as an island version of the late " Scotch house ". Its substantial ruins (a photograph of which faces page 208) lie within the steading at Ormacleit farm, nine miles to the north-west of Lochboisdale, in South Uist. It was built in 1701, as a place of residence, by the chief of Clan Ranald. Fourteen years later (that is to say, in the year of Sheriffmuir) it was destroyed by fire, some say by accident, others say by the Hanoverians, because of Clan Ranald's participation in 'The Fifteen', as the first Jacobite Rebellion is called. The gaunt ruins, with their steeply pitched gables, stand very much as the fire left them, more than two centuries ago.

Built on a T-shaped plan, Ormacleit Castle is two storeys

and an attic high. The main part of it measures, over all, seventy feet by twenty-five. At the south end, a wing, some twenty-two feet square, has been added. A stone partition divides the main block into two unequal parts, the larger of which looks as though it had been sub-divided by wooden partitions, and supplied with a wooden staircase. The masonry throughout is of harled rubble, with dressings of imported freestone. The windows in the upper storey are in a better state of repair than are those on the ground floor. Nothing remains, of course, of the dormers, which admitted light to the attics. In the north wall, above the castle's entrance, is an armorial panel representing—well, now, as I know singularly little about matters heraldic, I had better just quote from the Inventory once more. Above the entrance " is an armorial panel representing a helm, mantling and shield, the latter being parted per pale and charged in the upper dexter corner with a lion rampant above a hand couped, grasping a cross. The charge in the upper sinister corner is obliterated, but it may be either a burning mountain or more probably a castle, and below is a lymphad ".

I readily confess that these archiac words and phrases convey nothing to *me*; but I must assume that they may be easily understood by some of my readers.

Not a vestige is now to be seen of old Stornoway Castle, once the stronghold of the bellicose MacLeods of Lewis. The little that remained of it (see the illustration facing page 16) was demolished in 1882, when the port of Stornoway was being enlarged, and a number of new piers constructed. Its site lies hidden by the great piles and beams of No. 1 Wharf. According to tradition, it was built by the Nicolsons, a clan once numerous and powerful in Lewis, and a surname still fairly prevalent in that island. Indeed, the Nicolsons are said to have preceded the MacLeods as the dominant clan in these parts. If the supposed progenitor of the MacLeods of Lewis flourished about the middle of the thirteenth century, the oldest part of the castle, the ruins of which stood here well within the memory of the oldest natives of Stornoway, probably date back to that period. There is reason for supposing that the castle's site had been occupied much earlier by a fort of some kind belonging to the Nicolsons. If this were so, "it is a strange commentary on the mutations of Time," writes W. C. MacKenzie, "that the same family who built a fort at Stornoway for the purpose of repelling enemies of flesh and blood, should, seven or eight hundred years later, found a school in Stornoway to repel the more tangible foes of ignorance and vice".[1] The reference is to the Nicolson Institute, that excellent school founded by a Stornoway family of the name, and noteworthy for the number of Nicolsonians who have achieved distinction in every part of the world.

According to the authority just quoted, the earliest record in authentic history to old Stornoway Castle is that of 1506, when the Earl of Huntly besieged it and eventually took it. This castle is the *Castrum de Stornochway* denoted in a crown charter dated 1511. In 1554 the old fort held out against an attack made upon it by the Earl of Argyll, who brought artillery on the scene, probably the first artillery the Western Isles ever experienced. In a document, the date of which is uncertain, but which is thought to be early seventeenth century, a list is given of the castles then standing in Skye and in the Outer Hebrides. Therein we read that "the House of Stornowa in the Lewis is fallen, albeit it had bidden [resisted] the canon of the Erle of Argyle of auld, and by the gentilmen ventourares of lait". The latter part of the quotation alludes, of course, to the colonising campaign of the Gentlemen Adventurers from Fife, to whose trials and misfortunes we return in a subsequent chapter. In the years during which the Fifers had so precarious a foothold in the island, the old castle frequently changed hands. As a fortress, it was probably rendered useless by the MacKenzies in 1610, when, armed with a commission from the Privy Council to apprehend Neil MacLeod, then in possession of it, they attacked it and reduced it to impotence. Once the Mac-Kenzies had placed themselves in control of Lewis, however, they are pretty certain to have repaired the castle, and to have refortified it against further attack by the warring MacLeods, whom they had displaced.

But for the weakness resulting from internal strife, the MacLeods might have repelled the newcomers, and defied the

[1] *The Book of the Lewis* (Alexander Gardner, Paisley, 1919).

The Prince's Strand, Eriskay, with Barra in the distance

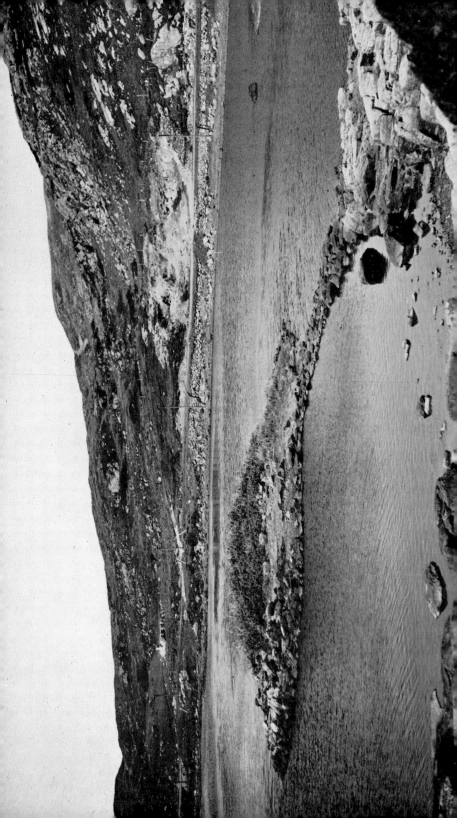

Privy Council. Their family feud is one of the longest, bitterest, most barbarous and calamitous in the all too sanguinary history of the Western Highlands and Islands. It far outmatched in ferocity even the feud between the Clan Donald and the MacLeans of Duart. Throughout this prolonged strife, Stornoway Castle figured much. It was constantly being besieged by one MacLeod faction or another, the winning faction of the moment murdering the leaders of the other, thus providing the surest incentive for retaliation in like terms, just as I believe the recent war trials, so-called, to have done. Not without justification is Ruairi MacLeod of Lewis referred to in a manuscript dated 1595 as an old man famous for the massacring of his own kinsmen! His notoriety as an assassin was even known in Ireland, as is shown by an account of this massacre written the same year by Dennis Campbell, Dean of Limerick, who appears to have been in touch with various sources of information relating to ongoings in the Hebrides. " Old McClod Lewis, by reason of many treacheries committed by himself against his kinsmen, inviting many of them upon a time to his house, and causing them to be killed at table, entertained such intestine broils and dissensions in his country, that I suppose he could neither help his friends nor annoy his enemies abroad." The truth of this statement is borne out by the fact that toward the close of the sixteenth century old Ruairi, Chief of Lewis, was a prisoner in Stornoway Castle, which had been seized by his disinherited son, Torquil Conanach MacLeod. Torquil was his father's gaoler.

Kisimul, in the Isle of Barra, is the only castle in the Outer Hebrides, the ruins of which are of any real archaeological interest. Indeed, they constitute the largest and most imposing secular ruins in the Long Island. The castle, a photograph of which faces page 192, and also page 240, is situated on a low rock at Castlebay, a couple of hundred yards offshore. Most of the rock is completely submerged at high water.

In the north-east angle of the site stands a fifteenth-century tower, doubtless the original nucleus of this ancient and historic stronghold. And here, for the last time, you must allow me to quote from the Inventory such details as archaeologists appreciate. From the tower run curtains to form an

L 145

Dun and causeway in Loch an Duin, Isle of Barra

irregularly shaped enclosure, measuring internally a hundred feet from north-east to south-west, by sixty-eight feet from north-west to south-east. At two places, the north and north-eastern angles of the enclosure, the curtains rise above the general level to form vantage points thirty-three feet above the rock. Against the curtains are subsidiary structures, one within the northern angle being original, the remainder being considerably later, *i.e.*, seventeenth-eighteenth century. The original entrance to the enclosure, which is now built up, adjoins the north-east angle of the tower. In front of the entrance is a harbour protected by an outwork built on a spur of rock.

The masonry throughout Kisimul Castle is rubble built of local stone in shell-lime mortar. Here and there slabs are bedded on edge, an unusual feature noted also in the case of Castle Calvay, the ruins of which are to be found on an islet near the mouth of Loch Boisdale.

Kisimul's tower, which is a continuation, as it were, of the wall below, is oblong on plan. From north to south it measures thirty-three feet, and twenty-nine from east to west, over walls averaging six feet in thickness. From its steeply battered base-course, it rises sheer to the crenellated parapets, a height of forty-nine feet. Beneath the crenellations occurs a series of apertures resembling windows. At the level of the parapet walls are those drainage openings termed " weep holes ". The walls of the tower are still almost complete. In looking down into the tower from the parapet, as far as the soil now occupying its lower part will allow, one observes that it had at least three storeys, each containing a single chamber. The removal of this accumulation of soil might reveal the existence of a fourth storey. The tower has been entered from a fore-stair rising along the north wall to the curtain parapet. From that level another stair, or possibly a movable ramp or ladder, rose to the entrance, above which is a machiocolation. The entrance, eighteen feet from the ground, is two-and-a-half feet wide. It opens on a lobby within the thickness of the wall from which a narrow stair descends to the basement, while another ascends to the chamber beneath the walk. From this room a stair, entered from the embrasure of the north window, ascends to the parapet walk.

The floors have been of timber. The roof, as in most of the old houses in the Islands, rested on the inner face of the walls. In the case of Kisimul Castle, the space between the roof-rest and the parapet is utilised as a parapet walk, above which the parapet itself rose nine feet, thus necessitating, in its lower part, the insertion of windows or outlooks. The crenellations above appear to have been reached from a narrow scarcement on two walls, the higher level being reached by steps on the west wall.

The chamber immediately beneath the roof, like the others, possesses no fireplace. To north and to south, there are windows furnished with aumbries in the ingoings. In the east is a window from which the stair leads down to the entrance. Since the apartment below this has no opening, it is thought that it must have been entered from a hatch. The lower chamber, however, has a window on the east, and on the west what looks as though it might have been a door. A couple of flues or chutes occur, externally, on the south wall of the tower. There is no trace of them internally, which prompts the notion that they may have been used for latrine purposes.

It would appear as though there once stood against the castle's north-west curtain a building older than the present structure, since there are evidences of a side gate at the base of the turret projecting near the pit. Traces of a second turret are to be seen at the other end of the curtain. This turret, which rose only one storey, and had a domed roof, may have been a latrine. The interior building, which the outer walls of Kisimul hide, except on the seaward side, where they are somewhat fallen, is a two-storeyed house built of rubble, and having tabled gables. A transverse partition probably divided it. The curtain has been thickened; whilst the wall heads and the roof-rest are quaintly corbelled out with slabs set on edge. An additional building having a crow-stepped outer gable has been placed against the south gable. Recessed into this newer gable is the well from which, according to tradition, Kisimul was so plenteously supplied in time of siege. The well, we are told, had a dome-shaped lid or canopy. Against the tower's west wall are the remains of a two-storeyed building, between which and the well stands the remnant of another such. Two one-storeyed buildings, little of which survives, have stood against the north and north-eastern curtains.

On the whole, the ruined buildings comprising the castle are regarded as being in a satisfactory condition by those responsible for the preservation of our ancient and historic monuments. Not very long ago, they were repaired in such a way as to secure them against too rapid decay at the instance of the normal epigene agencies. Shortly before the outbreak of the Second World War, they were visited by Robert Lister, who claims to be the XLVth chief of the MacNeils of Barra. Robert, who is an architect in New York, wrote me at the time, telling me that he had surveyed Kisimul's ruins with a view to restoring the castle as a habitable place, rather after the manner in which the late Lieutenant-Colonel John MacRae-Gilstrap restored Eilean Donan, in Kintail. The war intervened.

When in Castlebay last autumn, I procured a small boat, and rowed myself over to Kisimul. This I always like to do as a matter of course, when visiting Barra. I found the ruins just as I had known them when first I explored them with memorable enthusiasm, nearly a quarter of a century earlier. Not a stone seemed to have fallen from position in the interim. Kisimul's masonry would appear to be comparatively immune from the ravages wreaked by Time on many of the buildings of later centuries.

It was in 1427 that Alexander, third Lord of the Isles, granted to "Gilleonan Rodrici Murchardi MakNeill" the island of Barra, together with the lands of Boisdale. Throughout the sixteenth century, the MacNeils were still in possession of these extensive territories, as we see from the writings of Dean Monro, of Martin, and of other contemporaneous annotators. Early in the seventeenth century, Roderic Mac-Neil, the chief of Barra at the time, forfeited his estates through the repeated piracies for which he and his Barra sailors were responsible. These estates were bestowed upon Sir Rory MacKenzie of Kintail, who had succeeded in ensnaring MacNeil in a manner hereinafter described, and in bringing him before the crown authorities at Edinburgh to answer for his delinquencies. So far as Kisimul Castle was concerned, this did not make much difference, since MacNeil was to return there eventually as MacKenzie's tenant, upon the promise that he would behave himself.

It would appear that the MacNeils were still in occupation of Kisimul Castle at the beginning of the eighteenth century. "It has always been the residence of the Lairds of Barry till the beginning of the present century," says the *Old Statistical Account*, dated 1794.

Sixteenth-century references to Kisimul are numerous. George Buchanan, historian and celebrated Latinist, writing of Castle Bay, mentions that "this bay hath ane island in it, and therein a strong fort or castle ". At one end of the Isle of Barra, writes Dean Monro, " ther enters a salt-water loche, verey narrow in the entrey, and round and braide within. Into the middis of the saide loche there is ane ile, upon a strenthey craige, callit Kilcherin, pertaining to the MackNeill of Barray".

From a document on the Western Isles compiled between 1577 and 1595 we learn, with reference to the chief of Barra, that "his principall dwelling-place thair is callit Keissadull, quhilk is ane excellent strenth, for it standis on the seaside under ane great craig, sua that the craig cummis over it, and na passage to the place but be the sea, quhairof the entrie is narrow, but that ane scheip may pass throw, and within that entres is ane round heavin [haven] and defence for schippis from all tempestis. This Ile is five miles of lenth or thairby, and is 20 lb. land, and may raise on this Ile, with foure or five small Iles that he hes beside it, 200 gude men".

More valuable than any of these is Martin's description (*c.* 1695). "The little island Kismul," he writes, "lies about a quarter of a mile from the south of this isle. It is the seat of Macneal of Barray; there is a stone wall round it two stories high, reaching the sea, and within the wall there is an old tower and a hall, with no other houses about it. There is a little magazine in the tower, to which no stranger hath access."

The rest of Martin's account describes how the officer called the cockman treated his request that he might be permitted to land and see something of the castle's interior. Not until some weeks afterwards did he learn why the cockman had refused him admission. MacNeil and his lady were absent from Barra at the time of his visit; and the cockman feared lest the stranger should prove to be a spy sent by some foreign power for the purpose of obtaining information about the castle and its fortifications. It was the cockman's duty to act as sentinel, and to challenge the approach of any unauthorised person. Of his reception at Kisimul, Martin writes thus:

"I saw the officer called the Cockman, and an old cock he is; when I bid him ferry me over the water to the island, he told me that he was but an inferior officer, his business being to attend in the tower; but if (says he) the constable, who then stood on the wall, will give you access, I'll ferry you over. I desired him to procure me the constable's permission, and I would reward him; but having waited some hours for the constable's answer, and not receiving any, I was obliged to return without seeing this famous fort."

From the battlements of Kisimul Castle, according to history as well as to tradition, the cockman dropped through "a perforated stone" large boulders on the head of any who might try to surprise the garrison. In Castlebay some years ago, a native, well informed on matters relating to the piratical MacNeils and their island, told me that each boulder used thus had a rope attached to it, so that, when it had functioned in this way, it might be drawn up to the parapet and dropped again as occasion demanded. In the muniments room at Dunvegan Castle, in the Isle of Skye, I once saw an interesting document relating to certain legal proceedings at Edinburgh, and containing an account of how unwelcome callers were treated at Kisimul as late as 1690. That year a notary had travelled to Castlebay to serve a writ on Ruairi MacNeil of Barra.

"The said Rory MacNeil threw large stones from the roof of his house, whereby the said notary was in danger of being battered, and discharged four scoir shots from guns, pistols, muskets, hagbutts, and other invadive and forbidden weapons, whereby he was put in hazard of his life, and took from him all the papers he had in his company, and, in high and proud contempt of His Majesty's authoritie, did ofend and grieve the same."

Among the more celebrated occupants of Kisimul Castle was *Ruairi 'n Tartair,* or Roderic the Turbulent, who is said

to have been the XXXVth chief of the MacNeils of Barra.
Ruairi, one of the most reckless and daring of his race, carried
piracy to such lengths that he could boast his cellars at Kisimul
were at all times stocked with the finest wines of France and
Spain. Not content with what he obtained from foreign
vessels intercepted in West Highland and Hebridean waters,
he directed his attention to the Irish Sea, where many an
English ship fell victim to his sea-rieving crews.[1] Thus it was
that he annoyed Queen Elizabeth, who had to complain to
James the Sixth of Scotland that vessels belonging to her subjects were being plundered by the Barra pirates, and that
something must be done to bring Ruairi MacNeil to account,
previous warnings having in no way curtailed these lawless
enterprises of his. King James, knowing how elusive a fellow
Ruairi was, felt that the only person capable of capturing
him was the crafty Ruairi MacKenzie of Kintail. At the
King's suggestion, therefore, MacKenzie undertook, by one
means or another, to bring the Chief of Barra to justice. In
a small barque manned by a number of well-equipped henchmen, he sailed for Castlebay, and eventually dropped anchor
in the shadow of Kisimul. Posing as the skipper of a vessel
casually calling there, he proceeded to make kindly enquiries
for the Chief of Barra, who now felt so flattered that he
instructed the cockman to conduct the enquirer into his
presence. Thus-wise Ruairi MacKenzie gained admission to
Kisimul. In the course of conversation with MacNeil, he
mentioned that he had come from Norway and was bound for
Ireland, and that, during the voyage, he had fallen in with a
French vessel, from which he had purchased some very choice
wines. With the suggestion that MacNeil might care to
inspect his barque, and at the same time sample these wines,
the unsuspecting host was all too ready to agree. Thus Mac-
Neil was enticed aboard MacKenzie's vessel, accompanied by
none but his usual bodyguard, " for ", as one authority tells

[1] There is documentary evidence that these pirates even visited Ireland
when on plunder bent. MacNeil of Barra, " reputed the best seafaring warrior in the islands ", according to Dennis Campbell, Dean of Limerick, whom
we have already cited, often preyed upon the coast of Connaught, and
invaded Ulla, O'Malley's Country. " Whereupon," says the Dean, " Grany
ny Mallye and he invaded one another's possessions, though far distant. I
have heard some of MacNeil's sept to have come with the Malleys to prey on
Valentia, an island in M'Cartymore's Country, with the borders adjoining."

us, "there only appeared on board of the ship two or three mariners, and some ship boys, being what was only necessary to sail the ship".

Sure enough, Ruairi MacNeil did taste the wines. Abetted by MacKenzie, he was soon disposing of them too freely. On a given signal, the barque's hatches were fastened down. Roderic the Turbulent now found himself a prisoner. He had entrusted his life and his heritage to a mean trickster, whose vessel was already standing out to sea.

When, in course of time, the Chief of Barra was brought before King James in Edinburgh, he created a degree of surprise, for there now stood before His Majesty not some despicable fellow, as had been expected, but a tall, handsome chieftain, whose striking appearance called for consideration, if not actually for leniency.

Now, since MacNeil knew not a word of English, his captor, Ruairi MacKenzie, had to act as interpreter. When MacKenzie asked him in the Gaelic what explanation he had to offer for the "pyracies and robbrys" he had committed on ships belonging to Queen Elizabeth's subjects, he readily answered that only thus could he show his resentment at the Queen's having sent to the scaffold, at Fotheringay, King James's own mother, Mary of Scotland.

His Majesty was, indeed, nonplussed when, for his benefit, MacKenzie translated MacNeil's reply. "The devil take the carle!" said the King. "Rory, take him with you again, and dispose of him and his fortune as you please!" This Rory MacKenzie did. MacNeil was permitted to return to Kisimul Castle on condition that he behaved himself, and on the understanding that, henceforth, he held his estates with MacKenzie as his recognised superior, and at a yearly rental of forty pounds Scots. Furthermore, he had to undertake to furnish MacKenzie with a hawk, when required, and to provide him with armed assistance, should he be called upon to do so.

Roderic the Turbulent lived in Barra many a year thereafter. His adventures as a pirate, and his subsequent compearance in Edinburgh, in no way diminished his days upon the earth. On one occasion, he gave his age as "sex or sevin score of yeares"!

BALLAD OF MACNEIL OF BARRA

Once there lived a daring thief,
 Who did plunder ships at sea:
He of Barra was the Chief;
 And his name was Ruairi.

And he much annoyance gave
 To Good Queen Elizabeth:
He so reckless was and brave,
 That she wearied for his death.

Within Kishmul's walls he'd hide,
 And in creeks of Castlebay,
Till he spied upon the tide
 Merchant galleys for his prey.

In his stables were three pairs
 Of black steeds with golden shoes
Made from oriental wares,
 Captured on some rieving cruise.

And they say that in his stores
 He kept wines and Spanish goods:
From the ceilings to the floors
 Stored he casks and foreign foods.

Now the King of Scotland swore
 That, if he this thief could seize,
Ruairi would be no more
 Pirate on the western seas.

So he planned for his arrest;
 And a galley sailed one day,
To make Ruairi a guest,
 As she lay in Castlebay.

When she came 'neath Kishmul's wall,
 Ruairi was asked aboard
To inspect the galley tall,
 And to see her handsome hoard.

And, when he had stepped inside,
Where he thought a feast would be—
"Where's my skean-dhu?" he cried,
"Treacherous and vile are ye!"

So the ship sailed out to sea;
But her captive's heart was sore,
For in Barra Ruairi
Was a pirate Chief no more.

Barra and Kisimul Castle are, of course, the venue of *Kishmul's Galley,* one of the best known and most spirited songs in that famed collection, *The Songs of the Hebrides,* for which the late Marjory Kennedy-Fraser and Kenneth Mac-Leod were responsible.

Many of the folk-tales of this ancient keep concern the Norsemen—the *Lochlannaich,* or Lochlanners, as they are called in the Isles, because they came from Lochlann, which is the Gaelic for Norway, or for Scandinavia generally. One such tale, still recounted in Barra, describes how an early chief was driven out of Kisimul Castle by the Lochlanners, and how eventually the invaders were defeated, and the rightful occupant restored. Another tells of the occasion on which the Lochlanners arrived in Hebridean waters with a great fleet of war-galleys, and laid siege to Kisimul, having in the meantime ravaged the rest of Barra. As time wore on, starvation increasingly faced the stronghold's defenders. It was then that there occurred to MacNeil's bardess the happy idea of the ruse which ultimately saved the situation. Each day the sole cow-hide in the castle was dyed a different colour, and then hung over the battlements to dry, thus giving the besiegers the notion that the besieged were abundantly provided with food. In this way the Lochlanners were led to believe that the capitulation they had thought imminent was likely to be postponed indefinitely. So they became impatient, and sailed away from Barra, greatly to the relief of the besieged, whose plight was already desperate.

There is no place in all the Isles round which so much poetry and song, so much history and tradition, cling as round Kisimul Castle. Its chiefs, greatly daring, and enhanced in their own estimation by reason of the success with which they roved the seas, were a terror to their neighbours. Small wonder it was customary at Kisimul for the trumpeter to deliver himself from the top of the tower in those magniloquent terms with which some of my readers may already be familiar! "Hear, O ye people! and listen, O ye nations! The great M'Neil of Barra, having finished his meal, the princes of the earth may dine."

CHAPTER V

FOLKLORE AND TRADITION

In the Outer Hebrides where, as we have seen in the preceding chapter, the disbeliever in the Second-sight was inclined to be laughed at, one still runs the risk of being ridiculed for the expression of scepticism with regard to the faeries and the brownies, ghosts and witches, the *each-uisge* or water-horse, the Evil Eye, and so on. Indeed, in the remoter parts, even vague indication of such disbelief is liable to engender displeasure. If, for instance, the narrator of a fragment of faery-lore had the slightest inkling that his listener entertained any doubts about its authenticity, the narration would immediately cease, and the narrator show resentment in that dour and sulky manner so characteristic of the Celt. The hint that, in the smallest degree, the narrative might not be trustworthy would be deemed an unpardonable offence, nay, a slur on the narrator's integrity. I have been present at ceilidhs in the Isles at which someone has recounted a happening of a seemingly supernatural character, and a stranger from the sophisticated mainland has had the temerity to pooh-pooh it, with the result that the latter has been obliged to retire gracefully so as to prevent the scorn of storyteller and audience alike from finding physical expression. Many of the Islanders are extremely touchy on such matters. They believe that the Little Folk still dwell numerously amongst them, for good or for evil; while the appearance of ghost or witch is as common an occurrence as are the visible effects of the Evil Eye. Even yet, the water-horse is a reality with some, and is greatly dreaded. As for the Second-sight, I myself have had too much evidence of this phenomenon to wish to discredit other peoples'.

All manner of strange beliefs are prevalent in the Isles to this day. Superstition, much of it harmless, is by no means dead. A friend of mind has in his possession an old sixpence used as recently as 1938 in his native Island of Lewis to cure scrofula, the King's Evil.

Curious notions with regard to diseases and ailments are common. Both in the Highlands and Islands, many still hold the belief that the seventh son of a seventh son has the power of curing certain maladies. My own cousins at Sandwick, a populous village on the outskirts of Stornoway, firmly believe that the seventh son of a seventh son can cure the King's Evil. They have actually told me of instances in which the services of such a son have been sought. Morning and evening on three consecutive days, either a seventh son, or, better still, the seventh son of a seventh son, must bathe the wound of his patient. On the evening of the third day, he must pierce a hole in an old sixpence, and suspend it by a thread of green wool round the patient's neck. They declare that the patient's condition begins to improve the instant the green thread breaks, unbeknown to the person afflicted.

Apropos the King's Evil, one might mention an interesting obituary notice appearing recently in the *Stornoway Gazette*. It concerns a Lewisman named Donald MacLeod, who had just died in the United States at the age of forty-three. In 1922 Donald emigrated from the Lewis township of Carloway to Montana, where he worked on a sheep ranch. "Dotar Dhomhnuill Dhonnachaidh [that is to say, Dr. Donald, son of Duncan] as Donald was familiarly called, before he left for the U.S.A., was well known in these parts from his youngest days," runs the notice. Then follows this significant sentence: "Being a seventh son, his services for applying *eolas tinneas an righ* were often in demand." That is to say, his ability to apply the necessary skill or "charm" in cases of the King's Sickness, or King's Evil, by touching the sufferer.[1]

[1] As we go to press, the following letter concerning the King's Evil reaches me from Mr. G. E. N. Morison, a native of Stornoway long resident in Glasgow:

"DEAR SIR,—I learn that you are asking for cases of Second Sight, King's Evil cure, etc. Beyond the fact that one of my brothers was supposed to have Second Sight, I know nothing of that subject; but, so far as the cure of the King's Evil is concerned, I can give you an instance, the authenticity of which I can fully guarantee, *for the case was my own.*

"In my early thirties, I began to develop trouble on the right side of my neck, and, in spite of the efforts of my own doctor, this grew gradually worse until I was at last compelled to call for special aid in combating the disease. A severe operation was carried out by an eminent Glasgow surgeon (Dr. Parry) which resulted neither in a cure, nor in the discovery of the cause.

Another strange belief still prevalent is that a drop or two of blood taken from a man with the surname of Munro is efficacious in the case of certain diseases—perhaps in the case of scrofula, though I am not sure of this at the moment. In this context, however, I clearly recall a Gaelic conversation I overheard between my cousin, Mary MacDonald, and her

Then, after long weeks, and even months, during which two more minor surgical operations were carried out unsuccessfully, I entered the Victoria Infirmary, where Dr. Parry, as he said himself, thoroughly ' explored ' the diseased region, again without any good resulting, as the operation wound, though healing a little, stubbornly refused to cease discharging.

" After a while in the Infirmary as a walking-about patient, I was discharged, apparently incurable. Being on sick-leave, of course, I went up to Stornoway, to my home in Bayhead. As my neck had to have a wet dressing all the time, I saw old Dr. MacRae and his then partner, Dr. MacDonald, both of whom your father knew well. Neither of them could understand how I came to have this sort of thing, having regard to my family history, which was well known to both of them. But neither offered any advice, except that Dr. MacDonald told me to be as much as possible in the open air—' and don't be sitting at the fire ', as he put it.

" My mother and the other cailleachs [old women] near by now suggested trying to get hold of *a seventh son of a seventh son*, who might try his powers; and, though I hadn't any great faith, or otherwise, I agreed.

" As it happened, there was such a man (noted for his cures too) somewhere on the west side of the island; and he was got in touch with. One morning, before breakfast, he appeared at our house to ' do his stuff '. Taking a basin of water, he dipped the flat of his hand in it, and gently laid his open palm on my neck for a few seconds. This he did three times—that was all the first day. But he came back twice more, again before I had broken my fast, and did the same.

" On the last occasion he gave me a silver coin (6d.) to hang round my neck. That ended the treatment.

" I don't quite like that last bit! However, believe it or not, from that day, my neck gradually healed up, all discharge ceased, and nothing remained but the operation scars; and I was able to return to duty in a fairly short time. And when I tell you that I am now nearing 79 years of age, and have never since had the slightest sign or suspicion of a recurrence of ' the Evil ', 1 think you will agree that the Lewis cure was a success.

" The water used in the cure, I ought to have mentioned, was just ordinary water from Loch Airidh na Lic. [Stornoway's reservoir, situated on the moors a mile or so from the town.] It was applied without any mystic ' passes ' or other palaver."

Prompted by the receipt of this interesting letter, I now looked through my files to find a letter written to me some months ago by a Miss Campbell, a Lewis lady now residing at Saltcoats. Let me quote from Miss Campbell's letter the passage relating to the King's Evil. " I myself had the King's Evil between 1930 and 1933," she writes. " You are doubtless familiar with the cure used in Lewis—that of washing the affected part in water in which the seventh son, or even the seventh daughter, has washed his or her hands, and then, on the third day, the holing of the sixpence. It is important that the abscess should be washed in the morning, before either the person affected or the ' doctor ' has partaken of any food—also that the sixpences should not be removed from the neck whilst one has the disease. It is a fact that once, when I had the disease, I lost my sixpences, and the abscess became noticeably worse. On the recovery of the sixpences, it improved. . . . I can assure you that this cure is still prevalent in Lewis."

daughter, Catriona. Mary at the time was a woman of seventy; and Catriona, who was nursing in Glasgow, and had come home to Sandwick on summer vacation, was about thirty-five. Mary, in mentioning that a neighbour was suffering from some malady or other (the exact nature of the malady I never knew) added that it was a pity there was no one of the name of Munro at hand, so that the affected part might be smeared with a drop or two of his blood. She regretted that, just a few days before this neighbour's illness began to manifest itself, "Munro's Blood", as it is termed in the Isles, would have been available: the only male Munro in the locality had not then left the island to take up employment on the mainland. But, as Mary herself concluded, and on a hopeful note, another Munro, a member of a household she knew well, was expected home on holiday by the mail-boat on Friday evening. So the old, traditional cure, as she steadfastly believed, would be effected before the neighbour's condition could get much worse. When Catriona rebuked her mother for giving credence to such superstition, Mary quietly retired to the scullery, not prepared to argue the matter with so sceptical a daughter, adding that this particular Munro's arrival was being awaited anxiously by the relatives of the person afflicted.

Where birth and baptism were concerned, superstitious belief in the Outer Hebrides and elsewhere necessitated very special precautions, lest the infant should fall victim to harmful influences. It was firmly held that a child, until it had been baptised, was exposed to two particular dangers, namely, the Little Folk, and the Evil Eye. The former might steal it; and many of the folk-tales of the Hebrides describe how they *did* carry off infants from the care of mothers upon whom they had cast a spell. But there were recognised methods of averting this. The placing in the infant's cradle of something made of iron, such as a nail or a horseshoe, was a sure remedy. Sometimes a knife functioned as well. Such articles prevented the faeries from exercising their charm or spell over the sleeping infant. They *sianed* the babe, or "charmed" it, against anything of this nature. So, also, did the person who walked seven times round the house, *deasil*, or sunwise, thus surrounding it with an invisible ring, through which the faeries' influence could not penetrate. And just in case these precautions should prove inadequate, recourse was had to certain old incantations which, when uttered in traditional manner, rendered house and household, goods and cattle, doubly immune to faery interference.

Furthermore, until the child was at least a week old, no one must bear either fire or light from the house in which it lay. Great care was taken not to wash the palms of the child's hand, lest by so doing its chances of material prosperity in later life should be ruined. The washing of the palms was liable to wash away any "siller" to which it might fall heir.

Mention of "siller" recalls the practice whereby those coming to see an infant for the first time placed in its hand a silver coin, and watched carefully how it reacted thereto. If the infant grasped the coin tightly, it was assumed that it would grow up close-fisted: if it held the coin loosely, it was regarded as a sign that it would be open-handed: if the child repeatedly dropped the silver coin, it was destined to lead a life of kindness and generosity. The presentation of a spoon made from the horn of a live animal, whether bovine, sheep, goat, or deer, was believed to vouchsafe to an infant a life of material success, especially if such a gift were given to it while it was still but a day or two old.

Care was also taken to ensure that the newly born was never left alone in a room with a cat, since the cat might turn out to be a witch, and witches were given to stealing infants and to substituting changelings. A cat, even when not thought to be a witch in disguise, could not be left in the room with an infant, for it was believed that it might smother it, or suck its breath away.

It was held, moreover, that, when a child was being carried, for the first time, out of the room in which it had been born, it should always be carried *upwards*, that is to say, carried to a higher level. Since the apartments in the old cottages in the Isles were all on the ground floor, there was no need for a staircase. In order, therefore, to obtain the necessary ascent when first transferring an infant, the superstitious, when carrying it, mounted a chair placed in the doorway of the apartment from which it was being taken.

160

The Broch known as Dun Carloway, Isle of Lewis
The Standing Stones of Callernish, from the east

The infant was then handed down to a relative, standing ready to receive it just beyond the door.

.   .   .   .   .

In the Isles, as elsewhere, it was the belief that witches had the power of converting themselves into hares as well as into cats—*black* cats, as a rule. Either as cats or as hares, they could wander over vast tracts of the country, without much restriction, performing their evil deeds wherever they liked. To ordinary shot fired from a gun, their bodies were immune. Thus, many a man fired at a witch without even wounding her! If one wanted to shoot her dead, one had to place in the gun a small, silver coin, which explains how sixpences were coveted for this purpose. Was it not a sixpence—and a *crooked* one at that!—fired at Sheriffmuir, which, prevailing against the charm he carried, as you will see a little later, encompassed the death of Alan MacDonald of Clan Ranald?

Belief in the Evil Eye (that is to say, the power of casting at man or beast a withering glance, such as would cause either to sicken and even to die) prevails in the Western Isles even at the present day. Certainly, not so long ago most of the inhabitants took for granted the existence of such wicked practice. When ceilidhing at the house of friends on the outskirts of Stornoway a few years ago, my host, now a prominent schoolmaster in Glasgow, gave an instance which occurred in his boyhood. He told me that, when the bailiff's daughter was vacating Aignish farm, years before it was broken up into crofts, she sent for—well, his Highland designation is so long and complicated that we had better content ourselves with the first of his Christian names—she sent for Iain, my host's grandfather, and asked him to value her crops and stock. Iain, who lived near by, at a place called Old Holm, duly came to Aignish, and did as he was bidden. But his valuation did not give satisfaction. The outgoing tenant felt that he had given her too low an estimate. She therefore called in from the adjacent township of Garrabost another valuator, who appears to have pleased her with a higher assessment. This infuriated Iain, who, swearing vengeance upon the Garrabost man, now brought his occult faculties into play. Henceforth, matters went badly for the Garrabost man. His cows no longer prospered. His sheep were continually being bogged or lost.

M   161

St. Clement's, at Rodil, and the tomb Alasdair Crotach prepared for himself therein
St. Columba's, at Aignish, with Broad Bay in the background

His milk went sour. His sowing yielded but a meagre harvest. The reason for all this misfortune he well knew. So he decided to visit Old Holm, and ask Iain's forgiveness.

"Is it not time, Iain, that you allowed the *toradh*[1] to return to my stock?" he implored.

"It is not just out of your stock I took the *toradh*," replied Iain, "but out of your croft; and I cannot let it return until I walk upon it."

The upshot was that Iain promised to pace the croft the following week, when he expected to be passing by Garrabost on his way to visit an ailing friend at Point, a crofting area a few miles farther on. This he did, thus restoring to the croft its pristine qualities. And it is related that no fewer than six calves were born thereafter on the croft of the repentant valuator.

Let me add that I myself knew a man living at Sandwick, who once visited Iain at Old Holm with his churn, complaining that, though his wife had been churning all day long, no butter would come, and that he and his wife were convinced that a *bana-bhuidsear*—a witch-woman—was at work. Without comment, Iain took the plunger out of the churn. With an old auger he used in such circumstances, he bored in the plunger a few more holes, and then sent the man on his way with the assurance that all would now be well with the churning. An hour later he was home in Sandwick. After a few rapid strokes with the plunger, he told me, the butter came perfectly!

This recalls a tradition concerning a missing eye, a tradition still current in Lewis and on the west coast of Sutherlandshire.

The grandfather of yet another Hebridean friend of mine sailed in one of the small, open smacks engaged many years ago in transporting to Stornoway from Caithness quantities of slabs used as paving stones. When off the coast of Sutherland, this particular smack, together with all hands, was lost in a storm. The bodies of the crew were washed ashore at Scourie, where the natives buried them.

Now it was noticed that one of the dead seamen (my friend's grandfather, as it afterwards transpired) had only one eye. It

---

[1] Fruit or produce; the substance, as in dairy produce.

looked as though the other had been wrenched from its socket, or perhaps eaten away by some marine creature.

Oddly enough, a day or two after the interment at Scourie, there was found lying on the grave of the one-eyed man a human eye. The explanation for this, no one ever knew. It was thought that a bird may have carried it from the shore, and dropped it there.

A grandfather is one of the two principal characters in another witch story which comes to mind, and which one feels inclined to relate, although it actually belongs to the Highland mainland. My excuse for its inclusion here is that it was first told in Lewis by a young man named MacDougall, whom I met in Stornoway a year or two before the Second World War. It tells how the last witch in Glen Moriston met her death.

One night old Mr. MacDougall, the narrator's grandfather, a crofter in Glen Moriston, was proceeding homewards up the glen on horseback. In passing the dwelling of a hag reputed in the district as having been a witch, and much feared on account of the nefarious acts for which the country-folk held her responsible, he drew up and chatted with her for a moment, as he had often done. She happened to be standing in her doorway as he was about to ride by.

A little later, as he went a-galloping through the glen, his cap blew off. This he immediately attributed to the witch, for, as his grandson added, he knew the old hag was floating in the gust of wind which had carried it away. Convinced that her wicked art would be his undoing, unless he put an end to her, he wheeled his horse about and returned to her dwelling. Without a moment's hesitation he entered. There he found her, seated by the fire, and in the act of repeating a sinister incantation, meanwhile rubbing together, between her palms, two parts of the cap, in an endeavour to render it holed, or at any rate threadbare. According to the belief in witchcraft, as the cap began to get worn away in this manner, so would Mr. MacDougall's vitality diminish. However, he attacked her and killed her at her weird malpractice. Thus died the last witch in Glen Moriston; and Mr. MacDougall, like the heroes of Classical days, was thanked by his neighbours for having relieved mankind of one of the earth's evil creatures.

Fifty or sixty years ago, belief in witchcraft was the rule rather than the exception in the Western Isles. At any rate, so far as Lewis is concerned, this is shown in a paper read by my late friend, Norman Morison, before a learnèd society in Glasgow.[1] When visiting Norman at Campbeltown a few years ago, I had an opportunity of discussing these matters with him. He assured me that, in the eighteen-eighties, nearly everyone in his native village of Shawbost believed in witchcraft, and therefore took various precautions against it. The Lewis witches' favourite work was that of taking away the milk from the cows, or of abstracting from the milk its nourishing qualities. Norman himself, when a boy (he was born in 1869) was often shown milk with which a witch was said to have interfered. Such milk was thin and watery, and seemed devoid of its proper fat content. It was held in the populous township of Shawbost at the time that, if a witch wanted to tamper with the cow of a neighbour, all she had to do was to attach, clandestinely, a straw rope either to the byre or to the neighbour's cottage. The straw rope acted as a tube through which the milk or its substance was drawn away.

If some were accredited with the power of witchcraft, others were said to have the power of counteracting the harm of which witches were capable. A witch's spell could be broken by those recognised as witch-doctors. For a small considera-tion, these doctors undertook to restore to the milk its former qualities. For this purpose they prescribed a special medicine, which they themselves supplied. It consisted of a bottle of liquid coloured in some mysterious way. Morning and even-ing, the cow, whose milk had been affected, had to be sprinkled with some of the bottle's contents. I myself have been assured by old people in Lewis that, on more than one occasion, when their own cows were bewitched, the witch-doctor's bottle contained the remedy.

One of the commonest media through which a witch worked her evil was the *corp-creadh*, or clay body. When she had malicious designs on one whom she disliked, or whose death

[1] " The Mythology and Folklore of Lewis ", by Norman Morison, F.Z.S., appearing in the *Proceedings of the Royal Philosophical Society of Glasgow*, Vol. liv, 1926.

she wished to hasten, she made of that person a small clay image, into which she stuck a great number of pins, before baking it. The image was then placed in running water, usually a burn near her house. As it dissolved, so would the person it represented waste away. I remember an occasion about 1909, during my own boyhood in the Highlands, when the *corp-creadh* of a man we knew (a solicitor practising in the little town of Tain, in Easter Ross) was placed in a stream near our home by a widow who had put her witch's curse upon him, declaring that he had evicted her unlawfully from her croft.

Can it really be said that the Western Islanders still believe in witchcraft?

In answering this question, let us consider the following account of official proceedings at Stornoway.

As evidence that a man was feeble-minded and, therefore, unfit to make a will, it was averred, as recently as October, 1947, in the Scottish Land Court held at Stornoway, that an Islander believed in witchcraft, and that, when over seventy years of age, and in declining health, he talked of getting married. The Court, rejecting both of these arguments, held that the will was valid.

The matter arose when Mrs. MacLean, an isleswoman living at Carloway, asked the Court to declare her to be the tenant of a croft in virtue of a will left by the previous tenant, Angus MacKay, who was her cousin. Donald MacKay, another cousin of the testator, a constable in the Lanarkshire Police Force, residing at Kirivick, a township at Carloway, disputed the will, alleging that his cousin, Angus, had believed in witchcraft, in that he had accused a neighbour of having walked thrice round his croft, *anti-sunwise*, in order to extract the milk from his cow, and of having placed a spell on his sheep, with the result that several of them had gone lame. The constable contended, further, that Angus, besides having mentioned to him that he was going to marry at the age of seventy-two, was in a pretty low mental state at the time he made the will, and could hardly walk. The local doctor stated in evidence, however, that the testator was of sound mind when visited shortly before his death; and the headmaster of Carloway Public School spoke of him as a man for whom he had a profound respect—a man who was "intelligent, strongly religious, and good-living in every way".

Having heard evidence on both sides, my friend, Lord Gibson, Chairman of the Scottish Land Court, giving judgment, declared Mrs. MacLean the landholder in virtue of the will, awarded expenses against the respondent, Donald MacKay, and said there was little evidence that the testator believed in witchcraft. "Even supposing it had been proved that he was superstitious, there is not a tittle of evidence that any belief he held had affected his ability to make a will," said Lord Gibson. He made the further observation that Angus MacKay very sensibly thought of getting married when he had no one to keep house for him, and that it was proper for an old man to make a will leaving his croft to the lady who, when there was no one to look after him, had taken him into her house, and attended to his needs.

This case was widely reported in the press.

.   .   .   .

There is scarcely an isle in the Hebrides which does not have its *sithean*, or brugh, as the faery knolls are termed in Celtic Scotland. Even remote St. Kilda had its faeries, and indeed may still have, for all we know. Their underground dwelling-place on Hirta (the name of the principal island of the St. Kilda group, and the one which, for centuries, was inhabited) was well known to the last of the natives. In Barra one meets with folk who sing fragments of faery music which have been heard issuing from brughs among the Barra Isles. Not so long ago, faery music was heard on Mingulay by two people who disembarked there one summer's evening to explore its ruined village. The islanders themselves are quite unable to set down in musical form the melodies they have heard. In recent years, however, this has been done for them by musical friends who, from time to time, arrive from the south in order to collect such material.

In Uist you will learn of the arrows shot by the Little Folk at human children whom they are said to dislike. These faery arrows, so beautifully wrought, are indeed tiny, as I can well vouch, for I have seen them! A few years ago, an excellent specimen was picked up in Lochmaddy by a young woman who, when out in the dark one night, bringing in an armful of peats from the stack at the gable-end of her cottage, was startled at hearing something whizz past her ear, and drop at her feet. Returning to the very spot in daylight, she found a faery arrow.

The natives of Ness, in northern Lewis, will point out for you, near the Butt, a patch of ground believed to be a fief which the faeries cultivated; and in the midst of this fief is a stone with a faery's footprint clearly defined upon it. I have been shown another such stone in a burn near Cellar Head, in the same locality. This stone lies in mid-stream, and is used as a stepping-stone by those who cross the burn at this point when tenanting the summer shielings on the moors beyond.

The faeries of the Hebrides, from all accounts, resemble those dwelling elsewhere in Celtic Britain. They inhabit much the same type of dwelling. They subsist on the same foods, and wear the same clothing. They own livestock, and are much employed in the fashioning of agricultural implements. They make weapons both for offensive and defensive purposes. They experience the same joys and woes. They are heir to maladies and diseases not dissimilar to those from which ordinary mortals suffer. They borrow from their neighbours things which, like human beings, they sometimes forget to return. Their womenfolk, after they have attended to the cooking, the baking, and the churning, spin and weave and embroider. Indeed, from intimate descriptions I have been given in the Isles by people there, who have had dealings with them, or at any rate are on amicable terms with them, they greatly resemble those kinsfolk of theirs about whom the Rev. Robert Kirk wrote so authoritatively in *The Secret Commonwealth of Elves, Faunes, and Faeries*, before he himself was spirited away to Faeryland. According to this celebrated authority, who was minister of Aberfoyle and Balquhidder from 1685 until 1692, the faeries are of medium stature, " twixt man and angel, as were demons thought to be of old; of intelligent studious spirits, and light changeable bodies (like those called astral), somewhat of the nature of a condensed cloud, and best seen in twilight. Their bodies be so pliable, through the subtilty of the spirits that agitate them, that they can make them appear or disappear at pleasure.

Some have bodies or vehicles so spongious, thin, and defecate, that they are fed by only sucking into some fine spirituous liquors, that pierce like pure air and oil: others feed more gross, on the foyson or substance of corns and liquors, or corne itself that grows on the surface of the earth, which these faeries steall away, partly invisible, partly preying on the grain, as do crows and mice; wherefore, in this same age, they are sometimes heard to bake bread, strike hammers, and do such like services within the little hillocks, they most haunt: some whereof of old, before the Gospell dispell'd paganism, and in some barbarous places as yet, enter houses after all are at rest, and set the kitchens in order, cleansing all the vessels. Such Drags go under the name of Brownies."

The brownies of the Western Isles we shall deal with a little later on.

There is much faery-lore in these parts. For our present purpose, however, we must needs confine ourselves to a few pertinent incidents and tales.

On a memorable occasion (so the last of the St. Kildans told me when I lived among them in 1930, while Hirta was on the point of being excavated) two faery women, dressed in green raiment, visited a cottage in which a mother sat rocking a cradle. Though they bound the mother with a spell depriving her of the power of utterance, she heard quite plainly their conversation. Said one faery woman to the other, in looking into the cradle, "We must bestow upon this child the gift of the tongue, for he has surely drunk of the milk of the cow that ate the *mothan*." They told me on St. Kilda that, consequently, this child grew up to be the most fluent member of the community, and that, without showing the slightest weariness, he could talk any assembly into complete silence. Whether the faery woman's visitation was, therefore, regarded as a blessing or as a bane, they would not say when I asked them, for they were fearful of offending the Folk living in the Faeries' Brugh behind the village.

The folk-music of Barra includes a Gaelic song, the words of which concern a Barra girl with a faery sweetheart whom she used to meet every day at a secret trysting-place, when driving the cattle to the hills. After much persuasion, she finally consented to leave her people, and go off with him to the faery knowe. On her last night at home, her sister, with whom she slept, sensed that there was something on her mind, and coaxed her to tell what it was. "Well," she answered, "if you give me your word not to let on to a soul, I will tell you my secret."

"Your secret will be safe with me," the sister replied. "It will come *through my knee* before it will come *through my mouth*."

She then told her secret; and her sister was so astonished that she rose before dawn, and wakened her mother to tell her what was about to take place. The mother got up, and hastened out to gather a sprig of the *mothan*. This she now wove into her enchanted daughter's garter.

When the girl went to the trysting-place to await her faery sweetheart, she saw him at a distance coming towards her. Suddenly, instead of approaching in the usual way, he stood still some little way off. On calling out to him to ask what was keeping him there so long, he replied, " *Tha cearcal seun timchioll ort; agus cha'n fhaod mi dol thairis air:* there is a charmed circle round you, through which I may not pass."

Not until then did she know that her sister had betrayed her secret. And she returned home to compose the Gaelic song referred to, a song which Annie Johnstone herself sang to me recently in the traditional manner at a ceilidh in her home at Castlebay.

The *mothan* protected one against fire, and also against abduction by witch or faery. It was held of old that neither witchcraft nor faery influence could affect anyone who had partaken of cheese made from the milk of a cow given but the merest sprig of this plant to eat.[1] So firmly established was the belief in its protective properties that, when an islander recovered unexpectedly from a serious illness, or miraculously escaped death or injury, it was said of him that he must have had some of the milk of a cow which had eaten of it. A fragment was often sewn into women's bodices as an amulet; and men were given to carrying a sprig of it in a left pocket. The cow was put to graze in a field where the *mothan* was known

---

[1] See *The Peatfire Flame: Folk-tales and Traditions of the Highlands and Islands*, pp. 272-4. (The Ettrick Press, Edinburgh, 1947.)

to be growing; and that, as a rule, was how the cow, sooner or later, got it—among the grass.

There is some doubt among the Gaels as to precisely which plant the name, *mothan*, was applied in olden times. The bog-violet has been suggested by some authorities on such matters; but the bog-violet is quite unlike the tiny plant with tiny, white flowers, each about the size of a pin-head, which the islesfolk call the *mothan*. This minute plant flowers in June; and you might search a whole summer's day without finding even a sprig of it, so scarce is it, so tiny, so elusive. Nevertheless, Annie Johnstone, that admirable person who has done so much to rescue from oblivion the folk-lore and folk-music of her native isle of Barra, hopes to send me a sprig of it ere these pages go to the printer! [1]

Notwithstanding the belief in the *mothan's* occult powers, there were instances in which island mothers, knowing their infants were liable to be stolen from them, forgot to place in the cradle, or somewhere in the clothing, a sprig or two of this plant. The St. Kildans used to tell of the occasion on which a neighbour of theirs unwittingly placed her child on a faery hillock, while she reaped by the light of the harvest moon. She returned to the hillock to find a changeling.

The St. Kildans often heard within the Faeries' Brugh on Hirta the rattle of faery crockery and spoons, especially after their womenfolk had poured on the milking-stone behind the village the libation by which, for centuries, the faeries had been propitiated.

Among the iris-flags near this faery dwelling stand the tumbledown ruins of the building which the islanders called the House of Big Malcolm. This semi-underground house Malcolm, a lame man, unable to accompany the menfolk of the island on their several dangerous adventures, undertook to build for a special friend of his, who had gone on a fowling expedition to the great gannetry of Boreray. When the expedition returned to Hirta, it was discovered that, all in a single day, Malcolm had managed to erect this house, roof it with turf, and have it ready for immediate occupation. The natives were convinced that he had had the assistance

---

[1] It has arrived, and has been identified as the Purging Flax—*Linum catharticum*.

of the dwellers in the Brugh, so close at hand! No mere mortal, they declared, could have accomplished, on his own, so much in one day!

The St. Kildans frequently told the story of two of their neighbours who, in passing by a knoll, were surprised at hearing within what they were certain was the sound of churning. In halting to make sure that they were not trespassing on a *sithean*, they noticed a small door in the knoll. Soon the door opened; and out by it came a faery woman carrying a pitcher brimful of milk. To the passers-by she offered some of the milk. Only one of them accepted, however, doing so in the name of the Trinity. The faery woman, a little hurt at the other's refusal, then retired to her dwelling; and the two Islanders proceeded on their way. He who had taken of the milk, they say, lived long and prosperously: he who had declined it was killed shortly afterwards by falling over those stupendous cliffs for which St. Kilda is renowned the world over.

It was in the village of Sandwickhill, Lewis, that there lived a woman whom my kinsfolk knew intimately, and from whom we got one of the most explicit accounts of the Little Folk I have ever heard. The woman's name was Morag— *Mor Nic Dhomhnuill*, Morag, daughter of Donald, to give her the Gaelic name distinguishing her from the village's other Morags.

Now Morag, throughout the greater part of her life (she lived to an old age, and is not long dead) was in touch with the faeries living in Cnoc Dubhaig, a hillock near by, where plovers and curlews like to assemble. The villagers held that the faeries pestered her from the day she exposed to view the interior of their brugh on Cnoc Dubhaig by cutting a *ceap*, this being the name given in Lewis to the big divot placed at the back of the fire as a support for the peats. Never thereafter was she able to rid herself of them. They followed her wheresoever she went; and in her declining years, spite her objecting to their unsolicited attentions, they would sit with her in the evenings, and carry on long and intimate conversations. Knowing, as did her neighbours, that the faeries disliked sharp, metallic things, such as knives and nails, pins and needles, a plentiful assortment of these was always in evidence in her cottage. But the faeries of Gnoc Dubhaig seemed to pay little attention to them. Not even the crowded pin-cushion hanging behind her door deterred them from entering. Into this weighty pin-cushion Morag habitually stuck every pin she chanced to find. The villagers of Sandwick imagine they still see her stooping to pick up a rusty pin or nail she happened to see lying on the country road passing by her humble home. These all found their way into that well-known pin-cushion of hers.

Now the interesting thing about the Cnoc Dubhaig faeries was that Morag knew many of them by name. When she and they got to know one another better, towards the latter years of her life, they told her their names; but I now recall the names of no more than four of those with whom she eventually became so very friendly. There was Popar; and there was Peulagan: there was Conachag (a little shell); and there was *Deocan nam Beann,* the Sucking-plant of the Mountains, probably one of the milkwort family.

Morag's neighbours all knew about these faeries, for she would repeat the conversations she had had with them. She used to tell the schoolmaster at Sandwick how she sometimes overheard them discussing the pranks they proposed playing on her. When leaving her cottage to work at the other end of her croft, she often heard them whispering to one another that they ought to adopt this shortcut or that, in order to reach some particular spot before her.

Morag was careful never to leave her cottage without covering up such things as the butter and the crowdie, declaring that, when she omitted to do so, the faeries invariably spat on them. Not long before her death, she happened to go into the house next door, while one of the inmates was in the act of shaving. Noticing this, she insisted that, in order to scare away the Little Folk, he flourished his naked razor behind her back. This, she was sure, would keep them away for a whilie, anyway!

Whereas, in the case of the Pied Piper of Hamelin, the rats gathered round and followed him whenever he played his pipes, in the Western Isles the pipes are sometimes used so as to scare away these destructive creatures. In Lewis, if you should happen to have a troublesome rat in your barn, you

do not hesitate about asking a local piper to play in it a skirl
or two. Morag often induced the village lads proficient in
piping to play a tune in her cottage, believing that, although
the faeries had their own pipe-music, such strains played by
ordinary mortals had the power of inducing them to leave
premises where they were not wanted.

For all this, as my kinsfolk in Lewis well remember, Morag
was not slow to concede that there were occasions upon which
she found the Cnoc Dubhaig faeries kind and helpful. On
dark nights, for example, they escorted her safely home when,
otherwise, she might have lost her way; and, when she went
to the moor for a creel-ful of peats, she never found her load
too heavy, for, as she herself declared, the Little Folk not
only lifted the creel on to her back, but also shared with her
its weight throughout her homeward journey.[1]

Those who speak with authority on such matters say that
the bagpipes are the only musical instrument known to the
faeries. True enough, most of the faery music of which we
hear has been played on faery pipes. Yet, there are instances
of harp and fiddle music. The harp the faeries use is supposed to be a miniature of the clarsach, the small, Celtic harp
—so I am assured, anyhow, by one or two friends in the Isles
who claim to have listened to faery harping.

The story is told of how two young men, when passing by
a knoll at the witching hour, were surprised at seeing a green
light within. They halted in astonishment to find that the
knoll was in reality a faery dwelling, the door of which happened to be open at the time. From the heart of the dwelling
there came the sweetest strains they had ever heard: they were

[1] Oh, the Faeries! Bless them! I discover, as we go to press, that they
are believed in not only in the Highlands and Hebrides, but also in prosaic
Glasgow. The Director of Education in that vast city does not mind the
school-children's believing in them; but he is perturbed by the waste of
food resulting from this belief. Food is being wasted there because the
children served with school meals at midday (approximately 60,000 meals
are served there, five days a week) insist upon setting aside on their plates
a substantial offering for the faeries. So the faeries have been doing well in
Glasgow of late. The habit has spread from school to school throughout
the city; and teachers are trying hard to deal with it. Some of them have
told the children that the idea has nothing to do with the faeries—certainly
not with the *good* faeries—but has been inspired by the hobgoblins. Thus
a recent New Year Resolution in the schools ran " Clean plates and nothing
for the Hobgoblins ".

those of a faery orchestra. One of the men, being quite a good hand at the fiddle, could not tear himself away from so tuneful a setting: something irresistible drew him towards the green light. No sooner was he inside the brugh than its door closed behind him, shutting out his trepid companion, who now hurried home to give an account of what had occurred. The faery music fairly enchanted the fiddler; and the faeries, realising this, soon provided him with one of their own fiddles, and invited him to play with the orchestra.

When, in course of time, he returned home and began to explain what he believed to have been but a few hours' lateness, his relatives had difficulty in convincing him that his absence had lasted a year and a day, and that they never expected to see him again. His story that on the way home he had entered a faery brugh, and had been invited to join the faery orchestra, the islefolk readily accepted. How, otherwise, could his fiddle-playing have acquired so ethereal a quality?

Then there was the case of Finlay, Son of Iain, Son of the Black Faery, as his Gaelic name signifies. Throughout the Barra Isles everyone knew Finlay, partly on account of his comely countenance, but chiefly because he had a faery sweetheart. Finlay lived on Mingulay in the times when it still carried a fair population. One misty day he went to look for his sheep on MacPhee's Hill, one of the island's highest points. As he approached the summit, he began to hear the strains of faery music. Suddenly there stepped out of the mist a beautiful faery with whom he instantly fell in love, quite forgetting that he already had plighted his troth. Aware of her faery form, he took care not to invoke the Deity in her hearing, lest she vanished. In course of time she bequeathed to him the *Currachd Flath*, or Faery Cowl, with which she had been born. This bound him to her more than ever. Not as much as a passing thought did he give thereafter to his former sweetheart. The Mingulay faery had captivated him utterly. Henceforth, for all *he* cared, his sheep could go their own way.

But there was trouble in store. Near the top of MacPhee's Hill, in the haunted hollow which the Islanders were always careful to avoid, Finlay and the faery used to meet secretly. In that hollow lay a bottomless well. One evening, as Finlay

and the faery arrived at this spot for their wooing, there
emerged from the well an *each-uisge*—a water-horse— shouting " Death upon thy head, O Finlay, son of man! " Finlay
fought valiantly in the struggle that ensued, calling for help
from any who might hear him at a spot so far from the village.
No one heard him except his former sweetheart, who chanced
to be milking the cows at no great distance. When she arrived
on the scene, the water-horse seemed to be getting the better
of him. " O, God! " she cried. " Dear Finlay, it's myself
that's sorry for your plight this night! " At mention of the
Deity, the faery vanished, leaving Finlay and his former love
to their fate. The water-horse strangled the maiden and then
dragged Finlay into the depths of the well.

Somehow or other the faery music Finlay heard on Mac-
Phee's Hill, the day the faery stepped out of the mist, has
been preserved. Those bars of it appearing in one of my
earlier books were given to me some years ago by Miss Annie
Johnstone, whom at least some of my readers will recognise
as one of those from whom the late Marjory Kennedy-Fraser
derived much that went into those unique volumes, *The
Songs of the Hebrides*. While visiting Annie lately, she mentioned that the music Finlay heard on Mingulay was by no
means the only faery music she knew. She has collected several
other fragments. These have been handed down traditionally
in Barra and elsewhere, and are now being preserved in
staff notation, and by gramophone and ediphone recordings
made on the spot by the people who sing them.

One of the many folk-songs of faery origin, which Annie
herself sings, describes how a man belonging to Cille Pheadair,
in South Uist, when travelling post-haste to Benbecula to
fetch the aid-woman to his wife, who was in labour, arrived
at the ford to find the tide was in—or, as the Uist and Benbecula folk say, " *Bha am faoghal duinte*: the ford was
closed ". So he sat down by the shore to await the ebb. There
he fell asleep. How long he slept, we do not know. What
we do know is that he was wakened by the singing of a faery
woman seated beside him, reproving him for having slept
while his wife—" the young wife of the curly hair ", as the
faery's song has it—was being laid on the bier at his home.

Much more of this traditional music survives in the

Roman Catholic isles of the Hebrides than in the Protestant. This is clearly shown by recent research in this field. The collector of folk-music finds a rich harvest in Barra, Eriskay, and South Uist, where the natives are inclined to be less sophisticated than in North Uist, Harris, or Lewis. Thus they have preserved a legacy of poesy and song, legend and tradition.

In this context one must commend the work Father Iain MacCarmaig is now engaged on in Eriskay, an island teeming with a wide range of folk-music. When staying in Eriskay recently, I spent a happy and profitable evening with Father Iain, who entertained me far into the night with various ediphone recordings he has made among his flock. These included the original version of *The Eriskay Love Lilt*, a song now known all over the world. It is sung by a native of the island, Marion MacInnes, from whose mother Mrs. Kennedy-Fraser obtained this old, traditional rendering. The song in its present popular form, as Marion herself says, is very different from the simple version her mother used to sing to her when she was a child. Nevertheless, Marjory Kennedy-Fraser has made fine music of it.

No less fearsome than the water-horse is the *cu sith* or faery dog, a creature said to be about the size of a two-year-old stirk. It moves silently and rhythmically, and always in a straight line. Usually it is green. Those of the species possessing a tail have a curious habit of curling it over the back. Their footprints, which are large, being as broad as the average hand, have been seen on the sands, on mud-flats and on shell-banks at low water, and in the snow.

The faery dog's bark is coarse and clamorous. In the Hebrides it is held that the creature barks no more than thrice. Between each bark there is a sufficient interval of time to enable the hearer to seek adequate protection before the third and final bark, after which the faery dog overtakes and destroys any living thing in its path.

Faery dogs are not so common in the Outer Hebrides as in the Inner. Tiree used to be a favourite haunt of theirs, as is shown by that island's folk-tales.

Not so long ago, the grandfather of a friend of mine, living

LEFT: *Late fifteenth-century effigy at Aignish of one of the MacLeod chiefs of Lewis*
RIGHT: *Elaborately carved slab affixed to north wall of St. Columba's, at Aignish*

at Sandwick, in Lewis, happened to notice that the supply of potatoes in his barn was gradually contracting by some means which he had reason to believe were supernatural. Although the old man hid in the barn in the hope of catching the thief, the potatoes went on diminishing in quantity as before. At length, sticking out of one of them he saw what he took to be the fang of an ordinary dog. However, when he picked up the potato in order to examine it more closely, he found that it was a faery-dog tooth, a charm greatly prized on account of the occult properties it is said to possess. If placed in milk from which witches or other evil creatures have extracted the substance, the milk is instantly restored to its pristine quality. Ailing livestock, having drunk of water into which a faery dog's tooth has been dipped, soon recover.

Ten years ago, when last I heard of the faery dog's tooth my friend's grandfather picked up in his barn, it was in Canada, greatly revered by a branch of the family there. It is being handed down from generation to generation as a charm. One day it may return to Sandwick, whence it came.

It was while the Great Clan Ranald of the Isles still lived at Nunton, in Benbecula, that two men, while feeding the calves at night-time, were alarmed by a couple of faery dogs which, held together by a leash inlaid, as they said, with precious stones and precious metals, came rushing in upon them. Outside they heard a strange voice calling:

> *Slender-fay! Slender-fay!*
> *Mountain-traveller! Mountain-traveller!*
> *Black-faery! Black-faery!*
> *Lucky-treasure! Lucky-treasure!*
> *Grey-hound! Grey-hound!*
> *Seek-beyond! Seek-beyond!*[1]

The faery dogs stayed on the premises scarcely a moment. They rushed out, as they had rushed in, the men now sufficiently in possession of their faculties to be able to follow them to the doorway, and to behold in the sky the Spirit-host —the *Sluagh*, as the Gaels call it, whence comes the word,

---

[1] *Carmina Gadelica*, Vol. 11.

Eorapie Church showing (a) doorway, (b) south-east corner, with " squint " into the chapel, and (c) the east end

slogan—about to speed away on a hunting expedition, with hounds on leash and hawks on wrist. "Fortune follow them, and luck of game," wrote an ancient chronicler, as he watched these multitudinous spirits of the departed swing westward across the sky. "And, O King of the Sun, and of the Moon, and of the bright, effulgent Stars! it was they who put fear and fright, and more than enough, on the men and the calves of Clan Ranald."

Then there are the *crodh sith*, the faery cattle. As a rule, these strange creatures are dun-coloured and hornless. In Skye and Tiree, however, they are oftener red or speckled. It is said that there are few pastures on which they graze—not more than ten throughout the Highlands and Islands, I have been told. It is said, too, that they feed little on ordinary herbage, preferring certain kinds of seaweed, their staple diet.

These faery cattle have been found both in the Inner and in the Outer Hebrides. Tiree used to be a favourite haunt of theirs. So did Harris. Like ordinary cattle, they had their herdsmen and their herdswomen. In olden times, while they were being driven home to their byre at Guershader, in Skye, the herd-maiden might be heard counting them thus:

> *Crooked one, dun one,*
> *Little wing grizzled,*
> *Black cow, white cow,*
> *Little bull, black-headed,*
> *My milch kine have come home,*
> *O dear! that the herdsman would come!*

In South Harris you may learn of a herd of sea-cows which, long ago, came ashore at Nisabost, and which the natives tried to capture. Those they were able to prevent from returning to the sea actually settled down on the old farm at Luskentyre, near by.

According to Dr. Carmichael, who informs us that the sea-cattle are either red-eared or notch-eared, another herd, tended by a sea-maiden, once came ashore at Obbe, some miles to the south of Nisabost. After they had been on land for some little time, the sea-maiden herded them back to the

178

water, meanwhile singing to them in the Gaelic a herding-song, part of which has been preserved.

You may regard all this as a lot of nonsense; but do you know that not so many years ago, a water-cow was seen in a sea-loch in Gairloch?

. . . . . .

Several families in the Highlands and Islands had a brownie attached to them; and indeed, judging by reports I have had in recent years, some would appear to have them still. At Castle Lachlan, home of the MacLachlan of MacLachlan, for instance, there is still a brownie. On Cara, an isle situated off the west coast of Kintyre, dwells the brownie who presides over the affairs of the MacDonalds of Largie. The good offices of the Cara brownie still continue, and have been recognised quite lately. When I visited Cara a few years ago in company with the parish minister of Gigha (his parish includes Cara, which is now uninhabited except for the brownie and some wild goats) the minister, on disembarking, doffed his hat most reverently.

"To whom are you making such obeisance, Kenneth?" I asked him when he turned round to see whether I had observed what he hoped might have been an unseen gesture on his part.

"I'm paying my respects to the brownie," he answered, "for he protects many of my own parishioners, as well as the MacDonalds of Largie, across the water there."

The answer was partly in jest; but one could not help feeling it was also partly in earnest.

The brownies may be said to correspond with the *lares* and *penates* of the Roman household. They usually took up their abode in the castles and mansions of the wealthier classes, where they performed certain social and domestic duties, such as dish-washing and tinkering. They were of a genial disposition, though there are instances in which they took offence, and left their duties unperformed. Such was the case, at any rate, with the brownie at the Doune of Rothiemurchus, in Inverness-shire—the brownie who, in return for his long and faithful ministrations to the Grant family, was rewarded daily with "a cream-bowl duly set". *He* is one of those who left in a huff. One night his tinkering of the pots and pans in the

Doune kitchen was so noisy that it disturbed the laird who, groping his way to the stair-head, shouted down to him to make less din at his tasks, so that decent folk might have their sleep. The brownie took umbrage at this, and deserted the Doune. The following morning the maids found the kitchen in great disorder. It was bestrewn with half-mended pots and pans; and the fire, moreover, was out, a thing that had never happened all the years the brownie exercised his beneficent influence over the Doune, over its inmates, and all its contents.

Early in the seventeenth century, according to Martin, every family of substance in the Shetland Isles had its brownie, who did all sorts of helpful things; " and this was the reason why they gave him offerings of the various products of the place: thus some, when they churned their milk, or brewed, poured some milk and wort through the hole in a stone, called Browny's stone.

" A minister in this country had an account from one of the ancient inhabitants who formerly brewed ale, and sometimes read his Bible, that an old woman in the family told him that Browny was much displeased at his reading in that book; and if he did not cease to read in it any more, Browny would not serve him as formerly. But the man continued his reading notwithstanding, and when he brewed refused to give any sacrifice to Browny; and so his first and second brewing miscarried, without any visible cause in the malt; but the third brewing proved good, and Browny got no more sacrifice from him after that.

" There was another instance of a lady in Unst, who refused to give sacrifice to Browny, and lost two brewings; but the third proved good, and so Browny vanished quite, and troubled them no more."

Perhaps the best known and most lovable of the brownies in the Long Island was that which attached itself to the house of Sir Norman MacLeod of Berneray, in the Sound of Harris. On a number of memorable occasions this brownie made his presence known. One evening two of Sir Norman's guests sat long over a game of backgammon. Both had reached an impasse, as it were. As time dragged on and the other guests began to weary of this interminable delay, an attendant, who had been observing the play at some distance, came forward to say that he could indicate the move which would win the game. Owing to the lateness of the hour, the players agreed that the attendant should be allowed to make the move. This he did; and accordingly he won.

When on the point of retiring, the players asked him how he, a man who, so far as they knew, had never played backgammon, was able to step forward and move with such assurance. His explanation was that, although he had never played the game in his life, during the protracted interval when neither player seemed capable of winning, he had noticed the brownie alight momentarily on the empty square into which the next piece ought to be moved if the player hoped to win!

On an occasion when Sir Norman was absent from Berneray, and his employees were making merry in the hall, one of them, known to have been endowed with the Second-sight, interrupted their merriment to announce that at any moment the master would be returning, and that they ought therefore to leave the hall, which would soon be required by him and the guests arriving with him. The merry-makers paid little heed. Though they knew their informant to be something of a seer, they thought it highly improbable that Sir Norman would return so late, and on a night so dark. However, less than an hour later, one of the men who had accompanied Sir Norman on his journey furth of Berneray arrived unexpectedly on the scene, and bade the servants provide lights, and in other ways make preparations to receive their master and his guests. This they immediately did, resolved that never again would they doubt a pronouncement made by the seer.

When, eventually, Sir Norman was told of this instance of the Second-sight, he sent for the foreteller to ask him what manifestation he had had. He replied that, on several occasions during the evening, he had seen the brownie enter the hall in human form, and carry to the door an old woman seated by the fire. As the old woman insisted on returning to the fireside, the brownie in the end, seizing her by neck and heels, had to eject her. He added that he could not help laughing at the brownie's performance, but that his fellow-servants, unable to see anything such as might have justified his hilarity, merely thought he was being silly.

Not unlike the brownie was the loireag, a female sprite with an insatiable appetite for dairy produce, and one who was always invisibly present at any process connected with cloth-making. She frequently makes her appearance in the folklore of Benbecula and of South Uist. A Benbecula woman named Mary MacInnes described the loireag as " a small mite of womanhood, who does not belong to this world, but to the world thither ". A loireag at Hacleit, in that same isle, resentful because her services, during the weaving and the warping and the fulling of the cloth, were not being appreciated sufficiently, as evidenced by the Islanders' omission to provide for her an adequate libation of milk, took her revenge by placing a spell on all the township's milk-yielding stock.

Belonging to the same order, though of a more benevolent disposition, was the rock-gnome, a creature said to have been an inhabitant of the corners of the rocks farthest removed from the reach of men.

Now, it was MacVurich Mor himself, who insisted that from time to time the rock-gnomes of South Uist had food left here and there for them. When bread was being baked in his house at Staoligarry, he made it the rule that all scraps falling to the floor from the baking-board, or on the hearth from the girdle, should be left where they fell. MacVurich often rebuked the housewife whom he saw sweeping up such scraps, reminding her that she was depriving the hungry rock-gnomes of them. " Give a look to it," he would say, " for it's many a needy mouth that's waiting for it! "

. . . .

Tales of the water-horse are to be found throughout the Isles. Many of these are associated with the shielings, near which lie the lochs and ponds out of which these monsters have stepped to terrify and even destroy the maidens tending the cattle during the summer months.

In the west of Lewis, near the village of Shawbost, there is a shieling which, for several generations, has been known by a Gaelic name denoting the Shieling of the One Night. This shieling was established by two families who agreed to share alike their rights in it.

There came an evening in June when all was ready for its occupation. Two cousins known in Shawbost as Fair Mary and Dark Mary were the first, and indeed the last, to occupy it. The Maries were in their early twenties at the time. Having milked the cows at sundown, and seen to the churning, they seated themselves by the low entrance to their temporary summer dwelling. There they employed the twilight hour in knitting, and in lilting Gaelic melodies to one another. When they were putting a light to the rush-lamp, there arrived at the shieling a woman whom neither of them knew. She explained that she had come a long distance, and still had a good way to travel. She was tired, and therefore suggested to the two Maries that they might grant her a night's shelter. The young women saw no reason why she should not tarry. In fact, they were quite pleased to have her company on this first night at the new shieling. There did not seem to be anything unusual about her appearance. She wore the dress of the ordinary peasant women in the Isles; and she spoke the Gaelic as they themselves did. In the course of conversation it transpired that, although she and the Maries did not know one another, they had friends and acquaintances in common. The visitor, moreover, knew the countryside thoroughly. Indeed, she described her journey to them in such detail as to leave no doubt in their minds that she was just one of themselves.

As it was now getting late, preparations were made for a night's repose on the large shakedown of heather or bracken comprising the bed in the hut of stone and turf, wherein dwell those who take the cows to the shieling, and remain there with them during the summer. After the Maries had given the woman a little supper, all retired peacefully. At dawn, however, Dark Mary woke with a fright. She had felt a warm trickle by her side. She immediately sat up to find that the guest had departed, and that blood was oozing from the breast of her cousin, who was already dead. On pushing open the rude door of the hut, what did she see but an animal galloping away and away from the shieling! That explained everything: the galloper was nothing more or less than an *each-uisge* to which she and Fair Mary, in their innocence, had given a night's portion, believing it to have been a weary .

woman who had arrived at the shieling during a long journey.
They say in the Isles that this incident occasioned much grief
and dismay among the islesfolk, who buried Fair Mary on a
slope to the east of the shieling. The tumbledown ruins of
the hut are still to be seen at the very spot; but no one has
ever had any desire to rebuild it, and to re-habilitate this shieling. So, to this day it is called the Shieling of the One Night.

Close to the now tenantless crofters' houses on Ceann Ear,
one of the group of small islands known as Heiskeir, or the
Monach Isles, is a freshwater loch which goes by the name of
the Loch of the Virtues—a name somewhat inappropriate,
one would think, for a place reputed to be inhabited by one
of the largest and most fearsome of water-horses.

Ceann Ear has been uninhabited since the autumn of 1943,
when its last two smallholders, John and Alexander Mac-
Donald, two brothers, whom I knew, gave up their croft, and
retired to the mainland of North Uist, a few miles distant. In
the days when Ceann Ear carried a fair population, however,
the islesfolk, with little success, were continually devising
schemes to rid the loch of its evil occupant. Each succeeding
fatality due, as was firmly believed, to the sinister water-horse
made them the more resolved to extirpate it. Indeed, things
had reached such a state that they realised the necessity for
abandoning the island if they could not free the Loch of the
Virtues of a creature which, year after year, went on way-
laying and destroying the inhabitants.

At length one of their number—she was a woman named
MacLeod, I have been told—let her neighbours into a great
secret. For some time, as she now explained, she had been
feeding a young bull in the hope that one day he might be
able to engage successfully the island's dreaded water-horse.
So it was agreed that the evacuation of Ceann Ear should be
postponed until it could be seen whether this bull was to be
a match for the monster.

There came a day, then, when MacLeod led forth her bull,
and allowed him to graze by the fringe of the loch, while she
herself stood some distance off, eagerly watching for the emer-
gence of the water-horse. Before long the bull showed signs
of restiveness. Soon he commenced to stamp, and to gore the
sod with his horns, and toss great divots in the air. He was,

indeed, in fine fighting fettle when the water-horse, covered with mud and pond-weed, came out of the loch to accept the challenge. The contest began immediately; and it was soon realised that the water-horse was no match for the bull—not on land, anyhow. It was forced to give ground; but it did so with an eye to strategy, retreating all the time toward the water, the element in which it was as much at home as was the bull on land. The bull, not content, alas! with driving it back into the loch, followed beyond his depth; and it now looked as though the fortunes were to be reversed. A tremendous struggle ensued—so tremendous that the commotion of the water rendered it impossible for the onlookers to see clearly what was happening. At one moment they would be seeing a horn: at another a hoof. Suddenly the struggle ended; and the water subsided. Neither bull nor water-horse was to be seen. The loch lay still. The Islanders were mystified. Had the water-horse won? Had it dragged the over-confident bull down to the bottom of the loch, from which it would never emerge? Or had both creatures died fighting?

On the morrow there was found floating by the margin of the Loch of the Virtues a pair of lungs so mutilated that no one could tell whether they were the bull's or the water-horse's. Anyway, never since that day has the water-horse been seen in Ceann Ear. However, the hoof-marks which the bull left by the fringe of the loch, and also the indentations in the sod made by the horns as he challenged the water-horse to deadly combat, were pointed out to me when exploring the Monach Isles some fifteen years ago.

It may interest you to know that, while holidaying at Glenelg in 1932, I interviewed at great length an old man named John MacRae who was an eye-witness when, in 1870, a loch in Skye was publicly dragged with a view to capturing the water-horse believed to haunt it!

Unlike the water-horse, which had a reputation for malevolence, was the *each-tarbh*, or water-bull, a creature regarded as having been of a disposition relatively harmless. In the Highlands and Hebrides it was believed that calves born with short ears, or with ears which looked as though they had been notched with a sharp instrument, were the offspring of the water-bull, which was said to have no ears at all. At night-time the water-bull might be heard lowing by the edge of some tarn, whence it had just emerged to graze with the Islanders' cattle.

The species would appear to have been numerous in St. Kilda, the folk-lore of which embraces several references to it. The St. Kildans used to tell of the occasion upon which a woman, when returning to the village of Hirta with a creel of peats, noticed a tiny door open in the side of a hillock. With consummate wit, she stuck a knife into the ground close to the tiny door, thus preventing its being slammed in her face. As she continued to look into the interior of the hillock, a speckled cow came out and dropped a speckled calf, which grew up to be a speckled cow, which, in due course, dropped a speckled calf *without ears*. This was regarded as definite proof of the existence on St. Kilda of at least *one* water-bull.

The St. Kildans of old never doubted that a water-bull resided on Boreray, for the marks of its cloven hoofs were often seen upon the pasture there.

Bird and beast appear plentifully in the folklore and tradition of the Western Isles.

It is said that, when Christ was being pursued from one isle to another, a pair of oystercatchers, taking compassion upon Him, concealed Him under a heap of seaweed until His pursuers were well out of sight. And this, they say, explains how the oystercatcher was chosen to be the *gille*, or man-servant, of St. Bridgit, Christ's foster-mother, and also how this bird received its Gaelic name, *gillebridean*. Of all the birds frequenting the Isles, none occurs so often in their lore and legendary.

When the oystercatcher is flying toward one, its breast and wings resemble a white cross, a distinctive feature bestowed upon it because of its services to Christ, the white of its plumage having been originally black.

The oystercatcher's short, sharp, impetuous cry is still regarded by seafarers as a warning of a coming storm. The cry is rendered in Gaelic as *Bi glic, bi glic! Bi glic, bi glic!* meaning, "be wise!" "be careful!" "be prudent!"

There is current in South Uist a folk-tale describing how Christ, in His fugitive days, arrived at a croft in the Isles while a crofter was in the act of winnowing his corn in the open. Recognising the Christ, and anxious to succour Him, he hid Him in the heap of corn that went on mounting as he continued his winnowing. In order to make His conceal-ment doubly sure, he then sought to add to the heap from corn already in the barn. During his brief absence in the barn, the ducks and hens found their way to the heap. But, whereas the ducks ate the corn as they trampled it, the hens, by their thoughtless scraping, scattered much of it, and in so doing exposed a part of the Fugitive. It was thus, they say in Uist, that the hen and her progeny became earth-bound, and inherited a fear of water, a fear of snow and hail, of wind and rain. But not so with the duck and *her* progeny. It was decreed that she should be webbed, that water should be her natural element, that she should rejoice in the wind and the rain, and even in the thunder and the lightning which the hen and her kindred dread. Indeed, it was ordained that, henceforth, the duck should inherit the four supreme joys—the joy of land, of water, of under-water, and of air. And this explains how the duck is merriest when the hen is most miserable, most confident when the hen is most terrified. This ancient fragment of Hebridean bird-lore survives in two similes still in use in Gaeldom:

(a) *You are as happy as a duck expecting thunder.*
(b) *Your heart is shaking as would a hen in thunder.*

Swans, according to the legendary of the Isles, are devout women under spell, under enchantment. And so, to this day, the species remains comparatively free from molestation in these parts, as it does in the remoter parts of Ireland. The swan is looked upon as a bird of good omen. Seven of them seen together, or a multiple of seven, prognosticates the advent of seven years of peace and plenty.

I know people in the Western Isles who wince at the idea of shooting a swan. Some regard such an act as heinous because of the swan's being a metamorphosed human: others regard it as unlucky, because it is said in the Hebrides that in the tip of the swan's tongue there resides a drop of the devil's blood.

Once upon a time an old woman in the Isles found by the fringe of a lochan, near her cottage, a wounded swan, which she carried home with her. She dressed the bird's wounds; and for a considerable period it remained under her care. It so happened that the woman had an ailing child to look after at the same time; and she noticed that the child's health improved as the swan's wounds healed. The child was restored to perfect health the very day the swan was sufficiently recovered to take to the wing again. And so the woman concluded that the bird, upon which she had bestowed such care, was in reality a devout lady, enchanted.

There once inhabited Berneray, that fascinating isle in the Sound of Harris, a sept known as the Clan MacAndy, or the Clan Andy. Members of this sept suffered metamorphism: they were turned into widgeons, whose descendants to this day haunt the Sound of Harris in great numbers.

Now the MacAndys—so the legend goes, anyhow—had tilled the barren fields of Berneray with little to show for all their labour. And so there came a time when it was found necessary to seek, elsewhere, a livelihood less arduous. Thus the clan was divided into two communities, a land community, and a maritime community. While the latter railed at the former for the old-fashioned ways in which it pursued its agrestic affairs, its members were transformed by magic —by the touch of a Druid wand, they say in the Isles—into the long-tailed *lach*, or widgeon. And so it comes about that, when an islesman in these parts, tilling the stony soil laboriously, and with little to show for all his trouble, happens to see a widgeon, whether joyous on the wing or buoyant upon the tide, he will say that he wishes his ancestors had been as fortunate as those maritime members of the Clan MacAndy.

Do you realise that there actually exist some ancient fragments of the Clan Andy's language? These few lines, a rough translation from the Gaelic, are from those said to have been reduced to writing by that doughty cavalier, Sir Norman MacLeod of Berneray, aforementioned, who fought for King Charles at the Battle of Worcester in 1651:

Clan MacAndy!
Clan MacAndy!
Weakly clansmen!
Puny clansmen!
Vioch! voch! vuch!
Uv-uv! uv-uv! uv-uv!
Ur! ur! ah!

Berneray and the Sound of Harris bring to mind yet another metamorphosed race, namely, the Seal-folk. It is believed in the Outer Hebrides that the seals were attendants in the royal courts of Lochlann—of Norway—and that they came to the Isles long, long ago as secret emissaries from the Norse kings.

In North Uist there lived a sept of the Clan Ranald known traditionally as the Clan MacCodrum of the Seals. The MacCodrums, though they had been transformed into seals, were allowed to retain their human souls. Popular belief had it that they were seals by day, and human beings by night. Aware of their seal affinity, all members of the sept were particularly careful not to kill a seal, or even to disturb one unduly.

According to the Seal-folk tradition in the Western Isles, the MacCodrums sprang from one of the name who, when shore-wandering in his native isle, chanced to come upon a group of seals while they were in the act of divesting themselves of their skins. Seizing one of the discarded seal-skins, MacCodrum dashed home with it. When on the point of concealing it above the lintel of his cottage, there arrived on the scene its seal-woman owner, whom he detained, anxious though she was to return to the sea. He clad her in ordinary clothing; and in course of time he married her, and begat a large family by her. This family—this *clann*—became known throughout the Western Isles as the Children of MacCodrum of the Seals.

One day, when MacCodrum was away from home, his seal-woman wife searched successfully for her hidden seal-skin. She immediately got into it; and, by the time MacCodrum returned, she had rejoined, irretrievably, her sea-kindred.

189

The traditions of the Seal-folk are of immense interest. They are current not only in the Western Isles, but also in Ireland, in western Argyllshire, in Caithness and Sutherland, in the Orkneys and Shetlands, and even in Norway and in Greenland.[1] The MacCodrum tradition, as existing in Berneray and North Uist, provided Fiona MacLeod with the theme of *Dàn-nan-Ròn,* Song of the Seals, a tale in which one, Manus MacCodrum by name, is the principal character.

.   .   .   .

To Prince Charlie's landing on the sands at Eriskay a couple of centuries ago, and to all that befell him thereafter in these wild parts and, indeed, furth of them, the older natives of the Roman Catholic isles refer as though they themselves had been with the Prince throughout his wanderings, and as though he had quitted Scotland for final exile but a few days previously.

Pre-eminent among such natives is one living at Northbay, in the Isle of Barra, and known popularly throughout the Western Isles as the Coddy. Many who recognise him by this nickname may not even know that he was christened John MacPherson. On matters relating to 'the Fifteen' and 'the Forty-five' the Coddy speaks with one in terms so intimate, so urgent, so very personal, that one cannot but feel what he has to say is part of his own special mission in life. Prince Charlie's doings in the Hebrides, the few joys he experienced there, the hazards he survived when afloat with Donald MacLeod of Gaultergill, his trusty pilot after Culloden, are, as it were, the Coddy's own personal epic. You would think he had been present on every occasion of importance during the Prince's eventful time in Scotland, eye-witness of all that happened to him, partaker alike in his triumphs and troubles. When I visited the Coddy at Northbay as recently as 1948, he spoke of Prince Charlie with an intimacy which would have made me reluctant to disbelieve him, had he mentioned that he was one of the Seven Men of Moidart, returned from the dead, and now dwelling in Barra, committed to the sacred duty of keeping green, in that locality, the memory of the

---

[1] These traditions may be referred to at greater length in my book, *The Peatfire Flame: Folk-tales and Traditions of the Highlands and Islands,* Chapter viii. (The Ettrick Press, Edinburgh, 1947.)

luckless Jacobites. Indeed, nothing would have surprised me less than to have learnt from his own lips that he claimed to be the descendant of Cluny MacPherson, that valorous namesake of his, better known to Scottish history as Cluny of ' the Forty-five '.

"There's a bit more I should be telling you about Fuday," the Coddy interposed the other day, recalling a previous conversation he and I had had concerning this grassy isle lying in the Sound of Barra, at no great distance from his home at Northbay. "But wait a moment," he added, "while I get the magic wand I like to have in my hand when storytelling to the likes of yourself." Straightway he made for the sitting-room of his house, in order to take, from its customary corner there, the bamboo stick which, as he informs me, the harsh landlord occupying the north end of Barra after the Clearances used as a means of frightening anyone refusing to obey his commands.

In a few seconds the Coddy returned, bearing this eloquent emblem of past injustices. Before allowing him to continue with the narrative which this magic wand now inspired in him, I insisted upon taking the photograph facing page 193. Thereafter he proceeded as follows: "In the ' Forty-five ', MacNeil of Barra went over to Fuday to see a man, Donald MacInnes, who was then a prosperous crofter on the island. MacNeil explained to MacInnes that he came to Fuday to ask him for money to assist Bonnie Prince Charlie, who was about to land in Scotland to claim the throne of his ancestors. Without any delay, MacInnes put his hand on a *mogan*[1]—he had it hidden away behind the rafters: that was his bank, you see— which contained three hundred pieces of gold; and he gave it all to MacNeil for the good cause. *That's* worth recording, you'll agree! You won't collect the like of that one anywhere else than from myself! . . . A good cause it was; and we all know what happened to it, without criticising it in any shape or form. . . . We all know it was lost."

In words such as these, I heard many of the folk-tales and traditions concerning the Jacobite Rebellions from a man who claims to be on speaking terms with more than one ghost, to be very much *persona grata* with the faeries, and to know

[1] An old stocking, usually footless, often used in the Isles for keeping money.

the precise spot where the last faery washer-woman in the neighbourhood was seen rinsing the death-shrouds.

Several of the folk-tales and traditions of 'the Fifteen' and 'the Forty-five' described how the supporters of the Stuart cause were *sained* or "charmed" before leaving home, with the result that, when others were wounded or slain, either at Sheriffmuir or at Culloden, they survived, unscathed.

When Alan MacDonald of Clan Ranald—Little Alan, as they called him in the Isles—was on the point of leaving South Uist to join the Earl of Mar in the Rising of 1715, an agèd isleswoman put on him a charm that, assuredly, would have protected him at Sheriffmuir, had he not insisted upon taking to the wars with him the only son of a widow. True enough, the Hanoverian bullets showered upon Little Alan without doing him the slightest harm. Then the lad remembered the crooked sixpence his mother had given him at his departure —the crooked sixpence seven times cursed—and the curse that went with it. Better, said she, that her son should go forth to the wars with her blessing than with her curse. That crooked sixpence, fired by the lad from his flint-lock at the height of the battle, spelt death for Little Alan.

That day a further disaster befell the Clan Ranald family. The vision Lady Clan Ranald had had, some little time earlier, that Ormacleit Castle was to be the scene of a catastrophe, became a reality. On the day of Sheriffmuir, while Little Alan's corpse lay stiffening upon the stricken field, his home in South Uist was gutted by fire, leaving in its walls and gables just those ruins one sees to-day at Ormacleit.

As MacLeod of Berneray was about to join Prince Charlie at Culloden, it was a woman from Skye who put upon him the charm which rendered him immune to the enemy's bullets. When the clansmen disbanded after the Jacobite rout, those who eventually found their way back to the Isles bore testimony to the way in which the bullets fell on Mac-Leod without doing him any injury.

When all seemed lost, MacLeod flung off his coat, that he might be hindered as little as possible in his flight. That coat was picked up by Murdoch MacAskill, his foster-brother, who was following behind him. When Murdoch gained a

Ruins of Kisimul Castle, at Castlebay, Isle of Barra

few moments' respite, he examined the coat to find it riddled with bullet-holes. Not a bullet had as much as grazed the skin of MacLeod of Berneray, however: so potent had been the Skye-woman's *seun*, or charm.

It is traditional in the Western Isles that not a few of those who fought for the Prince at Culloden returned safely, having carried with them, throughout the campaign, an amulet in the form of a tiny bit of the king otter's skin.

.   .   .   .

Tradition dies exceedingly hard in the Isles; and the Islanders are by no means as free from superstition as some of the more emotional and superficial writers on the Hebrides in recent years would have us believe. It is Compton Mac-Kenzie, a convert to Roman Catholicism, who writes fulsomely of the Catholics of Barra as "a people who, whatever its material suffering in the past, has been spared the influence of the darker Calvinistic superstitions upon its spiritual health".[1] This statement is no more true of the Catholics of the Western Isles than it is of the Protestants, as I can vouch from a fairly intimate knowledge of both.

So far as the survival of ancient customs and beliefs are concerned, it is regrettable that Dr. Johnson and James Boswell did not find their way to the Roman Catholic isles of the Hebrides in 1773, for, had they done so, they assuredly would have recorded some interesting observations. "If we had travelled with more leisure," wrote the Doctor, "it had not been fit to have neglected the Popish islands. Popery is favourable to ceremony; and among ignorant nations ceremony is the only preservative of tradition. Since Protestantism was extended to the savage parts of Scotland, it has perhaps been one of the chief labours of the Ministers to abolish stated observances, because they continued the remembrance of the former religion. We, therefore, who came to hear old traditions, and see antiquated manners, should probably have found them among the Papists."

Barra is certainly the isle for old traditions. The entire gamut of Celtic folklore and belief is to be found there, even at the present time. When writing Annie Johnstone the other day on the subject of folk-music, I appended to my letter

---

[1] *The Book of Barra*, p. 2. (Routledge, 1936.)

The Coddy, at Northbay, Isle of Barra

the following tentative postscript: "When next you write, don't forget to tell me a little more precisely how long ago it is since the Barra folk believed in faeries! "

" To this very day, to this very hour," she responded, almost by return of post. " I am not going to be more explicit than that! "

Much folklore and tradition in the Western Isles have still to be preserved. At the present moment, the Irish Folklore Commission is in Benbecula, recording by dictaphone the Hebridean folk-tales which Angus MacMillan, a crofter living at Griminish, in that island, has been narrating in Gaelic for half a century. Night after night during the summer of 1948, Angus, now seventy-eight years of age, spoke into the dictaphone in a leisurely and expansive manner. One of his recitals went on almost continuously for eight hours. It took four nights, on an average of five hours a night, to record, on twenty-one records, the longest of his tales. According to Professor Delargy, head of the Folklore Commission, this feat has never been equalled by folklorists anywhere in the world.

At the time of writing, no fewer than six hundred records of Angus's folk-tales have been made. These deal with but half of his repertoire of forty tales, all of which he believes to be true.

CHAPTER VI

THE ISLANDERS AND THEIR WAYS

THE Western Islanders are Celts, with a strong admixture of Norse. They are almost entirely crofters, or crofter-fishermen, gaining a livelihood from cultivating their sparse holdings and from a certain amount of fishing, and also from any public monies to which they can lay claim. Crofting, so much of it uneconomic, is their main occupation. Fishing in recent years has become quite secondary. Lobster-fishing, however, has been an increasing source of income of late, and is now being conducted on a fairly large and profitable scale.

The language of the natives is the Gaelic tongue, which few of them can write. Those who write it spell it variously, for the orthography of the language is ancient, intricate, and highly controversial. The Islanders are bi-lingual, however, since nearly everyone can also speak English, a language in most cases acquired, and spoken with great accuracy and beauty, and with an intonation not unlike that one associates with the Irish use of it. The Outer Hebrides remain the stronghold of the Gaelic tongue, which is waning more rapidly in the other Gaelic-speaking areas of the Scottish Highlands and Islands. The entire rural and crofting population uses the language constantly, and with great fluency. Only in a semi-urban area like Stornoway does one find natives who neither speak nor understand it.

All the older inhabitants, even of Stornoway, *have the Gaelic,* as the saying is; and most of them still prefer to express themselves in their mother-tongue when dealing with problems the least complicated. This explains why the Scottish Land Court, which visits the Outer Hebrides from time to time to adjudicate in matters of dispute connected with crofting, embraces, statutorily, a Gaelic-speaking member, who acts as interpreter when necessary. When Mr. Murdo Montgomery was installed recently in this capacity,

Lord Gibson, chairman of the Land Court, remarked that circumstances had so altered that, nowadays, it was the distressed landlord, rather than the distressed crofter, who sought the Court's aid.

In the schools of the Gaelic-speaking areas, Gaelic is now taught compulsorily. Yet, it is a dying language, certainly as a *spoken* language. Its decay has been exercising the more pervervid of the Gaels for well over half a century. My own father was one of those who worked hard for its resuscitation. He spent much of his latter life deploring its decline when, as my mother used to say, he might have been engaged more usefully, if not also more gainfully, where the affairs of his family were concerned. As Bard of the Clan Gregor—of the historic Clan Alpin—he deemed it his bounden duty to revive interest in it, though in his eighties even *he*, who had written so much in the language, had to admit that the compulsory teaching of it in schools could not arrest a decay which, for a number of reasons, seemed inevitable. The efforts of An Comunn Gaidhealach, however, have done much to encourage a study of Gaelic, although one wonders whether, even with the best sentiment in the world, these efforts may not result in achieving an academic knowledge of the language rather than a prolongation of its use as the daily tongue of the people in districts where it is still spoken. To me, it seems, its value is already greater from the academic and cultural standpoint than that which can be expected from artificially stimulating its use as a spoken language. Many native-speaking Gaels, and also many of those possessing a superficial knowledge of Gaelic, which they may have acquired and are anxious to augment, continue to show an interest in it when they take up residence in cities where provision is made for further study. They take advantage of continuation classes. Every autumn, preparatory to the opening of a new session, one may see, in our Scottish newspapers, public announcements inserted by the Director of Education, on behalf of the Education Department of the Glasgow Corporation, concerning continuation classes for the study of Gaelic, and giving particulars of enrolment at a fee of seven-and-six for a session of twenty-four weeks.

Nevertheless, it would be ridiculous to suppose that all the united efforts of Scottish Gaeldom could stem the advance of English in the Gaelic-speaking regions of Celtic Scotland.

"There is the imperative need of taking practical measures, not merely for the preservation, but for the advancement of Gaelic," writes Compton MacKenzie, who is so essentially an Englishman. "We do not intend to rest until every official communication in the Outer Hebrides is printed in Gaelic and in English. We are tired of being put to sleep by Gaelic lullabies to dream sentimental dreams. That is the risk which lovers of the islands always run."[1] Official communications in Gaelic and in English! What nonsense!

It seems apposite to mention that, owing to the decline of Gaelic-speaking congregations in parts of the Highlands, the Presbytery of Lorne decided, as recently as March, 1948, not to insist any longer on the appointment of Gaelic preachers for certain parishes hitherto classified as charges where Gaelic was considered essential. The Presbytery unanimously agreed, therefore, to remove from the list of "Gaelic essential" charges the five Argyllshire parishes of Duror, Appin, Kilmore, Kilmelfort, and Muckairn, and to describe them instead as "Gaelic desirable" charges. It was agreed, in the case of Argyll Square Church, Oban, that Gaelic was no longer either essential or desirable.

The Islanders are well educated and exceedingly intelligent, though there has been a certain amount of inter-breeding amongst them. I doubt whether there exists anywhere in Britain a peasantry so well-read and so well-informed, despite its relative remoteness. The Islanders write the most excellent letters—grammatical, imaginative, and perfectly expressed—and in a beautiful hand. This is true of all the Hebrides, but it is particularly so of Lewis, where education was looked upon as a necessity of life certainly half a century before popular education became prevalent elsewhere in the country. Among the natives of Stornoway, whose resources were notoriously meagre, the desire for education was strong a hundred years ago. You will not find in Lewis the illiteracy to be met with in the Channel Isles.

[1] *The Book of Barra*, p. 29. (Routledge, 1935.)

An enormous proportion of the Hebrideans of both sexes graduate at our Scottish Universities, either in Arts or in Medicine. Many in the latter faculty go to Edinburgh. As a rule, those graduating in Arts do so either at Aberdeen or at Glasgow. For the most part, they become teachers or ministers. The teachers, like the many who become doctors, often receive excellent appointments throughout Britain and in the Dominions and Colonies. The majority of the latter, however, return to their native environment for the obvious reason that they must needs preach in Gaelic, and are therefore largely limited to West Highland and Island charges.

The number of graduates, both from the Roman Catholic and from the Presbyterian isles of the Hebrides, is higher in proportion to population than anywhere in the Kingdom. So far as the natives of Lewis are concerned, the number is amazingly high.

One cannot say when education first reached the Western Isles. As late as the close of the sixteenth century, in all likelihood, the inhabitants were almost wholly illiterate. When the Fife Adventurers came to Lewis in 1598, they brought with them a schoolmaster, whose services were intended for the improvement of the colonists themselves. He was probably the first member of the teaching profession to function in these wild and uncouth parts. Old Roderic, Chief of the MacLeods of Lewis at the time of the Fifers' arrival, was unable to sign his name. On the other hand, two of his sons, Neil and Murdoch, would appear to have been less illiterate than their father: unaided, and with a remarkable degree of legal precision, they actually drafted a bond.

It was not until Lewis came into the hands of the Seaforths, early in the seventeenth century, that anything in the nature of education began to circulate among the islanders generally. "Onlie for the tyme the countrie is possessed and safelie governed by the Earle of Seaforth, by whose industrious care and benevolence the people, formerlie inclined to rudeness and barbarity, are reduced to civilitie, much understanding, and knowledge by the flourishing schooll planted and maintained by the said Earle all the tyme in the toun of Stornoway." Thus, about 1680, wrote John Morison, a native of Lewis—an "Indweller", as he describes himself: "And not onlie the people of the Lews, but also those of the nixt adjacent Isles. The gentlemens sons and daughters are bred in that schooll to the great good and comfort of that people; so that there are few families but at least the maister can read and write: I do remember in my own tyme that there was not three in all the countrie that knew A.b by A Bible."[1]

This, doubtless, is the school at which, according to Martin, writing a few years later, both Latin and English were taught.

During the eighteenth century there was established at Stornoway a school for the teaching not only of these two languages, but also of writing and arithmetic. However, the principal channel along which education was carried to the Islanders at this time was the Society for Propagating Christian Knowledge.

Education was greatly extended throughout the nineteenth century, during the first quarter of which the Gaelic School Society of Inverness lent to it considerable impetus. Then followed the church schools. These were established by the Church of Scotland; and, after 1843, the year of the Disruption, their number was increased by the Free Church of Scotland, then instituted. The church schools did much to supplement the education already made available by the parish schools, which had been founded throughout the Long Island, as elsewhere in Scotland, towards the end of the previous century. In Stornoway, particularly, the church schools spread much knowledge and enlightenment. Their standard of education was high. In the eighteen-sixties, as my father used to tell me, no boy left the Free Church school at Stornoway without a thorough grounding in navigation, as well as in a curriculum of half a dozen ordinary subjects.

A decade later, with the passing of the Education Act, the Long Island was brought into line with the remainder of Scotland, where, henceforth, under the School Boards, education became free and compulsory.

The Lewis people, perhaps more than any other in the Western Isles, have long been noted for a leaning towards

[1] MacFarlane's *Geographical Collections*, 11, p. 215.

199

scholarly pursuits. The result of this must be patent to any-one studying the *Stornoway Gazette,* the only local newspaper published in the Hebrides, founded in 1917 by the late William Grant, and now edited by his younger son. During the war, when there were servicemen on every battlefront, most local papers established temporary contacts with the far corners of the earth. However, the *Stornoway Gazette* has always had such contacts, even in times of peace, since the Lewisman, though an inveterate wanderer, seldom loses touch with home. This weekly paper, consisting of eight pages in normal times and of four in abnormal, has its regular readers in every continent, and wellnigh in every country. This is especially true of the Western Hemisphere, where it is read from the Falkland Islands to the Yukon. Many Lewismen are to be found on the sheep stations of South America; and on one of the large farms in Chili it is customary for the manager, a native of Lewis, to ring up his fellow-countrymen at scattered outposts of the ranch, in order to read to them the latest news from home, whenever the month-old *Stornoway Gazette* arrives with his mails. Many distant readers of this paper pay their subscription years in advance.

A lively correspondence column has always been one of this paper's principal features. Recently, when wordy warfare over the erection of village halls broke out between the young folk of the island and the elders of the kirk, letters-to-the-editor came pouring in not only from the Lewis villages, but from Lewis people in lands as far apart as Egypt and Van-couver. The paper's policy has been to express the personality of the Island rather than to reduce to journalistic clichés items of external news. People in all walks of life supply it with news from the rural villages—school teachers, clergymen, mis-sionaries, crofters, fishermen, seamen, merchants, shoemakers, shepherds, and weavers. On the plea that, if anyone have anything worth saying, it might as well be said vigorously, every correspondent, as far as possible, is given his head.

The Hebrideans live mainly in thatched cottages, the oldest and most primitive of which are known as black houses. These, naturally, are numerous in places adapted to cultiva-tion and pasturage—that is to say, along the flat, sandy, coastal belt running down the west side of the Outer Hebrides, and at a level not much above that of the sea. Here one finds the principal machar-lands. Settlements occur on the east coast also; but these tend to be less numerous and more isolated, since the eastern regions are the more mountainous, rising in places to an altitude of over 2,000 feet. Population, as would be expected, is greatest where the soil is richest and most extensive. Thus many of the crofting townships on the western fringe are large and populous, whereas those on the eastern seaboard, or scattered about the fiords penetrating it, are sparsely peopled. A race almost exclusively pastoral in ancient times settled and propagated in communities situated where conditions were most conducive to crofting and herding.

Though the black house is still very common, especially in Lewis and South Uist, it should be mentioned that during the last thirty years many two-storeyed, slated houses have been built throughout the Western Isles, almost entirely with government help. These are cleaner and more sanitary. One or more of them may often be conspicuous in the midst of a township of black houses. From several of the less isolated villages, the black house has disappeared completely, in favour of these newer and more up-to-date homes. They have gone from all the villages on the outskirts of Stornoway, where, at the time of writing, only one thatched cottage now remains, and of a date much more recent than that of the black house.

The Hebridean black house is essentially the product of physical environment. Native stone, of which it is built, is abundant on every hand. Stones and boulders of every shape and size are plentiful, so that no dressing is necessary. The walls of these ancient dwellings are rectangular, or perhaps ovate. They vary in thickness from four feet to six, and are seldom more than six feet in height. As a rule, they consist of two walls, an inner and an outer, the space between them being filled in with earth and small stones, which tend to seal them. The black houses have no gables; and no mortar is used in the walls, which are known as dry-stone. At the corners they are rounded, so as to offer the minimum resistance to the winds for which, especially in wintertime, the Hebrides are notorious.

The wall of an ordinary black house is thus described by Dr. Johnson: " A hut is constructed with loose stones, ranged for the most part with some tendency to circularity. It must be placed where the wind cannot act upon it with violence, because it has no cement; and where the water will run easily away, because it has no floor but the naked ground. The wall, which is commonly about six feet high, declines from the perpendicular a little inward." From this it may be assumed that the black house, as then (*c.* 1773) existing on the Highland mainland, had only a single wall of no great thickness.

The thatched roof of the black house, resting on the top of the walls, has nothing of their durability. Owing to the scarcity of native timber, its rafters are inclined to be slight, except where sturdy driftwood, collected on the beaches after storms, has afforded a material stronger and more lasting. Logs and great tree-trunks from tropical America are often cast upon the Hebridean shores. The thatch is of heather, bracken, or machar-grass—bent-grass. It is seldom of straw, of which the agriculture of the Isles yields little. When, after several years, the home is re-thatched, the old thatch is spread on the ground as manure.

" Houses of venerable age," writes Werner Kissling in a learnèd treatise on the black house, " as well as of comparatively recent construction, with only their double walls of earth and stone, effectively withstand the onslaught of winds, and provide calm and shelter from the violence without. The rounded corners, and, sometimes, end walls which give these houses a rounded-rectangular or ovate-oblong form, leave nothing on the outer surface to catch the wind. Whether or not this ' tendency to circularity ' is to be explained as a stage in development from an earlier type of dwelling in the islands, it is undoubtedly suited to the conditions in a windy district, where man has lost the natural protection of his forests, and is dependent on stormproof shelter."[1]

There are several types and modifications of black houses. In outward appearance, those of Lewis differ much from those of, say, South Uist. The most primitive of them have but a

[1] *The Character and Purpose of the Hebridean Black House,* by Werner Kissling, Dr. Jur., published by the Royal Anthropological Institute of Great Britain and Ireland in 1943.

single apartment. The floor is of earth, and often slopes considerably, owing to a preference for building on a sloping site, rather than upon a cultivable plot of ground. Thus, too, one end of the house is higher than the other. Captain F. Thomas, R.N., that painstaking and thoroughly competent folklorist, who noted so much of sociological interest in the Outer Hebrides, refers to the floor of a ruined black house in Harris in 1869 as being so steep that a cask would have rolled from one end to the other.

To this day, the floor of most of the oldest black houses is at two levels, thus denoting two *de*partments, rather than two *a*partments. Both of these are entered from without by the same door. At the lower level is the byre: at the higher the living-room and bed recesses of the household. With the cow at one end, it is essential that the house should either be erected on a sloping site, or that the floor-level of the byre should be below that of the household's quarters.

The placing of a wooden partition between the byre and the rest of the interior is a fairly recent innovation. Such a partition is seldom carried up as high as the rafters, one reason for this being the desire not to do anything which might look as though the cow were being excluded. Man and beast have sheltered for so many centuries under the same roof in the Outer Hebrides that the Islanders residing in such habitations are loath to shut out the cow, the animal which has meant to them more than any other in their struggle for existence under conditions traditionally backward. "There is a prejudice against shutting out the cow from a view of the fire," wrote Captain Thomas. It must be remembered, moreover, that, even yet, the belief survives among the Hebrideans that their cows are liable to evil influences, such as witchcraft and the Evil Eye, as already noted, and that a sprig of ivy or of bramble may be hung over the lintel of the byre to ward off such influences. So far as the belief in the protective power of fire is concerned, let us again quote Kissling:

"Yet a lingering notion that the fire had the power to repel evil spirits from man and from his domestic animals, which survived in the Hebrides, as in other parts of Christian Europe, down to modern times, may partly account for the disinclination to cut off the cow from the fire. Such ideas, belonging properly to pre-Christian ages, clearly underlay various traditional acts performed with fire as late as the beginning of the nineteenth century, although their originally profane intention seems to have been subordinated to religious thought and ceremony. Fire, which, according to ancient faith, had been the source of its own strength, seems to have been regarded as a mere symbol of divine power, shining with spiritual light, attracting benevolent rather than repelling evil spirits, and inspiring faith and trust in the good. But the people had perhaps not abandoned faith in the fire itself, and were still expecting practical wonders from these supposedly symbolic performances. In venerating their sacred fires, they were no doubt clinging to a form of ceremony which was the product of an older faith. It is thus plausible that the Hebridean did not dare to cut off his animals from the light of the fire, even if he probably had only a vague notion of all that fire was supposed to do in the past. On the other hand, he had a very definite idea of the nature of the evil influences which might affect the cow's life and well-being."[1]

To-day, in the majority of cases, dwelling and byre are no longer under the same roof, though in the remoter townships such may still be found. The byre may adjoin the black house, or may be detached from it at no great distance.

Round the peatfire of many a black house the ceilidh—the "at home" of the Isles—is still held of an evening, especially in winter. At the ceilidh tales are recounted, and folk-songs sung—sung after a fashion.

.   .   .   .

It has often occurred to me as strange that the average Highlander and Islander, leaving the native hearth without any musical appreciation in the sense in which a musician would understand the term, seldom acquires any such appreciation, even after residence in a musical city sometimes extending over two-thirds of a lifetime. This is shown by the enthusiasm displayed at Gaelic and Highland concerts held

[1] *Ibidem.*

in such cities as Edinburgh and Glasgow, the audience, for the most part, being Highland-born, or the relatives and friends of persons Highland-born. Talk of bellowing, well, the biblical bull of Bashan never exercised his vocal organs in tones more raucous than does many a favourite songster at these concerts. How dare anyone discharge, and in the name of singing, the cacophony to be heard at the popular Gaelic concert! The songster is given a resounding applause, and sometimes two or three encores, for an exhibition which, if delivered before an audience the least critical, would be greeted with what is vulgarly called "the bird". With very few exceptions, and for as long as I can remember, the singers at these concerts (I have been familiar with them since I was but three years of age) have indulged in the most astonishing musical liberties, without criticism, without challenge. As for restraint, they do not know the meaning of the word. They bawl and bellow with every atom of their being, the better to eject, as if under high pressure, the noisy matter pent up within them. Would-be singers in the Western Isles perform exactly like this. In their native setting, it does not seem to matter so much. Dolled up on some city platform, however, they are often vulgar and ridiculous.

If they can be excessively noisy on the platform, they can also be excessively silent. Whereas their *fortissimo* notes are apt to shake the building to its foundation, their *pianissimo* efforts the most sensitive ear could not detect behind half a sheet of notepaper.

Treat their performance as a travesty, if you like—as a burlesque; but never let it be said that either performers or audiences are musical. I have seen Mod gold medallists give an exhibition of Gaelic singing from the platform of the Usher Hall, in Edinburgh, and of the City Halls, in Glasgow, that have made non-Gaelic members of the audience wince and squirm. One would think that, far from exercising restraint, the singer's intention was to look as though at any moment he might explode. This unsightliness arises from the Gael's crude belief that the criterion of good singing is volume, and that tunefulness, in-tune-ness, and time are very secondary considerations.

Highland concerts follow a recognised pattern, whether

promoted at home or afield. Their promoters are much given
to platform parties; and herein may often be seen the Gael's
love of patronage. Nothing pleases him better than to have
some titled nonentity in the chair, especially if such a nonentity is likely to bring with him a stylish entourage, in the
presence of which he can be civil and obsequious. The Gael
feels flattered by this. If some duke accept the invitation to
preside at a Highland concert in, say, Edinburgh, the concert's
success is assured, even if the musical level of the vocalists be
no higher than might be expected of a number of casual street-
singers. A duke or a noble lord in the chair supplies just
that glittering nucleus round which the snobs of Gaeldom—
and they are numerous—gather as do wasps round the honey-
pot.

Of course, one can easily endear oneself anywhere, if one
have plenty of money, and care to undertake a little patronis-
ing. The Scottish Celts, in their love of patronage, have
remained essentially feudal. They grasp, in the most naïve
manner, the flimsiest pretext for demonstrating an obsequious
loyalty to royalty; and, like all peoples preponderately peasant
in outlook, they worship money and titles.

A minimum of three persons is necessary to adorn the platform, though, as a rule, the platform party is an august one,
certainly so far as numbers are concerned. I have known as
many as two hundred in the case of concerts held in the St.
Andrew's Hall, Glasgow, a favourite place of assembly for the
several Highland and Island societies in that city. Three, as
I say, is a minimum—a *workable* minimum.

The proceedings begin at least a quarter of an hour after
the advertised time, when one of the three, usually wearing
the kilt, rises to introduce, as laboriously as he can, the chairman. (As if anyone present did not already know the chairman and all his very excellent qualities!) Throughout the
concert, though every member of the audience may have a
copy of the programme in his hand, the chairman announces
each item in turn, adding, as the spirit moves him, some
platitudinous comment of his own. The proceedings are
brought to a warm and heart-felt close when the third member of the platform party rises to thank the chairman for his
splendid behaviour in the chair, and for having been so good

—so *very* good—as to have travelled such a long distance to grace us with his presence. Number Three performs this rite religiously, making his motion for the vote of thanks as profuse, as profound, and as protracted as he possibly can, this being the mover's own part as one of the essential performers of the evening. What with votes of thanks here and votes of thanks there, it never seems to occur to anyone that a vote of thanks may sometimes be due to the audience for having sat peacefully throughout much musical discord, as well as a good deal of banality. But, then, one must remember that the majority of the audience loves this kind of thing, and never wants to listen to anything finer. It is completely in accord with the accepted standard for a public performance. Sensitive people, however, who, whether by design or by accident, find their way into the midst of such a large, carefree, uncritical family party, can scarcely look at the human exhibits. The sight of them, added to the unmusical sounds they emit, is as much as the discerning concert-goer can endure.

In recent years, one must remark, it has been found advisable not to confine the programme entirely to Gaelic folk. Thus many a concert has been redeemed through the inclusion of items by such fine artistes as the late George Campbell and the late Robert Burnett. To such singers as these, the Gaelic element in the audience accords a luke-warm reception. The non-Gaelic element, however, usually knows better.

Audiences on such occasions are much given to encoring. Thus it is usual to state on the printed programme that no encores can be permitted during the first half. This ruling the chairman, already getting a little long-winded, underlines in his opening remarks, promising, however, that during the latter half those who have paid for admission can have as many encores as the artistes may be prepared to give. As the printed programme begins to get exhausted, the concert tends to deteriorate into a sing-song, in which the audience itself is invited to join. The favourite songster retains his place in the hearts of his audience by selecting for his encores well-known songs, in the choruses of which the audience can participate lustily. To this piece of simple psychology, our

Highland and Island audiences always respond heartily, both with uplifted voice and with their beating feet, the latter often drowning completely the former.

Encores are demanded uproariously as a rule. The clapping of hands can barely be heard for shrill, deafening whistling, and for the din created when half the audience's feet are stamping the concert-hall floor in the traditional way which the Gael loves dearly.

But why should I be so ungenerous as to criticise thus, when I know how the audience revels in this kind of thing? I do so entirely in the interests of art, and in the interests of artistes who perform well, yet can scarcely make a living. Perhaps one should be more charitable in the matter of these Highland concerts, and regard them as domestic rather than professional, though quite good fees are paid to these unmusical songsters—vocalists they are called on placard and programme! I think a well-known concert accompanist in Edinburgh was correct when, recently, he answered my criticism by saying that I appeared to have the fanciful notion that the promoters of Gaelic concerts, even in a city like Edinburgh, were the least interested either in culture, or in what musical people would regard as an artistic performance.

An indispensable feature of the evening's proceedings is the generous interval at half-time. To this concession the "drouths" always look forward, since it enables them to slip out to the neighbouring pubs before closing-time. Meanwhile, the less drouthy members of the audience move freely and informally about the hall, speaking to their friends, many of whom they have not seen for a long time.

The opportunity of paying a visit to the pub during a public performance is an established right north of the Tweed; and many a Gael would be furious if it were denied him. Indeed, if a glance at his watch were to show that the first half of the programme was likely to run over its time, out of the hall he will stamp before the interval, unable to endure any longer his boredom and his thirst. I have witnessed as many as a score of men make a noisy exit in this way, quite indifferent to the feelings of the performer and of the remainder of the audience. And I have been present when, in an endeavour to rejoin their womenfolk during the

208

ABOVE: *Ruins of Ormacleit Castle, South Uist*
BELOW: *Castle St. Clair, Isle of Barra*

second half, these tipsy fellows have straggled back to the hall even more noisily. In Scotland this is by no means unusual at concerts, especially when Gaels are present in numbers.

The Highlander's love of whisky, as a rule, is uppermost on such occasions. The temporary sobriety enforced by his attendance at a concert, while the pubs are open, is often more than he can bear. But he sometimes makes up for it afterwards, when the concert is over. It is then that the *real* Celtic revelries begin. It is then that many an "artiste", male or female, adjourns with friends for the prolonged carousal in which alcohol supplies the main attraction. I hope no one will be so foolhardy as to contradict me on all this, for I write with some inside knowledge of what goes on, having been associated with Highland and Island affairs since infancy.

In my view, musical appreciation is always lowest in districts where pianos are scarcest. Music and a musical sense are more dependent upon the piano than upon any other instrument, although my own father, who never got much beyond the primitive musical standard of appreciation obtaining in the Highlands and Islands, or for that matter in any area populated almost exclusively by peasantry, always insisted that the criterion of musicality was whether a person liked or disliked the bagpipes! He who chose the pipes as the instrument he would listen to before all others was regarded by my father as having the best possible musical taste. Others plump for the melodeon, or for the fiddle, which is usually played out of tune in Celtic Scotland, where a good ear is looked upon as being unnecessary to musicianship. True, a few pianos may be found among the northern Celts, but nine-tenths of these are out of tune, and have been so for at least a quarter of a century. In addition, two or three notes have been permanently silenced by age, neglect, or rough usage. Pianos in these parts are inclined to be regarded as nice pieces of furniture, upon which the youngsters of the household, as a very special treat, are permitted to strum from time to time.

Let me add that I am by no means unsupported in my attitude to music as understood and executed (one might sometimes be justified in saying "perpetrated") by the

ABOVE: *Thatching operations, Isle of Eriskay*
BELOW: *The Old and the New at Tangusdale, Barra*

Scottish Gaels. Periodically, one reads in the correspondence columns of our Scottish newspapers the same strictures by critics well-informed on musical matters, and often highly qualified in that field. A spate of such criticism usually follows the annual Mod, an institution which is held under the auspices of An Cumunn Gaidhealach, and is the Gaelic counterpart to the Welsh Eisteddfod. I have before me a letter-to-the-editor which appeared recently in our principal Highland newspaper,[1] and in which the correspondent, commenting on the standard of singing at a Gaelic concert in Edinburgh, during the International Musical Festival held there in the autumn of 1947, raises the question of how far the singers were able to sing in accordance with the recognised canons of the art, excluding altogether the matter of general musicianship. "Since I came to Lochaber over three years ago," he writes, "I have been puzzled and concerned at the almost entire lack of any general musical development in the Highlands. Unexpected enlightenment on this point came to me a few days ago, when I was speaking to a young singer who had competed successfully at local Mods. I asked if she sang any songs other than Gaelic ones, and the answer was 'No'. She had been told that singing any other than Gaelic songs would spoil her as a Gaelic singer. If this attitude is general, and I have every reason to assume that it is, to my mind it accounts largely for the lamentable lack of musical development in the Highlands to-day. . . . Until such time as Gaelic singers generally realise that the widening of their musical horizon would vastly increase their possibilities as Gaelic singers, the present low standard of musical achievement will persist."

With every word of this I agree. So long as these songsters believe that Gaelic singing, and pretty crude singing at that, is the be-all and end-all of musical achievement, we shall have uncritical, undiscerning audiences applauding Gaelic folk-songs rendered in a manner which would not be tolerated in any other country. We would not give a hearing to the singer who rendered, in the way in which the Gaels render theirs, the folk-songs belonging to any other people in the world. What would we say if a Hungarian song, for instance, were

[1] The *Oban Times*, 13th September, 1947.

sung in public as the average Gaelic song is sung in public, and actually broadcast?

In short, performer and audience are fully satisfied with the naïve standards of the homely ceilidh. No one at a ceilidh, when asked to contribute a song, suffers from a surfeit of shyness. On the contrary, the request is acceded to with a degree of confidence liable to embarrass the stranger who may be present, though, if he be the least musical, he may be still more embarrassed while the request is being complied with. This primitive screeching and caterwauling may be all right round the peatfire of a winter's evening; but one must surely take exception to its being transferred, remuneratively, to the cities, there to be accorded professional status.

A ceilidh (pronounced *kay'-lee*) is simply a social gathering of friends and neighbours held of an evening in one's own house. We talk of going ceilidhing to such and such a house, or on such and such a person. The evening is spent in conversation, in the telling of tales, and in the spontaneous singing of songs by anyone present. Sometimes a fiddle or a melodeon, or even the bagpipes, may be introduced to lend variety.

Though this institution survives in the remoter parts, it is gradually being superseded in the more accessible, where alternative forms of entertainment are available. Nowadays, even in the Western Isles, the preference is for entertainment given in return for a cash payment. The box-office has a greater attraction than has the peatfire. The picture-house and the dance-hall are now preferred to the ceilidh, where admission is free and unrestricted, and where refreshments are often so lavishly and generously provided. Easy money in recent years, and the enormous increase in the motor-bus services in an island like Lewis, have made it possible for all who are not too old and decrepit to visit the picture-house at Stornoway, when, formerly, they would have been satisfied with creating their own entertainment in their own or in somebody else's home. In other words, the popularity of the ceilidh continued so long as the rural population remained isolated from commercial forms of amusement. The children are the chief patrons of the pictures in Stornoway. Their papas prefer the pubs.

For many a generation, dancing was frowned upon in the Highlands and Islands. Indeed, in these parts the Free Church of Scotland, and also the Free Presbyterians and the Seceders, still frown upon it, and may even summon an elder to explain his attendance at a dance. In the remoter parts of Ross-shire and Sutherland, and in the non-Catholic isles of the Hebrides, where these denominations predominate, a communicant is frequently haled before the kirk-session to answer for such conduct, such un-Godliness, such truck with things satanic. From time to time such cases are reported in the press.

In the autumn of 1944, as widely reported in the Scottish newspapers, the Free Church Presbytery of Lewis called on the Free Church Presbytery of Edinburgh to constrain Mr. W. Rounsfell Brown, one of the leading lay members of the Church, to withdraw a statement he had made at the previous General Assembly, a statement " in which he insinuated that secular dancing is not an evil to be repented of ". The Free Church Presbytery also declared that, although the Y.M.C.A. "encourages this form of sinful pleasure", Mr. Brown insinuated that this was not a sufficient reason why the Free Church should dissociate itself from the Y.M.C.A.

The Free Church Presbytery of Lewis, dissociating itself entirely from Mr. Brown's views, claimed that these views were not supported publicly by any other member of the Assembly.

The customary practice in the courts of the Free Church of Scotland towards any member "indulging in this form of worldly amusement", it was stated, "is to bring him or her under disciplinary action".

In Presbyterian Lewis, and likewise in Harris and in North Uist, there are still hundreds of natives who discountenance everything to do with dancing. They regard dancing as immoral, in the narrow, sexual sense, or at all events as conducive to sexual intercourse. Well, of course it is! There's no denying that it stimulates the desires, whether indulged in by primitive or by civilised peoples.

Most dancing, to a greater or less degree, denotes a people's temperament and sexual life. Mating dances are prevalent throughout the world, among both aboriginal and so-called

civilised races. It is doubtful how much dancing, except
perhaps the Greek, which is on a much higher intellectual
plane, is not fundamentally sexual. Certainly, modern
dancing, like modern dance-band music, both of which have
invaded us from the Americas, is negroid in origin and sexual
in suggestion. Take, for instance, the Bunny Hug, the
Charleston, the Woogie-Woogie, the Conga, the Rumba,
Bumps-a-Daisy, or the Black Bottom. These are primitive,
and primarily sexual.

But why should the narrow and bigoted, the holy and
censorious, object on moral grounds merely to dancing?
Other things, even in the Western Isles, are also conducive
to sexual intercourse between unmarried persons, which is
the only form of immorality the bigoted and censorious can
think of. The most notorious drunkards are often those who,
in the name of religion and of morality, are loudest in their
condemnation of dancing.

The Roman Catholics of South Uist and Benbecula, however, take a much broader view on such matters than do the
Protestants, and with results no more commendable. Their
chief social events are the local dances held throughout the
year, except during the summer, when some at least are too
preoccupied with their crofting duties. At Balivannich, in
Benbecula, stands the splendid gymnasium built for the air
force personnel stationed there during the recent war, when
the government constructed the great aerodrome which, to-
day, serves as Benbecula's civil airport. The war thus provided the island with excellent accommodation for public
functions. Dances at Balivannich are, therefore, very frequent
—*too* frequent, one would be justified in saying. Two or
three a week is the rule in Benbecula and in South Uist,
islands which, for this and for similar purposes, may be
regarded as a continuation of one another, now that the South
Ford has been bridged. With the increase in the Outer Isles
of motor transport, and the consequent ease with which one
may hire a bus at any time of the day or night, to travel quite
considerable distances—from Lochboisdale to Balivannich, for
instance, or in the opposite direction, a distance of at least
twenty-five miles—these dances have become more and more
popular and frequent. They seldom begin much before

10 p.m.; and it may even be an hour later. They go on with unabated fervour until three or four in the morning. The music is supplied solely by local musicians playing fiddle and drum, melodeon or concertina, and the bigpipes. The last mentioned is the only instrument to the music of which reels can be danced properly. The musicians, throughout the evening, beat time loudly with their feet, following the practice of Highland audiences when songs are being sung. They cannot resist the habit of beating out the rhythm. This they do noisily.

Prime favourite among the dances is the Highland schottische. In Benbecula it is danced with terrific abandon. All the old, square dances still hold their own in the Islands. Reels are danced with amazing vigour, if not too accurately. One sees in the reels something primitive and splendid—something which makes the onlooker wonder how the graceful patterns of the foursome and the eightsome originated.

The Islanders in their choice of dances are by no means conservative. They like English and foreign dances too. A slow waltz may be announced to enable the dancers to cool down after the exertions and excitement of an encored eightsome. You ought to see them dance the Boston Two-step in Benbecula, to music supplied by one of the dancers who has brought his pipes with him, in order to afford the island's recognised dance-orchestra (a father playing a very complicated accordion, and a son tapping dexterously on a jazz-band drum) a break for refreshments and for a smoke!

Doubtless, it is true these dances afford the occasion for much promiscuity. On the other hand, promiscuity would take place *somewhere* in any case, since morals, in the sexual sense, are extremely lax in the Western Isles, as we shall see when we come to dealing with illegitimacy, which has always been rampant in the Highlands and Islands. An island clergyman told me the other day that, during a dance held recently in a village school, a young woman, who was little more than a schoolgirl, suddenly quitted the floor to hurry out into the darkness. In the school-children's latrine, a little later, she gave birth to a baby. No one in the island seemed to think there was anything to complain about in this. It was looked upon as being quite normal. The natives treated the incident in the usual casual manner, their only regret being that the poor girl hadn't had sufficient warning to have enabled the birth to occur in surroundings a little more comfortable!

Even the most superficial reader will be inclined to ask himself what prospect for betterment there can be in communities where this sort of thing is regarded as quite natural and normal, and whether something ought not to be done before further vast sums of public money are spent upon the Islands. When he has read what I now have to say about bastardy, he will ask himself the question with increased concern.

Closely bound up with the problem of population and subsistence in the Isles is illegitimacy. Bastardy has long been common—nay, notorious—in the Highlands and Islands; and certainly, so far as the Outer Hebrides are concerned, its incidence shows no decline. It is prevalent in the Protestant isles: it is even more so in the Roman Catholic. Whereas in the former, for a time at any rate, it is apt to carry a social stigma, in the latter it tends to be regarded as normal, and might almost be said to be no more the exception than it is the rule. Let us examine the position in Benbecula, where I made some personal investigations last autumn. In that island, with a population of between nine hundred and a thousand, roughly one half of which is Catholic and the other half Protestant, it is often difficult to know who was born in wedlock and who was not. In Benbecula, at the present time, there are unmarried women with as many as half-a-dozen bastard children, each by a different father. I cannot but believe that persons dealing in official capacities with the Isles are aware of this; and one does not require a university education to be able to deduce the social and economic consequences of such a state of affairs.

While the Church of Scotland, which, of course, is Presbyterian, deplores all this, the Catholic Church would appear to do little to discourage it. Indeed, it may even be said to turn a blind eye. Furthermore, the Church of Rome is rigorously opposed to the use of contraceptives. Investigation has shown that illegitimacy in the Western Isles is proportionately higher among the Roman Catholics than it is among the Protestants. This may be due, in part at least, to the Catholic

Church's official pronouncement on contraceptives, and to its more lenient attitude towards bastardy.

What one finds in Benbecula in this connection may also be found in South Uist. A Protestant clergyman in the Outer Hebrides, with whom I discussed this problem recently, assured me that it is wellnigh impossible to enter a house in the Roman Catholic islands where there is not at least one bastard. This statement, as I found from subsequent enquiries at other sources, was true, and was in no way inspired by animosity toward the Catholic Church. The only point to be considered is whether it is true or not. I am convinced that it *is* true; and I consider myself a reasonably accurate investigator and observer.

In these communities, sexual life begins early. Girls have scarcely left school when pregnancy sets in. This condition of affairs may be attributed to a number of causes. The housing position is largely responsible. It must be borne in mind that the Hebrides have their housing problem, which is just as acute as in many densely populated urban areas. One cannot expect children to have much reserve or restraint in sexual matters where, as with tinkers, numbers of them occupy and sleep in the same small apartment, if not actually in the same bed, as that in which their parents cohabit freely. There is risk of incest under such conditions.

It does not follow, of course, that improvements in housing would necessarily reduce the incidence of illegitimacy. To accommodate, respectably, such large families as are to be found in South Uist, for instance, quite large houses would be required; and, as matters are administered at present, the taxpayer cannot be expected to find even greater sums of money for these wholly unremunerative—nay, increasingly burdensome—islands.

So many people huddled together, and often unable to venture far from the cottage doorstep for several consecutive days, owing to the wind and rain, drowsing over the peatfire, or lying about on their none too salubrious beds, cannot but fall to casual sexual intercourse, as do people similarly situated elsewhere in the world. Bad housing is largely responsible for early and indiscriminate mating.

The general standard of morality is low in the Western Isles. By morality I mean morality in the wide sense, and not merely in the narrow, sexual sense. This state of affairs is due largely to a complete absence of public opinion—at any rate, an absence of that public opinion which, in more civilised communities, tends to restrain the evil-doer. The Isles are wholly wanting in this. Not even in the town of Stornoway is there any trace of it. The want of a civic sense accounts for much that is wrong, and that cannot be rectified without it.

A good deal of mischief arises from loafing, and from lounging in groups, as does so much of the youth of these islands. Loafing and lounging are common even in the rural villages. The corner-boys are by no means confined to the big cities. They are numerous throughout the Hebrides. Stornoway has an abundance of them. So also have Tarbert and Castlebay. Indeed, they are to be found wherever there is any concentration of peasant population having neither hobbies nor interests when the day's routine is over. But many of these loafers have no daily routine. They are a species of spiv, never doing a hand's turn at any time.

Cross-roads in the Isles are a favourite rendezvous for such members of society. So, too, are pubs, post-offices, and the local shops at which, after the mail-steamer has called, the more sensational newspapers are to be had. At Castlebay, for instance, long after dark, and often an hour or two after the steamer has landed the mails, those living within a mile or two of the post-office congregate at its closed door, and hang about there until the entire mails for Barra and the adjacent isles have been sorted. Thus it is possible to obtain one's correspondence the day before the postman is due to resume his rounds. I myself have often waited in this way, and found it very tiresome, very boring. The Islanders, so many of whom are inured to hanging about, would seem to enjoy it, on the other hand, even when there is but slight prospect of there being a letter for them. There they stand, in furtive groups, against the post-office walls and door, chatting, chaffing, smoking, spitting, swearing, blaspheming, and not infrequently giving off alcoholic fumes. A swearing drunkard among them is by no means uncommon; and, indeed, there may even be two or three. These help to provide entertainment until such time as those with their ears to the post-office door detect the footsteps of the postmaster or of his assistant, as he approaches from within to unlock the door and allow the flood to burst in. Then it is that the Islanders, with one mighty rush, carrying strangers as well as neighbours with them, press like a lot of stampeding animals at a ship's gangway. The pressure is in no way lessened at the counter. If you should be among the first to enter, and unaccustomed to this unfailing and often unpleasant demonstration of bad manners, the weight of the herd behind you would soon crush the breath out of you. The herd instinct is strong in the Islanders. Only in a very narrow sense can they be said to be individualists.

No one the least liable to panic or to claustrophobia should risk being caught up in such a scrimmage round the post-office door, especially on a rainless evening, when the crushing is inclined to be so great that only the soundest in wind and limb can withstand it. Since everybody, old and young alike, knows everybody else, the stranger in their midst on such occasions is usually the object of much speiring, much curiosity and guess-work. Indeed, if, unbeknown to them, he have the Gaelic, he is pretty certain to hear about himself some truly uncomplimentary remarks! The few older and better mannered natives stand patiently on the fringe, disinclined to make for the post-office counter until the rude and unruly mob has abated.

Lounging and loafing have become usual also among young women and girls. During the war, more than one correspondent to the local press remarked on the number of young girls, hardly in their teens, to be seen lounging and smoking of an evening in the doorways of Cromwell Street, Stornoway's principal thoroughfare and shopping centre. " I believe in the rights of women," wrote one of them. " They have as much right to smoke as men; but I think it is time for action when large numbers of young lassies begin to smoke at an age when boys, if they smoke at all, do so furtively, and in fear of parental punishment. The difference between Stornoway and Glasgow is that in the city there are many girls living in lodgings, and out of all control; but in Stornoway all these girls are living at home, and should be subject to family discipline, if their parents care to exercise it."

The same writer drew attention to the way in which, after 11 p.m. each night, a group of young girls of school age went marching through the town, screaming a song the refrain of which was "But these bloody airmen are no bloody good". This familiar serenade showed a complete lack of parental control, and also how little influence narrow, sectarian religion has in matters of public behaviour. Stornoway is full of pious people, adhering to narrow and narrowing denominations, who make no effort whatsoever to curtail such conduct on the part of young people. How can one expect the pious to make any effort when one realises that many of these girls are the daughters of the pious who are habitually emerging from the pubs in a state of intoxication?

Nowhere does one realise more forcefully than in the Western Isles how much the future of the race depends on the proper use of leisure. A populace which can find so much time for gadding and lounging, and is so completely devoid of ideas as to how spare time might be spent usefully, must necessarily become increasingly burdensome to the nation, increasingly dependent upon grants and other forms of public charity.

The Islander on the rampage shows respect neither for persons nor for property. He will often assault his neighbour, even to the effusion of blood, or steal or damage his property, without any sense of shame, and quite often with impunity. Where there is no public opinion, there can be no concerted attempt to curb such lawlessness. When a crofter or a labourer assaults his wife (such cases are very frequent) little can be done about it, for the wife is either too timid or too ignorant to ensure that he does not do so again. I have known serious cases of assault where no proceedings followed. Such excesses are frequently the result of drink, the prime curse of the Highlands and Islands for some centuries now. Drunkenness is so common that no one—not even the police—seems to regard it as anything to take exception to. I shall have much to say on drink in our next chapter.

The only person in the community for whom the inhabitants would appear to have retained even a semblance of deference and respect is the sheriff; and the Islanders would,

indeed, be obsequious with *him* if he gave them the chance!
There is a sheriff-substitute at Lochmaddy and one at
Stornoway. Successive holders of this office have been obliged
to remain aloof from the populace. In a town like Stornoway,
there happens to be no social circle with which the unhappy
sheriff can associate without at once losing caste and authority.
Sociability in which he might become involved would bring
him too closely into touch with the merchants and their wives,
any of whom might have to appear before him on some charge
or other, though it is astonishing how seldom the better-to-do
inhabitants have charges preferred against them, for it is
doubtful whether they are any more law-abiding than are
their relatives, the ordinary crofters. With impunity, they
play all sorts of mean and despicable tricks on one another.
If they had recourse to the law every time they considered
their honour had been impuned, the sheriff-court would constantly be filled with pots calling kettles black!

The appointment of sheriff at Stornoway can be a very
lonely one, as I know from one or two friends of my own, who
have gone there in that capacity. They have found it advisable to keep at a distance even the few professional people in
the islands, most of whom are natives and remain essentially
peasant in outlook and behaviour. Even the local bailies
would scarcely be fit company for the sheriff. If, as the chief
officer of the crown, the sheriff permitted himself to get in tow
with the *élite* of the islands, he would soon be unable to discharge his duties. Certainly, he would be feared no longer;
and, in the complete absence of the more civilised sanctions,
it is perhaps necessary that he should remain feared as well
as respected. Otherwise, what authority would he have when
dealing with the miscreants brought before him?

For other people's property, movable or immovable, there
is remarkably little respect in the Western Isles. Towards
public property there exists an attitude of vandalism. "The
problem of vandalism is a big one," said one of Stornoway's
bailies recently. "And it is on the increase," added one of
the town councillors. This is adequately borne out by a
reference to the files of the *Stornoway Gazette*. Let me quote
some cases reported and commented upon in recent years in
that sober journal.

Vigorous comments were occasioned by a report of extensive damage done to the public conveniences on South Beach Street quay, at Stornoway, when, during one of the usual Saturday-night brawls, thirty men were drinking, fighting, swearing, and breaking bottles. "It is a reflection on the community," Commissioner MacIver observed, "that, when a public body went to the cost of erecting a modern convenience, they had also to put people in charge to make sure that the place was not wrecked."

In looking through some *Stornoway Gazette* cuttings I have in my possession, I find that, at any rate so far as such cases were reported in that newspaper, 1944 was a bumper year for vandalism. The burgh surveyor complained at a meeting of the Stornoway town council that the new parking sign in Shell Street had not been erected a week before it was twisted round, and that, on the same night as this damage was committed, four tobies and three gullies were thrown over the sea-wall at Newton, the old part of the town. At the same meeting the provost complained that sheep had got into one of the manor farm parks, and had eaten the corn. The farm manager had acted promptly. He had rounded up twenty of the sheep, and had coöperated with the police in having them taken to the pound. Ten minutes after they had been impounded, they were out at the other end of the pound, where it had been tampered with. The posts, the burgh surveyor stated, had been wrenched out of the ground, and the wires raised and tied up in that position.

What these vandals cannot remove by stealing, they will assuredly destroy. Witness, in support of this accusation, the damage they do to the furnishings of their own mail-boat! When they cannot make off with the saloon cushions, they rip them with knives! A lady told the Ross Police Committee a year or two ago that no kind of movable property is safe. Neither bulk nor weight, she observed, is any guarantee of inviolability; "and, once the theft has been committed, nothing more is heard about it".

A mainland newspaper, commenting on local affairs in Lewis in the summer of 1944, mentioned that the Territorial Drill Hall in Stornoway had been broken into more than once, and that this was not surprising when one recalled the vandalism committed at the Lewis War Memorial, situated on the outskirts of the town. The town councillors were alleged to have been shocked when the disgraceful condition of this memorial was brought to their notice that summer. One of them recalled that, a few years earlier, the whole place had been renovated after a previous desecration, and that now "the door and windows were broken, and the place was in a mess".

The Outer Hebrides provide us with some first-class examples of desecration. A visitor to the old cemetery at Gress, not far from Stornoway, found that, where the grave-stones had leaded letters, the lead had been removed with a pen-knife or other sharp instrument. Some of the tombstones belonging to his own family had been tampered with in this way. When making enquiries in the hope of tracing the vandals, he learnt that the lead had been removed to serve as sinkers for fishing-lines!

In 1944 a correspondent to the *Stornoway Gazette* reminded us that exactly the same thing occurred some years previously, when lead was taken for the same purpose from the war memorial at Eorapie, near the Butt of Lewis. Thus it is no longer possible to read the inscription which might have reminded future generations of how the men of Lewis gave their lives in the First World War, which they did in enormous numbers.

In post-office circles, the Western Isles have an unenviable reputation on account of the wilful damage continually being done to various installations and fixtures. More damage is done to telegraph insulators in these islands than anywhere else in the United Kingdom. Boys and youths are principally responsible for this. Sunday afternoon is regarded as the favourite time for insulator-breaking in Lewis and Harris, a part of the country where the numerous Protestant non-Conformists, at the slightest hint of a boat or of a train being run on the Seventh Day, or of an aeroplane landing in their midst, protest vociferously against the breaking of the Sabbath! Sabbatarianism in the Protestant isles of the Hebrides can take some extreme forms. I remember my being present on one of the quays at Stornoway one Monday morning some years ago, when a herring-drifter came into port with a catch. Owing to the hostile attitude displayed by other fishermen assembled on the quay at the time, the drifter's crew did not attempt to land the catch, but cast off at once and sailed for one of the mainland ports. The reason for the hostility shown to the drifter's crew was that it was suspected of having caught the fish the previous Sunday night! It seems a pity that those, who are so punctilious in such matters, cannot bring their Sabbatarian influence to bear when it comes to damaging public property and destroying public amenities.

No amount of warning as to how serious might be the consequences of interfering wantonly with the telegraph system makes any impression. The smashing of insulators continues on a grand scale. That men's lives may be lost through this destruction means nothing to the Vandals of the Isles.

The condition of the telephone kiosks erected in recent years is now giving the post-office authorities anxiety. Indeed, they have threatened to remove certain kiosks altogether, if malicious damage to them should continue. At a meeting of the Stornoway town council, at which an appeal was made to the ratepayers to coöperate in protecting the town's kiosks, it was stated that the same kind of thing happens where housing schemes are in progress. Local vandals, in invading partly built houses, remove or destroy the fittings, wrench the woodwork out of its place, break windows and window-frames, twist metal work until it is useless, and so on.

So rife was this type of vandalism in the autumn of 1947, that, as widely reported in the press, the town council of Stornoway had to ask the police to make a more adequate patrol of the burgh at nights. At the council's new block of houses at Manor Park, railings were being wrecked, and newly planted trees uprooted.

The state into which the kiosks and public conveniences get is often not much worse than that of the streets. Refuse is put out anywhere and anyhow; and pavements and gutters are often littered in a most unsanitary manner with garbage, entrails, and offal. It is nothing unusual to see in the gutter of a Stornoway street a sheep's head newly decapitated, and perhaps a few bleeding trotters. What with this, with bluebottles all over the food in the shops, and with the Islanders' general indifference to sanitary standards, it is amazing that there has been no serious epidemic in recent years. The town's refuse-dump must be one of the least salubrious and most unsightly spots in the world.

Stornoway is a town distinguished by what Shakespeare described as "a very ancient and fish-like smell". This is particularly true during a low ebb, when much of its primitive drainage comes to the surface. It is essentially a place of odours, most of them offensive, a few of them pleasant. Probably the pleasantest is that diffused through the town when the kippering-sheds at Newton are busy, sending forth from their ventilated roofs the smoke of smouldering wood shavings. A pleasant smell indeed, when wafted across the bay to greet the wanderer returning by the mail-boat. It is almost as nostalgic as is the scent of peat-reek.

To the Rev. Canon Meaden of St. Peter's Episcopal Church at Stornoway must be assigned the credit for having made the only serious effort in the Western Isles to mitigate these excesses, certainly so far as the boys and youths of Stornoway are concerned. The erection in 1909 of the hall now used by the Stornoway Sea Cadet Corps, which he founded in 1912, and which he still directs, marked an entirely new departure in the public life of the community. Until then, no organised effort had been made in this part of Scotland to cope with the great problem of how to occupy the leisure hours of youth in places which, to an exceptional extent, needed healthy occupation, discipline, and training. Since 1912, the hall has been in daily use, with the result that hundreds of men now scattered throughout the world look back with grateful appreciation to the happy hours spent there, and to the many useful things learnt within its walls. If other members of the clergy in these parts had done something along these lines, or had even coöperated, instead of piously burying themselves in a narrow theology based upon a belief in the everlasting flames of hell, the standard of conduct among adults, as well as juveniles, might have been higher. Canon Meaden has ploughed this difficult furrow almost entirely unsupported by the rest of the Island clergy.

In a recent annual report of the Stornoway Sea Cadet Corps, attention was drawn to the fact that, not only had the Ter-

224

Looking seaward down Loch Resort, at Crolà.
The territory on the left is Harris

ritorial drill hall and a number of ammunition dumps in Stornoway been broken into, but that, on no fewer than three occasions, the same boys had forced an entry into the Sea Cadets' hall, thus necessitating considerable expenditure on repairs, as well as on measures to prevent a recurrence of this lawlessness. "A great deal of foolish talk is heard about the cause of so much juvenile delinquency," runs a passage in that report; "and equally foolish remedies are proposed for curing it. The cause is perfectly obvious, namely, the complete failure of so many parents to make the smallest effort to control their children."

That matters were not improving is shown by this extract from the following year's report: "The difficulties referred to in the last report are not in any way lessened; and, apart from the utter indifference of a great many parents as to the proper control of their children, quite a lot of uniform is actually taken out of the Island by boys leaving the Corps, and it is most difficult to recover this stolen property. Talking—official or unofficial—will never improve matters; but, if parents who neglect their duties by allowing children to wander about at night, breaking into buildings, could be treated in the same way as if they had neglected to feed them, a rapid change would take place."

. . . .

In such matters as poaching, the natives of the Western Highlands and Islands have never recognised any standards but their own somewhat arbitrary ones. They feel no compunction about poaching, nor about committing, in other ways, offences regarded by the law as tantamount to stealing. A dual morality pervades their lives. They like to imagine that they honour God's laws, but that they are entitled to flout, whenever they can, such laws as their rather pliable consciences find it convenient to describe as man-made. Yet, no section of the king's subjects is louder in wail and protest when, to *its* disadvantage, others behave arbitrarily. The Islanders' attitude to poaching is clearly shown in a book written recently by an old friend of mine, the Very Reverend Norman MacLean, D.D., a past Moderator of the General Assembly of the Church of Scotland, and for many years minister of St. Cuthbert's Parish Church, Edinburgh. Refer-

October sundown at Creagorry, Isle of Benbecula

ring to an incident during the Evictions in the eighteen-eighties, and known as the Battle of the Braes, Dr. MacLean, a Skyeman, brought up at Braes, near Portree, and now living in retirement in his native Isle of Skye, writes: "That day in April, 1882, was the most tense I have experienced in a long lifetime. There was not a more law-abiding community in the Three Kingdoms than we were, and yet six of our number were dragged, hungry, insufficiently clad, unwashed, through a storm of wind and rain, walking seven miles to Portree, there placed in prison cells; and there these six men were, who had done no injury and broken no law. For, mark you, taking a salmon from a river, a grouse from the moor, or a deer from the high hills, was never a crime in the eyes of their race. God alone made these, and by His bounty they were fed, and He had not handed them over as a monopoly to any man. We carefully distinguished between man-made laws and God-made laws; and the latter we held inviolate. As for the man-made laws, we never deemed it a dishonour to anyone to disregard them; but we were hitherto careful to keep to the windward of these manufactured laws. No doubt in England, poachers had been sent to Botany Bay, but never in our Island. Deeply devout and most religious men would come home in the morning with a gleaming salmon; and having carefully cut off the dorsal fin before reaching their house, would afterwards declare solemnly, 'I have not taken a fin home this year'. We were, in very truth, a pious, God-fearing community; and it stabbed us to the heart that our neighbours should now be in a prison. Shivering, soaked to the skin, in these cells, which so far had only sheltered tinkers and drunks. It was intolerable."[1]

Generally speaking, this attitude to game persists throughout the Western Isles, where, for a variety of reasons, it is impracticable to maintain a sufficient number of keepers to curtail its results. Except, perhaps, the ministers, all sections of the community—crofters, shopkeepers, local officials, and professional men—poach with gusto, and usually with impunity. Who ever heard of a doctor being prosecuted in the Hebrides for poaching? A crofter, however, sometimes finds himself standing before the sheriff on this charge.

[1] *The Former Days*, by Norman MacLean. (Hodder & Stoughton, 1945.)

It is not uncommon after dark to see, or at any rate to hear, the local doctor sneaking off with the local postmaster on a poaching expedition in the former's car. Most native-born doctors indulge in a bit of poaching, a favourite activity of peasantry. The urge to poach is in the blood. Fanciful tales of wicked landlords dead a hundred years have perpetuated the tradition that the practice is perfectly legitimate. Even doctors imported from the mainland, and now permanently resident in the Isles, have succumbed to the temptation. The car has greatly facilitated this form of stealing in recent years, much to the deprivation and disappointment of the shooting or fishing tenant who, unaware at the outset of ways in the Isles, pays a stiff rent for bags he seldom gets. The keepers are helpless. The most they can do is to divest themselves of gruff imprecations—imprecations such as those uttered by MacAulay, the keeper in Neil Gunn's *Morning Tide.* "You wass after the saamons, you puggers! " MacAulay would say when he came upon poachers by the water's edge.

Personally, I regard our game laws as antiquated; but I also hold that, so long as there are such laws, the person paying for shootings or fishings, often exorbitantly, has cause for grievance when he arrives to find that land and water, alike, have already been denuded. Poaching, like drinking, is largely looked upon in the Highlands and Islands as being gallant and manly. No male is considered manly who does not *take a dram*, as the saying is! That is to say, a great number of drams, habitually! The more drams, the more manly! And there are few activities in which the Highland and Island peasantry indulges with so great an idea of personal prowess as that which deprives the shooting or fishing tenant of the rights he has paid for.

.   .   .   .

Where animals are concerned, the Scottish Celts, in common with the other Latin races, are a brutal and cruel people. This may be due partly to thoughtlessness and to lack of imagination. By the Roman Catholics, animals are treated roughly because they hold that they have no souls, and are therefore unworthy of compassion. From Free Church and other Protestant adherents, the animal receives but scant

consideration because—to use a favourite phrase among them
—"it's just a brute".

To the truth of these statements I can testify from personal
knowledge and experience, since I was brought up in a
northern parish where this attitude to animals was widespread, and have since witnessed much cruelty to them in
other parishes. On the whole, animals suffer more at the
hands of countryfolk than at the hands of townsfolk, as is
proved by an analysis of the prosecution for cruelty to them.
In this connection, I noticed the other day a statement made
at a meeting of the Hawick branch of the Scottish Society
for the Prevention of Cruelty to Animals. The president
remarked that such cruelty was inclined to be more prevalent
in the country than in the towns. Treatment often had to be
given to sheep-dogs whose ribs had been broken through
being kicked.

Children and adults alike, especially when conversing with
a stranger, will strike their dog, or kick it out of the way, even
when it isn't in the way at all. This is a fairly common
expression of authority over something which cannot retaliate.
Children do this kind of thing in imitation of their elders,
whether they be the children of the tinkers or the children
of the clergy. I have seen the children of both do it; and they
have looked very surprised when I have remonstrated with
them. The dog or cat, horse or cow, is often given a blow
or a kick by way of covering up embarrassment or gaucherie
on the part of the assailant.

This brings to mind that telling passage appearing in a
book published recently, which I now propose quoting in support of my own contention that, where animals are concerned,
the Islanders are a cruel and primitive lot.

"We have already noticed the tragi-comic dearth of good
dogs in the Isle of Skye, though there were a multitude of useless ones in all the townships. Here on the Green Island there
were no fewer than eight dogs, of which only one was any
good with sheep, and he had but one eye, and was going blind
in that. The remaining seven spent the greater part of their
lives chained up in the pitchy-blackness of a filthy stable for
days—aye, and for weeks—at a time, without an hour or a
minute off the chain. When not forgotten all day, they got a

small dishful of potatoes and a drop of skimmed milk. Their water-tins were always dry.

"In this neglect of their dogs there is no deliberate cruelty any more than there was in Donald the Red allowing his bitch to swarm with lice. No, that consummate insensibility of the average hill-farmer and shepherd, a natural compliment to their own hard and primitive living conditions and the narrow outlook bred of their lonely lives, which allowed Donald to speculate as to the thinness of his bitch, but do no more, so that he would not believe that it had lice until M. lifted aside the sparse outer coat and showed him the hairless skin alive with them—it is this mental callousness that is the main cause of neglect: this, and perhaps originally the narrow fundamentalism of the hill-folk's religion, which taught that one saved one's soul by a rigid and meaningless adherence to dead biblical precepts, and not by an understanding kindness to living creatures, which they, in common with many other persons and peoples, believed to have been put into the world for the material benefit of man—though the Highland *crofters* are mostly good to their dogs, who endure nothing worse than an eternal boredom of inactivity.

"Of all the hill-farmers and their sons, their wives and their shepherds I have known, few indeed regarded their dogs as anything better than mechanical, unfeeling brutes, born to work for them with a minimum of care, and no kindness at all. That a man should keep a dog for any other purpose than the work to be got out of it, or for financial gain, is not understood . . .

"There are, of course, instances of real barbarity in both Highlands and Islands among the younger men; and some shepherds are very cruel in their methods of training young dogs—slashing their pads with a knife to prevent their running the sheep too hard; breaking or filing down the teeth of any that show a disposition to grip a sheep; beating them unmercifully with crooks or rope-ends, irrespective of whether the animal is a dog or a bitch in whelp; or training them on a long halter with a running noose jerked tight whenever the dog gets too excited; while such beliefs as that a semi-starved dog works best on the hill, and that it must never be allowed in the farmhouse, are almost universal—despite the high incidence among collies of skin and hair diseases, rheumatism, and paralysis of the hind-quarters from lying in wet byres or on concrete, or boards over concrete; and an enormous mortality from a form of hysteria accompanied by convulsions, to which they succumb with a suddenness that bespeaks their poor physical condition.

"It may be asked, if conditions are as bad as I have suggested, how it is that such organisations as the R.S.P.C.A. have allowed them to continue. The answer is that the evil is too widespread and too anciently rooted in the powerful farming structure of Britain, and that farmers and shepherds are independent folk with a traditional contempt for Inspectors of any kind, and an awkward habit of pitching inquisitive ones into the nearest midden; while the Police have always turned a blind eye to animal cruelty; and in the Scottish Highlands at any rate the general public are apathetic, and the Scottish R.S.P.C.A. apparently ineffective, for farmers and shepherds may be seen lounging through the market towns with starveling dogs at heel with more sores on them than hair.

"Only a national commission with the full backing of Parliament can hope to impose a proper control of dogs on farms and sheep-runs, for this will necessitate a regular examination by the Inspector of all out-buildings in which dogs might be shut up, though what man with a first-hand knowledge of conditions would give evidence before the commission, except myself, I do not know, so blind and gladly indifferent are men to embarrassing evils on their own thresholds."[1]

[1] *I Went A'Shepherding*, by Richard Perry. (Lindsay Drummond, 1944.) Perry would be the last to affirm, however, that only in the Highlands and Islands does one find cruelty and callousness where animals are concerned. In his more recent book, *In the High Grampians* (Lindsay Drummond, 1948), he writes: "It is all a matter of perspective, dependent upon a man's individual interests and the stratum of society to which he belongs. It is at least as painful to me to see a great borzoi or mastiff being led docilely from shop to shop by some witless, high-heeled city minx as it is to witness a physical act of cruelty to a sheep-dog in some Highland glen. Compared with man's inhumanity to man and, worse, to children, his cruelty to animals may be deemed negligible; but if we are to make one last attempt to construct a civilisation that can survive, then, surely, tolerance, to both man and beast, must be the main pillar of such a civilisation; and the answer to both intolerance and cruelty is education. Cruelty in rural areas is due in ninety-nine cases out of every hundred to mental torpor and callousness induced by long hours of manual labour, a low standard of living, and a total absence of cultural background. No one, who has given any serious thought to the matter, can really suppose that petty police prosecutions can ever provide a

That the dogs are lousy is not to be wondered at, since so many of the Islanders themselves spend their entire lives in that unsavoury condition. Newer houses and the cleanlier methods introduced with them have, to some extent, mitigated this unpleasant state of affairs. Nevertheless, in regions where there is no proper sanitation, no running water indoors, and where bathing is almost totally unknown, and even frowned upon, lice cannot but be well provided for.

As for cruelty to animals, for my own part I fail to see that much can be done whilst we breed them to eat their cooked corpses, or the corpses of their young. Therein, it seems to me, lies the real cruelty. Therein, too, the real horror, the real shame.

. . . .

The Hebrideans show a marked predisposition for being night-hawks rather than early birds catching early worms. Of course, there is no reason why this should necessarily be regarded as a shortcoming, provided it does not leave all the essential work of life to those who rise early. Where people are dependent for their subsistence upon their own efforts and resources, and are not answerable to master or employer in the accepted sense, they naturally work when they feel inclined. Sparse though may be the independence gained from crofting and fishing, the Islanders prefer it to any form of regimentation or direction. This one could admire in them, were they also to assert their independence in other ways—were it not that so many of them are now largely maintained in their so-called independence by a variety of public subsidies and gratuities. At the present time, independence in the Western Isles, as also throughout much of the Highlands, is being maintained at considerable public expense; and it seems to me that a situation has now arisen justifying some drastic curtailment of public expenditure upon these islands, from which no public benefit whatsoever accrues, and which are likely to become an increasing liability. Nowhere in Britain has so much been spent with so little to

long-term solution. This can only be achieved by the education of the mind from the earliest years and by raising the standards of living among the rural population, so that the farmer and the farm-worker, themselves comfortably housed and well-fed, will have the more charity and kindliness to spare for their animals."

show for it. I do not deny that this public generosity has been well meant; but it has been entirely uneconomic, if not actually wasteful. It has resulted from an emotional and sentimental attitude to the Western Isles, rather than from a courageous and realistic policy devised to resolve their complex problems.

In the five places at which a mail-boat calls regularly—Stornoway, Tarbert, Lochmaddy, Lochboisdale, and Castlebay—few are inclined to go to bed on mail-boat nights before the vessel has arrived. Storms at sea, or unforeseen circumstances delaying railway connections, in no way perturb the inhabitants. They are confident that, eventually, the mail-boat will come—indeed, that she *must* come; and they regard it as a social duty to be up and about when she does. There is often more gaiety and hilarity on an evening when she is several hours late than when she berths on time. When the news goes round that her lights have been sighted, it is still customary for all the young people, and indeed for many of the middle-aged and elderly, to set out for the pier in time to see her come alongside. It is deemed essential, for purposes of gossip and local knowledge, that as many Islanders as possible should know just who arrived on such and such a night, what the passengers were wearing, how they looked in their city finery, what news they had of ongoings among relatives and friends on the mainland. Though aeroplanes now land regularly at Stornoway's airport, and though most of the inhabitants of the town and of the surrounding villages listen a good deal to the wireless, and are thus kept in touch with the outer world, the meeting of the mail-boat each week-night, as in the pre-flying, pre-wireless days of their parents and grandparents, is still the principal event of the day. Few of the able-bodied fail to observe this traditional visit to the quay at least once or twice a week; and many do so habitually, though it may entail a walk of some miles.

The Hebridean's nocturnal habits (alas! I can speak of them from personal experience, since I myself am usually most alert at the end of the day, and have never found early rising attractive!) explain his disinclination to rise o' mornings. To the average Islander, all the early worms in creation are not worth the assurance that he can take the morning—

indeed, the forenoon—as leisurely as he pleases. Add to this predilection the effects produced by alcohol consumed *Scottico more* the previous evening, and you will see that many an Islander is seldom fully awake much before noon! If the pubs be open then or shortly afterwards, it is doubtful whether, on certain days, he is ever entirely in full possession of his faculties. Drink certainly exaggerates his temperamental laziness.

And why should he not live his life in the leisurely way his ancestors did? he will ask. Well, there is much to be said for an existence free from gongs and bells, from factory whistles and clocking-in. To industrialisation, the average Hebridean is ill-adapted. He would rather semi-starve on his croft throughout the winter than be at the beck and call of an employer, even for good wages. And so he stays where he is.

However, those of his kinsfolk, who do feel the urge to be up and active, soon leave the island hearth, and fare forth into the wider, wickeder world, there to seek fortune. Many find fortune; but they have to work as hard for it as their island relatives scheme to eschew work. The Hebridean abroad is a different fellow from the Hebridean who clings precariously to his native soil. The former is industrious, and at times amazingly adaptable: the latter is happy in the old ways, dilatory and slow-paced, resisting every effort to turn him into ways more modern, more profitable, and socially more useful.

It must not be imagined that *all* the inhabitants of the Western Isles are lacking in drive and initiative. The few who possess these qualities do so in a remarkable degree; and such of them as remain in the islands often prevent their respective townships from stagnating completely.

One recalls in this connection the amusing war-time story of the two elderly brothers who, in all weathers and at all seasons, were up at cockcrow, tending their sheep, or visiting the lobster-pots moored in the bay fringing their croft. Neither of them, as the neighbours knew, owned a timepiece. Yet, they were always hard at work hours before the rest of the township had even stirred.

When one of the old brothers died, the survivor felt obliged to engage the services of two local lads, whom he agreed to recompense well, if only they turned up betimes each morning. Week after week, month after month, the lads put in a punctual appearance, much against physical inclination. But they had given an undertaking not to be late, even though this necessitated their having to waken of their own accord, and to prepare their own breakfast. Each morning, on reaching the scene of their employment, they found their agèd employer already there, hard at work. This punctuality in a man of his years and, moreover, in a man possessing no alarm-clock, they could not understand.

In course of time there came a morning when the lads turned up to find that they had anticipated him. As time wore on, and he failed to put in an appearance, they thought that, perhaps, he had taken ill, or even died in the night. So they went to his cottage. There they found him still in bed. Their entering had wakened him suddenly. Sitting up in bed, and turning his attention to an object in a dark recess, he began to fulminate in the Gaelic because he had not been wakened as usual. What was this object but a roosting hen, fast asleep! The explanation for his having overslept was now obvious. He had been in the habit of taking the *cock* into the cottage with him each night. Thus he had been wakened, unfailingly, at cockcrow. Owing to the blackout, it is said, rather than to his having had a dram too many, he had grabbed a hen by mistake!

. . . .

Two characteristics of the people, which the stranger to the Western Isles is swift to observe, certainly so far as the male population is concerned, are laziness and drunkenness. Many of the Islanders are now so indolent and so spoilt by easy money that they no longer deign to cut peat, even though it is to be had on their own crofts, often within a stone's-throw of their doorsteps. They prefer to purchase coal, brought a long way, and at great expense. There is some excuse for this among those now living at a distance from peat, the deposits nearer home having been worked out over the centuries that the Islanders, except for driftwood collected along the shores after storms, or for boles and trunks of trees found buried in the peat-mosses, burned peat exclusively. In such cases, especially where there are no young members in the family or township to win the peats and bring them home, the cost of a ton of coal might be less than what they would have to pay for the casting, stacking, and transporting of two or three cart-loads of peats. On the other hand, many families, spoilt by the present high rate of wages paid in the Isles for totally unskilled work during the recent war, purchase quantities of coal when, with no great exertion, and with but little expense, they could have a huge peat-stack by the gable-end of their cottages. As a Benbecula woman remarked to me the other day, when explaining how *her* small household always brought home peats for the winter, even under some personal hardship and often in inclement weather, the family next door, with no fewer than five able-bodied men doing little or nothing all day but smoking and yarning, has not cast a peat for years, although the peat-hags lay but fifty yards from its hearth. "They're too lazy," she concluded. "Just taking the coal all the way here from the mainland, where people requires it more!"

On the whole, no one need go cold in the Isles, with so much natural fuel there for the taking. During a severe winter, which, so far as actual cold is concerned, the Islanders seldom experience (snow falling but seldom, and never lying for any length of time) they are therefore more favourably situated than are most urban and rural dwellers on the mainland.

Comparatively little peat is now cut in the Dark Glen of Barra, though there is still plenty of it. Twenty years ago, as I well remember, nearly every family in the island cut peats there. At the south end of Barra, coal, brought by sea to Castlebay, has displaced almost entirely the burning of peat. The crofters inhabiting the valley debouching at Castlebay itself have already skinned the rocky hillsides in their immediate vicinity; and now they say that the peat of the Dark Glen is rather far away. By the time they cut, stack, dry, and transport it home, they find it cheaper to purchase coal, and have it delivered. The day has gone, even in the Western Isles, when, without payment, neighbours assisted one another on a coöperative basis. Now your neighbour expects to be paid for the most trifling service he may do you.

The pack-ponies which, in the summer and autumn months, used to bear peat-laden panniers straight from hag to doorstep, are now scarce in Barra. The introduction of the light motor-lorry has largely dispensed with their services, particularly in the transportation of fuel. The establishment of the local carrier on commercial lines means that few now carry anyone or anything free in the Isles when, formerly, most people with a vehicle or conveyance of any kind, whether cart, trap, or boat, were only too pleased to perform such a service gratuitously. The arrival of the motor-car in these parts has altered this. All transport has become commercial. Nowadays, you will have to pay quite a lot to be ferried from one isle to another: not so long ago, an Islander with a small boat near the point at which you wished to embark would never hesitate about ferrying you, and would scorn the offer of payment. Indeed, one had to be very careful not to offend by offering payment in such cases. To-day you offend if you do not offer a great deal more than any service rendered may be worth.

It may well be that many of those situated at a distance from peat, and unable themselves to do the work entailed in the winning of them, find the purchase of coal in every way cheaper. "Besides which," as a native of Barra put it to me the other day, when talking about the transporting of peats by pony, "you have to feed the beast all the year round, whether you're working him or not, whereas you only feed a motor when she's running."

Even during the recent coal shortage, only those hard pressed reverted to peat burning. Though coal itself was scarce, money was plentiful everywhere in the islands. Hence the preference for buying coal even at £4 5s. per ton. From the calorific standpoint, of course, one ton of coal is said to be better value than three of peat.

Though peat is now burned but seldom at the south end of Barra, it is still used extensively at the north end, since the natives there are in proximity to the peat-mosses. Indeed, in some cases the mosses occur on their crofts, if not actually within a few yards of their doors, thus requiring little or no transport. On the other hand, coal, if not unloaded at North-bay, has to be carted round the island from Castlebay; and carting, like much else, has become expensive—prohibitive, in fact, for the poorer natives, who may be too old to work for wages. The Castlebay folk tell me that, even at £5 a ton, they would find coal cheaper than peat.

There is, of course, a good deal of work attached to peat, though this work may be pleasant in fine weather. Peat-winning does require labour, which in turn demands a degree of physical fitness. Old-age pensioners, who comprise much of the population, since so many of the young people are obliged to leave the Isles for employment elsewhere, cannot cut peats and carry them home.

In former days, every member of the crofter's big, growing family, except the infants, lent a hand with the peats—lent a hand with their neighbour's peats as well as with their own —casting them, carting and creeling them all summer, until the peat-stack at the end of the cottage was large enough to maintain the household in fuel right throughout the winter, and even into the following summer, when all hands were at the peat-moss once more.

The first impression gained by the stranger to the Outer Hebrides—and first impressions are often correct—is that the womenfolk look careworn, sad, and prematurely old. A woman of forty in these parts often looks quite elderly. The menfolk, on the other hand, are better preserved, for they preserve themselves by leaving to the women all avoidable work or worry. When prolonged rains keep the male population indoors, smoking or dozing all day by the fire, the women have to be up and at it as usual, tidying up, refuelling the fire, feeding and cleaning the bairns, washing and mending the household's clothes, bringing in peats, milking the cow in the byre, baking scones and oatcakes, eternally infusing tea for someone or other, cooking for a large family from dawn till long after dusk, feeding the poultry, or shooing it away from the doorstep where it likes to congregate on wet days.

The Hebridean woman has her outdoor toils as well, once she has fed her children, and packed them off to the village school. In places where no tradesmen's vans call, it may be necessary for her to walk some miles to do her shopping. Withal, she has to be as active as the men allow themselves to be lazy. Strangers often remark how few men they notice working on the croft-lands, even when several of them may be seen lounging about. It is astonishing how the women who, until nature concedes some respite, appear to be continually child-bearing, manage to labour out of doors so hard and so long. They do most of the work entailed in preparing the ground for the sowing of seed or of potatoes; and they are usually foremost in the endeavour to garner the harvest in the autumn, before the winds and the rains have descended. The men do the scything, however; and they attend to the bull, which is usually rendered the more unruly, if not actually ferocious, by spending most of his outdoor life tethered to field or hillside. But I was interested to see in Barra recently that quite often the crofter menfolk milk the cows, as the men always do in the Channel Isles. In summer and autumn, pass at sundown along the road by the western seaboard of Barra, and you will notice shadowy figures moving silently among the cattle pastured on the machar between road and shore, as at Borve and Allasdale. They are, for the most part, the menfolk of the various townships out milking the cows in the open, or perhaps shifting to fresh pasture the tethered calves and sheep. The cows, as long as the weather is not too trying, and there is still some fresh herbage upon which they can feed, are left out all night. At sundown, also, you may see a dark form cross your path some distance ahead. In all probability, it will be an Islander setting out across the machar, carrying in one hand a long, lithe, homemade fishing-rod, and in the other an old pail. He is on his way to fish off the rocks fringing such parts of the coast as are not composed of sandy bays and sand-dunes.

Somewhat perfunctorily nowadays, the menfolk fish with rod or hand-line. The easy money already referred to makes possible the purchase of more expensive, if at the same time less wholesome, foods. An English lady, having noticed the indolence of the male population, said to me the other day in Uist, "One would have thought that, with the announcement of a further reduction in the weekly meat allowance, they would endeavour to counteract it with a little fishing off the rocks of that splendid bay, which must be full of fish." With the sea virtually at their doorsteps, she could not

understand this lack of initiative.[1] What she did not know
was that the meat-rationing, as understood elsewhere, hardly
exists in the Western Isles, since those concerned in the
slaughter and sale of butcher-meat observe few regulations,
and always have at the tip of the tongue a volume of plausi-
bility when questioned about irregularities. Here again one
notices the Islanders' utter disregard of rules and regulations.
Where rationed goods are concerned, they lack nothing.
Indeed, they appear to have more than their statutory share
of everything. It is difficult enough to ensure that producers
of food on the mainland render truthful returns: where the
Islands are concerned, anything even approaching such
returns is seldom attempted.

The youths are as indolent and dilatory as are the adult
males. When staying recently at Daliburgh, in South Uist,
I put this to the test. I had a puncture in the tyre of a bor-
rowed bicycle, which had no repair accessories. Outside the
local shop there stood a cluster of loafing lads, one of whom,
the shopkeeper informed me, was the recognised mender of
punctures in the locality. Tapping on the window to draw
this lad's attention, he beckoned to him, and asked him
whether he would see to my puncture. The lad, somewhat
reluctantly, said that he would; and I replied that I would
give him half-a-crown for his trouble. Leaving the bicycle
with him, I retired to a window of the house in which I was
living, there to watch his pretended progress at a distance of
a hundred yards or so. I will admit that he did actually turn
the bicycle over, and stand it on seat and handle-bars. Thereafter, however, he disappeared from view, leaving the bicycle
in this position. Twenty minutes later he came to the door
to inform me that he could not mend the puncture because of
his having no tools. I knew this to be a lie. He was simply

---

[1] This is no new development. On the contrary, many strangers to the
Hebrides during the last few centuries have commented upon the half-hearted
manner in which the inhabitants fished. Writing about the middle of the
seventeenth century to St. Vincent de Paul, founder of the Lazarists, Father
Duggan, one of the priests who came over at that time from Ireland to
Montana Scotiae—to the Scottish Highlands and Islands—in response to an
appeal for missionary aid made by Clanranald, who, together with his wife
and family, had just been converted to Roman Catholicism, alludes to it as
follows: "There is fish in the sea which surrounds the islands, but the
people, by temperament easy-going and unenergetic, make but little effort
to catch any."

too lazy to exert himself; and money is too easily obtained in the Isles these days to make half-a-crown for a job which would have occupied less than ten minutes, temptatious even where young, unskilled persons are concerned. During my schooldays in Edinburgh, a lad of his age would have considered himself handsomely remunerated with tuppence.

The women are never idle. Indeed, they are not allowed to be. Whenever they have a spare moment, they are busy with their needles, knitting jumpers, socks, mittens, gloves, cardigans, underwear, and bed-jackets, all conforming to instructions set forth in the various knitting periodicals they study so zealously. In fact, there frequently exists between townships an element of competition in the variety, quality, and quantity of knitting. The amount the women accomplish is shown to some extent in the hand-knitted garments worn by the children of both sexes. In the days when hand-looms were common in the cottages, they made great quantities of tweed, blankets, drugget, and *clo-gorm*, or navy-blue tweed, for the fishermen.

The Island women, on the whole, are plain; and many of them are exceedingly so. This applies to the young, as well as to the middle-aged and elderly. Yet, occasionally one comes upon a young woman of astounding beauty, of quite exceptional loveliness. The women of the Hebrides bloom early, and fade early, especially those who marry early, and begin immediately to the wearing routine of crofting and excessive child-bearing. Nearly all the married women are spent within a few years after marrying. They become creased and careworn. At an age when so many women in other places are at their best, the Island women are worn out.

So accustomed are they to doing the hard labour that they are apt to resent any suggestion that the menfolk should perform the more arduous tasks, such as carrying heavy loads. The wife of a schoolmaster in South Uist was indignant with me the other day, when I told her that she ought to get her husband to assist her in carrying the ponderous pails from the well. Indeed, she remarked that she would regard such help from her husband as undignified for him, as something *infra dig*. So used have the women become to incessant toil

240

A corner of the harbour at Castlebay, with Kisimul Castle

and to bearing loads. They are, in fact, still quite uneman-
cipated. Their existence is largely a form of slavery, though
they seem unaware of this, having for the male members of
their society an attitude fostered by the notion that the latter
are a better and finer race than they.

When in Eriskay last year, I asked two women, who were
panting heavily while carrying sacks of flour up a steep path
from a point on the shore at which they had just been landed,
why the womenkind appeared to perform all the onerous
duties on the island. "Och, well," answered one of them,
"*someone* will have to be facing the music!" When I
enquired of her why the menfolk were so seldom seen carrying such heavy loads, she replied that there were hardly any
young men in Eriskay. "They're away fishing, or in the
Merchant Service," she added. "There's nothing for them to
be doing here."

However, this did not explain why so many able-bodied
men, though not necessarily young, left all the heavy tasks
to the women, and saw nothing wrong in their being the
bearers of innumerable babies, and beasts of burden when
they did not happen to be too far gone in pregnancy. Truly,
in the Isles the women are the beasts of burden, for chivalry
in such matters does not exist there.

In the matter of drink, it should be emphasised, the older
womenfolk are as abstemious as so many of the menfolk are
intemperate. Only the younger and flightier women drink
—and smoke. Many of them acquired the cocktail habit during the war. In an island like Barra, where all the older
men smoke either bogie-roll or black-twist tobacco, and the
younger smoke the ubiquitous cigarette, one seldom sees a
native woman over forty smoking. Nearly all the old women
of the island, as well as the old men, take snuff, however; and
at the present time the snuff habit is growing among the
younger married women.

.   .   .   .

By no stretch of imagination can the Islanders be described
as a cleanly people. Yet, a few keep themselves clean, and
their cottages bright and tidy, and are a perpetual example
to their more slovenly neighbours. The cleanliest people are
always the most active and sober: dirt is the boon companion

R   241

*John MacDonald, the Uig postman, on his ten-mile
tramp between Morsgail and Loch Resort*

both of laziness and of drink. Nowhere is this more apparent than in the Western Isles.

Soap and water, even in the days when the former commodity was cheap and plentiful (and there is never any lack of the latter in the rainy Isles) have never found much favour in these parts. Such a thing as a hot bath—one of life's greatest solaces—is looked upon by nearly all the inhabitants as a piece of nonsense, wholly unnecessary. Few even of the comfortably-off merchants regard a bath as an integral part of the day's, or even of the week's, routine. Bath-night—well, there isn't such a thing, even among those possessing a bath! Half-a-dozen tepid dips a year is about as much as even the bath-owners permit themselves. They have the notion that bathing is not good for one, and may, indeed, be injurious to health. Chills which might prove fatal, they believe, are apt to follow so unnatural a practice. They are a long way from the state of mind where the bath becomes a pleasurable necessity. That anyone should want even one bath a week, they consider extraordinary: that anyone should desire a bath on two consecutive days, is, to them, indicative of some regrettable abnormality, if not actually a sign of daftness. I can testify to this from personal experience. On more than one occasion, when living with friends in the Isles who have a bath which they seldom use, I have made myself exceedingly unpopular by my habit of bathing, not because I was using up the hot water, but because I actually enjoyed immersing myself in it!

Many a rich merchant in the Isles never had a hot bath in his life. The suggestion that he might install a bath in his house would probably be countered with the boast that his parents and grandparents had lived to be eighty, ninety, or even a hundred, without ever having had a bath in their lives!

It must be mentioned, however, that baths are now provided in all council houses, and that the younger generation is beginning to feel the benefit of these installations. But we can hardly complain about the lack of baths in a region where laid-on water reaches but the merest fraction of the population, and where water-closets are still exceedingly uncommon. We must not malign the Isles unduly in this connection. Most readers would be appalled if they knew the proportion of homes throughout the United Kingdom possessing no sanitation of any kind.

We see, then, that personal cleanliness is at a discount among the Islanders, which explains how so many of them, parents as well as children, are perpetually in a verminous condition. In fairness, it ought to be added that this lack of cleanliness is by no means confined to the Isles. In February, 1948, during a discussion on prevailing standards of cleanliness, at a meeting of the Stirlingshire Public Health Committee, the medical officer, reporting on the incidence of scabies, declared that the public were dirtier than need be, and that a more liberal use of soap and water would improve Scotland! In fairness, too, it should be mentioned, apropos what I have just said about the verminous condition of so many of the Islanders, that people who, during the recent war, threw their homes open to children evacuated from the bombed cities and towns, were shocked at finding so high a proportion of these children in a similar state.

The health of the Islanders, on the whole, is good; and much has been done in recent years to alleviate sickness and physical distress amongst them. Few realise just what has been done for them in this regard, and what is still being done.

Since 1929, when the Local Government (Scotland) Act came into force, cases of tuberculosis from the Outer Hebrides have had equal treatment with those from the mainland. Such treatment is given not only at hospitals situated in the counties of Ross and Inverness (the counties to which the Outer Hebrides are attached for purposes of local administration) but at hospitals in the south. In fact, most of the Island cases have received attention at the latter hospitals. Recently, owing to the shortage of nurses and of hospital beds, there has been a diminution in the number of admissions; but this has not affected Island cases any more adversely than it has cases from other parts of these counties.

The removal of urgent cases is effected by air-ambulance from North Uist, Benbecula, South Uist, and Barra. From Lewis and Harris such cases are removed by car or by motor-ambulance to the Lewis Hospital, at Stornoway. The air-ambulance service runs between the Isles and Glasgow. This service is an expensive one; but patients are not expected to contribute toward the cost a sum beyond their means. The rest of the cost is shared equally by the Department of Health for Scotland and the County Council. This excellent service has responded well to the demands made upon it.

As there are no fever hospitals in the Outer Isles, fever cases are usually treated at home, where the necessary nursing services are supplied by that great, public benefactor, the district nurse. On occasions, infectious cases are removed by air to a central hospital.

At least once a year, an ear, nose, and throat surgeon, an orthopaedic surgeon, and an ophthalmic surgeon visit the Islands to give attention to such cases as can be treated locally. Under the School Health Administration and Child Welfare Schemes, all expenses in respect of pre-school and school children are paid.

Up to the date at which the new National Health Service became operative, the general medical and nursing services were subsidised by the Highlands and Islands Medical Services Fund. The doctors were also parish and district medical officers, for which post they were paid, and in respect of which they also enjoyed a rent-free house.

. . . .

The leisurely existence of so many of the Islanders may have something to do with their longevity, a matter upon which several writers have commented during the last few centuries. "The inhabitants of this island," says Martin, writing of North Uist, "are generally well-proportioned, of an ordinary stature, and a good complexion; healthful, and some of them come to a great age: several of my acquaintance arrived at the age of 90, and upwards; John Macdonald of Griminis was of this number, and died lately in the 93rd year of his age. Donald Roy, who lived in the Isle of Sand, and died lately in the hundredth year of his age, was able to travel and manage his affairs till about two years before his death."

Much more remarkable are the cases of longevity Martin cites in connection with Jura, an island of the Inner Hebrides, to which, at a later date, we propose devoting a further volume. "Several of the natives," he writes, "have lived to a

great age. I was told that one of them, called Gillouir Mac-
Crain, lived to have kept one hundred and eighty Christmases
in his own house. He died about fifty years ago, and there
are several of his acquaintances living to this day, from whom
I had this account. Bailiff Campbell lived to the age of one
hundred and six years; he died three years ago; he passed the
thirty-three last years before his death in this isle. . . . A
woman of the Isle of Scarba, near the north end of this isle,
lived seven score years, and enjoyed the free use of her senses
and understanding all her days; it is now two years since she
died."

A few years ago, when at Inverlussa, situated near the north
end of Jura, I photographed the tombstone marking the grave
known as *Uaigh Mhairi Rhiobach*, Hairy Mary's Grave. This
stone, the inscription testifies, denotes the place of burial
of Mary MacCrain who died in 1856 at the age of 128. Mary
is further described on the stone as having been a descendant
of " Gillouir MacCrain who kept a Hundred & Eighty Christ-
masses in his own house, and who died in the reign of
Charles I ".

The Western Islanders are certainly a long-lived race, as
one sees from a glance at the obituary column in the *Stornoway
Gazette* each week. A high proportion of the resident population consists of octogenarians, nonagenarians, and even centenarians. Out of a list of nine deaths notified recently in the
obituary column of this informative journal, there were four
octogenarians, two nonagenarians, and two centenarians. This
may have been a somewhat exceptional list; but deaths giving this high average of years are by no means uncommon
in these Islands. Even men who have spent the greater part of
their lives abroad, or as seafarers, return quite late in life to
their native surroundings, where they live on to a great age.
Though I cannot claim to have known anyone who lived as
long as the MacCrains, I may add that many of my own kinsfolk and friends in the Outer Hebrides have survived in full
vigour to a ripe age. The slower tempo of the Isles—their
freedom from hustle and bustle, their perfunctory ways of
life—seems to have vouchsafed to many of the inhabitants
a lengthening of their days.

If physical courage be the criterion of bravery, then the Islanders are exceedingly brave. For my own part, however, I regard moral courage, which is so rare, as a much higher form. The record of the Western Isles for courage in wartime is well known. As with most native races, an insensibility to those loftier feelings inspired by Christianity, and found in the more civilised members of human society—an insensibility bred of primitive belief and environment—renders them courageous and callous in face of danger. Real courage, real bravery, it seems to me, means something more than a mere disregard for physical danger: the most courageous are those who, recognising to the full the danger involved, do not allow themselves to be deflected from facing it.

Both in the First and in the Second World War, many of the men from the Isles served in the kilted regiments comprising the spirited Fifty-first Highland Division. Thus they were included among those troops known to the Germans as the Ladies from Hell. If we accept war as a grand and glorious thing, and as a necessary evil (as, indeed, some still do) then we must admit that the Western Islanders played a most heroic part in achieving what the last two major wars did achieve, though neither of them would seem to have achieved its declared objectives.

Only so far as Lewis is concerned am I familiar with the details of how these wars affected the Island people; but what I shall now have to say about Lewis in this connection must have been true, though perhaps to a lesser degree, of the other islands included in the Outer Hebrides. The record of Lewis is unique, however.

In the wild, wet darkness of New Year's morning, 1919, the Admiralty vessel, *Iolaire*, in making for the port of Stornoway, went off her course, struck the submerged reef close inshore known as the Beasts of Holm, and heeled perilously to starboard. In addition to her crew, she had aboard between two and three hundred naval men returning on leave to their native isle at the conclusion of a long and rigorous war at sea. They were getting their kit together at the time of the disaster, since the vessel was now but a few minutes' steaming from the safe and ample anchorage of Stornoway, metropolis of the vast island of Lewis.

More than two hundred of them were drowned that dark, fateful morn, literally within hail of the cliffs of their boyhood. And such corpses as were afterwards recovered from the wreck were laid out upon the green sward at Holm, whither the isleswomen came from the remotest townships to identify their dead. Scarcely a home remained unaffected by this tragedy. My own relatives were there, with the women of Lewis, questing among the dead. There is no more moving episode than this in the arduous history of the Long Island, where wartime must always be a time of anxiety and of sorrow.

Out of a population of roughly 30,000 Gaels inhabiting but sparsely Lewis's 400,000 acres of moorland and rock, more than 6,000 men, unconscripted, left for service on land and sea at the outbreak of war in 1914. As the war dragged on, this number was considerably augmented. So far as honours and casualties were concerned, every naval engagement and every battle on land affected the island—so much so, indeed, that Lewis was officially recognised as having contributed to the Great War, voluntarily, and in proportion to her population, more men than any other part of the Empire. Many of these men were in the Naval Reserve. They came of the blood of those who, for centuries, swore fealty, not to the Kings of Scotland, but to the Sea-Kings of Lochlann —of Norway—for it was not until the defeat of Haco and his vast fleet at Largs in 1263 that the authority of the Scottish Crown extended to their unruly ancestors.

From a strictly material point of view, Lewis's resources are neglible. She is a poor and barren isle, where indifferent crofting and casual fishing supplement one another in securing but the slenderest subsistence for the majority of her people. Yet, what men she has sent forth to the wars! In all the heroic annals of our country, there is no record comparable with that of Lewis.

Of her contribution to the Second World War we may obtain some idea by reference to the casualties she sustained, as well as by the deeds of valour for which so many of her sons were decorated. One recalls in this context the performance in November, 1939, of Malcolm Morrison, the young sailor-lad—the mere deck-boy—who received Admiralty recognition for the skill and tenacity with which he sailed an open boat for six consecutive days in tumultuous seas, after his ship, the *Arlington Court*, had been sunk by a U-boat. Five other shipwrecked mariners in that open boat owe their lives to the seamanship and endurance of this shy, red-cheeked son of the sea. His is but one of the innumerable acts of heroism redounding to the island's credit.

Where the Western Isles were concerned, casualties were heavy in the Second World War. Most of the men served at sea in one capacity or another—in the trawlers, in the mine-sweepers, in the food convoys, in the destroyers, and in the big ships of the Northern Patrol. Many of them fell victim to submarine warfare. There were twelve Lewismen aboard the *Rawalpindi*, eight of whom were lost, and four of whom were prisoners of war in Germany. The last seen of one of those who perished was when he leapt out of the boat, in which he would have been saved, to swim over to another boat in a vain but heroic attempt to right her. She was heeling badly, and ultimately capsized with the loss of her entire complement. The Admiralty, in announcing the *Rawalpindi's* survivors who were prisoners in German hands, also reported the loss of the *Exmouth*, with seven of our isles-men aboard. Then, at least a dozen Lewis lads were serving aboard the torpedoed *Forfar*, a vessel I myself knew well when she was the C.P.R. liner, *Montrose*.

As indicating the number of men from Lewis serving in the Merchant Service, let us consider the case of the *Lochavon*, torpedoed early in the war. In her deck crew of sixteen, she had thirteen Gaelic-speaking sailors, ten of whom were natives of Lewis. One of the men rescued from this ship sought further adventures immediately he set foot on *terra firma* again. He joined the Navy, and in no time won the Meri-torious Service Medal. One might also mention the Shaw Savill vessel, *Maimoa*, sunk by a German raider. Including the bos'n, she had aboard no fewer than fourteen men from Ness, the northern parish of Lewis. The island also sustained casualties at Narvik; and there were four natives among the *Altmark's* prisoners when she was intercepted by H.M.S. *Cossack* in Josing Fiord.

In April, 1941, when the war entered a new phase with the German invasion of Norway, Lewismen found themselves in the midst of fresh and daring operations, especially at sea. Some of our men were lost aboard the steamer, *Stancliffe*, when, at the outset of the invasion, she was sunk in an attempt to escape from Narvik Fiord. At least three of them were serving with H.M.S. *Warspite*, when she forced her way into Narvik, and smashed up a concentration of enemy destroyers. Luckily, all our men with the trawler, *Rutlandshire*, were saved when she was sunk by enemy action at Namsos; and none of those aboard the *Rodney* was injured when she was struck by a bomb.

Following upon the collapse of Holland in May, 1940, Lewis seamen took a leading part in the operations off the Dutch coast when Queen Wilhelmina and the Dutch Government were transferred to London with much gold. Many of our fellows were killed in that action, or died of wounds.

All the natives of Lewis aboard the torpedoed *Transylvania* and H.M.S. *Scotstoun* were saved. Of the ten serving with H.M.S. *Wren* when she was sunk, nine ultimately reached safety. Nevertheless, the heavy casualties at sea bore sorrowfully upon the people of Lewis. Though nine out of the ten natives on the *Dunvegan Castle* were rescued, eight perished eventually. Several others were seriously wounded when the destroyers, *Esk* and *Ivanhoe*, were sunk. One could extend indefinitely the list of ships in which islesmen served and suffered.

Turning from sea to land, we find a record equally formidable. Shall I ever forget the heroism of my own platoon on the Western Front during the First World War? This platoon of Seaforths was composed almost exclusively of men from Lewis. Never was there such dash, such nonchalance, in the midst of death. Before the war ended, and while I myself lay in hospital, they were killed to a man.

Those natives serving with the army in the Second World War were, indeed, unfortunate, in one respect at least, though it is doubtful whether many of them would have returned, had they been engaged throughout in fighting. The whole of the Lewis Territorials (the Ross Battery of Gallipoli fame) and the Harris Territorials (the 4th Camerons of the Highland Division) were surrounded at St. Valery. The 2nd battalion of the Seaforth Highlanders, the County Regiment, fighting with the Highland Division at St. Valery, suffered the same fate, so that the whole of the regular and territorial forces of the island were captured simultaneously.

Scores of our fellows came through the epic of Dunkirk; and there were many casual re-unions on the famous beaches there. Several of the vessels engaged in the evacuation had Lewismen in their complement. Indeed, one destroyer had as many as fifteen. Some of our men, fighting ashore, took to their natural element ere they got away. Certain units of the Dunkirk fleet were commanded by Lewismen. Prominent among them was the *Blackburn Rovers*, sunk by an enemy bomb. Dunkirk exacted heavy toll from Lewis.

To every clachan, to every township, came news of sons killed, drowned, wounded, taken prisoner, or posted missing. Not a village but mourned its dead or its lost ones. There was little to mitigate the island's sorrow but the homecoming of her sons on brief leave, or news of their exploits on the Seven Seas—and perhaps the hope that, in the end, some of those unaccounted for since the days of St. Valery and Dunkirk might turn up, as many actually did at the conclusion of the war.

Daisies, I should tell you, were in flower in Lewis early in January, 1941—a bad omen! The year was but a day or two on its way when the old folks shook their heads, and murmured that, for *them* at all events, it would inevitably be a year of sorrow. *A hind had been seen in the village of Breascleit, in Bernera.*

The arrival in Bernera a week later of the crew of the torpedoed Swedish steamer, *Gothia,* was the first sign of bad times ahead. To the exertions of a naval reservist who, while home on leave, glimpsed the sail of her life-boat off the coast in the waning moonlight, the survivors owe their lives. Though weary through lack of sleep after travelling home to remote Bernera, he persisted in his search until he located the life-boat, now bumping heavily on a ledge of rock, its crew too exhausted to fend her off. The survivors were entertained in accordance with traditional island hospitality. It happened that a wedding was being celebrated next day in Bernera. The bride was among those who succoured the

Swedish seamen; and they were the first to partake of the wedding feast.

. . . .

Hospitality, in the old, traditional style, is still to be met with, despite a noticeable increase in the greed for money among the Hebrideans. Though a few of them will still perform, gratuitously, many a service, often at considerable personal inconvenience and physical discomfort, the number so disposed is rapidly diminishing. In recent years, high wages paid for quite unskilled labour, and various forms of public money all too easily obtained, have made them avaricious. Even if you travel by the motor-boat carrying the mails across the Sound of Eriskay from South Uist—from Ludaig or Kilbride to Haun, a distance of not much more than a mile—you will have to pay the boatman at least five shillings, although the boat is crossing in any case, and is subsidised by the Post Office for doing so. On occasions you may have to pay as much as ten.

On landing in Eriskay lately, I was afforded a good example of the commercial values now to be encountered almost anywhere in the Outer Hebrides, as elsewhere. By the jetty at Haun several white ponies bearing panniers were waiting, ready to transport along the island's footpaths mails and sundry stores consigned to the inhabitants. I speedily erected my camera on its tripod, and was about to photograph this picturesque assembly when a middle-aged man, the owner of one of the ponies, standing idly but a few yards from it, promptly got in front of it, in order to obscure it from the camera. After a cocky observation in the Gaelic to a bystander, he turned defiantly to ask me, in English, what I proposed paying him for permission to include his pony, adding in a knowing way that some newspaper would certainly be paying *me* for it. To his astonishment, I rebuked him in Gaelic, more in sorrow than in anger, and picking up my camera and tripod, proceeded inland, remarking that I regretted to find the greed for money had reached even Eriskay.

Money, obtained preferably without working for it, now has a firm hold of many of the Islanders; and they show no compunction about indulging in the deceits and subterfuges

251

employed more usually by the trading classes than by the rural and crofting. A few months ago, thirty-seven women were among forty-two Islanders from the Leverburgh district of Harris charged at Stornoway Sheriff Court with selling Harris tweed above the permitted price. The excesses ranged from a few pence per yard to three-and-nine. Fines amounting to £500 were imposed. The accused were not regular dealers in Harris tweed. They included crofters, spinners, weavers, housewives, domestic servants, grocers, motor fitters, and a postal official. All of them, it was reported, made an occasional length of tweed as a subsidiary to their main occupation. The offences came to light when an inspector of the North of Scotland Price Regulation Committee examined the books of the firm which had purchased this tweed, all of which, it was said, had been bought by a London firm doing business in the Isles from premises resembling a hen-house. Enormous profits had been made by buyers who took the tweed to London, and cut it into suit-lengths. Most of the accused swore on oath that they knew nothing about the Board of Trade regulations governing prices!

The Islanders are capable of being vindictive in a degree unbelievable to those strangers who, arriving amongst them for the first time, are impressed by their charm and naïvety. At times they pursue their neighbours with extreme avidity and bitterness. Thus some of the remotest island communities are characterised by feuds which go on from generation to generation.

Not long ago, a lad, while driving a van, came into slight collision with the wing of a doctor's car. After the lad had been fined at the police court for negligent driving, the doctor had the insolence to send him in a bill for repairs amounting to several pounds. The lad, however, was able to ascertain from the mechanic, who did the repair, that, at a cost of but a few shillings, he had gently malleted out the dents in the wing, this being the only repair the car required. The lad thereupon called on the doctor, abused him, and flung in his face a bill about which he has never heard another word.

The more enlightened of the Western Islanders would endorse the criticisms enumerated in the preceding pages.

Certainly, so far as Lewis is concerned, this is true, as may be seen from the correspondence columns of the local paper. This was clearly demonstrated in a controversy which arose a few years ago out of a B.B.C. broadcast on the island, for which a well-known and scholarly native was responsible. "A perfectly true picture of Lewis," wrote one of the Islanders contributing to this free and frank expression of opinion on the natives and their shortcomings, "would be a work of art; and Lewismen have no use for works of art. Not that we lack emotion. In fact, to a sane mind the most revolting thing about Lewis Presbyterianism is its unrestrained emotionalism . . . In brief, Lewis life is a thing of extremes. If you are not dissipated, you are expected to be excessively pious, and *vice versa*. The Greek virtues are almost unknown. And a 'temperate' man, in the widest sense, is something of a curiosity. . . . Leaving aside drunkenness (the chief 'active' vice of the Lewisman, if lifting the elbow be activity) let us consider the devout section of the community. Why this cant in print, when those of us who are outside their free-masonry freely admit among ourselves that the average 'pious' person in Lewis is a humbug? They could hardly be portrayed without being satirised. No doubt, there are sentimental Lewismen, curled up in whelk-shells of self-deception, who picture venerable elders mature with heavenly wisdom. Will someone tell me where I can meet them? A grey beard is as often the mark of black superstition as of the white light of philosophy.

"The stranger sees the Lewis peasant at his best—courteous, hospitable, and intelligent. These virtues are real enough; but there is an obverse side to the medal, which the stranger never sees, namely, the rude, vulgar, superstitious life of the dweller on the soil, a life in which loud tongues, underhand strife, and bursts of something not far from savagery are as common as idyllic peace.

"Even the supposed independence of the crofter is largely an illusion. He is a slave not only to his poverty, and to the dictators of the church, but also, as much as any bourgeois, to the opinion of his neighbours. The standards differ—that's all. Especially must he not pretend to be superior to the herd. If he be so, he must conceal his superiority, or get out of the

Island. That is why most actively intelligent Lewismen live outside Lewis."

The Hebrideans certainly *are* a people of extremes. They can be extremely greedy and extremely generous, excessively cruel and excessively kind. If they know you, and like you, their hospitality can be overwhelming. In this connection, I recall the Stewarts, my recent host and hostess in the glen at Castlebay. When first I knew Seumas Stewart, a quarter of a century ago, he was the postman taking mails over from Castlebay to the small-holders then lately settled on Vatersay; and I well remember pleasant trips with him to that isle. The stormy evening I disembarked at Castlebay from the mail-boat in 1947, Seumas was at the pier to welcome me.. As we proceeded up the glen to his home, and he insistent on carrying my suitcase, this old man, with tears welling in his very blue eyes, halted for a moment to say to me one of the most felicitous things anyone ever said to me in my life. "I couldn't be more pleased supposing Conan Doyle himself, or even Barrie or Bernard Shaw, came to stay with us."

A happy note upon which to conclude this somewhat searching chapter.

CHAPTER VII

THE SCOURGE OF THE ISLES

THE observant and alert of ear, when travelling among the Western Highlands and Islands, cannot but learn what is uppermost in the mind of the travelling Gael. As the boat comes alongside some pier at which the Gael is not disembarking, he may be heard putting to the mate (meantime busy supervising the fixing of the gangway) the burning question, "*Will there be time to go up to the hotel?*"

Little is of greater moment to the average Gael than this. When at home or when travelling, drink is all too often his preoccupation. When his train stops at a station, the one and only enquiry he makes of any railway official he may see is whether there will be time for him to visit the refreshment bar.

This recalls the Islander's reply when asked, on his return home, what he thought of Oban, where he had never been before. "Man, it was just grand!" he said. "You couldn't throw a stone without hitting a public-house!"

The drink problem is no new one where the Western Isles are concerned. So serious was it in the time of King James the Sixth (that is to say, at the beginning of the seventeenth century) that stringent measures were taken by the Privy Council to suppress the excessive consumption of intoxicating liquors. These measures throw much light upon social conditions as then existing in the Hebrides. They show how the deplorable drinking habits of the natives were provocative of many of the cruelties and barbarities practised in these parts, and how they led to the most appalling destitution among the people, and to wholesale thefts committed by the impoverished, in order to obtain such necessities of life as the squandering of their resources in drink had deprived them of. From the preamble to an Act passed by the Privy Council in 1622, we learn that the Islanders, whenever they had the opportunity, devoted "bothe dayis and nightis in thair excesse of drinking". Smuggling, like poaching, was deemed an honourable calling; and illegal distilling was carried on everywhere. In Lewis such distilling continued *overtly* as late as 1827. One of the two principal stills in the island at that time was at Coll, but a few miles from Stornoway: the other was at Gress, a few miles farther on. Both were famed for quality, as well as for output. It is said that, when an excise official visited Lewis, it was the practice, when treating him, to ask which he preferred—" Coll " or " Gress "!

In the nineteenth century, Stornoway was a drunken place, as, in fact, it still is. In 1833 this quite small town had, in addition to many notorious shebeens, no fewer than a score of licensed premises.

. . . .

If there be one topic with which the social literature of Celtic Scotland deals amply, during recent centuries, it is surely that of wakes and funerals, and the excesses associated therewith, in open defiance of the efforts of the Church. In Protestant as in Roman Catholic communities, the lykewake or death-watch was regarded as a social function of first importance, the cost and extravagance of which varied according to the status of the deceased. The preliminary expenses incurred between the death and funeral of a chief or laird, for example, were often very high; and, comparatively speaking, so also were those upon which the relatives of the poorest crofter or cottar embarked, by way of celebrating the passing of their kindred.

Glance at the items purchased for the wake of the Laird of Ardnamurchan in 1651:

	(Scots) £	s.	d.
52 gallons of ale at 20/- per gallon	52	0	0
5 gallons and 1 Quart Whisky at £16 per gallon	84	0	0
8 wethers at £3 each	24	0	0
2 pecks salt	2	0	0
2 stones cheese	4	0	0
1¼ lbs Tobacco		11	0
1 Cow	23	6	8
	£189	17	8

A typical scene in Eriskay

When The MacKintosh—MacKintosh of MacKintosh, as he is sometimes called—died at Moy Hall in 1659, his lying-in-state was much protracted owing to the time it took his heir-male to arrive at the family seat. In the interim, funeral feasting went on, unabated, and on the most lavish scale. For this occasion, expert cooks and confectioners were actually brought North from the Scottish Capital. Two months after this Chief's death, the heir at last managed to reach the ancestral home; and so great were the expenses incurred in respect of the wake and funeral, that the family exchequer was straitened for several decades!

Some years later, The MacKintosh's domains became so notorious for these licentious excesses that the minister of Moy was instructed by the Presbytery of Inverness " to pro-hibit dancing, piping, and fiddling at lykewakes, and to punish the guilty with church censure ".

About this time, too, the Synod of Moray, " being deeply weighted with the superstitious and heathenish customs at lykewakes in many places within the diocese . . . ordains that the ordinary crowding multitude of profane and idle persons be debarred, and that none frequent or countenance these meetings but those of the defunct's nearest relatives, or those that may be useful for Christian comfort to the mourners and afflicted . . . spending time in reading the Scriptures, and in conferences upon mortality ".

Among the most memorable old-time funerals was that of The Chisholm in 1817. This chief of his clan died in the town of Inverness, several miles from Erchless Castle, his ancestral seat, in Strathglass. In Inverness his corpse lay for several weeks, during which time wines and refreshments were dispensed freely among those who travelled thither to pay their last respects. When, eventually, the burial took place at Beauly Priory, the two hundred and forty representa-tives of county families who attended were provided with a sumptuous funeral dinner in the upper storey of a neighbour-ing granary, while mourners of the lesser orders were regaled with claret and whisky on the ground floor. Liquor is said to have been so plentiful at this funeral that the local people carried away the surplus in buckets!

At the historic funeral of Flora MacDonald, in Skye, the

The Sound and Isle of Eriskay from South Uist

procession was estimated to have consumed no fewer than three hundred gallons of whisky on its sixteen-mile trudge to the graveyard with her coffin.

Only in scale did the lykewakes and funerals of the poorer classes differ from those of the chiefs and the petty lairds and their kinsfolk. The story is told of an old Highland woman who died in Glen Moriston, midway between two kirkyards. By the time the mourners reached the point at which the roads to these kirkyards led off in opposite directions, most of them were thoroughly intoxicated. A dispute now arose as to the kirkyard to which they were to bear the coffin. Dispute soon led to angry words, and angry words to fisticuffs. While there ensued a drunken brawl, in which several were injured, the more sober mourners solved the problem by burying the old woman on the spot!

One of the last Highland funerals conducted according to the old, traditional style, was that of the Laird of Dundonell, who died in Edinburgh about 1830. The coffin containing his remains was brought by sea as far as Inverness, where, on its being unshipped, several days' feasting and drinking followed. From Inverness, in course of time, the funeral procession set out for far Dundonell, in Wester Ross, by way of Garve, where, in those days, the road ended. At Garve, therefore, the entire male population of Dundonell awaited it, in order to bear the coffin home across the hills and moors. But dusk was falling by the time they were ready to fare forth; and, since no night's accommodation could be found for them in the neighbourhood of Garve, they decided to sit up through the darkness with the coffin, among the heather, and to enjoy the excellent refreshments provided. At dawn they started out for Dundonell; and they had travelled many a rough and rocky mile before one of the less inebriated noticed that the coffin had been left behind at Garve. Back they had to go for it!

"Drinking of ardent spirit at funerals," according to the *New Statistical Account*, was a lamentable feature of social life in Tiree in 1843 and, indeed, remained so until fairly recently. It cannot be said that, even yet, the practice has wholly disappeared. The chronicler instances poor families parting with their last horse or cow, so as to provide the wherewithal for funeral refreshments; "and thus what might have contributed to their support for a twelvemonth is wasted in a day, to keep up a savage and disgusting custom". This, together with smuggling (mainly from the north of Ireland), clandestine stilling, and the abundance of "low, illicit tippling-houses", or shebeens, was responsible for much depravity during the first half of the nineteenth century.

At many a funeral in the Western Highlands and Islands, the providing of a copious supply of whisky is still deemed a matter of prime honour, and one which the natives observed to the full until very recently, when it was agreed that too much brawling and fighting took place afterwards, and that few of them could really afford the traditional dramming associated with burial.

Between death and committal to earth, however, it is still customary in Tiree for relatives and friends to send or take to the house of the deceased all sorts of provisions, such as butter, eggs, cheese, and biscuits. Those actually visiting the house are expected to sit with the corpse for some twenty minutes—not nearly so long, I might add, as in Lewis, where the formalities connected with the death-wake are observed in even greater measure, and where the period between death and interment is sometimes protracted, owing either to the expected arrival of a near relative from afar, or to the time required to procure, for the funeral party, a sufficient supply of alcoholic beverages. On such occasions, soft drinks are conspicuous by their absence.

On the day of the funeral, the female mourners in Tiree gather in large numbers *inside* the house of the deceased. The male mourners, with the exception of ministers, dominies, and the like, wait *outside*, where, on arrival, they are treated to the traditional dram. When an adequate number of carriers for the coffin has assembled, a short service is conducted just outside the door of the house. The coffin, raised on two short poles, is then borne on the shoulders of four mourners. Two of the principal mourners, who are usually the deceased's nearest relatives, stand by the coffin, one in front of it, the other behind, each holding a black cord attached to it. The other mourners precede the coffin. A local worthy leads the procession and, at intervals of between forty and fifty yards, calls on the next four mourners to stand out. This they immediately do, in order to relieve the first four bearers, who now walk in front of the coffin, but in the rear of the main part of the procession. This direction is repeated until the island burying-ground is reached.

No matter how cold or wet the day, no matter how distant the burying-ground, most of the inhabitants of Tiree adhere to the practice of carrying the coffin. In cases where the burying-ground lies in close proximity to the house of the deceased, the mourners often enter into open competition with one another for a turn of carrying, if only the distance of a few yards.

One funeral I witnessed necessitated the "fours" changing over every ten yards, to ensure that everyone had had his spell before the graveside was reached, so numerous were the male mourners, and so near at hand lay the cemetery. Female mourners in this Presbyterian isle follow the coffin for a short distance only. Before returning to their *own* "refreshments" at the house whence the coffin has been carried, however, they observe the custom of kissing it, and of the laying-on of hands. In Tiree nowadays there is no halting between the deceased's house and the place of interment.

On arrival at the graveyard, the coffin is immediately lowered and covered with earth. Those Islanders, who are expert in the use of spade and shovel, trim the sods, and generally tidy up the grave. This process occupies some twenty minutes, during which the main body of mourners lingers idly through the graveyard, re-reading the inscriptions on its tombstones, or resting on the surrounding dyke. When all is in order, a brief committal service is held—*brief* it certainly used to be, because by this time the cart conveying the "refreshments" had arrived on the scene, and the mourners were drouthy with their exertions! Biscuits and cheese were then distributed, and drams freely dispensed. The greater the number of rounds of the latter, the greater the honour the natives believed they were paying to the dead.

The mourners' homeward journey was often boisterous and hilarious. Not infrequently, the least sober of them were carted home in the horse-drawn vehicle that had brought the whisky to the scene of their revels. There was a day, not so long ago, when more than one cart accompanied the procession, in order to carry home those defeated in brawling and overcome in dramming.

A good story is told of the way in which the natives often vied one with the other in the quantity of alcohol consumed at funerals. When X's wife died, she was honoured in eleven drams. Shortly afterwards, X's son returned home from a funeral at a neighbouring township with the disconcerting tidings that thirteen drams had been given. This so annoyed his father that he threatened to dig his wife up, "and we'll have *fourteen* rounds!"

When I was staying in Tiree some years ago, there took place a memorable departure, when a local worthy had the coffin of his late sister conveyed to the graveyard by motor lorry. The mourners numbered five—just as many as the lorry could accommodate, together with the coffin. In the chief mourner's own words, "it was all over in ten minutes, with just one bottle". Not so very long ago it was customary in the Highlands and Islands to attend a funeral armed with a good stick, in anticipation of the inevitable brawl. Clan feuds often broke out afresh at funerals.

A Tiree minister did inaugurate a petition with a view to putting an end to these pagan and unseemly observances; and a member of the Argyll family (the island belongs to the Duke of Argyll) actually went so far as to offer the natives a hearse. However, the first funeral to take place after the signing of the petition happened to be that of a near relative of "a pillar o' the kirk", a prominent signatory who, when the crucial moment arrived, had not the heart to break away just so suddenly from age-long tradition. Liberal supplies of whisky were procured, therefore; and the humble petition became a very humble affair indeed!

These funerals in Celtic Scotland, quite often, are boisterous and irreverent, even at the present day. Solemnity, in any marked degree, is seldom exhibited at them. Animated conversation on earthly topics, such as the price for cattle and sheep at the Oban marts, absorbs the mourners' attention until dramming-time.

I can recall the case of an Islander, who had some odd pieces of furniture he wanted to dispose of. As his house lay close to the township's burying-ground, he arranged that the sale should take place immediately after the interment, in the hope that the mourners, now somewhat inebriated, might be attracted to it. A schoolmaster on this particular island assured me that never had there been such keen bidding. In the estimation of all present, it was a good funeral, and a very good sale. No one had had anything to complain of.

Invitations to these Island funerals is usually delivered orally. One or two respected members of the community are honoured with instructions to call with it at every house. A friend used to tell me that a voice in the dark, outside his front door or sittingroom window, always summoned *him*, and in the recognised terms: "The presence of your company is expected at the funeral of —— from —— to —— at twelve noon to-morrow." An hour or two after noon, the proceedings usually begin.

I have heard it said that dramming at funerals had some connection with the ancient ritual into which seven, the mystical number, entered. Seven drams were given before setting out with the corpse, seven each time the bearers halted with it, and seven at the graveside.

Two other occasions are regarded by the Western Highlander and Islander as justifying the most liberal consumption of intoxicants—the celebrating of the New Year and a marriage. The pagan tradition that there must be plenty of drink at marriages and funerals, and on New Year's Day, is dying hard in these parts.

Right up until a few years ago, it was customary in Barra, both at Roman Catholic and at Protestant funerals, to hand round among the mourners whisky, bread or biscuits, and cheese. No sooner had the menfolk begun to shovel the earth over the coffin than the deceased's relatives took out the refreshment basket, and supplied the fifty or sixty mourners who, by now, were standing in one long line with their backs to the sheltered wall of the church. By means of no more than one or two tumblers, passed from one to the other when emptied, everyone present got a good, stiff dram. This was never sipped. It had to be thrown over the throat—"knocked back", I believe, is now the correct term—in traditional style. Nowhere is whisky consumed with such speed as in the Highlands and Hebrides. It's down the gullet in a jiffy!

The first funeral to the parish burial-place at Cuier, in Barra, at which whisky was not served, took place in 1941, when, owing to war-time scarcity of this precious—nay, this *sacred*—commodity, the relatives of the deceased were able to procure no more than one solitary bottle. Finding it impossible to obtain what they would have considered enough for at least half a hundred expectant palates, they agreed to dispense with refreshments altogether. Indeed, a courageous decision in a part of the country where the natives are such moral cowards!

The young minister who officiated at this funeral told me the other day that the chief mourner, the deceased's eldest son, asked him to explain to the assembly why there were no refreshments, and to make some kind of apology on behalf of himself and his family. This the minister innocently did. Anyhow, so far as Protestant funerals in Barra are concerned, the drinking custom has now been broken; and I learn that its revival is unlikely.

No funeral in the Highlands or Islands was regarded as having been conducted worthily unless it concluded with a series of fights, to the effusion of blood, among those attending it, to whom plenty of whisky had been given. The traditional idea of what, in many parts, still constitutes a successful funeral is humorously alluded to in the note upon which ends a story well told by the Very Reverend Dr. Norman MacLean, in a recent book of his.[1] " Johnnie is buried, and not a bloody head in the churchyard!" exclaimed Peggy Nighean Uisdean, after her husband's burial. "Shame is on me, for they will to saying of me that I spared the whisky at my husband's funeral."

Only eleven residents and sixty-eight visitors were convicted of drunkenness at Brighton in 1947—a total of seventy-nine convictions. Vigilance and police efficiency in the Outer

[1] *The Former Days.* (Hodder & Stoughton, 1945.)

Hebrides, with a total population but a tenth that of Brighton's, would secure as many convictions for the same offence in a single week-end.

A decade ago, when I brought to the notice of the Secretary of State for Scotland the appalling amount of drunkenness in Stornoway, with a population but a fortieth of Brighton's, it certainly would have been possible to obtain this number of convictions over a week-end, had the police been resolute, and adequate in numbers to deal with the situation, and had there existed in these parts any public opinion whatsoever on the subject of drink. My letter to the Secretary of State was designed to bring to public notice the lax condition into which police administration had degenerated in Stornoway, particularly in regard to drunkenness, disorderliness, and the overcrowding of public vehicles with drunken and riotous passengers. I pointed out that, when residing with cousins at the adjacent village of Sandwick in the autumn of 1937, I was frequently obliged to return from Stornoway, by the regular bus, under the most disgusting conditions. Out of fourteen passengers aboard this public conveyance one evening, I was the only passenger sober, apart from a schoolboy. On five consecutive Saturday nights, to my own knowledge, this bus stopped at the same place at Newton to enable a number of drunkards, residing in some of the new houses there, to topple out on to the roadside in the dark, and find their way to their respective homes as best they could. On several occasions I was a passenger on that same bus when it was obliged to stop, in order to allow a drunkard to alight before he spewed on the laps of his fellow passengers. Spewing is a common occurrence in our island buses, especially at week-ends. On one journey made on the Stornoway-Sandwick bus at this time, a Member of Parliament, his wife, a local child, and myself were the sole passengers who were not drunk and incapable. There were eleven passengers in all. Any Friday or Saturday evening, one may find the buses leaving Stornoway for neighbouring and distant townships dangerously overcrowded with drunken men.

In 1937 the Gaelic Summer School was held at Stornoway. This brought to the island of Lewis many strangers from the mainland cities, several of whom assured me that they had never seen such a spectacle as the streets of Stornoway, and that nothing would induce them to return to a place where, under the very eyes of the police, such unseemly conduct was the rule rather than the exception. I myself have seen police officials standing by, and turning the blind eye, when brawling drunkards were being taken aboard the island's buses, and when the buses already had aboard almost as many people standing as were seated. I have observed the police pass quietly on the opposite side of the street while drunken men have been endeavouring to gain re-admission to public-houses from which they had been ejected; and I have frequently watched the same officials saunter by as these ejected drunkards were banging at the door of the Caledonian Hotel, trying to re-enter the pub attached. It is seldom that one attends a concert or a public meeting in Stornoway which is entirely free from drunken interruption. The inhabitants think little of this, for they are so accustomed to it.

With all this information I supplied the Secretary of State for Scotland in 1938, adding that I could put him in the way of obtaining much corroborative evidence. Notwithstanding, he wrote me some weeks later saying that, "after exhaustive enquiries", he had been informed by the police authority of Ross and Cromarty (to whom my communication had been submitted for comment and report) that nothing could be found to suggest that there was any foundation for my complaints. That the meeting of the Police Committee, before which my letter came, was devoted to denials and irrelevancies, is shown by the press reports in my possession. One of Stornoway's more voluble councillors described me as a writer of fiction, who had allowed his imagination to run riot; and with that irresponsibility so often exhibited in matters of serious import, he appealed in a big-hearted way to the Police Committee to do everything in its power to contradict my statements, which it promptly did. And thus the matter stands. Drunkenness and drunken disorder are as rife as ever.

Many an Islander is amazed that anyone should object to drunk persons being conveyed on the buses. They think that this is just what the buses are for—indeed, that they have a public charity—nay, a public duty—to perform in getting them safely home and off the roads!

In the Isles on a Saturday night it is no unusual thing to see a native quitting a public-house with a pailful of beer—literally, a pail overflowing with beer. He is probably on his way to some ceilidh, to some week-end carousal, near at hand.

Sunday morning in Stornoway, before the clamour of the church-bells rouses the inhabitants to a sense of righteousness, is as silent as the previous evening has been roisterous. Scarcely a soul is to be seen abroad, scarcely a sound heard. Not even a dog is allowed out, lest his bark should disturb the holiness of the Sabbath. A few straying sheep may have wandered into the streets from the town's refuse-dump, where they feed on garbage, and get their fleeces in an indescribable mess. Otherwise, to all outward appearance at any rate, one would think the inhabitants had vanished overnight. This silence before the church-bells begin to peal is attributable, in the main, to two causes. One of these is the natives' puritanical piety: the other is the number of "hang-overs" from the previous evening's intemperance. Nowhere do piety and insobriety exist so amicably, side by side, as in the Highlands and Islands. There you will discover that those adhering most strictly to Sunday Observance are often the most dissolute members of the community on Friday and Saturday nights. To these pious people, it does not seem the least sacrilegious, or even incongruous, that on Sunday mornings church grounds and graveyards should be littered with empty bottles thrown into them by revellers homeward bound the night before.

In fairness to Stornoway and to Lewis generally, it must not be supposed that drunkenness is relatively less prevalent elsewhere in the Western Isles. It is pretty bad in Castlebay, for instance; and this recalls a well-known Barra teacher, now dead, whom I habitually saw lying in a drunken stupor by the roadside in a very protracted endeavour to return home to Greian, a township situated several miles away. So long as he remained sober during school hours, I was assured, no one felt there could be any ground for complaint. He could do just as he liked in his own time, especially at the week-ends. The example he set the children of the island was unimportant. No one, to whom I spoke of the matter locally, would concede that this habitual performance of his in any way reduced the community's respect for the schoolmaster, or influenced adversely such esteem as the island's juvenile population had for him. The real tragedy, it seemed to me, lay in the fact that this was true, both as regards parents and children.

Quite early in life, the Islanders are taught to revere whisky —to deem it one of life's chief glories. They are broken in, so to speak, early and gently, as the following anecdote shows. A friend of mine expressed astonishment the other day that a boy of ten should have been given whisky at an island wedding. "Oh, but they mix it with lemonade for us!" said the boy, equally astonished that anyone should take exception to such a trifle.

A mother at a New Year's party was much amused when her own child, to whom she had given a glass of wine, complained that he felt hot and funny. The child was only three!

When in Castlebay in the autumn of 1947, taking notes on the spot with a view to presenting in these pages an up-to-date picture of ongoings in these parts, I noticed one Saturday evening a brightly lit vessel making for the pier, just after dark, and shortly after closing-time at the local bar. A little later, and out of curiosity, I made for the pier to find that she was a Fleetwood trawler, full of fish, calling for water while on her voyage south from the Icelandic fishing-banks. Silhouetted against her powerful deck-lights, I counted seventeen "locals". They were standing in an uneasy line at the pier's edge; and I observed them closely for a considerable time. No more than two of them, I do solemnly declare, were in complete possession of their faculties; and, in fact, most of them were very little so. When not forming part of this slouching, swearing, swaying line, bantering with a member of the trawler's crew, who declined to give them any fish, though his tips were literally overflowing, and who himself had just returned from the local bar none too sober, they retired in twos and threes to urinate against the empty bread hampers lying on the pier awaiting transhipment by Monday's mail-boat to the Glasgow bakery, whence comes so much of the bread now eaten in the Outer Hebrides. The traditional Scottish Saturday Night is, indeed, an ugly institution.[1]

It must not be assumed from the foregoing pages that everyone in the Western Isles is drunken and dissolute. On the contrary, there are several, particularly in the burgh of Stornoway, who have worked hard to relieve the community of the evils of drink, notable among them Mr. Roderick Smith who, on more than one occasion, has been provost of the town, and upon whose shoulders fell the main part of the responsibility for putting into effect a new but thoroughly inadequate law of local government purporting to deal with the drink problem. What *can* be assumed is that, in relation to population, the Outer Hebrides—and I fear one must include much of the Highlands as well—are the most drunken part of the United Kingdom.

Let us look at the efforts made some years ago to introduce into Lewis a measure of sobriety, and see how these efforts were frustrated.

The Temperance Act, passed in 1913, was new legislation designed to deal with intoxicating drink. It provided for a delay of seven years after the passing of the Act before it took effect, in order that publicans, hotel-keepers, and other holders of liquor licences might be afforded the opportunity of recoup-

---

[1] The farther north and north-west one travels in Scotland, the more pronounced becomes the reverence for alcohol, with a corresponding disregard for temperance and the licensing laws. When we come to Orkney and Shetland, we find few hotels in Kirkwall or in Lerwick where the *bona fide* traveller can be vouchsafed a night's rest undisturbed by rowdy men going noisily and hilariously to their beds in the small hours, after a long carousal somewhere downstairs. Many hotel-keepers with licences to sell intoxicants take very lightly their obligations to the non-drinking resident in the Northern and Western Isles of Scotland. The visitor from the more civilised and considerate parts of the country, turning on his bath-water at 11 p.m. with some trepidity, lest he should disturb the slumber of others, soon loses any such sense after a night or two in most of these hotels. In many of them there is no apartment except one's own bedroom where one can sit comfortably of an evening, free from the intrusion of bottle parties, often conducted in contravention of the licensing laws. The farther one penetrates into these regions, the more one discovers that the bar assumes the sanctity once vested in the temple. Thus, the average innkeeper shows little interest in the wayfarer requiring lodgings, and will often turn him away on the pretence that he cannot provide him with food and shelter. The sale of drink brings all the profit he wants, and with the minimum of inconvenience to himself. Brochures and booklets designed to attract visitors to Scotland make no mention of this. Yet, it is assuredly a situation to which those interested in the tourist traffic will have to devote some serious attention.

ing themselves in view of the prospective loss of their trade in liquor. During this long interval, licence-holders made the most of things. Few failed to compensate themselves against the possible loss of " goodwill " which, it was claimed, they would suffer if their trade were extinguished. It was 1920, therefore, ere effective steps could be taken under the Act to contest the existing position by demanding a poll of the electorate in any area in Scotland where the temperance party might desire to put to the test the wishes of the people in respect of licences for the sale of liquor.

This Act of Parliament, it may be recalled, was " an agreed measure "—the type of legislation which, in my opinion, is always fatal where matters of high principle are involved. The temperance party, not fully alive to the dangers, accepted the Act, believing half a loaf to be better than no bread.

In 1920 the temperance workers in the town of Stornoway demanded a poll, having secured the signatures of a tenth of the electorate, as the law required. The number of voters who went to the poll was 874. They voted as follows:

No Licence	720
Limitation	149
No Change	5
	874

These figures showed that the community was almost entirely opposed to the Liquor Trade. The bad practices of the drink shops seemed to have had their day: henceforth, these evils, it was thought, would diminish, locally, at all events. The opportunity for habitual and excessive indulgence in intoxicating liquor was to be effectively stopped, and the drunken rowdyism, then so prevalent in Stornoway, positively curbed.

From the end of the war in 1918 until the closing of the liquor shops under the Temperance Act, the streets of Stornoway presented a shameful spectacle of drunkenness. This was greatly accentuated by " treating ", a practice which was common after the war. Yet, despite the lawless and disgusting condition into which the town's highways and byways had fallen, there was relatively little prosecution for drunkenness by the police.

The opponents of the temperance party were not long quiescent, once the result of the local option poll became known. They soon discovered ways and means of evading the spirit of the Temperance Act. The immediate sequel to the closing of the public-houses was the flagrant practice of open-air drinking, in direct contravention of the voice of the electorate—indeed, in barefaced defiance of the big majority of the ratepayers who had voted against it.

The attitude of the customs and excise authorities was one of complete indifference to the temperance cause. They and the police connived at the extensive shebeening in the town, and at other serious irregularities which developed apace with the shutting down of the public-houses.

The excise authorities now granted wholesale licences. These permitted the sale of $4\frac{1}{2}$ gallons of beer and of 12 bottles of whisky to any purchaser within a " dry " area, as well as to any purchaser outside such an area, anywhere in Scotland. This subversive practice seriously vitiated the purpose of the Temperance Act, which granted to the people the right of local option. In fact, it made it impossible for social workers to cope with the evils arising from the lavish consumption of alcohol. The local bench of licensing justices had no control over the granting of these wholesale licences, which could be held by anyone, anywhere, whether a community voted " wet " or " dry ". The cause of temperance was further obstructed by the refusal of the customs and excise officials to supply information regarding such licences—the dates on which they were applied for or granted, the names and addresses of the licensees, and so on. Though the secretary of the local No-Licence Committee made every endeavour, no particulars regarding the wholesale licences held by two hotels in Stornoway could be obtained.

The Temperance Act required that such licences should have been held in the district for a whole year prior to a poll which might result in that district's going " dry ". If not so held, they had to be given up with the ordinary retail certificates.

Such were the first bitter fruits of the measure "agreed" between the temperance advocates and "The Trade". Until the Act is amended, this state of affairs must necessarily continue in any area where the electors may desire to vote "dry". The position is an untenable one, an insufferable one. It has led to much drunkenness and much corruption. Exactly the same circumstances prevailed in Wick, which also went "dry", but which is now "wet" again.

At the inauguration of the "dry" regime in Stornoway, two hotels—the Imperial and the Lewis—held a wholesale excise licence. To the credit of Mr. Carnegie, the licence-holder at the former, let it be recorded here that, whenever he realised what had happened, he gave up his licence. His premises were afterwards sold to the Education Authority, and became a Girls' Hostel connected with Stornoway's famous school, the Nicolson Institute.

The proprietor of the Lewis Hotel held on to his wholesale licence, despite the contention that it was illegally held, it being alleged that it had not been taken out in due time before the first poll in the town. This licence continued throughout the whole period of six years of "No Licence"! It must have brought its holder a considerable fortune. In Stornoway "the four-and-a-half" now became proverbial. After the drunken orgies on Friday and Saturday evenings, empty containers were to be found on the doorsteps of the temperance workers in the town. In ways, drinking now became more excessive than ever. If you were obliged to purchase a minimum of twelve bottles of whisky, you might as well drink them. The dissolute clubbed together to raise the money for these quantities; and, having done so, felt obliged to consume it all that night.

At the beginning of the "dry" period, shebeening was not very common. As time went on, however, it became rampant. Neither the police nor the excise officials gave the temperance party any assistance whatsoever in its efforts to stamp out the various forms of shebeening now being carried out openly on the highways, round the quays, in the public urinals, and in houses throughout the town. Much of this shebeening, and of the disgusting spectacles it occasioned, I myself witnessed at this critical time.

Without avail, the local No-Licence Committee called on the government, on the excise, and on the police to take action for the suppression of these excesses. The Committee asked the government to amend the Act, so that, in any area in which a No-Licence Resolution was in force, the sale of excise-able liquors *by wholesale* should be prohibited. Besides, it was well known that smaller quantities than the legal $4\frac{1}{2}$ gallons were being sold to the shebeeners. Men were found openly carrying $2\frac{1}{2}$ gallons from the wholesaler, and deposit-ing this quantity on premises known to be shebeens. Yet, although the police were informed, evasive ways were always found to frustrate the efforts of those who desired to clean the town of the drink curse. By all and every means, the electors' expressed wishes were defied.

By 1923, when a fresh poll was demanded by "The Trade", after much agitation among the working-class people of the town, the temperance party had slackened in its efforts to teach the Islanders by propaganda. The position had deteriorated much when there went to the poll 976 voters. The voting that year was as follows:

Continuance of No Licence	565
Repeal	401
Spoiled papers	10
	976

Shebeening and open defiance of the law increased year by year. The members of the town council of the day were not such eager reformers as their predecessors had been. An unfortunate weakening of the support for temperance crept into the body politic, with a noticeable falling off in sobriety. As a result of the poll held in 1926, the town went "wet" again.

The Stornoway No-Licence Committee did all in its power to stop the rot, hoping that the community would successfully stand the test that year. The vote was lost by a majority of 74, when the electorate voted thus:

Part of the bay and mountains of Uig, seen from Carnish

Continuance of No Licence	393
Repeal	477
Spoiled papers	5
	875

During the six years that Stornoway remained "dry" (at any rate, nominally) the *Stornoway Gazette* declined advertising contracts, worth some thousands of pounds, from firms seeking to get round the local veto by supplying wines and spirits through the post. When the next poll fell due, however, and on the pretext that it believed in freedom of speech, and that it was the only local paper in the island, it published the advertisements of the "wets" as well as those of the "drys". This distinction between advertisements seeking to circumvent a ban imposed by the vote of the people, and advertisements designed to persuade the people to change its views, puzzled many ardent temperance advocates.

"The evil forces set on foot by the publicans and their helpers, who found coöperators in places where they should not have existed," wrote Roderick Smith, that champion of the cause for a sober island, "aided by authorities who failed to work with the electorate . . . gave 'The Trade' a win, obtained by constant catering to all the baser elements of human nature and by stimulating the craving for strong drink."

This frightful fiasco resulted, in the main, from police indifference, if not actual hostility, to the new order. The local temperance party readily admitted defeat in face of odds so overwhelming as those created by the wholesale licences. It was a defeat without disgrace, however. The *real* disgrace may be seen in Stornoway any time. There cannot be a more drunken place in all Britain.

The annals of the Scottish Isles contain innumerable references to protracted orgies of drinking occasioned by shipwreck upon them. Martin, for instance, mentions that, among the advantages accruing to the inhabitants of the lesser isles of

T   273

The Parish Church of Barra, at Cuier

the Shetlands, when an Amsterdam ship was wrecked among them in 1664, was "the pleasure of drinking liberally of the strong drink, which was driven ashore in large casks for the space of three weeks".

Several shipwrecks brought drink in this manner to the Western Isles, but none so abundantly as did the *Politician*, a British merchantman of approximately 12,000 tons, registered at Liverpool. On a February evening in 1941, this vessel went ashore upon a rock immediately at the east of Calvay, an islet in the shallow Sound of Eriskay. How any ship of her size, under control, as one presumes the *Politician* to have been, came to grief at this spot, even under the black-out conditions of war-time then prevailing, is a mystery. The supposition is that her navigator mistook the Sound of Eriskay for the Sound of Barra. The latter separates the south end of Eriskay from Barra: the former intervenes between the north end of the island and South Uist, is much more constricted, and is so shallow that, when crossing it by small boat at low water, even on a moderately calm day, the eye can follow the sandy sea-floor all the way, but a dozen feet below.

"Och, well," replied an island fisherman, when I enquired of him some months ago how the *Politician* was wrecked, "it would be the whisky aboard that would be putting her off her course." Thereby hangs a tale of orgy and drunkenness surpassing any in the history of the Outer Hebrides. The drunken condition which the Statutes of Iona sought to assuage early in the seventeenth century was as nothing compared with that which followed the wreck of this vessel, now popularly known throughout the Western Highlands and Islands as the *Polly*. The full story of this mishap and all that ensued was not made public at the time, owing, one supposes, to the secrecy enshrouding incidents of this kind in war-time. Little mention of it appeared in the press until the autumn of that year (1941) when but a few of those who had helped themselves too liberally to the *Polly's* cargo were brought before the sheriff at Lochmaddy, and sentenced to varying terms of imprisonment up to two months for offences against the excise laws. Otherwise, one knew little of what had occurred except that the Islanders were said to have enjoyed the most convivial spell on record.

The first indication the inhabitants of Eriskay had that anything unusual had occurred was given by the steamer's siren, the insistent blare of which rudely disturbed the peace of this historic and romantic isle, and even filled many of them with fear. Young and old hastened in the direction from which the blare was coming. They arrived at the beach opposite Calvay to find a great ship firmly aground, roughly a hundred yards offshore. Soon the crew was landed in Eriskay; and there it remained for some days, receiving at the hands of the inhabitants the hospitality for which that isle has long been renowned. The *Polly* meanwhile lay stranded and completely abandoned. For several weeks no one came near her. Soon it began to be whispered among the Islanders that whisky comprised the bulk of her cargo. This prompted verification. Some of them now visited her at high water in small boats and found her full of whisky. Cases of it lay partly submerged in her enormous hold. With this discovery there now began what some have described as "the greatest Saga of the Outer Hebrides in modern times", but what certain members of the clergy in this locality told me was probably one of the most disastrous episodes in which the Islanders had ever been involved.

News of this palatable treasure spread like wildfire throughout the Isles. People arrived on the scene from as far north as Lewis, from as far south as Mull. They came armed with rods, ropes, hooks, and all manner of ingenious contraptions for the fishing out of the ship's interior as much as possible of the whisky she carried. Rumour had it that the vessel contained a million bottles! In point of fact, she had less than a fourth of that number, her whisky cargo being precisely 20,300 cases, or 243,600 bottles, there being a dozen bottles to a case. This whisky—the best Scotch, and overproof at that!—was on its way to the American "millionaire" market.

Eye-witnesses have told me that the unloading of the whisky presented an amazing sight. It continued day and night, according to the state of the tide. At the outset, the vessel's iron sides stood so high at low water that even the longest ladders in Eriskay and South Uist scarcely enabled the Islanders to board her. When, a little later, she slipped back some distance into the water, their ladders proved ade-

quate at *high* water, since the stranded ship no longer rose
with the tides.

The unlawful removal of the intoxicating cargo went on
unceasingly. In the dead of night, as many as fifty men,
black beyond recognition with oil, might be seen in the hold
with their bright Tilly lamps, standing up to the thighs in
oil and sea water, probing, tugging, hauling, and slinging
cases of whisky to the upper decks. "You couldn't visit the
Polly without meeting someone you knew," I was told by one
of those who took a prominent and profitable part in this
epic of the Isles. "You would meet people there from the
other islands that you hadn't seen for years."

"Going aboard the *Polly*," said another, "was like arriving at the Highlandman's Umbrella," the allusion being to
that part of Argyle Street, Glasgow, which is roofed in by the
railway lines passing overhead, close to the Central Station—
a favourite rendezvous of Highlanders residing in the city.

As news of the ship and her cargo continued to spread,
small boats arrived in increasing numbers from farther and
farther away, so that, before long, consignments of whisky
were being cached down all along the West Highland and
Hebridean coast. Cases were removed from her by the hundred; and in Eriskay itself, as also in Barra and South Uist,
whisky was now so plentiful that the Islanders thought nothing of sprinkling half a bottle of it over a fire, in order to
make it burn more vigorously. I have been told by many,
who boasted that they partook freely of this commodity at
the time, that it became the practice to use it in this way
as a substitute for paraffin. The *Polly's* whisky revived many
a sluggish peatfire in the Isles.

Never had liquor been so ubiquitous. Young and old made
merry on it. In Eriskay, especially, life became a perpetual
revelry. Nearly everyone fell under the influence of this
drink. Many a house became a veritable bar at which drinks
might be had at any time, free of charge. Many an Islander
sat up drinking till early morning. Little work was done
without liberal potations. Thus the Islanders' capacity grew
at an alarming rate—their capacity for laziness, as well as
for drink. The injunction, "Thou shalt not dilute whisky"
(the Eleventh Commandment, as it is called in Scotland) was

strictly observed. Whisky, and plenty of it, must be " knocked
over ", neat. So plentiful was the beverage that, when some
of the crofters went out to till the soil, they found it helpful,
if not actually necessary, to have a bottle in readiness at each
end of the furrow, wherewith to restore their flagging efforts.

The very poultry were drunk in Eriskay. While pecking
about the crofts or on the sands of the machar, they would
sometimes come upon dregs in broken bottles. These they
sipped; and I had it from those who saw them that their
antics thereafter were fantastic—the most astonishing exhibition of fowl play, a native told me! "If only Hogarth had
been among us at the time," he added, "he could have
depicted drinking comedies in the Isles as memorable as any
he ever did in eighteenth-century London."

It was hardly to be expected that, with so much whisky in
circulation, Eriskay could continue indefinitely and unmolested in so blissful a state. Gradually, stories of this era of
abounding hospitality began to filter to the mainland. A
native, when sober enough to return from leave in these parts,
would carry south with him not only the tidings of excessive
conviviality, but also evidence in the form of a bottle or two
of Johnnie Walker. So, after several weeks, during which
many an inhabitant, without interference from anyone, indulged himself to capacity, the attention of the Ministry of
Shipping and of the Customs authorities was at last directed
to Eriskay. A night-watchman was now placed aboard the
Polly, and the island invaded numerously by police and excise
officials. This intrusion, wholly unexpected, occasioned great
alarm. No one had come near for weeks; and, since the war
was still raging, it never occurred to the revellers that anyone would ever land to claim the wreck and her contents.

The method of the ancient fiery-cross was now resorted to,
lest any inhabitant should be caught unawares. In attempts
to conceal the great quantities of liquor still unconsumed,
every imaginable deception was adopted. Bottles were hung
as far up the chimneys as possible, and stuffed into the thatch
of cottage, barn, byre, or hen-house. Expedients had to be
adopted quickly: with the excisemen probing the thatch
next door, there was no time for elaborate plans. There are
natives who proudly declare that, on the whole, they were

equal to the invaders, and managed to save much from the general comb-out. Like Achan of old, they buried their treasure in the ground. Deep down among the potatoes and the sown corn of Eriskay, of Uist, and of Barra the bottles went. Never had there been such Digging for Victory!

The great bulk of the salvaged cases was buried on the moor or by the shore. Interment took place at night, or in the early hours of the morning. Burying became second nature. Young and old alike turned zealously to the spade. "If you happened to go out on such a night," an eye-witness told me, "you would see illuminations before which the lights of Blackpool at its merriest would have paled into insignificance. Lines of flickering lantern lights could be seen creeping along the hillside. The sand-dunes by the shore were dotted with weird spectral lights as the people cunningly hid their treasures from the dreaded excise officers. Many a comic yarn will yet be told about this amazing episode in the history of our quiet, little island. A bottle of whisky was the merest trifle. With the good weather, there came a spiritual resurrection; and certainly in the theological sense. Drinking the first drink to the captain of the ship became a solemn ritual; and a delightfully apt toast in his honour was composed for general use throughout the Islands. As Calvay was about the only thing in the Sound of Eriskay which a ship could strike, the Gaelic toast for the occasion ran " Health to the one who did not see Calvay".

Scarcely a stook, scarcely a stack of corn or of peat, but concealed the amber treasure: scarcely a chimney but had its bottles hung away in it. Spring mattresses were found very serviceable. With care and patience, each could be made the hiding-place for the entire contents of a case. On the approach of the inquisitors, elderly natives, though hale and hearty, were bundled off to bed. There, surrounded by heaps of bed-clothes in which a round dozen bottles might be secreted, they remained until the danger seemed past, feigning mortal illness. Some of them lay with hot water-bottles full of whisky.

The ingenuity of one old woman is often cited. When news reached her that the excisemen had landed in the neighbourhood, she assembled her bottles in a heap by the door of her byre. Over them she threw a fork-load or two of hay, and then brought her cow on the scene. The cow ate contentedly of the hay. The ruse was successful. No other fodder escaped the probing of the officials. The winds of the wildest Hebridean winter never knocked over as many haystacks as *they* did!

The search continued unabated. So thoroughly were the little crofts examined that not a dung-hill escaped attention. Receptacles were ransacked. The very caves by the shore were explored. The silver sands, upon which Prince Charlie disembarked from the French frigate just two centuries earlier, were probed with prying appliances.

Many a good dram, as they confess in Eriskay and the neighbouring islands, was lost in the confusion, and as the result of subsequent forgetfulness. Bottles were buried in places which the natives afterwards failed to locate. When, some weeks later, the ground was being prepared for the spring sowing, an odd decanter would be turned up. Occasionally, the tragic breaking of glass might be heard as the ploughshare tore its way through some forgotten cache. " That was the cruellest cracking sound that ever we heard! " a native of South Uist observed when boasting to me of the enormous number of bottles *he* had retrieved from the wreck.

Last autumn a ferryman told me that he himself had salvaged, clandestinely, no fewer than 2,000 bottles. These he sold, by the score, at ten or twelve shillings each, while some of his less-grasping accomplices were asking no more than half-a-crown or five shillings. There was nothing in his life he regretted so much, he added, as that he had not held on to his whisky until its abundance had turned to scarcity, for people were now offering him not a meagre ten shillings for a bottle, but ten pounds! He did not confide to me (a wretched teetotaller! !) whether he still had some bottles left.

It is well known that some of the more adventurous and farseeing possessing their own boats, amassed small fortunes. Indeed, this was an easy matter in a region where, at the time, money was ridiculously plentiful, and where whisky at all times is deemed the most precious commodity on the face of the earth.

There is an amusing story which I must tell. A certain

brand of whisky carried by the *Polly* was contained in firmly corked decanters labelled " Highland Nectar ". To the neck of each decanter was attached a glass stopper, the like of which the natives had never seen before. One day Donald Campbell, the island schoolmaster, entered the cottage in which Lachlan, a worthy of the island, lived with his wife, Anna, and his sister, Bellag. Than Lachlan, Anna, and Bellag there never was a more unsophisticated trio. Here they were, in heated dispute over a glass stopper, which they mistook for a very little bottle. Lachlan believed its content to be a colourless liquor more precious than all that being poured so freely out of ordinary bottles throughout the Isles at this time. Anna thought it wasn't whisky, anyhow: it was probably a special wine. Bellag counselled caution. It might be poison, she said; and Lachlan had better throw it away rather than take any risk with it. But Lachlan would do nothing of the kind. He must needs break the wee bottle open, because he could not unscrew the head of it even with the pliers. A knock with the back of a hatchet would settle the matter, he urged. Anna, however, pronounced against anything so drastic. How could you break open so small a bottle without losing most of the precious liquid it contained? Better ask the schoolmaster for his advice, suggested Bellag. They were greatly disappointed when Donald Campbell dispelled their problem by explaining that what they were trying to open was not a wee bottle at all, but a fancy stopper for their decanter, now empty of " Highland Nectar ".

In course of time, a salvage-tug reached Eriskay and dragged the *Polly* off the rock on which she had gone. She was then cut in two. The fore-half of her was towed into Lochboisdale to await suitable weather for the long voyage to Rothesay, where she ultimately arrived. The stern-half got stuck beyond recovery on a submerged sandbank between Eriskay and Calvay. There she is gradually sinking deeper and deeper, taking with her, the Islanders say, some hundreds of cases of the precious liquor they had had no opportunity of salvaging. At low tide, a small part of the stern-half may still be seen awash.

Some months later, several of the natives of the Isles came before the sheriff at Lochmaddy, charged with concealing, or with having unlawfully in their possession, whisky and other things removed from the wreck. Many of them were sentenced to a month's imprisonment in Inverness. They returned to their homes in no way critical of the treatment they had received when under detention. The prison authorities, they like to impress upon one, did not regard them as felons in the ordinary sense, and, indeed, were sympathetically inclined towards them, if not also disappointed that they had not brought a bottle or two with them! Those convicted returned to the Isles as conquering heroes. Had there been a brass band, it assuredly would have turned out to welcome them home. It was the complaint of some of them that several, who actually had been guilty of the anti-social crime of *selling* the stuff, and at a considerable profit, went scot-free. That rankled more than anything. *They* had not commercialised their good luck, as had some of their mercenary neighbours. And what about those who, without let or hindrance, had trafficked so remuneratively in liquor with the military and air force personnel then stationed in Benbecula!

The Islanders' dealings with the *Polly* have left their mark on some of the Isles. When in these parts as recently as the spring of 1948, I had occasion to ask a native to oblige me by carrying a message to a neighbour of his. Politely he declined to do so, adding that he could not very well explain his attitude. I afterwards found that there existed a feud between his household and his neighbour's. The one accused the other of having acted as informer.

Whisky was not the only cargo the ill-fated *Politician* had aboard her. She also carried some thousands of yards of shirting, lengths of which were used to great advantage in raising the whisky cases, parbuckle-wise, from hold to deck, and in lowering them to the small boats clustered round the stranded leviathan.

Dozens of bicycles were also taken off her unlawfully. These became popular in Eriskay, both with the young and with the agèd. Many of the natives of this quiet, sequestered isle had never seen a bicycle before. Old men and old women, to many of whom even walking was now possible only with the aid of a stick, strove hard to become proficient in this new mode of transport in an island where there are no roads, and where nothing whatsoever on wheels—not even a cart—travels its two-and-a-half miles of footpath. The bicycles occasioned many a spill and many a laugh. Never before had road accidents occurred in Eriskay.

Scores of bottles of perfume were also taken from the *Polly*. Many of these the children brought with them to school, having already applied to themselves so much of their contents that the schoolroom was scented like a beauty parlour. More troublesome to the teachers than the perfume was the abundance of tooth-paste, hundreds of tubes of which were removed from the wreck. The children found diversion in squirting the paste at one another. It was smeared upon everything—clothes, hair, limbs, seats, and school-books. It took the teachers weeks to rid pupils and premises of this clammy bane.

To the Eriskay folks, one of the most unusual objects picked up in the *Polly* was the telephone receiver, salved by an elderly native who triumphantly brought it home to his wife. "There, now, Catriona," says he, "we can speak to our son, John, in Glasgow, any time we like!" The old man proceeded to demonstrate the marvel of this find. Lifting up the ear-piece, he riveted it to his ear for several minutes. Not a sound could he get from it, however. "Damn it!" he exclaimed impatiently, in slamming it down, "I can't hear a whisper after all my trouble in taking it ashore!"

The *Polly* had aboard her a beautiful, little German piano. This the Eriskay schoolmaster sought permission to bring ashore for use in the island school. He wrote to authority after authority, offering twenty pounds for it, and adding that the local fishermen had agreed to transport it gratuitously from wreck to schoolroom before pounding seas smashed it to bits, as it lay on deck, exposed to the elements. No permission was received; and the much-coveted piano now lies deep in the salten sands of the Sound of Eriskay.

The *Polly's* misfortune, a local clergyman assured me, brought incalculable harm to these Island communities. It was, indeed, one of the greatest calamities that ever befell the natives of the Outer Hebrides. Those already addicted to drink just became more so. The confirmed drunkard took the opportunity of re-dedicating himself to Bacchus. In some districts the young—even the very young—were encouraged to sample the whisky. Owing to prolonged insobriety attributable to this free and bountiful measure of liquor, persons lost positions of responsibility. The higher percentage of alcohol this cargo contained—much higher, I am informed, than that of the whisky procurable at the local public-houses—sent some of its partakers raving mad.

A native of Barra testified to what I already had heard elsewhere, namely, that some of the Islanders actually died, following upon their orgies. Where the metal caps of the bottles were corroded by sea water, a little of which got in among the whisky, the contents appear to have been rendered even more potent. Thus a number of the Islanders became dangerously ill. The stomach-pump was now brought into use by the local practitioners, some of whom had, themselves, partaken plenteously of the *Polly's* popular cargo.

To revert to the somewhat serious social matters alluded to in this chapter and in the preceding one, the question naturally arises as to how this unhappy state of affairs might be mitigated. In other words, how can the standard of integrity and social discipline be improved in the Western Isles?

In seeking the answer to this, one must take into the fullest account the origin and type of people presenting such social problems. It must be remembered that the population of these islands is composed almost entirely of peasants employing themselves casually in crofting or in fishing, or assiduously in petty trading. Many of them, irrespective of whether they be Catholics or Presbyterians, or whether they be simple crofters or sophisticated shopkeepers, retain wellnigh irradicable notions and superstitions associated with peasantry the world over; and it is to be regretted that many of those returning from college to take up professional positions among them remain peasant in mentality, in outlook, in habit and custom, to the end of their days. To a large extent, this is due to the complete absence from their midst of a middle class, from which better standards might have been copied. Even the natives who have been a-field for several years, and have been accustomed to more civilised standards, soon revert to the wild, as it were, when they come back to live in their native environment.

Furthermore, the Western Isles are now without a landlord class in the old sense. This class, with all its shortcomings, did maintain certain standards of conduct, although it may be objected that the Isles were largely denied the better influences of such a class through the fact that the landlords were seldom, if ever, resident. Absentee landlordism has been one of the major drawbacks of the Highlands and Islands.

Where the professional classes—doctors, clergy, solicitors, teachers, and the like—are drawn almost solely from the native peasant population, one cannot expect any high degree of cultural appreciation or of moral integrity. As a rule, they are no better than the townspeople or the villagers among whom they function. The same limitation applies to the civic authorities. They, also, are recruited from the people. The bailies, town councillors, and county councillors, elected almost entirely from the petty merchant and shopkeeping members of the community, are no improvement on those who elect them, with the result that their electors, only too aware of this, show them no respect, and frequently flout their authority flagrantly. Take, for instance, the town of Stornoway, which, from a social and administrative viewpoint, may be looked upon as one big family, the members of which all know one another, and often know too much about one another. Here you have a community in which few dare criticise for fear of incurring fiercer criticism, together with the mutual raking up of past misdemeanours and dishonesties.

The rigid exclusion from public appointments of natives, as well as of the relatives of natives, over a long period of years, seems to me the first step towards betterment. As things are at present, this may be regarded as impracticable. But things will have to be altered fundamentally ere any improvement can take place in the ways and habits of the native populace. I would begin by seeing that all appointments, such as that of procurator-fiscal, went to persons imported from the mainland; and I should certainly insist, *as a matter of principle*, that in a small town like Stornoway, or indeed anywhere for that matter, the procurator-fiscal be debarred from carrying on in the town a private legal business of his own. The best public prosecutor in the world cannot but have qualms about pursuing his duties *ad vindicam publicam* where his personal friends and clients are involved. This state of affairs should be rectified on principle.

Then the main post-offices should be staffed by strangers; and so should the police force. Fortunately, so far as the latter is concerned, this is already largely the case in Stornoway. Otherwise lawlessness—bad enough at present—would be unimaginable. The townspeople usually dislike a constable who isn't a Highlander like themselves, for he is inclined to be less lax with them, and to demand certain behaviour to which they are little accustomed. This is always a good thing. For the position of sergeant and of inspector in Stornoway, a member of some mainland police force should always be chosen.

The ministers—well, they are not public appointments, of course. Yet, it must be obvious how little moral influence is exercised by those of Island origin.

One obvious difficulty is that, when dealing with a peasantry so preponderately Gaelic-speaking, it is assumed that many of the public appointments must go, as at present, to those of Gaelic-speaking peasant stock. So long as the teaching of Gaelic is compulsory in the schools in Gaelic-speaking areas, it will remain largely impossible to improve the children's standards, since the teachers themselves must needs be drawn wholly from the crofting and shopkeeping peasantry to which their pupils belong.

Whatever may be the solution, to the outsider the social problem of the Isles is a very real one. They have become an enormous public expense in recent years; and it is only right that the taxpayer should insist upon a standard of local administration more in keeping with statutory requirements.

CHAPTER VIII

THE TANGLE O' THE ISLES

WHEN we speak of the tangle o' the Isles, we usually have in mind the seaweed, *laminaria*, the nostalgic smell of which is carried to our nostrils by one of the most famous songs of modern times:

> *Sure, by Tummel an' Loch Rannoch an' Lochaber*
> *I will go,*
> *By heather tracks wi' heaven in their wiles;*
> *If you're thinkin' in your inner heart braggart's in*
> *my step,*
> *You've never smelt the tangle o' the Isles.*[1]

The tangle with which this final chapter deals is a very different one, namely, the complex social and economic tangle which the Western Isles have presented continuously for two centuries at least, and which successive governments, often imbued with the loftiest motives, have failed to solve. My own view is that the economic problem of the Hebrides, like that of the world at large, is incapable of solution upon the existing basis of population in relation to food production, either actual or potential. The popular, political slogan, " There's plenty in the world for everybody ", is a mischievous half-truth.

The problem of the Isles dates roughly from the middle of the eighteenth century, though it must not be supposed that, formerly, the Islanders lived by any means free from grinding want. On the contrary, their earlier poverty and squalor must have been inconceivable, especially in those parts where population was so much higher than it is to-day.

[1] *The Road to the Isles*, written for the lads in France during the First World War by the Rev. Dr. Kenneth MacLeod, D.D., until recently parish minister of the island of Gigha. (See page 244 of his book, *The Road to the Isles*, first published in 1927 by the Moray Press, Edinburgh.)

Islands which, a century or two ago, carried a fair population are uninhabited at the present time. How they could have borne the population they did, except in the condition of economic slavery for the barest subsistence, it is difficult to imagine. This point should be reasoned out by those who, on emotional and sentimental, as well as on narrow nationalist, grounds, deplore the depopulation of certain areas of the Highlands and Islands where they themselves would never dream of settling.

The Western Isles, in common with the rest of Celtic Scotland, underwent a radical social change following upon the final defeat of the Jacobites at Culloden in 1746. That defeat brought to an end, almost precipitately, the clan system, so patriarchal in character, so feudal. Ostensibly, the old relationship between chief and clanspeople disappeared, though here and there fervent efforts were made to retain at least some semblance of the old order, long after it had become an anachronism. Considerations of kinship and clanship were now displaced by those which came into existence as between landlord and tenant and, later, as between employer and employee. The authority of the chiefs was gone for ever. No longer could they exercise their ancient and hereditary power in the matter of jurisdiction. Their right of pit and gallows was finally extinguished; and the social and economic revolution now inevitably overtaking the people could be no more than delayed by a waning adherence to clanship, based largely upon sentiment for things traditional.

Whether the change was to the advantage of those whom it directly concerned at the time must remain a rather moot point. The early transitional stages were grievous, and indeed oppressive. Certainly, at the outset, many found themselves parlously placed. The old system, for all its evils, had vouchsafed, as regards land tenure, a measure of security, whereas the state of affairs under the new landlords not only bereft the Islanders of the contentment they had enjoyed in their old and primitive ways of life, but eventually confronted them with such excesses as eviction, and even transportation. The story of the peasants' sufferings during the latter half of the eighteenth century and the former half of the nineteenth is, indeed, an appalling one. Only by mass emigration did there appear to be any relief from poverty, and from the exactions of many a landlord or of his factor.

It was the factor's tyranny which, in 1773, resulted in the great efflux from Lewis to America. By this time, emigration had become a sort of epidemic in the Western Isles; and many found it to their interests to encourage it. Few of the emigrants, on their arrival in the New World, discovered anything even approaching the rosy conditions they had been led to expect. They found themselves in a position rather comparable with that of some of the " G.I. Brides " who have sailed for Canada during the past year or two. Several who, with high hopes, quitted Barra about 1794 for Nova Scotia and Prince Edward Island, were stranded there. Emigrants from the Uists, similarly induced to leave their homes on the promise of prospects held out to them, reached America to discover that they were homeless, helpless, and penniless. Their experiences soon became known throughout the Western Isles, whence many were about to follow them, with the result that there was now a temporary falling off in the numbers drifting away across the seas.

Wholesale emigration was resumed in the nineteenth century. During its opening years, both proprietors and peasantry gained appreciably by the boom in kelp-making, fostered so largely by the war with France. Kelp is the calcined ash of seaweed. The cessation of hostilities was soon followed by a slump, which in turn brought famine to much of the native populace, and ruination to many a proprietor. This was particularly true of the Uists and Benbecula, where, during the winter months, the great stems of the laminarian seaweed—" the tangle o' the Isles " which we smell, and about which we sing—were gathered in huge quantities, distributed along the shores in such a way as to allow of their being dried by the keen winds of spring, and then heaped and burned on the seashore for the ash. In the days when small sailing smacks and coasting vessels were commoner in the Isles than they are to-day, the transference of this ash to the mainland ports presented no problem.

Distress became widespread. Emigration seemed the only means of lessening pressure on diminishing subsistence; and the proprietors were only too glad to avail themselves of it.

288

Islanders returning to Vatersay after
Sunday Service at Castlebay

Indeed, some of them reverted to the earlier practice of evicting the people from their crofts. Among the more notorious of these was Colonel Gordon of Cluny, who, in the eighteen-fifties, banished across the seas many of his South Uist and Barra tenants. So ruthless was this expatriation said to have been that, even to-day, the more dastardly episodes connected with it are related at the ceilidhs in the Outer Hebrides.

It was at this time that Cape Breton and Nova Scotia received from the Western Isles the colonists whose descendants there, at the present day, speak the Gaelic language as fluently as did their emigrant forbears. There are communities in Canada as Hebridean as any in the Isles, since the racial identity of the original settlers has been preserved not only in the language, but in many ancient customs and observances peculiar to the Celt.

Though it cannot be said that the proprietors were wholly blameless for this state of affairs, one finds difficulty, when examining the matter in historical perspective, in assessing just how much blame should, in justice, have been attached to them. On the other hand, it must be borne in mind that, during the years of prosperity, attributable to the inflated value of the kelp, many of them were notoriously extravagant. Few estates in the Highlands and Islands could bear the high living in London, which now became fashionable among them. The tyrannical efforts of factors to finance such costly conduct by increasing the rents paid by a peasantry already impoverished are one of the grimmest passages in the troublous agrarian history of the Western Isles. As W. C. Mac-Kenzie remarks, there was an aptness in Dr. Johnson's dictum that " the Highland chiefs should not be allowed to go farther south than Aberdeen "! [1]

[1] " The advent of kelp to the Outer Hebrides was an event of the greatest economic importance," MacKenzie writes in his *History of the Outer Hebrides*. " A state of fictitious prosperity was created, which appeared for a time to have solved the problem of poverty. As with the potato, so with kelp, a knowledge of its manufacture was first brought from Ireland to Uist by MacDonald of Boisdale (or, according to other accounts, by MacDonald of Baleshare). Since 1722, kelp had been made in the Orkneys, and it was first manufactured in North Uist in 1735, an Irishman named Roderick MacDonald having been brought over by Baleshare to instruct the people in its manufacture. In 1748, it was first made in Harris, on the initiative of MacLeod of Bernera. The date of its introduction to Lewis is unknown.

" The vicissitudes of the industry in the Long Island were remarkable. The high-water mark was reached at the commencement of the nineteenth

Loch Kentangaval with Castlebay beyond, from Ben Tangaval

Apart from the profitable manner in which, during the last decade or two the tweed and the lobster-fishing industries have been conducted, the fishings around the Western Isles have always been the basis of any regular commerce they have enjoyed. Yet, the land, so limited, so impoverished, has remained the foundation of the Islander's existence. His troubles, therefore, have always been mainly agrarian, in the peasant sense of the word. Throughout the last two centuries or thereabouts, and indeed up until fairly recently, a determination on his part to dig himself in the more securely on his croft or holding produced not merely friction, but also strife, and even flagrant law-breaking. Land agitation led to riots and land-raiding, stimulated largely by the reaction to harsh absentee landlordism, and to emigration. One recalls in this connection the Bernera Riots in Lewis, in 1874, and the raids carried out ostensibly by ex-servicemen in the early nineteen-twenties on the farms belonging to the new proprietor of Lewis, the late Lord Leverhulme. To these raids we shall make reference at a later stage.

By no means has raiding been confined to the northern end

century, when as much as £22 per ton is said to have been paid, but that must be considered quite an extreme figure. For this inflation of value, the war with France was chiefly responsible. For the twenty-two years ending 1822, the average price was £10 10s. A succession of heavy blows played havoc with kelp. The high duty on the imports of barilla from Spain was removed; the duty on salt was repealed; and potash salts from Saxony were added to the list of competitors. In 1831, as low a price as £2 per ton was reached. The increasing uses of iodine saved the trade from extinction; but when, about 1875, iodine was imported from Chili, and, subsequently, from Peru, the manufacture of kelp was again rendered unremunerative. An effort was made in 1863 to revive the industry in Tiree, and subsequently in North Uist, on more scientific principles than had formerly obtained; but the attempt had to be abandoned in Uist, and last year [1902] the works in Tiree were closed.

" The revenue derived by the proprietors of the Long Island from kelp, during its palmy days, was considerable. To the proprietors of Uist, especially, it proved a veritable gold mine. In 1812, the net proceeds of kelp in North Uist exceeded £14,000, and for several years afterwards, they fell little short of that sum. By 1837, the profits had dwindled to an insignificant amount. About 1790, the rental of South Uist was £2,200. As kelp increased in value, the rental rose rapidly to £15,000. By 1837, it had fallen to £5,000. In 1825, the net proceeds from kelp in Harris were about £2,180; in 1826, about £800; in 1828, about £280; and in 1829, the balance was on the wrong side. While the boom lasted, the people were in a state of comparative comfort, though their share of the profits was not commensurate with the terribly arduous labour which kelp-burning entailed. But the proprietors lived up to their inflated incomes, and the people saved nothing from their increased wages. When the bubble burst, ruin stared proprietors and people alike in the face."

of the Long Island. Early in the present century, the Barra Isles became embroiled in this arbitrary method of settlement. At that time there were three families living on Barra Head, in addition to the lightkeepers. On Sandray (now a sheep-run belonging to the small-holders on Vatersay, and conducted by them as a club for a fixed number of sheep, the profit or loss on which they share equally) there lived only a shepherd and his family, the ruin of whose solitary home may yet be seen about the centre of the island. On Pabbay in 1900 there were two families. These were joined a little later by another two. No one lives on Pabbay now. On Mingulay there was a township with a population of between thirty and forty. Vatersay was occupied solely by MacDonald, the tacksman, or tenant-farmer, together with his family and the shepherds he employed.

So extreme was the discord between landlord and peasant throughout the Highlands and Islands during the latter half of the nineteenth century, that in the end parliamentary intervention became inevitable. This led, in the first instance, to the Crofters' Act of 1886, and later to the Congested Districts Board. These did much to alleviate conditions amongst the native population, though no reasoning person could ever have expected that they would have solved the land question in localities where land, especially productive land, is so limited, and where the numbers seeking to derive direct sustenance from it have always been greatly in excess of what it can maintain, even under the most modern methods of agriculture. Through the Crofters' Act, Highland and Island crofters did achieve their two main objectives, namely, fair rents and fixity of tenure. But it cannot be said that the Congested Districts Board, with the best intentions in the world, could ever have done much to relieve the press of increasing population in districts where the sub-division of crofts was so common and so notorious a practice, and the soil, owing to natural causes, so poor and restricted.

Disputes still occur in these crofting regions, of course—disputes as to title, succession, soumings, boundaries, and the like. To-day, these are adjudicated by the Land Court, upon which now devolves the functions formerly performed by the Crofters' Commission. As the Land Court visits the crofting areas from time to time, in some sort of rotation, it means that investigations can be made on the spot; and, since, as we already have seen, one of its members must always be Gaelic-speaking, applicants and complainants appearing before it are at no disadvantage when they feel themselves "not too good at the English ", as the saying is.

That, on the whole, the crofters of the Western Isles are content with the present arrangement whereby the Crofters' Act, on the one hand, guarantees to them the security of tenure their rebellious grandfathers fought for, and the Land Court, on the other, disposes, in law and equity, of their local troubles, is surely shown by the fact that, when Lord Lever-hulme offered the Lewis crofters their crofts as a free gift, they declined them without thanks, preferring to remain as tenants under the Board of Agriculture than become peasant proprietors. Perhaps, they realised for the first time that the landlord was not necessarily the tyrant who took nothing but profit, and accepted no financial obligations. Though their ancestors had warred against landlordism for generations, they showed themselves more than reluctant to accept the land, even when offered to them for nothing. The very excellence of Lord Leverhulme's offer raised in their minds those suspicions to which they are so prone. " Better the De'il we ken than the De'il we dinnae! " was the attitude they adopted toward his magnificent gesture.

. . . .

From a report made by the factor for the Congested Districts Board, we learn that, arising out of a demand by cottars living in the vicinity of Castlebay, the Board, in 1902, bought from Lady Cathcart, for the sum of £600, sixty acres intended for potato plots in that part of Vatersay known as the Uidh, belonging hitherto to the island's farm. The cottars grew potatoes there for a season, and then complained that the land was unsuitable for the purpose. So another piece of Vatersay farm was rented for potato growing from the farm tenant. In 1907, cottars from the same locality, together with a number of crofters and cottars from Mingulay, which was also Lady Cathcart's, squatted on Vatersay farm, where they proceeded to erect for themselves temporary dwellings in the form of wooden huts. Some of these squatters put cattle, sheep, and ponies to graze on the farmlands, which were already fully stocked. Eventually, the Congested Districts Board purchased for £6,250 the entire island and farm of Vatersay (2,278 acres, apart from the Uidh's 60) and, in addition, the neighbouring islands of Sandray, Flodday, Lingay, Biruaslum, and Greanamul, having a total area of 1,178 acres. The Board sensibly resolved that any proposed settlement should be on Vatersay only, that it should consist of holdings suitable for the accommodation of crofter-fishermen, and that not more than sixty such holdings should be created. The remainder of the farm was to be assigned as common grazings to the four townships to be formed. In 1909, after public notice had been given in Barra, inviting applications for holdings from landless cottars or squatters residing within the parish, Vatersay was divided into the fifty-eight holdings still in being there. From a total of eighty-three applicants, this number was selected from amongst those who, in the Board's view, after credentials and references had been examined, seemed best fitted to occupy holdings. Half of the holders came from Barra, and one-third from remote Mingulay. The remainder were those who had already squatted there, and who, in the meantime, had informed the Board of a desire to be regarded as applicants. Five of the original applicants renounced their holdings, which were subsequently given to five others. In the interim, proceedings instituted by the Board in the sheriff court against certain squatters were decided in its favour.

At this juncture one might usefully give details of how Vatersay was ultimately settled. After a careful survey, the townships and holdings decided upon were as follows:

Township	Number of crofts	Rent per croft per annum
Uidh	14	£2 12s.
Caolis	16	£2 17s.
Eorisdale	8	£3 10s.
Vatersay	20	£3 10s.

A total annual rental from fifty-eight crofts of £180!!

In addition to each township's share in common grazings

on the island itself, Sandray (1,003 acres) was assigned for such purposes to the townships of Eorisdale and Vatersay, while Flodday (67 acres) and Lingay (66 acres) went to Uidh and Caolis.

The Board, of course, had to undertake various works of adaptation, such as roads, fences, drainage, and a wholesome and abundant water supply for each township and its live-stock.

It seemed to me, when spending a day on Vatersay recently, that the Islanders were reasonable prosperous. Yet, one could not but feel that, in the long run, a third fewer holdings on this island would have been wiser. The tendency is to over-populate such settlements at the outset, forgetting the rate at which peasants in these circumstances are apt to breed.

.   .   .   .   .   .

One cannot but express regret at the disappearance of the farms from the Western Isles, and the substitution of crofts upon which little is produced abundantly except babies, legitimately or otherwise. This transformation has taken place during the last thirty or forty years. I myself knew many a farm which is now no more.

When in Benbecula in 1947, I could not but notice the farmhouse and steadings of what, formerly, was the prosperous farm of Nunton. Here the arable fields seem more extensive and more generous than any I can remember having seen else-where in the Long Island. Nunton, like the rest, was broken up into small-holdings. One of the holders, to whom I hap-pened to remark on the unusually large fields then being harvested, was not slow to remind me that " we didn't *get* this farm, you understand! We raided it in 1923; and we've been here ever since! " He was proud to be in a position to com-municate this piece of information to one whom he imagined knew little of ways in the Isles. " Ay," he concluded, " we wouldn't be here yet, if we hadn't raided it! "

I am far from convinced that the division into small-holdings of farms more than economically self-supporting has been to the Islands' betterment. The crops raised on the old farmlands of Benbecula in a normal year far surpass those raised on the same area elsewhere in the Hebrides. What-ever case may have been made against the large farms (and one is inclined to think it was wildly exaggerated) their past owners have left a legacy in the splendid fields one sees in Benbecula, both at Borve and at Nunton. The good husbandry of former years has bequeathed to the small-holders now occupying these lands much excellent arable won and improved conscientiously, and with considerable diligence, at a period when agricultural labour was comparatively cheap, when mechanised farming was almost unknown, and the hours worked were twice what they are to-day.

The Islanders' conservatism in regard to the introduction of anything likely to improve their condition was well demonstrated in their early opposition to the potato, brought into the Western Isles from Ireland about the middle of the eighteenth century, and against which they and their mainland neighbours protested vehemently. In Lewis, the outcry against the tuber, which has since become one of the principal articles in the Islanders' diet, was considerable. In South Uist, where Clanranald had introduced it a few years previously, the tenants resolutely refused to have anything to do with it. They looked upon it with disgust; and many of them were actually threatened with imprisonment because of their attitude to it. "You made us plant these worthless things," they told Clanranald; "but, Virgin Mary! will you make us *eat* them?" Later, some of Clanranald's tenants relented a little and, under protest, did plant potatoes. However, when in due season they lifted the crop, they conveyed it to his home, setting it down at his gate, declaring that, sooner than eat of it, they would go to prison.

What a change was soon to come over the Islanders in regard to the potato! The tuber they despised during the eighteenth century was to become their mainstay during the nineteenth, when they would have cheerfully gone to prison rather than *not* have eaten it. The famine following upon the failure of the potato crop in 1846-7 brought them to a realisation of the part this humble plant now played in their slender economy.

Prejudice against the potato was by no means confined to the Hebrides. Even in England it had its opponents. One of the fiercest of these was William Cobbett—"the noblest

English example of the noble calling of the agitator ", as G. K. Chesterton called him. Referring to the Agricultural Committee of 1821-2, before which evidence on such matters was given, Cobbett deplored " that many labourers, especially in the West of England, use potatoes instead of bread to a very great extent, and I find from the same evidence that it is the custom to allot the labourers a ' potato ground ' in part payment of their wages. This has a tendency to bring English labourers down to the state of the Irish, whose mode of living, as to food, is but one removed from that of the pig, and of the ill-fed pig, too ".

Cobbett, in support of his hostility to the potato, quotes a certain Dr. Drennen, who described it as " the root of slovenliness, filth, misery, and slavery ". Drennen advised Englishmen to " leave Ireland to its lazy root ". Even the famine felt by much of rural England in 1822 did not turn Cobbett and his followers from their denunciation. On the contrary, Cobbett wrote that he was " glad to find that Edward Wakefield, the best informed and most candid of all the witnesses, gave it as his opinion that the increase which had taken place in the cultivation of potatoes was injurious to the country, an opinion which must, I think, be adopted by everyone who takes the trouble to reflect a little on the subject ".

The agrarian problems of the Western Isles are clearly reflected in their political history. Prior to 1917, when Lewis formed part of the parliamentary constituency of Ross and Cromarty, and all the Outer Islands to the south of it (that is to say, Harris, the Uists, Benbecula, and the Barra Isles formed part of the parliamentary division of Inverness) the electorate was Liberal—nay, Radical—owing largely to the influence of the Highland Land League and its efforts to combat those powers which had produced the historic Highland Clearances and Evictions. Traditionally, therefore, the Western Isles have been so consistently anti-Tory that the votes cast there during general elections more than counteracted any pro-Tory sympathy in the two mainland constituencies with which they polled, and in both of which there also was a strong Radical bias for similar reasons.

Apart from the growth of the Labour Party, the Liberals

might have retained Ross and Cromarty indefinitely, had they been able, as aforetime, to count upon the Radical vote of Lewis, which was very considerable. The same applies to the parliamentary constituency of Inverness. For some years now, both of these constituencies have returned to Parliament a member described as a Liberal-National, a species of Liberal for whom all the Conservatives are only too happy to vote, in order to ensure the defeat of the Labour candidate.

In 1917, the Boundary Commission for Scotland set up the Parliamentary County of Inverness, and Ross and Cromarty with its three divisions, namely, Inverness, Ross and Cromarty, and the Western Isles. In 1918, at the first general election thereafter, the Western Isles voted for the first time as a parliamentary constituency of its own. The Islanders were still predominantly Liberal in sympathy. This was shown by the fact that in this election, as also in that of 1922, two Liberal candidates fought one another for the seat. This was explained by the split in the Liberal ranks, as between the Asquithians and the supporters of Lloyd-George. The population of the Western Isles at this time was just over 44,000, and the electorate numbered roughly 21,000.

In the general elections of 1923, 1924, and 1929, both the Conservatives and the Labour Party joined in the contest. The Liberals held the seat, however, though in 1923 the Conservatives came within a couple of hundred votes of winning the seat.

In the Western Isles, as elsewhere throughout the country, the decline of the Liberal Party synchronised with the rise of the Labour Party. Labour polled well in the Western Isles in 1929, but did not contest the seat in the scare election of 1931, when a Liberal-National candidate, opposed by a full-blooded Conservative, won it. In 1935, by which time the population of the Western Isles had fallen to about 38,000 and the electorate was roughly 28,000, the seat, in a three-cornered fight, was won for the first time by Labour, in the person of Malcolm K. MacMillan. Malcolm was then twenty-two years of age, and a student at Edinburgh. He retained the seat at the first post-war general election of 1945. Being one of the brightest and most active of the Scottish Labour members, he has been chairman of the Scottish Parliamentary Labour Party, and of the Highlands and Islands Advisory Panel, set up in 1946. As a writer and poet, he is a regular contributor to several of our leading periodicals. He has published a volume of poetry; and a collection of his essays is expected as soon as supplies of paper will allow.

Many ancient usages connected with agriculture still obtain in the Western Isles. Where parts of the croft are too tiny, too steep, or too isolated for even a small, horse-drawn plough, the ground is worked quite effectively by the old *cas-chrom* or "bent-foot" plough. This implement, which might be described as a cross between a flat, wooden spade and a light, wooden plough, still functions well when manipulated by a crofter who is expert with it. Those who, at ploughing-time, turn the soil with it, declare that the crops raised thereon are better because it enables them to make a deeper furrow than would an ordinary plough, even were it possible to use the latter on patches so small and uneven. These patches are often no more than a few square yards in area. They may be seen on the hillsides, in hollows between out-cropping rocks. In the Hebrides they are known as lazy-beds. They are made by trenching in two parallel lines, five or six feet apart, and then piling up between these lines what soil is available. On these tiny, raised beds, potatoes grow well; but grain crops, often rather poor owing to the want of sun and to too much moisture, are also grown on them. From time to time the lazy-beds are manured, either with cow-dung or with seaweed. They are reaped by sickle when too small for scythe.

For centuries, the limitation of good pasturage in the Isles necessitated the retention of the shieling. Indeed, in parts of them the *airidh*, or shieling, is still to be found. There are several in Lewis, for instance; and only the other day I read of an octogenarian lady belonging to Ness who, while at the Cuishader shieling, where her family has spent the summer months for many years, went down the precipitous cliffs in the neighbourhood to rescue a sheep stranded on a ledge of rock.

The shieling is the moorland or hill pasturage to which the

Islanders—usually the womenfolk—drive their cattle at the beginning of summer, and where they remain with them until the autumn, living in temporary and somewhat primitive shelters built of stone and turf. These shelters are not unlike those used by shepherds on wide expanses of moor, or erected on uninhabited islets by lobster-fishermen engaged in adjacent waters. Doubtless, it was after such shelters, used by fishermen in olden times at the mouth of the Tyne, that the towns of North Shields and South Shields were named.

From the remoter townships of western Lewis, the annual exodus to the shieling has gone on, uninterruptedly, for centuries. Fifty or sixty years ago, women from almost every family went to the shieling, as the saying is, taking with them the churn, the spinning-wheel, a minimum of utensils, and perhaps one or two of the younger children. There they stayed for eight or ten weeks, according to the weather. A wet shieling-time was misery: a dry shieling-time idyllic. Sometimes two families shared the same shieling, thus effecting a saving in labour. It was just as easy to prevent a couple of families' cows from straying among the hills as to prevent one family's. This yearly removal kept the livestock off the township's unfenced crops, and at the same time gave the home pastures some respite.

Space will hardly permit of our dealing with the many quaint customs associated with the sparse and primitive husbandry of the Outer Hebrides. However, we might just mention the *sugan*, which is the Gaelic term for a rope of straw or heather or, perhaps, of bent-grass. "None of his people that *we* ever heard of, anyhow, ever dropped a sheaf from the *sugan*", was the proverb to which the old folks had recourse when testifying to a man's probity.

The *sugan* had a loop at one end of it. Towards the other end there were three knots, each about six inches apart. In the days when the wintering of the township's bull had to be undertaken by the entire community, a meeting was held, after the harvest had been gathered in, to decide what the bull's allowance should be throughout the winter months. The precise measure was fixed by the *sugan*, which was laid flat on the ground so that the agreed number of sheaves might be laid upon it, in order to allow of its being tied at the knot appropriate to that particular season's harvest. When the harvest was a plentiful one, the *sugan* was tied at the last knot, so as to permit of its embracing the maximum number of sheaves. Conversely, when the harvest was a bad one, the first knot denoted each crofter's obligation in respect of the bull's fodder. When the harvest had been of middling dimensions, sheaves bound by the *sugan* tied at the middle knot were the agreed sufficiency. Each evening the *sugan* was passed on, in rotation, from croft to croft by the crofter who, that day, had provisioned the bull.

Now, the number of sheaves the *sugan* held was determined not merely by the knot at which it was tied, but also by the degree of tightness of the binding. And there was no greater disgrace than when a sheaf or two, because of the looseness to the *sugan*, fell out while the crofter was in the act of conveying to the bull its daily feed. When this occurred, it was held that the crofter was trying to defraud the bull of its rightful portion; and there existed no more damning evidence of his meanness and badness of heart. So this explains why, to this day, in the remoter parts of Celtic Scotland, it is proverbial to speak of a man or of his family or ancestors according to their record when the township's bull had to be provided for in this way. There could be no more admirable estimate of a man's honesty than that a sheaf was never known to have slipped from his *sugan*. That was the hallmark of integrity.[1]

. . . .

The only commercial enterprise which has been of any enduring benefit to the Western Isles is the herring fishing industry. The success or failure of the herring fishings meant prosperity or hardship to many a Hebridean home, especially in Lewis and in Barra, where they were prosecuted on a large scale. In prosperous times, the port of Stornoway retained prime place among Scottish herring centres; and during the summer fishing season, its population was greatly increased by the numbers of East Coast crews operating from it, and to the many supernumeraries connected with the purchase, sale, curing, and transport of the catches, both to home markets

[1] An interesting account of all the *sugan* implied appears in Colin MacDonald's intimate volume, *Highland Journey* (The Moray Press, Edinburgh, 1943).

and to markets as distant as New York, the Baltic States, and Russia.

Though Stornoway still has its fishing fleet, Castlebay now has none. Twenty years ago, however, Castlebay was a thriving port with a fleet of two or three hundred boats nightly fishing the southern waters of the Minch. The steam-drifters, which, as at Stornoway, formed the bulk of Castlebay's fleet, have gone. Even the old coal-hulks, alongside which they replenished their bunkers, have disappeared. A harbour once so full of craft of every size and shape is now deserted. Occasionally a drifter does tie up at the pier; but the curing of herrings and the transportation of them straight from Castlebay to foreign markets is a thing of the past. Not so long ago, as I well remember, drifters and small motor fishing-boats were unloading their catches at no fewer than twenty landing-stages erected round this excellent natural harbour. Castlebay was then the hub of busyness. Coopers, gutters, and curers, after the landing of exceptionally heavy catches, worked continuously from early morning until the small hours of the following morning. The stages, as well as the pier at which coasters called to load this cargo, were stacked with barrels packed with cured herrings, most of which had been landed from drifters owned and worked by the East Coast fishermen, who have always been the backbone of the herring fishing industry, even in the Isles. However, many of the smaller fishing-boats were then owned locally, and worked by Island crews. But these fell into disrepair during the First World War, when they lay beached. The few that survived at Castlebay went to bits during the Second World War, while the lads who operated them were serving either with the Naval Reserve or with the Merchant Navy, or perhaps with the Army. So there is no longer any curing at Castlebay.

With Castlebay's decline as a fishing port, Mallaig, a rail-head, situated on the west coast of Inverness-shire, has developed. Herring drifters now sail direct from the fishing grounds to Mallaig with catches which can be consigned straight to King's Cross, if desired, since Mallaig is the northern terminus of what used to be the West Highland Railway, a component of what until recently was known as the London and North-Eastern. The Argyllshire port of Oban has also been expanding as a herring port in recent years. Oban is the northern terminus of the old Callander-Oban Railway, a branch of the Caledonian, which was incorporated in the London, Midland and Scottish. So herrings landed and packed at Oban can travel direct to Euston or to St. Pancras.

Stornoway, of course, is still famous for its kippers; and in this connection it should be noted that the kippering industry is also being developed at Mallaig as part of the general expansion of the fishing industry there.

The herring is the only fish caught abundantly in Hebridean waters which has been commercialised to any extent. Line-fishing has been pursued, of course; but of late years it has declined greatly, owing partly to the destruction caused by trawlers operating illegally within the statutory three-mile limit. Many of the natives, for their own immediate consumption, still fish with lines, though rather more apathetically than in former years.

One of the chief recreations of the boys and younger men of the townships situated on the western fiords, or close to suitable rocks, is fishing for the saithe or cuddy. "Plenty of cuddies," I see from my *Stornoway Gazette*, "are being got at Carloway these days by rock fishers hardy enough to stand the finger-numbing cold sufficiently to be able to bait the hooks."

Fishing boats and gear have altered much in recent years. During the last quarter of the nineteenth century, half-decked boats were being displaced by fully decked and larger ones. At the beginning of the present century, Lewis had an enormous fleet of those sailing-boats known as wherries. Summer, autumn, and winter, they were engaged in the pursuit of the herrings. In spring, they were profitably employed at the White, or Great Line, Fishing.

The Lewis wherries followed the fishing all round the East Coast ports, and also to the English fishings at Lowestoft and Great Yarmouth. Until about 1928, fishing was an all-the-year-round occupation for our Island fishermen. By 1938, however, it had so decayed that no more than three or four months of the year were devoted to it.

The introduction of the steam-drifter at the beginning of
the present century gave a tremendous fillip to the Scottish
herring industry. The running expenses of these boats were
then comparatively light. Coal was only 15s. to 19s. the ton.
Other charges were correspondingly low. An East Coast
drifter making five landings a week, as against the sail-boat's
two or three, could then be run on about £14 a week. Besides
this, their capacity was so much greater. They held thrice
the number of cran the wherry could contain.

Not until 1912 did steam-drifters reach the Outer Isles and
participate in the fishings there. They were so much easier
to work, their running costs comparatively low, and their
profits therefore so much larger, that the East Coast fishermen,
with the enterprise the Island fishermen have always lacked,
steadily developed the importance of Stornoway as a herring
port. The native fishermen, either through lack of initiative
or of capital, stuck to their old, picturesque wherries as long
as they could. Of a fleet consisting in 1912 of roughly a
thousand wherries, no more than two were surviving at
Stornoway when the recent war broke out. And now we
learn that the *Muirneag*, the last of Stornoway's wherries
(named after a hill in northern Lewis) has been to sea for the
last time, and is about to be broken up.

From 1900 to 1914, the herring fishermen enjoyed a considerable measure of prosperity. The years 1914, 1919, and
1920 were highly profitable. So were the years 1926, 1927,
and 1928. Thereafter, a serious deterioration set in. Fishing-
boats no longer brought a return either to owners or to crews.
During the prosperous period, Lewis fishermen began to
acquire motor fishing-boats. Many of them were old sail-
boats fitted with Kelvin or Gardner engines. These, together
with two modern drifters and a small fleet of motor-boats,
comprise the Stornoway-owned fleet at the present time.

The report of the Fishery Board for Scotland, published in
1938, showed the alarming rate at which the fishing industry
had declined all over Scotland. For some years, the number
of fishing vessels registered in Scotland had been falling consistently, and with it, of course, the value of the fleet and its
gear. During the preceding decade, the decrease in the number of full-time fishermen, as well as of crofter-fishermen,

amounted to several thousands. It has been estimated that no fewer than two thousand fishing-boats disappeared from the Scottish fishing fleet; and, whereas roughly 35,000 persons were employed in the fishing industry in 1923, by 1930 the number had dropped by a third. The general decline in what was once one of Scotland's chief industries—indeed, for many years her staple—has had serious economic repercussions in the Outer Hebrides.

In the autumn of 1947, the Stornoway town council urged the Herring Industry Board to expedite such plans as it had for the provision of quick-freezing plant, emphasising at the same time the restriction placed on fishing at Stornoway throughout the previous summer (an exceptionally hot one) by marketing difficulties. The council sought to point out that Stornoway had transport problems peculiar to an island port, and that kipperers suffered heavy losses during 1947 through their consignments having been delayed in transit. It was argued that, if better facilities could be established for the disposal of the great catches of herrings landed at Stornoway, there would be a considerable contribution toward the nation's food supply, especially as the fishing season lasts longer at this port than at any other Scottish herring port. The difficulties Stornoway is now experiencing are just those which so recently took the fishing industry away from Castlebay, and led, as we have seen, to the development of Mallaig and of Oban.

While travelling among the Isles in the autumn of 1947, I met the members of the Fishery Group of the Highlands and Islands Advisory Panel set up shortly before by the Secretary of State for Scotland for the purpose of investigating the fishermen's problems. They were working their way northward from Castlebay, studying various problems on the spot—" panelling their way through the Isles ", as Naomi Mitchison, one of the group, put it. A competent body, it must be conceded. Yet, one could not resist the comment that the country might well have been saved the expense of such " panelling ", having regard to the numerous investigations of one kind or another which have been carried out in this field during the last few decades, and to the great accumulation of material which must have been gathered in

The MacKelvie brothers crossing the moorland of Eriskay to fish for cuddies (saithe) at sundown

The Isles of Gighay and Hellisay, with the old farmhouse and steadings of Eoligarry in the foreground

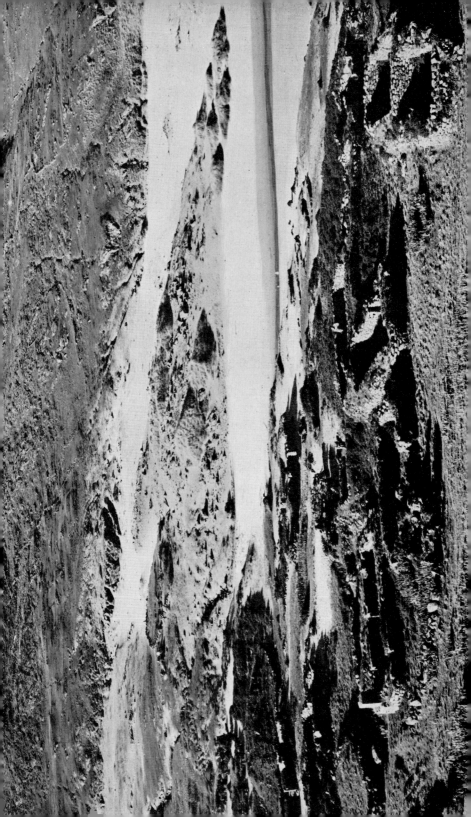

the course of them. Surely, there is already available sufficient evidence to have spared us the expense of these redundant groups " panelling their way through the Isles " !

To some extent, the decline of the herring fishings has been counterbalanced by the growth of the lobster-fishing industry. All down the Atlantic coast of the Outer Hebrides, lobsters are plentiful. The industry is carried on from March or April until September or October. It may even continue into November, if weather be favourable. In recent years, the Barra Isles have profited greatly by it. The crofters there have augmented their incomes appreciably by consistent lobster-fishing. Many of the small-holders on Vatersay sink lobster-pots as far south as Barra Head. Lobsters are to be had in plenty off the west side of Mingulay, Pabbay, and Sandray. The Islanders hold that, if they possessed bigger boats, they could venture farther seaward with good results. There is scarcely a crofting township in Barra at the present time which is not deriving benefit from lobster-fishing.

Although twenty years ago, lobsters brought the natives little money, to-day they are in great demand, and fetch good prices. Consignments are sent by private individuals direct to London, often at the rate of three or four shillings the pound. In the early spring, when they are scarcer and surer of reaching their destination in good condition, the price paid for them is often much in excess of this. Many an Islander should be paying income tax who isn't !

The lobsters, of course, must be alive on arrival : otherwise, they are valueless. During the season, great numbers of those caught off the Barra Isles are shipped by the mail-boat from Castlebay to Oban, whence they travel by rail to the cities with expensive hotels and restaurants. Owing to the unusually hot summer of 1947, many perished en route.

In Lewis, and for many a year, lobster-fishing has been centred mainly at Bernera, in Loch Roag. Indeed, lobsters were being despatched to London from Bernera long before the Barra Isles began to take a hand in this profitable pursuit.

At varying intervals during the past three or four centuries, and with results anything but encouraging, attempts have

The sands of Mingulay Bay encroach
upon the ruined and deserted village
Vatersay Bay with Sandray Isle in the background

been made to develop the economic potentialities of the Hebridean fishings. This is especially true of those pertaining
to Lewis. One of the earliest endeavours to exploit this
"hitherto most barbarous Isle of Lewis" was that made by
the Gentlemen Adventurers from Fife, with whom King
James the Sixth and First entered into a contract, hoping
that, when they succeeded in colonising it, there might at last
accrue to him some of the revenue the wild and redoubtable
MacLeods had denied him. He had been led to understand
that Lewis was "inrychit with ane incredibill fertilitie of
cornis and store of fischeingis and utheris necessaris, surpassing far the plenty of ony pairt of the inland".

Most of the Adventurers—the "partners", as they were
styled in official documents—were Fifeshire lairds. Prior to
their actual agreement with King James, two Acts of Parliament had been passed, virtually bringing under the Crown's
ownership islands such as had been selected for commercial
treatment. This preamble suited both King and prospective
colonisers. It lent to the Adventurers' subsequent charter the
semblance of authority and legality, and at the same time gave
to James some slight promise of revenue he so greatly needed.
But any suggestion that the motive behind the scheme was
purely one of profit was disavowed. The Adventurers were
to be not merely traders, but also benefactors: they were
pledged to the civilising of the natives, though one may ask
how far such a mission could have been consistent with
extirpation—"ruiting thame out", were the actual words—
which was one of their declared intentions. Indeed, there
was even a proposal to transport to the mainland any who
might obstruct their schemes. Though, at the outset, Lewis
was selected for the experiment, it was obviously intended
that at later dates the rest of the Hebrides should be subjected to this arbitrary benevolence.

Opposition the Fifers certainly encountered when, late in
1598, they first arrived in Lewis. We learn from the *Book of
Clanranald* that they had to contend not only against the warlike MacLeods of Lewis, but also against their collaterals in
Skye, who appear to have been equally ready to take a hand
in harassing and plundering their ships. In 1616, we find
Sir Rory MacLeod, chief of the MacLeods of Skye and Harris,

receiving stolen goods at Dunvegan Castle. These consisted
mainly of wines and other merchandise taken in the summer
of that year by his Harris tenants from trading vessels belonging to Kinghorn and Burntisland. The tenants brought them
across the Minch to Skye; and Sir Rory and they "maid
publict and oppin mercat" with this plunder in the court-
yard of Dunvegan.

In spite of the fiercest antagonism, the Adventurers managed to take Stornoway Castle, and to obtain sufficient foothold in the town of Stornoway itself to enable them to make
a beginning with their plans for reducing the island from
chaos to profit-making order. To begin with, the natives
seemed half-hearted in their hostility. But, as time wore on,
opposition grew apace. The doughty Neil MacLeod, one of
the last of the MacLeods of Lewis, started to organise his followers against them. So, too, did others who thrived on lawlessness and internecine strife. Such were Torquil Conanach,
and Tormod, the younger brother of Torquil the Black, each
of them representing MacLeod factions within the island
itself.

Opposition even more formidable than theirs was pursued,
sub rosa, by that arch schemer, Roderic MacKenzie, the
resourceful Tutor of Kintail. Though at bitter enmity with
one another, all these interests were so united in their hostility
to the Fifers that the latter, after three years' attempt to settle
and trade, had to abandon their enterprise. Final capitulation resulted from the ruthless attack upon their settlement
led by Tormod MacLeod, who, with his partisans, fired their
fortress, killing most of its defenders. The few survivors were
glad to accept terms which included the surrender to Tormod
of their trading rights in Lewis.

To anyone who reads the documentary accounts of the
Fifers' struggles and losses, it seems remarkable that they had
not abandoned hope earlier. By this time, the fate of their
cause had been fully recognised in the county of their origin,
where:

> *Some say the Fife Lairds ever rews*
> *Since they began to take the Lews;*
> *That bargain first did brew their bale,*
> *As tell the honest men of Creil.*

The Adventurers' efforts to colonise Lewis were renewed in 1605. Although now better equipped to withstand the ferocity of the natives, as well as the rigours of the Hebridean climate, they made little headway, however. The Islanders' hostility was much intensified by this time; and they also had to contend against the schemings of others with an eye on Lewis. In a part of Scotland where no one cared a whit for the Crown's authority, all the legality the King could bestow upon the Adventurers' speculation, together with the rights and favours he had extended to them in their hazardous undertaking, availed them little. By this time, moreover, the clansmen of the rest of the Western Isles were alive to the consequences which would inevitably follow, if ever the Adventurers succeeded in establishing themselves in Lewis. So the MacNeils of Barra and the MacDonalds of Uist now took to harassing the colonists. In the main, however, the failure of the Fifers' second attempt was due to the resolute opposition of the MacLeods of Lewis, directed by Neil Mac-Leod, whose courage and craftiness again forced them to withdraw.

In 1609, they made their third and final attempt to reduce Lewis. Yet again a combination of force and of cunning proved too much for them; and they were at last convinced of the futility of further designs on the Western Isles. With no small relief, they sold to Kenneth MacKenzie of Kintail their rights in Lewis, as well as those they had obtained in the Trotternish district of Skye. For his so-called "services" to the Fifers, Kenneth had now been created Lord MacKenzie. With the aid of his brother, Roderic, and a considerable force of his clansmen, he was not long in subjugating Lewis. The MacLeods, already much reduced in power, owing chiefly to inter-family feuds, were no match for these subsequent invaders.

The ancient MacLeods of Lewis—the Siol Torquil, as they were called—now begin to disappear from the annals of the Western Isles. Their power waned as quickly as that of the MacKenzies waxed. Poor Tormod MacLeod (he whom the Islanders acknowledged as chief among the several claimants) was soon reduced to impotence. He sought refuge in Holland. In his penniless condition, he was happy to make a little money by selling his sword to Maurice, Prince of Orange. He died in Holland. As for Torquil Conanach, the claimant referred to by a contemporary writer as "the poor unable", he, likewise, vanishes from the scene. The only MacLeod of any standing still in open rebellion against the MacKenzies was Neil, who, along with thirty or forty of his clansmen, dug himself in on Berisay, one of the islands at the entrance to Loch Roag. From Berisay he conducted a campaign of attrition against the MacKenzies in particular, and of piracy against everyone in general. One may still see on Berisay the ruins of the fortress he built there, and which he and his men occupied for about three years.

It was while he and his desperadoes held out on this rocky island against the MacKenzies that there sailed into Loch Roag the pirate vessel, *Priam*, full of rich prize taken from English and Dutch ships, and commanded by the well-known pirate, Captain Peter Love. Neil and Peter had much in common. Both of them were "wanted" by the authorities. Soon they made a bond for mutual aid. This bond, it was agreed, should be strengthened by Peter's marriage to one of Neil's relations. The marriage never took place, however, for Neil in the meantime seized the *Priam*, together with captain and crew. The vessel he handed over to the State. In 1611, Peter Love and seven of his crew—"wicket impes of the Devill", as they are called in the indictment—were hanged on the sands at Leith. In recognition of his part in the capture of the *Priam*, Neil received from the Privy Council a temporary pardon for all his past offences.

Neil's ultimate displacement from Berisay provides us with an example of the resourcefulness of Roderic MacKenzie of Kintail.

For about three years, as we have seen, he and his pirate partisans held out on Berisay against the MacKenzies, who were now in full legal possession of Lewis. Some say that at last the pirates wearied of their existence on the island, and agreed to surrender to Roderic MacKenzie. But Sir Robert Gordon, in his *Earldom of Sutherland*, tells us that they were dislodged from it by Roderic's stratagem, when, at low water, he put their wives and children on a tidal rock situated sufficiently close to Berisay to enable their cries of distress to be heard as the tide rose to engulf them. Thus, says Sir Robert (whose account must be apocryphal) Neil was forced to surrender. With his son, Donald, he fled to Harris, where Ruairi MacLeod of Harris, acting under pressure, detained him, ultimately handing him over to the Privy Council. Neil was tried in Edinburgh on innumerable charges; and in the spring of 1613 he was hanged at the Mercat Cross there. He was one of the last of the MacLeods of Lewis. According to Sir Thomas Hamilton, writing to the King in his capacity as Lord Advocate, " Neill MaKcloyde died at his executioun verey christianlie ".

Meanwhile, other displaced members of the MacLeods of Lewis had also taken to piracy. Notorious among these was Malcolm MacLeod, one of Tormod's several illegitimate brethren. Malcolm was one of those who found a purchaser in Sir Rory MacLeod at Dunvegan Castle, at a time when the latter was giving to the Privy Council an assurance that neither he nor his clansfolk would have anything to do with such a rascal!

Not even the skill and cunning of the MacKenzies could bring Malcolm MacLeod to account. He successfully evaded capture for the rest of his days, though in 1626 a commission and fire and sword had been invoked against him. Eventually, the Western Isles became unsafe even for him. So he retired to Ireland. There, one presumes, he died.

Such was the end of the MacLeods of Lewis, who, so consistently, had harried the Fife Adventurers in their endeavours to exploit at least some of the economic possibilities of the Western Isles.

Further efforts to commercialise the fishings were made by King James's son, Charles the First. Lewis by this time had passed into the possession of Colin, first Earl of Seaforth, who had succeeded his father, Lord MacKenzie of Kintail. Colin realised that, in order to develop the fishings of his vast island, it would be necessary to seek external assistance. So he invited a number of Hollanders to come over to Lewis with their busses, and at the same time sought to obtain for Stornoway the status of a royal burgh, because of the trading privileges attached thereto. This brought him into conflict with the Convention of Royal Burghs, whose champions saw in the employment of foreign fishermen a threat to their privileges.

A few decades earlier, an English corporation had been established to exploit the Hebridean fishings, with special reference to those of Lewis. But its promoters soon found themselves confronted with that ignorant and pig-headed local opposition which has defeated every attempt to unravel the tangle o' the Isles up to the present day. The corporation's activities extended to Harris and to North Uist. On Hermetra, one of the several islands situated off the north-east coast of North Uist, may still be seen the ruins of the fishing-station they erected there. Martin Martin, writing of Hermetra at the close of the same century, tells us that he saw " the foundation of a house built by the English, in King Charles the First's time, for one of their magazines to lay up the cask, salt, etc., for carrying on the fishery, which was then begun in the Western Islands; but this design miscarried because of the civil wars which then broke out ".

During the reign of Charles the Second, yet another endeavour was made to organise, on a commercial basis, the fishings of the Outer Hebrides. Owing to a number of causes, not the least important being the lack of adequate financial backing, it failed.

The Seaforths, although their estates soon became so heavily encumbered and entailed, were not wholly indifferent to the economics of their vast Hebridean property. Certainly, Francis Humbertson-MacKenzie, the last Seaforth in the male line to own Lewis, tried to improve conditions in the island. He greatly encouraged building in Stornoway, with the result that by the seventeen-eighties it had become one of the most important centres on the west coast of Scotland. No place between the Mull of Kintyre and Cape Wrath had half as many inhabitants. Francis also did much to increase the island's agricultural yield; and, as a director of the British Society, formed in 1786 to develop the fisheries and to improve the sea-coasts of the Kingdom, he promoted the extension of Stornoway as a fishing port. In addition to this, he interested himself in kelp-burning, and was the first to undertake the arduous task of road-construction in an island hitherto almost completely devoid even of cart-tracks. He built the road across the moors from Stornoway to Barvas, on the west side of the island, and another from the town to the populous peninsula of Point. He invited the government to halve with him the estimated cost of £5,000 for making a road from Stornoway to Loch Roag, undertaking to pay out of his own pocket any charge in excess of the estimated cost. With this road he made a beginning; but he died before its completion.

In the midst of all these activities, Francis devoted serious attention to army recruitment. He raised the recruits who became the first Seaforth Highlanders.

Contemporaneous with the efforts of the last Lord Seaforth to improve the economy of Lewis were those of Captain Alexander MacLeod in regard to Harris. In 1779, MacLeod, late captain of the East Indiaman, *Mansfield*, had purchased Harris, together with St. Kilda, for £15,000 from the commissioners acting on behalf of General Norman MacLeod who, in 1772, had inherited, from his grandfather, the chiefship, and a debt on the property amounting to £50,000. Captain MacLeod did all he could to ameliorate conditions in Harris. He stimulated the fishing industry there. In the face of much opposition, and even ridicule, he established the rightness of his contention that the success of the herring fishing industry meant the seeking of catches much farther a-sea than the lochs beyond which the local fishermen seldom ventured. He improved the island's harbour accommodation, and erected a storehouse for salt, casks, meal, and the like. He built a factory for spinning woollen and cotton thread, and twine for herring-nets. He advanced to the local fishermen money for the purchase of boats and gear; and he provided them, rent-free, with cottages, and with ground upon which to grow potatoes. He built a boat-house capable of holding nine fishing-boats and their tackle. He constructed roads between the village of Tarbert and the two jetties he made there. He erected a schoolhouse and an inn; and, of course, he was responsible for one of the restorations of St. Clement's, at Rodil. In short, he worked hard to put Harris on an economic basis, but with no permanent result.

On the whole, the policy pursued by the Seaforths brought little, if indeed any, betterment to the Lewis people. Had earlier members of the family shown something of Francis's foresight, things might have been different. The Seaforths did, however, introduce to the island a more orderly form of government, and at the same time turned the natives from a few of their more primitive and boorish ways. But their wild extravagance pressed heavily on their tenantry, whose economic plight at the close of the seventeenth century would appear to have been no less acute than when the first Mac-Kenzie took over from the MacLeods at the beginning of that century. Nor were matters any better during the eighteenth century. " But I can assure yee [yee] shall find one rugged hag that will resist both King and Government, vizt., Poverty." So wrote Zachary MacAulay, Seaforth's chamberlain, in 1721.

That social and economic conditions were equally bad at the end of the eighteenth century is evident from the account written by the Rev. John Lane Buchanan, who, to a large extent, blamed the tacksmen for the deplorable condition in which he found the peasant population. With financial liabilities mounting on every hand, the Seaforths were power-less where their tacksmen were concerned, so that the tyranny of the latter grew, unchallenged. The island's agriculture in these circumstances received scant assistance: indeed, it seems to have been in a worse state towards the close of the eighteenth century than at the beginning when, in all con-science, it was primitive enough, and its yield far from com-mensurate even with the barest needs of the people.

How does one account for the Seaforths' failure even to assuage the island's poverty over so long a period? " Their old masters," writes W. C. MacKenzie in *The Book of the Lews*, " had exploited them to sustain their wars and feuds, and their new masters had neglected them for larger interests across the Minch. To be sure, the Seaforths were not respon-sible for an uncertain climate, nor for bad harvests, nor, directly, for the harshness of tacksmen. But to them Lewis was merely an appanage of their larger estates on the main-land, with the unavoidable result that Lewis was treated as a ' poor relation '."

This, surely, is not the entire explanation, since it takes no account of the root cause of poverty, whether in territory like the Hebrides, or in the industrial regions of the world, namely, the pressure of increasing population on static or diminishing subsistence.

If Nature have dealt uncharitably with Lewis in the matter of climate and fertility, fortune has favoured her bountifully. In 1844, when Mr. James Matheson (afterwards Sir James) purchased the islands from the trustees of the Seaforth Estates for £190,000, it passed into the hands of one of the first of three wealthy men to expend vast sums upon it.

Matheson, a native of Shinness, in the parish of Lairg, was born in 1796. Early in life he decided upon a commercial career, and at the age of seventeen travelled from his Highland heath to London, where he spent a couple of years in a mercantile house. At nineteen, he proceeded to Calcutta, where he was employed in the counting-house of MacKintosh & Co. Brighter prospects soon attracted him eastwards to China, where, almost at once, he became a founder of the house of Jardine, Matheson, & Co., of Canton and, subsequently, of Hong Kong, where he amassed a splendid fortune. In 1842, this opulent merchant returned from the Far East to his native Scotland, and in 1844, as we have seen, bought Lewis, an island the backwardness and poverty of which provided him with ample scope for his philanthropic turn of mind. He died on the last day of 1878, beloved, but without issue. To his widow, who survived him until 1896, he bequeathed the life-rent of the heritable estate. When she died, Lewis, in virtue of the entail, passed to Donald Matheson, her husband's nephew. In 1899, Donald, who died two years later, handed the island over to his son, the late Lieutenant-Colonel Duncan Matheson, my father's friend and contemporary.

Sir James Matheson's expenditure on various enterprises for the improvement of the island and its people was lavish. It has been estimated that he spent roughly half a million pounds, an enormous sum at a period when labour was so very cheap.[1] He drained the land and reclaimed much of it.

---

[1] The sum actually spent on the island from first to last was £574,363. This included the purchase price of £190,000 which worked out at roughly 9s. 4d. the acre. A sum of more than £100,000 was spent in building Lewis Castle and in laying out the grounds. All this provided his impoverished tenants with work; and much of what he spent remained in the island.

He planted trees. He built roads, bridges, and quays. He stimulated interest in the fishings, and erected extensive premises for fish-curing. He built a patent boat-slip for the construction and repair of fishing and other craft. He established schools, and paid the teachers' salaries. He subsidised a steamer service between Stornoway and the mainland, in place of the sailing mail-packet. He founded a gas and a water company. He built brick-works, and also chemical-works for the distillation of paraffin from peat—an experimental undertaking which failed in its objective after a small fortune had been lost on it. He imported meal and seed potatoes to the value of £33,000, in order to relieve the famine stalking the island so soon after he had come into possession of it. He interested himself in afforestation, as well as in land reclamation.

The fruits of his efforts at sylviculture in a treeless island may be seen in the wooded policies of the present Lewis Castle, which he also built. Though much of this woodland was uprooted by the great gale which swept the Hebrides in the spring of 1921, it still remains the only plantation of any size in the Long Island. At Cliascro, one of Lewis's few inland villages, a small plantation no more than survives. When last I saw it, a few years ago, there was every sign of its dying out, partly on account of the unsuitability of the soil, and partly owing to the site's exposure to blasting winds.

Apart from Lewis Castle and its wooded amenities, and the roads he constructed, little of enduring value, in the material sense, seems to have survived the Mathesons' regime. Their memory is perpetuated, however, as is also that of the Seaforths, in the name of one of Stornoway's streets. In Matheson Road lives Stornoway's *élite*!

Sir James Matheson, in furtherance of his plans for land improvement, enlisted the services of a certain Alexander Smith, one of the best known "speculative" agriculturists in Scotland at the time. Smith, who already had transformed the Carse of Gowrie from bog-land to a fertile tract, belonged to Deanston, in Perthshire; and the memory of his sojourn in Lewis survives in Little Deanston, the name of the small hamlet where he lived, situated some seven miles from Stornoway.

Of economic conditions then prevailing in Lewis, and as

assessed by an outsider, Smith gave a faithful portrayal after his first visit to the island, whither he had gone for the purpose of reporting to Sir James on the practicability of its improvement. At a meeting of the Glasgow Philosophical Society in 1844, he submitted an account of what he saw there.[1] The cultivation of the soil, he said, was as primitive as the Islanders' manufacture of cloth. He thought it extraordinary that there did not appear to have been any change in the island's economy over a very long period, and that the inhabitants were at least a century behind the times. They still used the ancient distaff, although a hundred years had passed since the Dutch wheel had supplanted it elsewhere in Scotland; and nothing diverted him more than seeing the womenfolk leave Stornoway for the remoter parts of the island, carrying with them spinning-wheels " to commence what they conceived to be a novel and vast improvement ". The advantages the best machinery possessed over the distaff, he said, was as a thousand to one. " Yet, by means of the distaff, these people managed to manufacture their clothing, which, under the circumstances, was very comfortable." The inhabitants he found in no way deficient by nature. They were social, in their own style. Speaking as a phrenologist, he remarked that they had very good heads—" that is, for people not accustomed to habits of thought ".

Their houses resembled huts. " The walls were from six to eight feet thick, composed of bog in the centre, and faced with stone inside and out. There was sometimes only one apartment, but generally two; and under the same roof the people lived and kept their cattle. There was this distinction, however; namely, a fall of eighteen inches from the apartment in which the family lived to the adjoining one, in which the cattle were kept. This might seem to some to be rather a queer arrangement; but the people themselves considered that there were points in it which contributed to their comfort. The room in which the cattle were kept was the entrance one, and, as the air passed through it, it came into the adjoining portion of the house appropriated to the family in a warm state."

[1] A synopsis of this account appeared in *Chambers's Edinburgh Journal* on December 21st, 1844.

So far as agriculture was concerned, Smith added that nothing in the way of draining the land had ever been attempted. Nor had any effort been made to penetrate the hard sub-soil. The great scarcity of timber, he held, had been a serious handicap, when it came to agricultural implements—to their renewal, repair, or possible improvement. After dealing in detail with those primitive customs and observances associated with the raising of crops, which he believed had greatly retarded progress, he showed himself more than convinced that, under proper direction, all this could be altered to the considerable benefit of the island; and he concluded by adding that he hoped the period of this improvement was not far off, and that, when members of his audience visited Lewis, " they would find a green, pastoral land instead of a dreary waste ".

Yet, for all Sir James Matheson's high hopes, and for all the munificence of at least two other benefactors during the present century, Lewis remains essentially the dreary, unproductive waste primordial chaos made of it.

In 1918, the island of Lewis was purchased by Lord Leverhulme from the aforenamed Colonel Matheson, Sir James's grand-nephew. Leverhulme had first visited the island in 1884; and now he returned with the ambition to transform it from its poverty-ridden condition to one of commercial prosperity. He planned to convert the natives from peasant communities dependent upon the poor soil to an industrial, or at any rate semi-industrial people dependent upon the bountiful sea. He was not indifferent to the problem of the land, however, as was to be seen in his attitude to the island's milk supply, to which we shall revert.

Leverhulme asked for ten years' freedom in which to develop fully the schemes he had in view: at the end of but half that period, he was obliged to abandon his gigantic projects, after the expenditure of some hundreds of thousands of pounds. The Islanders, tenacious of their old ways, became carping and critical, suspicious and subversive. They did not want to be looked upon as no better than mill hands in Lancashire. They were too proud and independent in their predial poverty for that! They really wanted to be left to their crofts. Of course, they would take out of the new

317

proprietor what money they could, as indeed so many of them did. But he mustn't disturb them too much, nor try to foist upon them a mere Englishman's ideas of what constituted security and comfort!

In the Islanders' mentality, this man, genuinely interested in their well-being, found himself up against something impregnable. I so well remember hearing my father tell him that, in the people of the Western Isles, though they always voted Radical, he was dealing with the most stubborn Conservatives in Scotland, and that he would find ample scope for pouring wealth into their peat-hags, from which the most astute industrialist would never retrieve a penny.

Greatly concerned that large quantities of milk were brought daily to Stornoway from the mainland by rail and mail-boat, Leverhulme thought the only practical thing to do was to help the Lewis people to graze a sufficient number of cows to make this unnecessary. Not far from Stornoway were the two farms of Coll and Gress, where he decided to make a beginning in this direction, not only with a view to supplying with good milk the town as then populated, but the larger town he believed his schemes would eventually create. Over Coll and Gress his Lewis ventures came to grief. The government, through the Scottish Office, had promised that these farms would be broken up into small-holdings— into crofts. When a number of young men returned to Lewis after the First World War, there began a clamour among them for settlement on the land. Much misplaced sympathy went into such ex-servicemen's claims. The Scottish Office, anxious to fulfil its promise, sided with the prospective crofters. Leverhulme, on the other hand, still thought the milk situation one which deserved prior treatment.

So far as the island's milk supply is concerned, the position to-day remains much as it was when Leverhulme arrived on the scene. Indeed, it may even have deteriorated. To-day the crofters are at liberty to raise on their crofts what crops they like, whereas in former times they were obliged to grow primarily what they needed, contending as best they could against unfavourable weather conditions and the poorness of the soil. The one crop the islands, generally, are capable of producing abundantly, and with a minimum of labour and expense, is grass. Yet, rather than alter their ways, and submit to the sensible reorganisation of their agriculture with a view to dairy-farming, and possibly also to stock-raising, many of them, possessing alternative and more remunerative sources of income than crofting, such as lobster-fishing and tweed-making, are allowing their crofts to revert to moorland or bogland. Meanwhile, the small town of Stornoway continues to import annually, through the Milk Marketing Board, between twenty-five and thirty thousand pounds' worth of milk! This milk, by the time it reaches the consumer, is already three days old; and it may even be four. Leverhulme was desirous of rectifying, among much else, this wholly unnecessary state of affairs. But no one concerned would coöperate with him. On the contrary, everyone seemed bent on obstructing him. At this interval of time and in the light of subsequent happenings, an examination of all the facts and circumstances then obtaining—an examination of a judicial and impartial nature, free from Celtic prejudice, ignorance, and emotion—would reveal how right he was in the main, and how wrong were those who did so much to bring about the abandonment of his efforts.

In my view, if Leverhulme had had reason to believe his giving way over the farms of Coll and Gress would have solved the land unrest in the island, he would have done so, and allowed them to be broken up. But he discovered that, even if the Scottish Office divided all the farms it had in mind, no more than 143 crofts could be provided, whereas the number of applicants was between two and three thousand!

Leverhulme still felt that the more sensible plan was to go ahead with his schemes for providing dwelling-houses suitable for these crofters near the place where wages could be earned to pay their rents, and to provide at the same time more of the necessities and amenities of life than they had been accustomed to. In all this, I do not think for a moment that there was anything of compulsion in his mind, anxious though he was that there should be an influx of population to Stornoway and its immediate neighbourhood. Those wishing to avail themselves of his proposal were at liberty to do so, if they cared.

The squabble over the farms of Coll and Gress continued

from 1918 until 1923, during which time the crofters raided them, drove off the farmers' stock, and began to till the land. The depression of 1921 aggravated matters, since Leverhulme felt obliged to curtail, if only temporarily, many of his projects.

The peasants, in their attitude of obstruction and hostility, were greatly abetted by the petty bourgeoisie of Stornoway —by those ignorant shopkeepers who feared lest one day Leverhulme might open a multiple store in the town in competition with them, and thus break their monopolistic and exorbitant prices—prices which, by the way, dropped very considerably when, a few years later, Messrs. Lipton, Woolworth, and the Scottish Coöperative Wholesale Society arrived on the scene. Not until then did the crofting populace of Lewis realise how little it would have had to fear from Lord Leverhulme's schemes!

From the outset, it should be remembered, many Highlanders objected to Lord Leverhulme's purchase of the Island of Lewis. In their false pride and provincial patriotism, they loathed the idea of a "soap magnate", as they called him, lording it over the Hebrideans, either from Port Sunlight or from his palatial castle at Stornoway. They showed deeper resentment than did their grandfathers when an indigo and opium magnate, in the person of Sir James Matheson, built, and later occupied, the same castle three-quarters of a century earlier.

Before long they were expressing publicly their indignation that a captain of industry—and an *English* one at that!—had proposed, for the alleged betterment of the Islanders, schemes which they maintained would rob them of their freedom and independence, and reduce them to the status of wage-slaves. With this extravagant assumption originated the myth, so widely accepted even in England, that the upright and freedom loving Islanders eventually compelled his lordship to retire ignominiously from the field of battle, leaving them in supreme control. They declared, in effect, that they preferred their poverty to working for anybody who would dare suggest their assisting in the building and running of a canning factory. *They* weren't going to be regulated by a factory's whistle, like the Lancashire mill hands! Indeed, no!

Lewis Castle from the wharf-side at Stornoway
Mountains of North Harris and the head of West Loch Tarbert

How farcical was this attitude may be seen to-day in Lewis, which now *has* its factories, to the whistles of which the natives cheerfully respond, having dropped all their nonsense about wage-slavery, and being as covetous of money as any section of the community.

In recent years the Harris tweed industry has grown enormously. It has been estimated that the present output exceeds 4,000,000 linear yards per annum, involving a turnover of more than £1,000,000. In Stornoway there are now no fewer than four large spinning-mills. Six days a week, yarn goes out from these mills to weavers in almost every hamlet and township in Lewis and Harris. "The reputation for quality and long life established for the cloth by the crofters of the Isles," says the editor of the *Stornoway Gazette* in a well-informed article he contributed during 1948 to *Scotland's Magazine*, "is still the foundation on which the industry must rest in normal times, but without a centre like Stornoway, possessing port facilities and power, the growth of the spinning industry to feed the island looms could not have taken place, and without the motor-bus the distribution of yarn and collection of tweeds on the present scale would be impossible.

"The people of the Highlands and Islands," he continues, "are not generally credited with enterprise, but it is a fact that the ordinary crofters of Lewis and Harris in recent years have sunk well over £100,000 of capital in equipping their industry with efficient modern looms, quite apart from the erection of spinning-mills in Stornoway by the four firms which produce the yarn.

"The function of the bus in the tweed industry is rather an odd one, and those who worship at the shrine of efficiency may think it economic madness to have one of the main processes of a textile industry scattered in a hundred villages over an area of eight hundred square miles, when the work could be done with closer supervision, at less cost, by power looms under the factory roof, a few yards from Stornoway pier.

"But the system has the great advantage for Lewis that it enables the industry to be spread over the whole island. Fortunately the cost of transport is relatively light, and the Harris tweed industry has not so far suffered for its 'inefficiency'. The terms of the Harris Tweed Association's mark provide

Y   321

The cattle auction at Castlebay, May, 1948
Brevig Bay from Scudag, with Heaval in the background

that the cloth must be hand-woven by the people at their homes, and that helps to stabilise the industry in its present position. If the power-loom is ever introduced, it will not be by the Stornoway mills, but by the crofters themselves, when they get electric power. But that is dipping some way into the future."

In the last twenty years or thereby, motor transport has completely revolutionised the social and economic life of the Western Islands. The greater the area served by such transport, and the more remote the inhabitants now enjoying the benefits of it, the greater the changes it has brought, as may be seen throughout the length and breadth of the Isles. These changes are very apparent in Lewis, where the more enterprising natives take full advantage of the network of internal transport now available to them.

The extent to which the advent of the motor-bus has altered things was demonstrated in the summer of 1948 when the Traffic Commissioners, sitting at Stornoway, heard an application by Back-Stornoway Transport, Ltd., for permission to run tours and excursions from its terminus at Back to all parts of Lewis and Harris. Back, a crofting township situated seven miles from the burgh of Stornoway, is probably the only community in Scotland of its size and kind which is sufficiently enterprising to possess its own bus service, and to conduct tours and excursions in competition with those of a neighbouring town.

This application brought to attention several salient facts about rural life in the Outer Hebrides. For instance, it showed that the villages of Lewis are not small communities such as one finds in the crofting areas on the Highland mainland. Many of them, on the contrary, have a population of five hundred. That of Tolsta is nearly a thousand; while the almost contiguous villages fringing the roadside at Ness for several miles have an aggregate population of more than two thousand. To-day the rural districts know little of the isolation in which so many of them were enclosed but a couple of decades ago. Except in the most inaccessible parts of Uig and of Lochs, most of these villages have their football teams in the Island Football League; and as many as two thousand spectators are known to attend matches, thanks to the ubiquity

of the bus. Rural concert parties and dance bands exchange
visits, often travelling thirty or forty miles by bus to do so.
To the picture-house in Stornoway the younger people travel
regularly by bus from the less remote townships. Grocery
vans belonging to Messrs. Lipton, the " Co-op ", and some of
the Stornoway shopkeepers go as far afield as the most indifferent of roads will allow, bringing to the crofter's doorstep com-
modities for which he formerly had to travel by cart or on
foot any distance up to thirty-six miles. The townsfolk now
convey their merchandise to the countryfolk.

And what of the crofter who has a little cash to put by?
No longer does he require to visit Stornoway to bank it there.
The savings bank now comes to *him*. Quite recently the
National Bank of Scotland introduced into the Western Isles
the first mobile bank in Britain.

In the matter of the canning factory mentioned earlier,
Lord Leverhulme saw much farther than did his unreasonable and myopic critics. Acre for acre, as he put it, the seas
surrounding the Hebrides were infinitely richer than the
land. In other words, in any programme for the improvement of the Islanders' economic position, fishing must take
precedence of crofting. Leverhulme recognised that, in order
to exploit to the full the potentialities of these seas, it would
be necessary to protect, to a much greater extent than hereto-
fore, the flat fishings from depredation and wholesale destruction by trawlers operating within the areas already prohibited
by statute. Trawlers had wrought havoc among the ling and
haddock beds, and had thus ruined many a line-fisherman.
Leverhulme held that not only was greater vigilance called
for on the part of the Fishery Board's cruisers, but also that
certain areas *beyond* the statutory three-mile limit should
likewise be closed to trawlers.

Furthermore, where the herring fishing industry was concerned, he urged that recognition should be given to a possible
change in taste and in transport facilities. How were the
herring fishings of the Hebrides to fare if the export market
for salt herrings declined through such a change? Here one
sees the wisdom of his attempt to make Stornoway a centre
of the canning industry. The herring caught in the Minch,

it is claimed, is the finest of all British herrings. Before the Second World War, it remained the only herring which, when cured, readily found a market in America. Moreover, it commanded the highest price for herrings exported to the European continent. Incidentally, it might be mentioned that the most remunerative years enjoyed by the Lewis herring fishermen were those which followed Leverhulme's retiral from the island. Indeed, the best period of all occurred after he was dead.

Now that the world market for salt or cured herrings has contracted almost to vanishing point, and the island ports of Stornoway and Castlebay can no longer compete with Oban, Mallaig, and Kyle, situated at rail-heads on the mainland, whence a perishable commodity like fish can be conveyed to the home market with a minimum of delay, one realises how far-seeing Lord Leverhulme was in his desire to establish a canning industry at Stornoway, where, to-day, the catches landed from but thirty or forty fishing-boats may cause a glut. In prosperous times a fishing fleet of five hundred boats operated from this port.

The decline of the herring fishing industry there is to be regretted all the more when one considers this port's advantages. Firstly, it has the longest fishing season of any British port. Secondly, the herrings caught in Hebridean waters and landed there are the finest in quality of any herrings in Europe. Thirdly, the fishing-grounds, with the exception of those in the Clyde area, are the most sheltered in Britain, and the most economical to work. Fourthly, Stornoway harbour is safe, accessible, and commodious in all weathers, and is reasonably well equipped with wharfage facilities. That hope of its regaining at least part of its former prosperity as a herring port has not been abandoned entirely is shown by the fact that the harbour, with the aid of a government grant, is to be developed still further at a cost of approximately a quarter of a million pounds. At the same time local fishermen are making some effort to rebuild the fishing fleet which, during the years immediately preceding the outbreak of war in 1939, had dwindled to insignificant proportions. It has been pointed out, however, that, unless the Herring Industry Board assists in providing modern refrigerating and processing plant, capable of handling the large catches likely to be landed there with any considerable resuscitation of the herring industry in these parts, much of this expenditure will be of little permanent value.

.   .   .   .

Sick at heart with all the local jangling and wangling, Lord Leverhulme decided in 1923 to abandon his many bold and ambitious schemes then being pursued in Lewis. He now proposed giving the island, in its entirety, to the people.

When he offered to the Lewis crofter his own croft as a free gift, and Lewis Castle and its policies, together with all his property in Stornoway, to the people of that town, there was consternation. At first, they couldn't believe it. Then they thought there must be some subtle snag. Such excess of generosity made them suspicious; and they are a suspicious lot at the best. They declined the offer of the crofts, as we have already seen. This amazed Leverhulme, because for years, through the Land League and other organisations, these peasants had been clamouring for the land. " The Land for the People " had been the slogan—nay, the war-cry—of the Highlands and Islands for many a day. Now they were being offered the land for nothing, and would not accept it.

The explanation for their refusal was fairly obvious. As crofters, under the Crofters' Act, they had security of tenure, so long as they paid their rents, and small rents they were. Indeed, they felt pretty secure, even when they failed to pay them. But, if once they allowed themselves to become owners, they might have to find owner's and occupier's rates; and they might be imprisoned, and have their properties confiscated, for refusing or failing to do so. They, therefore, felt on surer ground as crofters. They also argued that, as individual proprietors, they would forfeit the advantages of the Scottish Land Court in dealing with their disputes, and any litigation resorted to in its place might be costly. Moreover, they would be debarred from obtaining loans through the Department of Agriculture for Scotland for the improvement of their houses and holdings. They feared that, as individual proprietors, they would forfeit their share of the common grazing rights, and that, should they desire to leave their holdings, they would be obliged to find a buyer in the open market, instead of renouncing to their landlords, and receiving valuation. Furthermore, immediately they became landlords, the Assessor would increase the assessment of their holdings for rates and taxes. In short, they now wanted none of the responsibilities and liabilities of the landlord class, which they had been fighting so consistently for generations.

The town of Stornoway decided to accept Lord Leverhulme's gift, and formed a Trust to administer it. The castle grounds are now a public park, known as the Lady Lever Park, in memory of Leverhulme's wife, who died when he was still Sir William Lever. The Trust has found it necessary to let the castle and the sporting rights attached thereto, for the outgoing expenses have been greater than were anticipated at the time of acceptance of the gift. The castle, in fact, has been something of a white elephant, and deservedly so, though, unfortunately, most of the town councillors and others, who subverted Leverhulme's schemes, are dead, and cannot now be induced to take their share of the muddle their cunning created.

In the end, the island (apart from the parish of Stornoway) was divided into small estates, and sold. Many of these estates found purchasers at absurdly low prices—a few pence per acre. The Galson property, for example, went at $2\frac{1}{2}$d. the acre! With the introduction of de-rating a few years later, those who bought them soon discovered that they were an excellent investment. Several of them were purchased by sporting syndicates, some of the individual members of which have shown an interest in the island, and have contributed generously to local causes. Others are but absentee landlords, having no interest whatsoever either in the people or in the place.[1]

[1] The manner of Lord Leverhulme's withdrawal from Lewis was, indeed, dramatic. Let us read of it in his son's words, which I believe to be a veridical account of all that happened:
"On September 3rd, 1923, he invited to a meeting in Stornoway the members of the Stornoway Town Council, the Lewis District Committee, and the Parish Council of Stornoway, and, after referring to the motives which had brought him to the island, his hopes and his disappointments, his efforts on behalf of the inhabitants, and their frustration by the raiders and by the attitude and actions of the Scottish Office, he explained to his audience that he could no longer remain in Lewis. 'I am like Othello,' he said, 'with my occupation gone, and I could only be like a ghost of Hamlet's father, haunting the place as a shadow.' He then offered as a free gift to the people of Stornoway all his land within a seven-mile radius of the Stornoway Post

The collapse of Leverhulme's enterprises in Lewis meant the complete cessation of work there. With no prospect of fresh employment, renewed emigration seemed the only alternative for at least part of the surplus population. Some hundreds of the younger people now left the island.

Leverhulme must have expended on Lewis a sum far in excess of that spent by Sir James Matheson, and with perhaps even less to show for it in the way of permanent, public benefit. The figure has been put at a million sterling. This, one imagines, must be an exaggeration, however.

The failure of his endeavours there was a great grief to him. Many, in whom he had placed confidence, turned against him after they had got out of him what money they could. His niece, Emily MacDonald, whom I have known for a great number of years, puts the position fairly in a letter written me from Lewis the other day. "In the town of Stornoway, all their supposed admiration for my uncle was tinged with suspicion. 'What is this man going to get out of us, and how will his schemes affect our businesses?' . . .

Office, including the Castle and its grounds and woods. The Castle, he suggested, should become the Town Hall and the official residence of the Provost, replacing the former Town Hall, which had been destroyed by fire some years earlier. The ' policies ', including a fine road he had made along the harbour front through the Castle Woods to the mouth of the River Creed, he offered as a public park, and suggested that it should be called Lady Lever Park in memory of his wife. To enable the Castle and grounds to be kept up, he proposed, he said, to transfer to local trustees the Stornoway Gasworks and other undertakings in the town. The remainder of Lewis he offered as a gift to the inhabitants, to be administered by trustees appointed in part by the Lewis District Committee and in part by the Parliamentary voters, but each crofter was given the opportunity of becoming the proprietor of his own croft. He asked for an answer by October 6th. It was the general expectation that both offers would be accepted, for surely, it was thought, those who had for so long championed the cause of the crofter in his desire for land would see to it that this unique opportunity for putting into practice the principle of public ownership was seized. To most people's surprise, however, while the Town Council of Stornoway readily accepted the offer made to them, the Lewis District Committee, by 6 votes to 3, declined Leverhulme's offer, although a few crofters became proprietors of their own crofts. But the reason for the rejection is not difficult to understand, for it followed the lines of Mr. Micawber's immortal argument, ' Annual income twenty pounds, annual expenditure nineteen nineteen six, result happiness. Annual income twenty pounds, annual expenditure twenty pounds ought and six, result misery.' The crofters discovered that for every 10s. received in rent, they would have to pay 10s. 6d. in rates, and in some districts even as much as 54s. in the pound. They appealed to the Scottish Office for financial assistance, but in vain, and the majority came to the conclusion that it was better for the people to remain as they were, leaving the landlord to receive the 10s. as rent, and pay the 10s. 6d. or more as rates." (*Viscount Leverhulme*, by his son, pp. 218-20; Allen & Unwin, 1927.)

But my uncle saw more in life than mere material gain. To a man of his temperament, it was greatly satisfying to see well-made roads reaching where, formerly, there were no means of travel except by foot over the moors, and to see well-built houses displace those made with stones, earth, and straw of the countryside, and driftwood gathered by the shore. If he could have produced an industry which would have brought an adequate wage to the Lewis people, and have run farms which would have supplied Stornoway with milk, he would have considered his colossal expenditure more than justified. He was genuinely interested in the prosperity and happiness of the islanders. . . . The situation in Lewis has changed drastically of recent years. The island is rolling in money, what with tweeds, slip-overs, hosiery, not to mention all the various kinds of dole."

Briefly, the circumstances culminating in Lord Leverhulme's abandonment of his programme for Lewis may be summarised as follows:

1. The peculiar psychology of the natives, which made them as suspicious as they were plausible. Leverhulme could not understand their outlook any more than they could understand his.

2. The unsatisfactory attitude of the Scottish Office.

3. His realising that even those already benefiting as the result of his enterprises were apathetic, if not actively hostile.

4. The state of financial stringency affecting the entire realm of commerce at the time. The tightness of money offered little immediate prospect of a return on his very considerable capital outlay. Leverhulme may have felt obliged, therefore, to cut at least some of his losses.

I do not think there was the slightest ground for the view, so freely expressed afterwards by those who had thwarted him, that impaired vigour and vision were in any way responsible for his decision in this matter. Of course, there may have been *other* factors, of which we know nothing. Those emunerated above could have been the only weighty ones, however.

Leverhulme's exit from Lewis did not mean his renouncing all interest in the Western Isles. On the contrary, he now applied himself with renewed zest to Harris, the proprietor of which he had become in 1919, about a year after he had entered into possession of Lewis. South Harris he bought from the Earl of Dunmore, and North Harris from Sir Samuel Scott. (Incidentally, it was while Barrie was the guest of the latter at Amhuinnsuidhe that he conceived the idea of *Mary Rose*. The Island which Likes to be Visited is situated in that part of Harris.)

With the transference of affections from Lewis to Harris, Borve Lodge now became Lord Leverhulme's island home. His undertakings in Harris were to be similar to those he had attempted in Lewis; and, as the inhabitants displayed a keener desire to combine with him than their northern neighbours had shown, he had hopes of carrying to fruition schemes no less colossal than those which he had so recently abandoned.

Harris, it should also be mentioned, had not been entirely free from the activities of land raiders. Shortly after the outbreak of the raiding epidemic in Lewis, sporadic raids were made on one or two of his Harris farms. But these were openly denounced by the Harris people, who seemed anxious to avoid a repetition of the mistakes which had occurred in Lewis. The little raiding received prompt repudiation by the Harris crofters. In fact, everyone appeared so amenable to reason that Leverhulme had no difficulty in getting the Scottish Office to agree that no Harris farms should be broken up into holdings until his policy for the island's development had been given a ten years' trial.

Thwarted in his efforts to develop Stornoway as a port of the first importance, he now concentrated on Obbe instead. So he set to work in South Harris with this object in view. The harbour at Obbe lacks the natural advantages of the fine harbour of Stornoway. Its sea approaches are studded with perils; and the tides run vigorously, and even dangerously, everywhere about it. Notwithstanding, no money was spared in improving it from a navigational standpoint. Enormous piers were constructed at this tiny place, hitherto so quiet and secluded. Rocky obstacles were blasted out of existence, in order to obtain navigable channels; and numerous buoys and beacons were established to guide the vessels which he intended should land herring catches there. Indeed, everything was going so very well at Obbe that the natives, as a mark of their appreciation, suggested that it should be re-named Leverburgh. This was done; and Leverburgh is to-day its name for all official purposes.

In proximity to the new quays were erected kippering sheds, and buildings necessary for the curing and packing of herrings, heavy landings of which had been assured through Leverhulme's arrangement with the MacLine Drifters and Trawlers, Ltd. This subsidiary of MacFisheries agreed to operate from Leverburgh during the herring season.

It now became necessary to provide at Obbe accommodation for the influx of workers and fisherfolk. This Leverhulme encouraged by granting building sites at the nominal annual ground rent of one shilling; and at the same time he gave a grant to the applicants enabling them to purchase certain building materials. This grant, when added to the government's allowance for the purpose, made it possible for many to build their own homes. As this nucleus of industry and activity was developing, Leverhulme laid out a recreation ground for the people, and built a public hall, which he named the Hulme Hall.

Among his other undertakings in Harris were the erection of a mill for the making of tweeds, and the construction of much-needed roads. He bore half the cost of the five-and-a-half miles of road between Leverburgh and Finsbay: the Ministry of Transport met the other half. He shared with the Unemployment Grants Committee, in like proportion, the cost of two other roads in Harris, each five miles in length.

Everything was proceeding satisfactorily in Harris when, in 1925, his death occurred. This brought his schemes to a speedy end. So all his efforts to establish the herring industry at Leverburgh came to nought. Leverburgh, to-day, is a place of tumbledown sheds, of bare, concrete foundations, of rusting iron, of rotting piers. Things are now much as they were before he went there, but sadder. From his vast expenditure upon Harris, little of permanent value accrued to the island except the roads.

Early in 1922, the question of the style, "of the Western Isles", assumed by Lord Leverhulme on his being created a viscount, was raised at a meeting of the Gaelic Society of Inverness, at which a resolution of protest was adopted. The Society's secretary, speaking to the resolution in that unctuous way in which the Highlanders have specialised when dealing with titled and moneyed personages, sought to make it clear that the Society's council, in proposing the resolution, was anxious not to say anything which might offend his lordship, but felt very strongly that he had been badly advised when he adopted the style, "of the Western Isles". The secretary expressed regret that Leverhulme should have departed from the propriety with which Englishmen purchasing Scottish estates had always respected Scottish feeling; and he was bold enough to add that he knew of no Scottish sentiment which had been more grievously offended. The passing of the resolution, he claimed, was the least the Society could do in defence of national rights. The truth of the matter was, however, that most people in Scotland did not care a hoot. Indeed, they knew little of Lord Leverhulme except that he had some connection with soap, and had bought some of the Western Isles. To his new territorial title they were largely indifferent. Nevertheless, the caucus, which can always be relied upon in Scotland to be vociferous on such occasions, got busy, and soon magnified matters out of all perspective. To the opposition to Leverhulme's schemes in Lewis there was now added this extravagantly publicised objection to his assumption of the style, "of the Western Isles". This engendered complications; and complications have a way of generating ill-feeling.

At the meeting referred to, the Society's secretary begged to propose the following motion, which, after some discussion was adopted unanimously:

"The Gaelic Society of Inverness has learned with deep regret and disapprobation that the Right Honourable Lord Leverhulme has assumed the style of 'of the Western Isles' on his being created Viscount, as in so doing he is trenching on the dignity of an ancient title, *viz.*, that of Lord of the Isles, which is now borne by His Gracious Majesty, the King. The Society would like to believe that the assumption of the said title arose out of thoughtlessness on the part of his lordship, and that, if he but realises that the assumption of that title by him, or any other, is an encroachment on a Royal and ancient title, and an offence to Scottish sentiment, he will at once take steps to change his title to one which would be more in keeping with present-day conditions and actual fact. That a copy of this resolution be sent to Lord Leverhulme, and also to the Prime Minister, the Secretary of State for Scotland, the Members of Parliament for the Highland constituencies, and the Lyon King of Arms for Scotland."

The copy of the resolution sent to Lord Leverhulme was accompanied by a covering letter, pointing out, somewhat irrelevantly, that the Lords of the Isles were MacDonalds, and that even the assumption of the title by a MacDonald not belonging to the acknowledged branch of the family would have been resented—a declaration which might well prompt one to enquire as to the *King's* entitlement to this ancient title! It might have been argued that, on territorial grounds, Leverhulme had a better claim, for it cannot be held that the King, automatically, carries all the territorial titles in his kingdom.

It was suggested to Lord Leverhulme that he might assume the title of, say, "of the Lews", which would not merely remove the grievance, but would also justify the high esteem in which he was held. But what would the *MacLeods* have said, had Leverhulme adopted Lewis as his territorial title? That, assuredly, would have provided further ground for rancour and dispute. All the MacLeods in the world would have been up in arms!

A futile and fatuous correspondence now ensued.[1] The matter was brought to the notice of Bonar Law, then Prime Minister, in writing to whom the Society's secretary asked that this wrong—"this outrage on the feelings of all Scotsmen, particularly on the feelings of Highlanders not only at home, but also in the Dominions"—should be rectified by

---

[1] It is reproduced in full in the *Transactions of the Gaelic Society of Inverness,* Vol. XXXI, published in 1927.

the cancellation of the title. The secretary enquired of the
Prime Minister whether the Lyon King of Arms had been
consulted, and, if so, whether *he* had sanctioned this usurpa-
tion. Replying by return of post, the Prime Minister mentioned, *inter alia*, that he had caused enquiry to be made, and
had found that the King had approved a submission, based
on the recommendation of the College of Arms, under which
Lord Leverhulme was created Viscount Leverhulme of the
Western Isles, in the Counties of Inverness and Ross and
Cromarty, and that letters patent were issued accordingly. It
was pointed out at the same time that Leverhulme's title, as
approved, was Viscount Leverhulme, and that the addition
of the words complained of was a descriptive designation
which did not form part of the title itself.

Subsequent letters passing between the Gaelic Society of
Inverness and Lord Leverhulme were of a rambling character.
The former cited instances in which, in deference to local
feelings, the intention of adopting certain descriptive designa-
tions had been abandoned. The latter, on the other hand,
could not agree that his using " of the Western Isles " was in
any way an encroachment on that ancient and heroic title,
Lord of the Isles, to which frequent reference had been made
throughout this silly correspondence, and into which Leverhulme, with great subtlety, now introduced economics, setting
forth in dignified terms what he had hoped to do for the
betterment of Lewis and of Harris, but had been prevented
from doing. " Unfortunately," he added, " the Scottish Office,
notwithstanding the adverse reports of Royal Commissions,
especially the Royal Commission of some twenty years ago,
that farms are essential to the life of a community, are determined to convert the farms into crofts, thus hampering me,
and crippling me in the work I have undertaken.

" I do not know whether you are aware, but the milk for
the people of Stornoway has always to be drawn from Aberdeen, and it is 36 hours old before it can reach the consumer
in Stornoway, and at week-ends even up to 96 hours old.

" There will soon be no farms left in Lewis: the Scottish
Office have given me notice again this week to take another
farm. They have the power to do so, and disregard the
warning of their previous experience in following this line

of policy. It can only lead to the forced exile of the rising generation—the sons and daughters of the people of Lewis and Harris."

When Leverhulme was reminded that, in any case, he did not own the *whole* of the Western Isles, and that his title was therefore an inaccurate one, he responded with the retort that the Duke of Argyll by no means owned the whole of Argyllshire!

A final appeal to his lordship to remove "this blot, and restore to us, unsullied, a title which belongs to the heroic age of Scottish History, and which is enshrined in the song and story of the West", proved abortive.

It should be remembered that the style objected to merely resembled that of the Lordship of the Isles, the title of the MacDonalds of Clan Ranald, whose suzerainty, so far as the Western Isles were concerned, never extended beyond the Uists and Benbecula. This ancient Lordship never included those parts of the Western Isles purchased by Leverhulme, and in respect of which he appended the offending words —"this offensive designation", as the Society's secretary described it in a further communication to the Prime Minister. However, it did include several of the *Inner* Isles or Inner Hebrides, together with much of the adjacent mainland of Inverness-shire. Moidart and the Small Isles were once theirs, for example.

In 1928, and in the person of the late T. B. Macaulay, a Montreal magnate, Lewis was to find another benefactor anxious to follow the example of Sir James Matheson by experimentally sinking wealth in peat. Dr. Thomas Basset Macaulay, LL.D., who died at Montreal in 1942 at the age of eighty-two, had been president and manager of the Sun Life Assurance Company of Canada. Though Canadian-born, he claimed descent from the MacAulays of Uig. Not until the summer of 1928 did he first set foot on the island of his ancestors. There he, too, found ample scope for beneficence.

His favours were not confined to Lewis, however, once he had discovered Scotland. Then approaching his seventieth year, and with a great deal of cash at his command, he began to spend lavishly. Shortly after his Lewis scheme had been put into operation, he made to Fraserburgh (his father's early home) the gift of a memorial hall, and founded there a Widows' Fund and an Educational Trust. At Craigiebuckler, Aberdeen, he established the Macaulay Institute for Soil Research. To the Animal Breeding Research Department of Edinburgh University he gave £30,000. Little wonder he was, in no time, an LL.D. of Edinburgh and Aberdeen, as well as of McGill! (Our universities frequently give preferential treatment in this way to wealth. Scholarship they also recognise—occasionally.)

Macaulay's initial contribution to the solution of Lewis's economic problem was the gift of £10,000 for an experimental farm there. This project was entrusted to the chairman of the Board of Agriculture for Scotland, as it was then called; and the said chairman appointed Dr. W. G. Ogg, at that time Director of Rothamsted Experimental Station, and Mr. W. G. Coles, then on the point of retiring from the position of chief engineer to the Board, to superintend its working. These two experts toured peat-land reclamation works in Germany, Norway, Sweden, Denmark, and Holland, whence they returned so favourably impressed with what they had seen that it was decided to run the Lewis scheme, as far as practicable, on continental lines.

A peaty site, typical of nearly 400,000 acres of Lewis, was now chosen on the Arnish Moor, not far from Stornoway. In the winter of 1928-9, work was begun there, at what has since been known as the Macaulay Farm, when about fifty acres of peat land were drained by a system of wooden box drains placed twenty-two yards apart, and leading into parallel open ditches a hundred yards apart. As the spring of 1929 was an exceptionally dry one, especially for the Outer Hebrides, the draining scheme gave misleading promise of its being effective.

The agricultural part of the undertaking was placed under the supervision of Mr. Angus MacLeod, County Organiser of the North of Scotland College of Agriculture, and affectionately known in Lewis by the nickname of Page Eight. Cropping was begun on a small scale in 1929. The following year, about twenty acres were under crops. By the end of that year, however, the partial failure of the drainage system became apparent; and it was, therefore, with difficulty that the crops were secured, although there had been quite a satisfactory growth of oats and grass, as well as of some vegetables. Cows and poultry were introduced to the farm in 1930. Both crops and stock were increased during the ensuing year or two. The farm, as a whole, was not on an economically sound footing, however. Though crops were grown, and milk was produced, the cost of production was too high, largely owing to the inadequacy of the drainage scheme. The problem of the satisfactory drainage of peat, in order to convert it into good, arable land at reasonable cost, has yet to be solved.

Unfortunately, two years after this experiment was inaugurated, the great depression came, with the consequence that funds were no longer available to continue it as originally planned. Work was therefore slowed down. At last, the deficit on the farm became so large that it could no longer be run on its earlier basis. Thus, in 1939, it was let to a tenant. By this time, about seventy acres had been either cultivated, or improved as grazing. On this improved grazing the tenant pastures his dairy cows, continuing the system, previously in vogue there, of producing high grade milk. This he has been doing for nine years; and he appears to be making it pay. The farm he is not cultivating, with the result that the pasture is rapidly deteriorating.

It cannot altogether be said that this experiment in peat-land reclamation has failed, since it has never been pursued as primarily intended, because of the lack of funds, and because experimental work of this nature takes many years to achieve results of permanent value.

The Macaulay Institute for Soil Research is being supported by the Department of Agriculture. Much of the research work on soils, formerly carried on by the three Agricultural Colleges in Scotland, was transferred to, and concentrated round, this Institute, to which the Macaulay Farm is attached, and where there is a peat specialist of the highest scientific attainments, who is conducting research into peat, composts, and the like.

The Lewis experiment, so far as reclamation from peat is

Approaching Gramisdale, Benbecula, by the North Ford (note the cockle-beds in foreground)

concerned, has now been abandoned; and the farm is quickly reverting to moorland. One beneficial result of this effort which should be mentioned, however, is the method of improving rough hill grazings by dressing simply with shell sand (of which there are unlimited quantities on the shores of the Western Isles) and with some form of phosphate, such as slag or mineral phosphate, and seeding with cheap mixtures of Wild White Clover and ryegrass cleanings. For this, no cultivation whatsoever is required.

The farm has also given a stimulus to the improvement of poultry and of milk production. As regards the latter, it has introduced a quality and a standard of cleanliness hitherto almost unknown in these parts.

How much Macaulay sank in the peat of Lewis, I have no immediate means of ascertaining. Though the amount cannot have been as great as that which Sir James Matheson vested in a similar venture, it must have been considerable.

In addition to what he spent on this experiment, he gave an endowment of £12,000 to the public library at Stornoway, a contribution of £700 towards the purchase of books, and a handsome sum for the fireproofing of the building. And not only did he erect a new wing at the Lewis Hospital, but he also endowed that institution to the tune of £17,000. To the Town Hall building fund, he gave £5,000, after paying half the debt of £1,400 which existed on the old building. Further, he created the Macaulay Education Trust for the Lews, with a capital of £5,000.

What colossal sums have been poured into these uneconomic and intractable Isles!

. . . . . .

From an economic survey of the Western Isles one must not omit mention of the generous part played by the Department of Agriculture, especially when, either through ignorance or ingratitude, it is repeatedly being said by the Islanders and their advocates that governments have done little for them. Let us now examine in some detail the Hebrideans' indebtedness to the Department under various headings.

Land Settlement: On privately owned estates, it has created 802 holdings and enlarged 567 others. These embrace a total

High tide at Ardmhor, on the southern fringe of the Great Cockle Shore

area of 128,500 acres. On estates acquired by the Secretary of State, it has been responsible for 309 new holdings and 54 enlargements, occupying a further area of 39,900 acres. These two methods of settlement, then, have resulted in the creation of 1,111 new holdings and 621 enlargements, with a total area of 168,500 acres. To these should be added 195 fishermen's holdings occupying another 734 acres.

Buildings: In connection with its land settlement scheme, it provided, in the decade ending December, 1938, loan assistance for the erection of no fewer that 435 new houses, and for the improvement of 56 old ones. Under a provision of the Small Landholders (Scotland) Act of 1911, it also helped with new dwelling-houses and steadings, or with the improvement of existing ones. Thus 847 new houses were built and 697 improved, 56 new steadings built and 21 improved. Loans made for such purposes during these ten years amounted roughly to £300,000.

Equipment: Crofters erecting new buildings, or improving old ones, obtained grants through the local authorities under the provision of the Housing (Rural Workers) Acts and the Housing (Rural Population) (Scotland) Act. And, as if all this were not enough, the Department of Agriculture supplies building materials at reduced prices for cash, or against the loans it provides. Between 1929 and 1938, the Western Islanders received such materials to the value of £205,000.

Crofters in the Highlands and Islands usually erect or repair their buildings at reduced costs by providing their own unskilled labour and, to some extent, the semi-skilled as well.

The Department also gives assistance in matters of fencing, drainage, water supplies, and roads. Expenditure on these items has been considerable.

Public Works: During the same ten years (1929-38) under the Congested Districts (Scotland) Act of 1897, it made to local authorities and others grants totalling £22,500 in respect of road and pier works in the Outer Islands. Some of these works had further financial help from the Ministry of Transport to the extent of £8,410.

Improvement of Cattle: The Department's scheme for this has been in operation since 1911. Under it, bulls are supplied on loan to Crofters' Common Grazing Committees, or to other duly constituted bodies in the Congested Districts. A Committee must agree to provide for the keep and attendance of the bull, and to be responsible for its care during the prescribed period of the two or three years it remains in its custody, the period varying according to the breed of the animal. Where Committees are unable, satisfactorily, to winter their bulls in the townships, the Department, at a small charge, is prepared to do so at its stud farms at Inverness. The animals are delivered free of charge to the nearest or most convenient approved station or port. During the past ten years, some 85 bulls, half of them Highland and half of them Shorthorn, have been located annually in the Outer Hebrides.

Improvement of Sheep: This scheme, which has been in operation for a considerable number of years, is designed principally to improve the quality of flocks in the congested areas. Selected rams of the Blackface and Cheviot breeds are hired by the Department to Crofters' Common Grazing Committees for the service season, which extends to approximately ten weeks. The present hiring fee per ram is 70s., a pound of which is refunded when the ram is returned to the Department's stud. All transport charges between the stud and the island townships are borne by the Department. During the past ten years, about thirty rams of the Blackface breed have been supplied annually to North Uist, South Uist, and Barra.

In addition to the foregoing, the Department introduced in 1944 a special scheme for the improvement of the sheep stock in Lewis and Harris, whereby selected townships were offered a limited number of good, commercial ram lambs at 35s. each. This included delivery charges. To suit the conditions applicable to Lewis and Harris, the animals were of the short-coated and upstanding type. They became the property of the Township Committees. Since the inception of this scheme, the demand for ram lambs has steadily increased. In 1947, as many as 95 were supplied.

Highland Pony Stallion Scheme: Highland pony stallions from the Department's stud have been travelled annually for a number of years in Barra, Eochar and Benbecula, South

Uist, and North Uist. The service fee for mares belonging to crofters and small farmers is £1 per service. For mares belonging to other persons, it is £2 10s.

Veterinary Services: The Department also provides a reasonable veterinary service in the crofting counties of Scotland at reduced rates for the livestock belonging to crofters, landholders, and other occupiers of agricultural holdings, the aggregate rentals of which, as shown in the Valuation Roll, do not exceed £75 per annum, provided that the occupier is either (*a*) wholly dependent on the holding for his or her livelihood or (*b*) that, where he or she has other sources of income, the economic status does not differ materially from that of a holder who *is* so dependent. Holders known to derive the bulk of their income from some other enterprise, such as hotel-keeping, shop-keeping, or contracting, are not eligible, even though their holdings may fall within the category described above.

The scale of fees which may be charged by veterinary surgeons is as follows:

Occupiers of agricultural holdings with rentals of:
£10 and under	2s. 6d. per visit
Over £10 and up to and including £25	4s. 6d. per visit
Over £25 and up to and including £50	10s. per visit
Over £50 and up to and including £75	12s. 6d. per visit

The fee payable by shepherds, gamekeepers, and such as do not pay rent is 4s. 6d. per visit, plus the usual mileage charges; and the veterinary surgeon, in addition to his fee, may charge travelling expenses on an approved scale.

The veterinary surgeons are appointed by the local authorities, with the approval of the Department, which pays grants in aid of the cost. At present, there are twenty-two surgeons employed under the scheme, three of these being in the Outer Hebrides, with headquarters at Lochboisdale, Lochmaddy, and Stornoway.

Poultry Improvement: A scheme for this has also been in operation for a long time. It is designed to improve the poultry stocks in the crofting districts by making it possible for residents in these areas to obtain from approved station holders, and at prescribed maximum prices, limited quantities of eggs for hatching, and of day-old chicks bred from selected birds of pure breeds. An approved station holder is paid a bonus by the Department, based on the number of eggs or day-old chicks sold. In 1947, there was one approved station holder in Lewis.

Withal, a record of generosity and diligence, and an adequate answer to those who, in agitating for even further public expenditure on the unremunerative Isles, would have us believe that government departments have neglected them.

. . . .

Despite all the agricultural assistance given to the crofters, one frequently finds these "lassitudinarians" criminally negligent. For instance, often after the government subsidies have been paid to them on their crops, they cease to have any further interest in them. In South Uist, you will see potatoes being imported at Lochboisdale, while the crofters' potato crops lie rotting in the ground because they are too indolent to lift them. Even the officials of the Department of Agriculture, with the best intentions in the world, are powerless in such a situation, since the crofters recognise no authority. The one and only person they truly respect is John Barleycorn. He is their idol. Yet, they have no compunction whatsoever about laying baseless claims to public funds. Their speciality, on the pretext of asserting their "rights", is organised begging; and it is one which they have found too highly profitable in recent years.

. . . .

Money meantime is plentiful among the Islanders. In addition to such as is obtained through fishing, deep-sea sailing, weaving, lobster-fishing, and perhaps domestic service, they derive a disproportionately large revenue from public funds—from state pensions, unemployment insurance, public assistance, and various forms of allowances. Their pride where superficial values are concerned never stands in the way of their concentrating on methods whereby public monies may be obtained on the flimsiest of pleas. On the whole, therefore, most of them have little to complain of. Bear in mind that they have few expenses as generally understood.

In Lewis unemployment has given rise to sharp controversy. Many hold that much of it is not genuine. Certainly, there are numerous cases in which this can be shown to be true. To some extent at least, the explanation is that, in these crofting regions, regulations designed mainly to deal with unemployment in industrial areas offer loopholes for the lazy who, existing on their crofts in comparative comfort, can work just enough to keep their insurance contributions in order, thus enabling them to draw the maximum benefit for the minimum of useful work. That this statement is not an unfair one seems obvious from the fact that quite recently, after the Ministry of Labour tightened up the regulations governing unemployment, some hundreds of names disappeared from the live register in Lewis alone.

It may be pointed out, however, that this fall in the number of Islanders receiving unemployment benefit does not necessarily mean that a greater number is working. It may well mean that there is now a good deal of *under*-employment —a condition of affairs which may eventually have serious repercussions on the tweed industry, especially where Lewis and Harris are concerned, since their weaving capacity is rapidly exceeding their spinning capacity, and weavers are already crying out for yarn to keep their looms going.

Nevertheless, there *is* a core of real unemployment in the Western Isles; and it was with a view to some temporary alleviation of this that in 1947 the Department of Agriculture organised, in Lewis, the cutting of 1,300 tons of peat for sale as solid fuel.

What would happen if, for one reason or another the tweed industry died in the Isles, one can scarcely imagine. It must be borne in mind that, in the making of textiles, the Outer Hebrides possess no natural advantages over the more accessible mainland, though tweed-making would appear to be complementary to the crofter-fisherman economy. Moreover, the present prosperity in the tweed industry is due to a vogue which at any moment may pass. A slump in Harris tweed would, indeed, be serious. Tweed may suddenly go out of fashion. And what then? Large-scale emigration may again be the only alternative.

Hardly less precarious is the herring fishing industry. It is true that war-time restrictions on fishing elsewhere brought a measure of prosperity to the Lewis fishermen; but at times the herring, too, has a way of being elusive!

The conflicting claims of crofting and fishing create one of the greatest dilemmas in the Western Isles. While the Department of Agriculture is anxious that the crofter should be an efficient crofter, the Herring Industry Board is equally anxious that he should be an efficient fisherman. To this contradiction there would appear to be no solution. If both crofting and fishing are to be regarded as equally important sources of subsistence, the one is likely to be neglected for the other. Indeed, while the tweed boom continues, both may be neglected for weaving.

On the other hand, one must consider whether the Western Islander is temperamentally fitted for full-time employment, either as a crofter or as a fisherman. It is true, *on paper* at any rate, that, in the former capacity, he must satisfy the Land Court that he is cultivating his croft properly. Many a crofter fails to do so, however. This explains why the planning consultant for the mainland of the County of Ross (to which, it will be remembered, Lewis belongs) made the suggestion recently that all new tenants of crofts, and also the present tenants' heirs to crofts, should be compelled to satisfy the authorities that they are making the best use of the land apportioned to them, and that failure to do so should render them liable to having their crofts resumed.

The contradictory state of affairs in the crofting areas of the Western Highlands and Islands was ably set forth by the editor of the *Stornoway Gazette* in the article to which we alluded earlier, and from which we make this concluding quotation: " Lewis is an island of contradictions. It is a backward crofting community and an industrial centre producing for two important export markets. The people are 'notorious' for their attachment to the old home and the old ways, but they roam the seven seas, and are settled in every continent. An industry for which the Island has no natural advantage is booming. The industry for which it has every advantage is passing through grave difficulties. Social legislation has eased the lot of many Islanders in poor circumstances, but has also set up stresses which are changing the whole structure of the local economy. The bus has given the Island a unity it never had before. The aeroplane has brought Stornoway closer to the big cities than many mainland towns will ever be, but the Island is still isolated by heavy transport charges, which add, it is computed, about five per cent to the cost of living. There is unemployment in an island threatened a few years ago with a rapidly declining population. Fortunes are being made by a few, while many still struggle along on public assistance. The whole social and economic structure of the Island is changing rapidly, the cinema is popular, football fever runs high, but the Free Church holds the people's loyalty, and the induction of a new minister in a rural district still draws a bigger crowd than dance-hall, cinema, or even football match."

. . . .

As a rule, those who express concern about the depopulation of the Highlands and Islands are full of specious programmes, plans, and "deals" to arrest it. They clamour for the setting up of local industries, or for the resuscitation of those which, through various economic causes, have declined and disappeared. What they seldom consider is how far the Islanders would truly coöperate if such industries *were* introduced. Their response to Lord Leverhulme's requirements hardly gives one reason to expect that the promoters of new industries in the Outer Hebrides would receive from the natives much encouragement. Indeed, it is highly problematical whether, in connection with any serious undertaking, they could be relied upon. Let me tell you of an attempt which at present is being made to establish a local and profitable industry in South Uist.

In 1943, despite much discouragement and local opposition, efforts were begun with a view to reviving in the Outer Hebrides the seaweed industry, which had been dead for more than a century. An organisation, backed at the outset by Cefoil, Ltd., and latterly becoming Alginate Industries, Ltd., was set up for the purpose of collecting, and conveying to premises they had erected at North Boisdale, seaweed cast upon the shores of South Uist and Benbecula. This area was chosen because of its possessing the longest unbroken coast-line where seaweed is plentiful. Its great, sweeping bays, along the margins of which enormous quantities of it are cast in winter, makes the gathering easy there, as compared with, say, Argyll, or the west of Ireland, both of which are interrupted by rocky indentations. The sandy beaches of South Uist alone stretch a distance of nearly twenty-five miles without any appreciable interruption.

Owing mainly to the apathy and laziness of the natives, as also to their having considered the offered rates of pay too low, and the work too arduous, the first two years of collecting were certainly disheartening. At this period, the natives were being ruined by the high wages paid them by mainland contractors engaged on such public undertakings as the Benbecula aerodrome and the South Ford bridge. Add to money thus obtained the high subsidies paid on the Islanders' small crops, and one sees there was little inducement to work at the seaweed. A further drawback was their inherent suspicion of any new enterprise. It has been held that a minimum of five years' acclimatisation is necessary before they even get accustomed to the idea of something new in their midst.

On many government undertakings during the war, the method of payment was by "time and stuff". That is to say, the time taken to complete the job, together with the material used—a quick and easy way of making money. When all this extravagant wartime expenditure ceased, there remained no alternative means of employment for the Islanders. Nevertheless, there still persisted amongst them the demand for high rates of pay. In South Uist at that time, the unskilled labourer was receiving, and indeed expected, half-a-crown an hour—the rate which *skilled* workers were earning in the cities, except in the case of London, where the rates of pay have always been higher because of the relatively higher cost of living. In the Western Isles, men are paid standard trade union rates for work much inferior to that performed by workers on the mainland, so many of whom are perfect craftsmen. For example, joiners in the Western Isles, whose workmanship would not be tolerated on the mainland, where a minimum standard of efficiency is demanded and maintained, receive the same rates of pay as do those most accomplished at their craft.

Even though the company met with all this stupid opposition, it persisted in its endeavour to re-establish this ancient home industry in South Uist. Many crofters continued their hostility to it, although their material prosperity was bound up with that success which only their coöperation could ensure. For the processing factory then being built and gradually expanded at North Boisdale, they refused to collect the seaweed; and, indeed, at one stage, the police actually had to be called in to investigate cases of sabotage, especially where the company's motor-lorries were concerned. Large chunks of metal had been inserted in the engines.

So fierce was the Islanders' opposition in 1945 that, in order to keep the plant working, it was found necessary to import from Connemara a thousand tons of air-dried seaweed. This aroused considerable indignation locally, on the ground that there was plenty to be had in Uist. But, abundant though it was, no one seemed interested enough to collect it. Articles derogatory to the company now began to appear in the Scottish Catholic press. The promoters of the scheme were accused of importing from Ireland seaweed obtained by sweated labour. To this the managing-director promptly replied that importation was the company's only alternative, so long as the local people preferred to allow thousands of tons to rot on the beaches, rather than collect them, even at the high wages offered.

The unshipping of this Irish seaweed at Lochboisdale, seven miles from the factory at North Boisdale, awakened the local hauliers to the possibility of their earning money by hauling *local* seaweed. So a group of people primarily interested in transporting the seaweed now began to collect it. This had an instantaneous effect on the more recalcitrant, who now thought that they, too, might do a bit of collecting. In this way, the amount gathered gradually increased until, at length, the factory could be operated to capacity by local weed. On the Atlantic seaboard of South Uist, along a coastline of, say, a dozen miles, as much as 20,000 tons of weed might be thrown up by one wind and one tide. The next wind and tide, of course, might bear it all away before it could be gathered, with the result that the following day the bulk of this great harvest might be deposited on shores fifteen or twenty miles distant.

In the autumn of 1947, the quantity of seaweed gathered locally was in excess of what the factory could cope with. This was due partly to the discovery that the factory turned out to be better suited to deal with rock-weed than with tangle. The rock-weed (*ascophyllum*) is cut at low tide nearly all the year round, whereas the tangle (*laminaria*) is cast on the shore, and may be gathered roughly from October until March. The tangle harvest is still gathered; but most of it is now shipped from Lochboisdale to one of the company's other drying-plants on the mainland, such as that at Kames, on the Kyles of Bute. This means that, in practice, any amount of weed, whether tangle or rock-weed, can be harvested remuneratively.

The gathering from the beaches must be done speedily. Otherwise, great quantities of ·cast weed, as we have seen, may rapidly be carried off to inaccessible shores, and finally lost. To deal with this, the company organises teams of local workers, whom it provides with tractors and trailers. These mechanical units, when operating efficiently, guarantee a constant stream of weed arriving at the beach-heads. Here the weed is weighed roughly, and then walled for air-drying—laid across wooden walls erected for the purpose, and often consisting of no more than a series of planks stretched between empty tar barrels. Tractor and trailer teams operate as far away from the factory as half-a-dozen miles.

The company weighs and purchases tangle at the drying-sites. That is to say, at any of the spots along the shore where the crofters may care to collect it and air-dry it. Thereafter, either by the company's own lorries, or by local hauliers working on a sub-contract basis, it is conveyed to the factory, where it is stored, thoroughly dried, and eventually milled.

The function of the North Boisdale factory is solely the scientific drying of the weed, and its reduction thereafter to a fine powder. In other words, the weed is enormously reduced in bulk by its being dried and milled.

From this powder, all manner of products are now˙ being made. Among such are calcium alginate rayon, used so extensively in synthetic silks; alginade, an ice-cream stabiliser; and coldsett, a dessert sauce powder. These alginates are also used in welding, in textile processing, in foodstuffs, and in pharmaceuticals and cosmetics. And they have medicinal and surgical uses, too. From them is manufactured the gauze used by surgeons for stopping internal bleeding. This gauze is gradually absorbed into the body, and thus it becomes unnecessary to remove it during an operation. I have also seen some very light-weight wool spun by Courtauld with the aid of calcium alginate yarn.

The crofters gathering wet weed are paid whenever it is weighed, or on a cumulative total paid weekly. The rate of pay is ten shillings per wet ton. At this rate, an industrious Islander can earn as much as £15 to £20 a week. The average weekly wage is £7. Air-dried weed, on the other hand, is paid for at the rate of £3 5s. per ton. This is payable to any crofter who may care to gather and dry it.

When in Uist and Benbecula in the autumn of 1947, I discovered that, despite the high wages offered by the company, out of a population of approximately 5,000, only 56 of the natives were showing any interest in collecting seaweed— about one per cent. Yet, there is employment here for hundreds, were it not for laziness, and for the ease with which so many of the natives get public monies of one kind or another without having to do a hand's turn. It has been estimated that the factory could give permanent employment to at least 220 persons. Last autumn, about 70 were employed there. In order to comply with the requirements of the 44-hour week, they were working in four shifts—eight hours a day, five days of the week. This meant that the factory was running, continuously, night and day.

Absenteeism was rife, however, for the Islanders, as we have seen, are completely autonomous, and have no sense at all of civic responsibility. The manager never knew who was going to turn up at work, and who was not. He never could tell from one shift to another whether a sufficient number would put in an appearance to enable him to keep the factory going. Here, again, the croft was the all-important thing. The natives would rather fiddle about on their crofts, and live on various forms of public benefit, than work for good wages. Let me just give a rough estimate of what might easily be distributed in wages at North Boisdale by fifty-six men collecting, and another fifty employed at the factory:

Collecting force of 56 men at an average weekly wage of
£7 = £392. Say, roughly £400.
Factory operated by 50 men at an average weekly wage of
£7 = £350.
Aggregate weekly earnings of 106 men = £850.
Aggregate yearly earnings of 106 men = £850 × 50 =
£42,500.

Let us be conservative in our total estimate, and put it
at £40,000—an enormous wages bill for unskilled labourers
paying annual rentals of a mere pound or two, and having
practically no expenses as ordinarily understood.

Much of these earnings goes in waste: much of it in drink.
Many a crofter spends £4 or £5 a week on alcohol alone.
Never was money so plentiful in South Uist as at present. A
local butcher told me the other day that, whereas before the
war a sheep's carcass would lie on his counter for several
days, he could now sell a carcass every hour!

Those who started this industry at North Boisdale, and
have maintained it in face of such odds, should receive some
public acknowledgment, if only for their perseverance. Not
merely did they have to contend with serious physical dis-
advantages, such as weather, remoteness, and transport,[1] but
they had to survive the laziness, pettiness, prejudice, intrigue,
obstinacy, and unreliability of the inhabitants. Only those
who know them, and do not allow sentimentality to obscure
judgment, can have any idea how difficult it is to help the
Hebrideans to help themselves, particularly in these times
when, in common with so many people elsewhere in Britain,
they have the notion that, now we have a Labour Government
in power, they are permanently secure without any obligation on their part to contribute to the common weal.

The tenacity of the company's representative on the spot,
especially in the factory's early days, must have been pro-
digious. The knowledge of all he had to fight against locally
—not just the lack of coöperation, but overt acts of hostility
and obstruction—gives one, in retrospect, a considerable

---

[1] The company even had to construct a road suitable for its motor-lorries,
and also re-surface a considerable stretch of cart-track, in order to link its
factory with the main road running north and south through the entire
length of South Uist.

measure of sympathy with the late Viscount Leverhulme in his efforts to work with the people of Lewis.

There is no point in agitating for the establishment of industries in the Outer Hebrides until one can be assured that the attitude of the natives will be different from that which has manifested itself right throughout every attempt made to ameliorate their condition. Public expenditure on these Islands cannot but be a sheer waste, so long as this attitude persists. Indeed, one greatly doubts whether it is possible to improve the great mass of the inhabitants while they breed so heavily beyond their means, and decline to accept, in return for grants, subsidies, and even good wages, any civic obligation. They have no sense of contract. They will break a bargain with an employer, often without any pretext whatsoever, and without even letting him know. They simply fail to turn up at a job when he expects them, and often awaits them urgently. As employees, therefore, they are, on the whole, thoroughly unreliable. But they can always be relied upon to turn up for any bit of public money they can get their fingers on, without committing themselves to doing a stroke of work or performing any service in return. This is individual freedom carried too far, for it is individual freedom maintained on a " spiv " basis—a point which ought to be noted by those who say that the Islander is an individualist, and therefore cannot, and will not, be regimented. Many of them continue as individualists on their crofts only so long as they are a burden to the state, a burden to the ratepayer, a burden on industry as a whole, which is merely another way of saying that they are a burden on all who truly work and produce.

.   .   .   .

Sentimentalists and emotional writers (where the Isles are concerned, the latter are usually non-Gaels) are always crying out for what they term practical measures to maintain the existing population of the Highlands and Islands. In my view, however, there can be no economic solution for either, so long as population remains as high in relation to economic possibilities—indeed, so long as population is maintained at a figure much in excess of what these areas can support. Take South Uist, for example, where, besides the parents, you will find eight or ten children inhabiting a corrugated-iron shed or a shack, or a veritable hovel by the roadside, or on the moorland, with a floor area of no more than twenty square yards! There are scores of such miserable habitations among these Islands, especially in the Roman Catholic parts, where the great idea is as many babies as possible. No wonder the women of South Uist are old and haggard at forty! In addition to their being the Island's beasts of burden (the menfolk never carry anything if they can help it) they are worn out by then with excessive child-bearing. Whatever may be the shortcomings of the Protestant communities among the Isles, and they are many, their condition is not quite so bad.

The other day I overheard, in the lounge of the inn at Creagorry, a conversation in which a Roman Catholic priest, speaking to some minor officials about the building of more houses in Benbecula, said he was certain that the island could carry comfortably half as many people again. This meant, approximately, another five hundred. "If only we could get the young people to stay!" he concluded.

But what is there in these Isles for young people with any ambition, with any desire to improve themselves? So many of those who remain become loungers and scroungers. The bottle becomes their principal mode of entertainment. Any attempt to retain the young would be doomed to failure. Nothing but the establishment of industries, which, in any event, must necessarily be uneconomic, could keep them there, and then only until such time as the enormous cumulative losses on these industries compelled their being closed down. We have seen that millionaires attempted something along these lines in the Isles, and failed.

The realism of the economics of population in relation to subsistence—and frequently diminishing subsistence at that! —is appreciated by few. Population in relation to food (not forgetting, *inter alia*, the inexorable Law of Diminishing Return) is the most urgent problem facing mankind at the present time, and one which politicians of every party avoid.

The tangle o' the Isles is but part of the tangle o' Mankind.

INDEX

2A